THE FUTURE OF LEADERSHIP DEVELOPMENT

THE FUTURE OF LEADERSHIP DEVELOPMENT

Edited by

Susan Elaine Murphy
Associate Director

Ronald E. Riggio
Director

Kravis Leadership Institute
Claremont McKenna College

LAWRENCE ERLBAUM ASSOCIATES, PUBLISHERS
2003   Mahwah, New Jersey   London

Senior Acquisitions Editor: Anne C. Duffy
Editorial Assistant: Kristin Duch
Cover Designer: Kathryn Houghtaling Lacey
Production Manager: Sara T. Scudder
Full Service Compositor: TechBooks
Text and Cover Printer: Sheridan Books

Lawrence Erlbaum Associates, Inc., Publishers
10 Industrial Avenue
Mahwah, New Jersey 07430

Library of Congress Cataloging-in-Publication Data

The future of leadership development / edited by Susan Elaine Murphy,
    Ronald E. Riggio.
       p.   cm. – (Series in applied psychology)
    Includes bibliographical references and index.
    ISBN 0-8058-4342-6
    1. Leadership.   2. Executives–Training of.   I. Murphy, Susan E.
II. Riggio, Ronald E.   III. Series.

HD57.7.F88   2003
658.4'07124–dc21

                                    2003012175

Printed in the United States of America
10 9 8 7 6 5 4 3 2 1

THE KRAVIS-DE ROULET LEADERSHIP CONFERENCE

The Kravis-de Roulet Leadership Conference, which began in 1990, is an annual leadership conference funded jointly by an endowment from financier Henry R. Kravis and the de Roulet family. This perpetual funding, along with additional support from the Kravis Leadership Institute and Claremont McKenna College, enables us to attract the finest leadership researchers, scholars, and practitioners as conference presenters and participants. The Conference topics alternate between leadership research and more practitioner-oriented topics. The 11th annual Kravis-de Roulet Conference, The Future of Leadership Development, was held March 23–24, 2001.

In 2002, the first edited book was published by Lawrence Erlbaum Associates, entitled *Multiple Intelligences and Leadership.* The forthcoming book, *Improving Leadership in Nonprofit Organizations*, is expected in 2004.

THE KRAVIS LEADERSHIP INSTITUTE

The Kravis Leadership Institute plays an active role in the development of young leaders via educational programs, research and scholarship, and the development of technologies for enhancing leadership potential.

KRAVIS
LEADERSHIP
INSTITUTE

SERIES IN APPLIED PSYCHOLOGY

Edwin A. Fleishman, George Mason University,
Jeanette N. Cleveland, Pennsylvania State University
Series Editors

Gregory Bedny and David Meister
The Russian Theory of Activity: Current Applications to Design and Learning

Michael T. Brannick, Eduardo Salas, and Carolyn Prince
Team Performance Assessment and Measurement: Theory, Research, and Applications

Jeanette N. Cleveland, Margaret Stockdale, and Kevin R. Murphy
Women and Men in Organizations: Sex and Gender Issues at Work

Aaron Cohen
Multiple Commitments in the Workplace: An Integrative Approach

Russell Cropanzano
Justice in the Workplace: Approaching Fairness in Human Resource Management, Volume 1

Russell Cropanzano
Justice in the Workplace: From Theory to Practice, Volume 2

James E. Driskell and Eduardo Salas
Stress and Human Performance

Sidney A. Fine and Steven F. Cronshaw
Functional Job Analysis: A Foundation for Human Resources Management

Sidney A. Fine and Maury Getkate
Benchmark Tasks for Job Analysis: A Guide for Functional Job Analysis (FJA) Scales

J. Kevin Ford, Steve W. J. Kozlowski, Kurt Kraiger, Eduardo Salas, and Mark S. Teachout
Improving Training Effectiveness in Work Organizations

Jerald Greenberg
Organizational Behavior: The State of the Science, Second Edition

Uwe E. Kleinbeck, Hans-Henning Quast, Henk Thierry, and Hartmut Häcker
Work Motivation

Martin I. Kurke and Ellen M. Scrivner
Police Psychology into the 21st Century

Joel Lefkowitz
Ethics and Values in Industrial-Organizational Psychology

Manuel London
Job Feedback: Giving, Seeking, and Using Feedback for Performance Improvement, Second Edition

Manuel London
How People Evaluate Others in Organizations

Manuel London
Leadership Development: Paths to Self-Insight and Professional Growth

Robert F. Morrison and Jerome Adams
Contemporary Career Development Issues

Michael D. Mumford, Garnett Stokes, and William A. Owens
Patterns of Life History: The Ecology of Human Individuality

Kevin R. Murphy
Validity Generalization: A Critical Review

Kevin R. Murphy and Frank E. Saal
Psychology in Organizations: Integrating Science and Practice

Susan E. Murphy and Ronald E. Riggio
The Future of Leadership Development

Erich P. Prien, Jeffrey S. Schippmann and Kristin O. Prien
Individual Assessment: As Practiced in Industry and Consulting

Ned Rosen
Teamwork and the Bottom Line: Groups Make a Difference

Heinz Schuler, James L. Farr, and Mike Smith
Personnel Selection and Assessment: Individual and Organizational Perspectives

John W. Senders and Neville P. Moray
Human Error: Cause, Prediction, and Reduction

Frank J. Smith
Organizational Surveys: The Diagnosis and Betterment of Organizations Through Their Members

George C. Thornton III and Rose Mueller-Hanson
Developing Organizational Simulations: A Guide for Practitioners and Students

Yoav Vardi and Ely Weitz
Misbehavior in Organizations: Theory, Research, and Management

Contents

About the Authors

Susan J. Adams is currently a Visiting Lecturer at Northeastern Illinois University in Chicago. Additionally, Susan has been with the Leadership Academy at the Illinois Institute of Technology for approximately 2 years, where she has been involved with both the selection of scholarship recipients, including assessment center methodology, and the development of leadership skills within the undergraduate student population. She is currently enrolled in a doctorate program for Industrial/Organizational Psychology at the Illinois Institute of Technology and has a master's degree.

Roya Ayman is Professor and Director of the Industrial and Organizational Psychology program at the Institute of Psychology, Illinois Institute of Technology. She is the author of numerous articles and chapters on leadership and on culture and diversity in the workplace. Among her research contributions, Dr. Ayman was the coeditor of a book with Dr. Martin M. Chemers titled *Leadership Theory and Research: Perspectives and Directions.* She is on the editorial boards of *Applied Psychology: International Review, International Journal of Cross-Cultural Management* and was on the *Leadership Quarterly* editorial board. She also served two terms on the executive committee and program committee of the Organizational Psychology division of the International Association of Applied Psychology. As an active practitioner, she has provided assessments on organizational climate, effectiveness, and diversity; in addition, has designed and conducted leadership training and development programs for many private and public sectors, multinational, international, and national organizations, as well as for local nonprofit companies. She also has served two terms on the education and training-working group of the Governor's Commission of Status of Women in Illinois. Roya Ayman received her PhD, in Cross-Cultural Social Organizational Psychology from the University of Utah.

Leanne E. Atwater is a Professor of Management and Chair of the Management Department at Arizona State University West. She received both a bachelor's and a master's degree in Psychology from San Diego State University. She received a PhD in Psychology from Claremont Graduate School. She has worked as an Assistant Professor of Leadership and Psychology at the U.S. Naval Academy and as an Assistant Professor of Management at the State University of New York at

Binghamton. She has authored or coauthored 32 refereed journal publications in journals such as the *Journal of Applied Psychology, Personnel Psychology, Journal of Management*, and *Journal of Organizational Behavior*. She has been the recipient of over $800,000 in grants from agencies such as the Army Research Institute. She also has coauthored a book entitled *The Power of 360 Degree Feedback* with David Waldman. Her teaching interests are in the areas of Human Resources Management and Organizational Behavior. She is the president of a small management consulting firm, Atwater Management Consulting, which does leadership training and feedback interventions for public and private companies. She serves on the editorial board of *Group and Organization Management, Military Psychology*, and *Leadership Quarterly*. She is a member of the Academy of Management, the Society for Human Resources Management, and the Society of Industrial and Organizational Psychology. Her research interests include 360-degree and upward feedback, self-perception accuracy, and gender and discipline.

Bruce Avolio was the previous Codirector of the Global Center for Leadership Studies, State University of New York at Binghamton. He currently holds the Donald and Shirley Clifton Chair in Leadership at the University of Nebraska in the College of Business Administration and is a Gallup Senior Scientist. Professor Avolio has an international reputation as a researcher in leadership, having published over 80 articles and 5 books. He consults with a large number of public and private organizations in North America, South America, Africa, Europe, Southeast Asia, Australia, New Zealand, and Israel. His research and consulting also include work with the militaries of the United States of America, Singapore, Sweden, Finland, Israel, South Africa, and Europe. His latest books are entitled *Transformational and Charismatic Leadership: The Road Ahead* (Oxford Press: Elsevier Science, 2002), and *Made/Born: Leadership Development in Balance* (forthcoming with Erlbaum, 2003). His last two published books were *Full Leadership Development: Building the Vital Forces in Organizations* (Sage, 1999) and *Developing Potential Across a Full Range of Leadership: Cases on Transactional and Transformational Leadership* (Erlbaum, 2000).

Joan Brett is an Associate Professor in Management at Arizona State University West. She was on the faculty of the Edwin L. Cox School of Business at Southern Methodist University in Dallas from 1990 to 1999. She earned her PhD in Industrial Organizational Psychology at New York University in 1992. Her research on motivation and performance issues has been published in journals such as the *Journal of Applied Psychology, Academy of Management Review*, and the *Academy of Management Journal*. Her research has been discussed in the *Wall Street Journal* and *Harvard Business Review*. Dr. Brett is a member of the American Psychological Association, the American Psychological Society, the Academy of Management, and the Society for Industrial and Organizational Psychology. Prior to her academic career, Dr. Brett worked in the insurance and banking industries for 8 years and held various management positions in Human Resources. She currently consults with finance and insurance companies on a variety of issues related to human resources and organizational behavior.

Joanne B. Ciulla is Coston Family Chair in Leadership and Ethics at the Jepson School of Leadership Studies at the University of Richmond and is one of the founding faculty of the Jepson School. She has also held the UNESCO Chair in Leadership Studies at the United Nations University International Leadership Academy in Jordan, where she directed and designed leadership development programs for emerging leaders from around the world. Dr. Ciulla has a BA, MA, and PhD in philosophy. She publishes in the areas of business ethics, leadership studies, and the philosophy of work and is on the editorial boards of *The Business Ethics Quarterly* and *The Journal of Business Ethics*. Dr. Ciulla is the editor of the series, "New Horizons in Leadership," for Edward Elgar Publishing, Ltd., and is a member of the Board of Directors of the Desmond Tutu Peace Foundation. She is also a consultant who helps develop programs on ethics and leadership for universities, companies, and government agencies in the United States and abroad.

Jay Conger is a Professor of Organizational Behavior at the London Business School and Senior Research Scientist at the Center for Effective Organizations at the University of Southern California (USC). He received his BA in Anthropology from Dartmouth University, his MBA from the University of Virginia, and his DBA from Harvard. Before his affiliation with USC as the former Chairman and Executive Director of the Leadership Institute, he spent 10 years teaching business management at McGill University in Montreal. His passion for leadership development is reflected in over 70 articles and 10 books, including *Charismatic Leadership: The Elusive Factor in Organizational Effectiveness* and *Spirit at Work*.

David V. Day is presently Director of Graduate Training and Professor of Psychology at the Pennsylvania State University (University Park). He is also a Fellow of the American Psychological Association. He received a BA degree in psychology from Baldwin-Wallace College, and MA and PhD degrees in Industrial-Organization Psychology from the University of Akron. Day has published more than 40 journal articles and book chapters, many pertaining to the topics of personality, leadership, and leadership development. Journals that have published his scholarly work include *Academy of Management Journal, Journal of Applied Psychology, Journal of Management, Leadership Quarterly, Organizational Behavior and Human Decision Processes*, and *Personnel Psychology*. He serves on the editorial board of the *Journal of Management*, is an Associate Editor of *Leadership Quarterly*, and is presently editing a book titled *Leader Development for Transforming Organizations* (Lawrence Erlbaum Associates, 2004). Day is also an Adjunct Research Scientist with the Center for Creative Leadership and has recently served as a civilian member of the U.S. Army Panels for Training and Leader Development (Officer, NCO, and Army Civilian panels), which reported to the Army Chief of Staff on the state of the Army's practices in the areas of training and leader development.

Bruce Fisher is Director of the IIT Leadership Academy, where he is responsible for designing and implementing an undergraduate curriculum for leadership skills, including education programs and mentoring systems. In addition, as Director of the Center for Research and Service in IIT's Institute of Psychology, he manages applied research projects and provides services in the areas of managerial selection, retention of top performers, leadership development, and team skills training. Prior to joining IIT, Bruce worked for the Chicago-based consulting firm, Organizational Psychologists, from 1984 to 1998, achieving the role of partner. Bruce is a graduate of Illinois Institute of Technology with a PhD in Industrial/Organizational Psychology.

Erica L. Hartman is a doctoral student in Industrial/Organizational Psychology at the Illinois Institute of Technology, where she earned her MS. Her research interests include empowerment, leadership development, organizational assessment, and selection. Erica is currently a consultant at Stanard & Associates, a consulting firm that specializes in the development of selection systems and employee opinion surveys. Specifically, Erica is involved with job analysis, the development of structured interviews, assessment center development, and test development and validation. Previously, she was an associate consultant at the Center for Research & Service, an external consulting firm, where she worked on a variety of projects including survey development, test development, and validation and performance management systems.

Surinder S. Kahai is an Associate Professor of MIS and a Fellow of the Center for Leadership Studies at the State University of New York at Binghamton. He earned a B.Tech in Chemical Engineering from the Indian Institute of Technology, an MS in Chemical Engineering from Rutgers University, and a PhD in Business Administration from the University of Michigan. Dr. Kahai's research has been published in journals such as *Creativity Research Journal, Decision Sciences, Decision Support Systems, Group & Organization Management, Journal of Applied Psychology, Journal of Management Information Systems, Personnel Psychology,* and *Small Group Research.* Along with his colleagues at the Center for Leadership Studies and elsewhere, Dr. Kahai has a program of research that attempts to understand what affects group process when groups interact electronically, and how the group processes, in turn, influence the effectiveness of groups. Much of his work has focused on group leadership as a determinant of group process and outcomes by itself and in combination with features of electronic groups such as anonymity, rewards, and virtuality. He has worked with numerous organizations on the topics of using the Internet for e-business, information systems strategy and planning, and leadership development. He has been awarded the School of Management Professor of the Year in 1993, 1999, and 2002.

Edwin A. Locke is a Professor Emeritus of Leadership and Motivation at the R. H. Smith School of Business at the University of Maryland, College Park. He received his undergraduate degree from Harvard University and his MA and PhD in Industrial Psychology from Cornell University. Dr. Locke is an internationally known behavioral scientist whose work is included in leading textbooks and acknowledged in books on the history of management. He has worked on research contracts supported by the Office of Naval Research, the Office of the Army Surgeon General, the National Institutes of Mental Health, and the Civil Service Commission on the subjects of goal setting, incentives, feedback, job satisfaction, and job enrichment. Dr. Locke has been elected a Fellow of organizations such as the American Psychological Association, the American Psychological Society, the Academy of Management, and the Society for Industrial and Organizational Psychology and is a member of the Society for Organizational Behavior. He was a winner of the Outstanding Teacher–Scholar Award at the University of Maryland, the Distinguished Scientific Contribution Award of the Society for Industrial and Organizational Psychology, and the Career Contribution Award from the Academy of Management (Human Resource Division). He is a member of the Board of Advisors of the Ayn Rand Institute and is interested in the application of the philosophy of objectivism to the behavioral sciences.

Gregory G. Manley is an assistant professor at the University of Texas at San Antonio in the Department of Psychology. He received his MS and is currently completing his PhD in the area of industrial-organizational psychology at the University of Oklahoma. Mr. Manley teaches undergraduate and graduate courses in I/O psychology, psychological measurements, research methods, and introductory psychology. His research interests include background data personality measures, leader assessment, business ethics, and multivariate modeling. Mr. Manley has published his research in the *Journal of Education for Business* and has presented research at the annual meetings of the Society for Industrial and Organizational Psychology, Industrial Organizational–Organizational Behavior, and the Southern Management Association. Prior to graduate studies, he received his BS in psychology with honors at Montana State University and served in the US Navy as a missile systems analyst aboard the aircraft carrier USS Constellation.

Michael D. Mumford is a Professor of Psychology at the University of Oklahoma and Director of the Program in Industrial and Organizational Psychology. Prior to joining the University of Oklahoma, Dr. Mumford was a research fellow at the American Institute of Research. He served on the faculties of George Mason University and the Georgia Institute of Technology after receiving his PhD from the University of Georgia in 1983. Dr. Mumford has written over 120 articles concerned with the assessment and development of high-level talent. His books include *Patterns of Life Adaptation, The Biodata Handbook*, and *An Occupational Information System for the 21st Century*. He serves on the editorial boards of *Leadership Quarterly*, the *Creativity Research Journal*, the *Journal of Creative*

Behavior, and *Scientific Effectiveness*. Dr. Mumford is a Fellow of the American Psychological Association and the American Psychological Society.

Susan Elaine Murphy is an Associate Professor of Psychology at Claremont McKenna College and Associate Director of the Kravis Leadership Institute. She earned her PhD, MS, and MBA from the University of Washington. She is an Adjunct Professor at Claremont Graduate University. She has published articles and presented research investigating the contribution of personality characteristics and early leadership experiences in effective leadership and the role of mentoring in career and leadership development. Her most recent published work is an edited book, *Multiple Intelligences and Leadership* (Lawrence Erlbaum Associates, 2002). Prior to joining Claremont McKenna College, Professor Murphy worked as a research scientist at Battelle Seattle Research Center, where she designed and delivered leadership development programs for senior-level managers in a wide range of industries.

Patricia M. G. O'Connor is a senior faculty member at the Center for Creative Leadership (CCL). She received a BS degree in human resources from the University of Illinois (Urbana-Champaign) and an MBA degree with honors from Bernard M. Baruch College (CUNY). Since joining CCL in 1995, Patricia has worked nationally and internationally with over 500 senior managers and executives in the design and facilitation of leadership development initiatives. Her research, publications, and presentations have addressed the topics of corporate communication, 360-degree feedback in the development of learning cultures, systemic approaches to leader development, and context-based approaches to leveraging leadership capacity in organizations. She is coauthoring a new chapter for the second edition of CCL's *Handbook of Leadership Development*, which presents a model that calls for a departure from the traditional understanding of leadership and development (i.e., individually based) for organizations to more effectively address complex challenges. Before taking on a faculty position, Patricia served as the Director of Business Development and was responsible for developing enterprise-wide business development strategy, leading an international team of business development professionals and serving on the Center's management team.

Craig L. Pearce is an Assistant Professor of Management at the Peter F. Drucker Graduate School of Management at Claremont Graduate University. He received his PhD from the University of Maryland (College Park), his MBA from the University of Wisconsin-Madison, and his BS (with honors) from Pennsylvania State University. Dr. Pearce's areas of expertise include leadership, teamwork, and change management. He has won several awards for his research including an award from the Center for Creative Leadership for his research on shared leadership. His research has appeared or is forthcoming in *Organizational Dynamics*, *Journal of Management*, *Strategic Management Journal*, *Journal of Organizational Behavior*, *Journal of Occupational and Organizational Psychology*, *Group*

Dynamics: Theory, Research, and Practice, Journal of Managerial Issues, Advances in Interdisciplinary Studies of Work Teams, Journal of Personal Selling and Sales Management, Journal of Applied Social Psychology, Human Resource Management Review, Journal of Management Systems, and *Handbook of Nonprofit Management* as well as other outlets. His new book, entitled *Shared Leadership: Reframing the Hows and Whys of Leadership,* coedited with Jay A. Conger, was published by Sage in 2003. Dr. Pearce serves on the board of directors of Small Potatoes, Inc., an agricultural biotech company. Prior to beginning an academic career, Dr. Pearce worked as an international management consultant in the area of process reengineering, organizational development, and turnaround management. Dr. Pearce's clients have included AAI, ACNielsen, American Express, British Bakeries, GEICO Insurance, Land Rover, Mack Trucks, Manor Bakeries, Pickering Foods, Rayovac, The Rouse Company, Rover Cars, and Serono.

Ronald E. Riggio is the Henry R. Kravis Professor of Leadership and Organizational Psychology at Claremont McKenna College and Director of the Kravis Leadership Institute. His early research interests focused on the measurement of communication and social skills, with a particular emphasis on the communication of emotion and the role of communication skills and emotion in charisma and charismatic leadership. He is the author of more than 50 journal articles in organizational psychology, social psychology, management, and education, as well as author or coeditor of several books, including *Assessment Centers: Research and Practice* (Select Press, 1997), *Multiple Intelligences and Leadership* (Lawrence Erlbaum Associates, 2002), and his textbook *Introduction to Industrial/Organizational Psychology* (Prentice Hall, 2003), now in its fourth edition.

Chester Schriesheim is the University of Miami Distinguished Professor of Management and the Rosa R. and Carlos M. de la Cruz Leadership Scholar. He received his PhD at Ohio State University. Previously, he was a tenured Professor at the University of Florida and a tenured Associate Professor at the University of Southern California. Dr. Schriesheim's teaching and research interests are primarily in leadership, power and influence, and applied research methods. He has received numerous professional recognitions for outstanding teaching, service, and research. He is the author or coauthor of almost 200 books, articles, and scholarly papers, with six dozen published in top-tier scholarly outlets such as the *Academy of Management Journal,* the *Academy of Management Review,* the *Journal of Applied Psychology, Psychological Bulletin,* and the *Administrative Science Quarterly.* Dr. Schriesheim has been selected a Fellow of the American Psychological Association and the Southern Management Association and has held numerous offices in various professional associations, including President of the Southern Management Association and Chair of the Research Methods Division of the Academy of Management. Professor Schriesheim has done extensive training and consulting for government and industry, including Burger King, Chrysler Corp., Eagle Brands, Mt. Sinai Medical Center, and United Distillers. He has also served as an advisor to the Leadership Analysis Directorate of the U.S. Central Intelligence Agency and held various grants with funding agencies such as the Office of Naval Research.

Georgia Sorenson is a Visiting Senior Scholar at the Jepson School of Leadership and Founder of the James MacGregor Burns Academy of Leadership. A founder of the leadership studies movement, she has consulted to hundreds of leadership development and leadership studies programs around the world. A presidential leadership scholar, Sorenson also holds appointments at Williams College and at Ewa University in Seoul, Korea. She also serves as Professor and Advisor to The National School of Administration of the People's Republic of China and is on the International Board of Tokyo Jogakkan University in Japan. Sorenson is on the board of directors of many leadership institutions, including Kellogg National Fellows, Asian Pacific American Leadership Institute, Leadership Learning Community, Education in Action, LeaderNet, and New Voices. Before coming to the University, Dr. Sorenson was a Senior Policy Analyst in the Carter White House for employment issues and later served as a consultant to the Executive Office of the President. During her White House tenure, she served on the White House Productivity Council and Vice President Mondale's Youth Employment Council. Dr. Sorenson has published in professional journals such as the *Harvard Educational Review* and *The Psychology of Women Quarterly* and is a frequent contributor and commentator on social issues in the popular media. Sorenson is currently editing a four-volume Leadership Encyclopedia with Al Goethals and James MacGregor Burns for Sage Press.

Gretchen Spreitzer is a Clinical Professor of Organizational Behavior and Human Resource Management at the University of Michigan, School of Business Administration, where she received her PhD. Her most recent book, *A Company of Leaders: Five Disciplines for Unleashing the Power in Your Workforce* (2001), with Robert Quinn, brings together 10 years of research and practice on this topic. Her extended research program focuses on the changing essence of leadership in contemporary organizations, particularly within a context of organizational change and decline. Recent research focuses on how to move leadership down throughout the organization, what leadership looks like in a virtual context, and how leadership practices translate or fail to translate across cultures. She is an editor of the *Journal of Management Inquiry* and is on the editorial boards of *Organization Science* and the *Journal of Organizational Behavior*. She is the Past President of the Western Academy of Management and on the executive board of the Organizational Development and Change Division of the National Academy of Management.

Ginka Toegel teaches Organizational Theory and Behavior and Industrial Psychology at the London School of Economics. She received her undergraduate and MA degrees from Humboldt-University, Berlin, and her PhD in Psychology from Leipzig University. Currently, she is at the last stage of her second PhD in

Management at London Business School. Dr. Toegel has been deeply involved in 360-degree feedback applications for executive programs at the London Business School. Her research interests focus on the conflicts, contradictions, and dilemmas that are created when 360-degree assessment is stretched to uses beyond its original application for management development. Currently, she is working on two other empirical studies. One examines the so called "toxic handlers," or people who process negative emotions in organizations, and the other focuses on the function of the perceptions of control in the strategic decision-making process.

Mary Uhl-Bien is an Associate Professor of Management at the University of Central Florida. She received her MBA and PhD from the University of Cincinnati. Her work has been published in top management outlets, including the *Academy of Management Journal*, the *Journal of Applied Psychology*, the *Journal of Management*, the *Leadership Quarterly*, *Research in Personnel and Human Resources Management*, and *Human Relations*. She serves on the Editorial Board of both the *Academy of Management Journal* and the *Leadership Quarterly*. Dr. Uhl-Bien specializes in relational leadership theory, and her work on complex leadership received recognition from the Center for Creative Leadership as the best paper for the *Leadership Quarterly* in 2001. She has been involved in grant work in the Russian Far East and was a visiting professor in Spain in 2002. She has consulted to leading U.S. corporations, including State Farm Insurance, Walt Disney World, British Petroleum, and Sears, as well as to the U.S. Fish and Wildlife Service.

David A. Waldman received his PhD from Colorado State University in Industrial/Organizational Psychology. He has taught at SUNY–Binghamton, Concordia University in Montréal, and is presently at Arizona State University West, where he is a Professor of Management in the School of Management. He is also an affiliated faculty member of the Department of Management at Arizona State University Main. His research interests focus on leadership, 360-degree feedback, and cross-cultural management issues. His accomplishments include approximately 70 scholarly and practitioner articles and book chapters, approximately $450,000 in grant money, and current editorial board memberships, including the boards of the *Journal of Applied Psychology*, the *Academy of Management Journal*, and the *Journal of Organizational Behavior*. He recently published a book on 360-degree feedback, coauthored with Leanne Atwater. Other areas of expertise include survey construction and validation and assessment center methodology. Professor Waldman is a Fellow of the American Psychological Association and the Society for Industrial and Organizational Psychology. He has consulted for a number of Fortune 500 companies and governmental agencies in the United States, Canada, and Mexico.

Series Foreword

Series Editors
Jeanette N. Cleveland
The Pennsylvania State University

Edwin A. Fleishman
George Mason University

There is compelling need for innovative approaches to the solution of many pressing problems involving human relationships in today's society. Such approaches are more likely to be successful when they are based on sound research and applications. This *Series in Applied Psychology* offers publications which emphasize state-of-the-art research and its application to important issues of human behavior in a variety of societal settings. The objective is to bridge both academic and applied interests. This book, The Future of Leadership Development accomplishes this objective with respect to leadership development within organizations.

Three quarters of U.S. organizations with over 10,000 employees spend $750,000 or more on leadership development each year. According to the book editors, Murphy and Riggio, this figure represents nearly $8,000 per person and a large portion of organizational training budgets. The study of leadership, including what it is, how it operates, and the identification of characteristics of effective leaders, historically has been the focus of broad based multi-disciplinary attention. Yet leadership *development* is an understudied topic. As Schein (1992) indicates."we basically do not know what the world of tomorrow will really be like except that it will be different" (p. 361). "That means that organizations and their leaders will have to become perpetual learners." (p. 361).

In "The Future of Leadership Development," an impressive slate of scholars were brought together at the 11th annual Kravis-de Roulet conference to address critical issues about the current state of thinking on leadership and provide future directions for bridging the gap between leadership research and theory and leadership development in actual organizations. Globalization, knowledge-based organizations, rapid technological changes and the permeability of organizational boundaries have been discussed as critical factors in shaping organizations and

leaders of the future. Murphy and Riggio have skillfully organized the contributions of these scholars into 13 chapters (further organized into five sections) of the
current book.

In the first section, the importance of defining and articulating the domain of
leadership, including the necessary skills, abilities, traits and behavior needed to
implement a vision is stressed by Locke. Day and O'Connor develop this theme
by challenging researchers to go beyond defining leadership to understanding the
process of leadership development.

In the second section, emerging workplace challenges of leadership including
"e-leadership" and leadership within virtual organizations are presented in chapters by Avolio and Kahai (chapter 3) and by Spreitzer (chapter 4). Both chapters
discuss how technology affects leadership development, including emerging leader
challenges in situations with fewer face-to-face interactions and employees who
are physically dispersed from one another.

Innovative techniques for leadership development are presented in the third section of this book. Atwater, Brett, and Waldman specifically discuss the use of multisource feedback for leader development in Chapter 5. Conger and Toegel apply the
concepts of action learning to the development of leaders in the workplace. Rather
than viewing multiple source feedback and action learning as distinct leader development techniques, these authors suggest the use of them in complementary ways.

In section four, current leadership theory and its development implications are
explored. Uhl Bien (Chapter 7) and Cogliser and Scandura (Chapter 8) both extend
leader-member exchange theory to the development of relationship skills among
leaders and show how positive leader relations can be a leader development experience for followers. Cox, Pearce, and Sims present expanded conceptualizations
of the transformational, transactional leaders and shared leadership to include development in chapter 9. In chapter 10, Schriesheim critiques current leadership
theories in relation to leadership development.

Much of the research on leadership has focused on the characteristics of leaders in organizations and powerful social positions including those in industrial,
political, religious and government organizations. The current book broadens the
discussion of leadership development to include considerations of potential development for individuals "prior" to entering organizations. In the final section of this
text, three chapters are devoted to examining leadership development in higher
education. Ayman, Adams, Hartman, and Fisher present a general examination of
leadership education in university settings in chapter 11. In chapter 12, Riggio,
Ciulla, and Sorenson describe how such issues as ethnical leadership, good citizenship, social responsibility and the meaning of leadership are developed in programs
in liberal arts schools. Finally, in the concluding chapter of the book, Mumford
and Manley provide an insightful discussion of the inclusion of a developmental,
life-long perspective of leadership development.

The set of chapters and authors represented in the book reflect expertise and
scholarship across scientific and applied domains. This ground-breaking book sets

a research agenda for the future that addresses how leaders' careers unfold over time, what skills are needed by people occupying leadership roles, and how the skills are acquired.

The book is appropriate for students in industrial and organizational psychology, management and education including courses in leadership and motivation, training and development, and performance feedback. Professionals who are engaged in the development of leaders in organizational and academic settings will find this book essential to their work.

THE FUTURE OF LEADERSHIP
DEVELOPMENT

Introduction to The Future of Leadership Development

Susan Elaine Murphy
Ronald E. Riggio

Leadership in today's organizations is a tough business. Organizational leaders face a number of significant challenges as their jobs, and the world around them, become increasingly complex (see Zaccaro & Klimoski, 2001). Trends such as organizational "delayering," rapid technological advances, the proliferation of team-based organizations, and increased employee empowerment require that leaders adapt their techniques and styles of leadership to meet these new challenges. In the face of all these changes, researchers and management education specialists are working to find methods to develop more effective leaders. Old techniques of development are criticized and questioned, and new techniques are created—often before they are adequately tested and thoroughly understood. New techniques can become instant "fads."

The current economic environment is also tough. The same economic environment that challenges leaders in both for-profit and nonprofit organizations to do more with less squeezes the budget for developing organizational leaders, so there is an ongoing search for both highly effective and highly cost-effective leadership development methods. Still, 75% of U.S. companies with over 10,000 employees spend $750,000 or more on leadership development annually; that is almost $8,000 per person. These expenditures represent a large portion of their training budgets (as much as 25% for one third of all organizations) going to leadership/management

1

development (Delahoussaye, 2001, survey sponsored by Training Magazine and American Management Associations).

Programs for developing organizational leaders are far-ranging. They include programs that focus primarily on individual leadership enhancement as well as large-scale leadership development programs that focus on entire organizations—and view leadership development from a holistic approach of developing the entire organization's leadership capacity (Giber, Carter, & Goldsmith, 2000). Some organizational leadership development is expected to take place in settings other than the work organization as companies rely on colleges and universities to produce "emerging leaders" who can easily step into leadership positions in their organizations—thus the rise in college-based leadership programs. Moreover, there is the expectation that ongoing leadership development takes place outside the walls of the organization—thus the rise in popularity of personal leadership development books and the companies' encouragement of employees to take advantage of community service opportunities that build leadership skills.

What do most of the various organizational leadership development programs have in common? Many of them start with an assessment of business needs, onto which is mapped a set of leadership competencies. These competency-based programs are used in many organizations with some success (Conger & Benjamin, 1999). Competencies and broad-based skill sets are important in today's broadly defined jobs (Cascio, 1995). But do we truly understand the competencies required for today's organizational leaders and those that are needed for the leaders of tomorrow?

Another common element of organizational leadership development programs is that they are grounded in principles and theories of learning. However, one common criticism of leadership development programs is that they often are not strongly enough grounded in learning theories (Day, 2000). The age-old problem is the disconnect between the scholars who study and understand development processes and those who provide leadership training.

A great deal of energy, as well as substantial research efforts, goes into creating and evaluating specific leadership development techniques, such as 360-degree feedback, mentoring, goal setting, and the like. Problems arise, however, in the implementation of these programs, leading to a decrease in their potential effectiveness. Failures to match training needs to programs; failures to transfer training from the "classroom" to the workplace; failures to integrate new leadership behaviors into the workgroup or team; and even too great a focus on the leader, ignoring the realities of team-shared leadership (Pearce & Conger, 2003), all work to weaken development efforts.

In recent years, there has been an explosion of interest in leadership. The bulk of research efforts has gone into trying to understand leadership—how it operates—and into identifying the characteristics of effective leaders. Leadership development, although it consumes the energy of leadership trainers, as well as the training budgets of companies, is clearly a much understudied topic. Fortunately, that is changing. Influential organizations, such as the Center for Creative Leadership (see McCauley, Moxley, & Van Velsor, 1998) the Gallup Organization (Buckingham & Clifton, 2001), as well as many centers associated with universities around the world and noted leadership scholars are turning their attention to the difficult topic of truly trying to understand the process of leadership development. This book is an effort to continue that forward movement.

The 11th annual Kravis-de Roulet Conference brought together an impressive slate of contributors to explore current thinking and future directions in the field of leadership development. Collectively, this group of scholars has been thinking about questions of leadership effectiveness and methods for developing leaders for many years. The chapters they wrote ask and answer questions about the current state of the field and provide future directions for research to help bridge the gap between leadership researchers and leadership development practitioners. They also provide research evidence for the efficacy of many of the cutting edge techniques.

The first section addresses both the "how" and "what" of leadership development. David Day and Patricia O'Connor provide an initial assessment of the current state of leadership development by examining its underlying processes. In particular, they call for a theory that gives solid solutions for improving leadership development rather than merely explaining what leadership is. Concepts from the various learning and development literatures, such as reflective judgment, ego development, and continuous growth and change, are brought together to provide focus for future work in development of theory, or a "science of leadership development." Another important contribution of this chapter is the view that leadership development is a multidimensional and multilevel phenomenon. Although the chapter provides a rich set of ideas for theory development, it provides, more importantly, many practical solutions that leadership development specialists can use to design programs that work for their organizations.

The fact that organizations face many changes in today's workplace, affecting leadership research and practice, does not suggest that we should throw out our old ideas about what makes an effective leader. In chapter 2, Edwin Locke underscores the importance of enduring leadership requirements that have stood the test of time. After stressing the importance of defining leadership and delineating the domain of leadership, Locke provides a number of examples showing the role of vision, core values, and a summary of the necessary traits, skills, and abilities and actions to implement an organizational vision. His overview has a number of implications for developing leaders to learn and exhibit the skills to be successful and in providing important background for considering future leadership development challenges.

Chapters 3 and 4 explore the newest forms of leadership: "e-leadership" and leadership within the "virtual" organization. These aspects of leadership will affect the "what" of leadership development and highlight more forms of indirect leadership. Bruce Avolio and Surinder Kahai present their thoughts on "e-leadership." They address questions relevant to leadership mediated by technology, such as "how does technology change leadership?" According to Avolio and Kahai, technology influences leadership in many ways. For example, on virtual project teams, communication channels, decision making, and membership change frequently. Additionally, technology leads to fewer face-to-face interactions with leaders, yet at the same time, increases the opportunities to be in contact with leaders, as well as increases access to large amounts of information for all employees. Next, Gretchen Spreitzer uncovers the more specific challenges of leadership in today's workplace of virtual organizations. A virtual organization consists of employees who are physically dispersed from one another and may even be members of different organizations—but all work toward a common goal. According to Spreitzer, leaders must meet these challenges by developing high-level technological savvy, effective communication skills, comfort with and ability to empower employees, and cross-cultural dexterity.

These new leadership challenges suggest the need for cutting-edge leadership development technologies. The next two chapters focus on the use of specific types of very popular leadership development tools and their potential benefits as well as possible misuses. Leanne Atwater, Joan Brett, and David Waldman explore how 360-degree feedback is used and how this feedback can be presented more effectively for better leadership development results. They summarize the results of numerous studies attempting to ascertain the effectiveness of this technique. Their chapter summarizes research on the validity of the impact of feedback interventions, the factors that influence change, and the potential risks and negative effects of 360-degree feedback. Jay Conger and Ginka Toegel focus on action learning—a technique that has gained much recent attention. Action learning takes managers out of traditional classrooms to work on actual organizational problems, to learn leadership and management skills while responding to a specific organizational challenge. Conger and Toegel assert that both 360-degree feedback and action learning have not been used to their potential for developing leaders and managers. Each chapter in this section provides extremely practical advice for leadership development and human resource professionals, based on sound research with these popular techniques.

The next section delves into the leadership development implications of two very popular leadership theories. The first, which is discussed in the first two chapters, is a well-researched theory of leader and follower relationships: Leader–Member Exchange (LMX) (Graen & Scandura, 1987). According to this well-researched model, leadership is first, and most importantly, a relationship. Some leader–member relationships are more successful in fostering increased follower satisfaction and group effectiveness, whereas others are less successful. In a comprehensive review of LMX theory, Uhl-Bien and Graen (1995) reported that the next step for the evolution of this theory is to encourage leaders to develop these effective in-group relationships with their followers and to focus research that uncovers this process. The chapters in this section attempt to take LMX theory to the next level.

In chapter 7, Mary Uhl-Bien explores leadership development implications derived from LMX, by highlighting the importance of "social capital" in the relationship-building process. Because many leaders find themselves working in either team-based leadership positions or organizations with little true hierarchy, leadership power is now much less likely to come from the position, but rather from the leader's ability to develop and maintain relationships. Uhl-Bien utilizes Day's (2000) distinction between *leader* development and *leadership* development in understanding the importance of relationships in LMX. Relational skills, such as those involved in the larger constructs of social and emotional intelligence, and self-management skills are important for understanding relationships, for being able to engage in effective self-presentation in dyadic relationships, and for effectively delivering feedback (see also Riggio, Murphy, & Pirozzolo, 2002, for a discussion of the importance of different forms of intelligence for effective leadership). Uhl-Bien's chapter generates an important set of propositions for future research by providing both an overview of relationship development processes and delineating skills necessary for leaders to build and maintain effective relationships.

In chapter 8, Claudia Cogliser and Terri Scandura further extend Leader–Member Exchange theory by exploring how a leader's relationship with followers can be a leader development experience for the follower. How does this occur? They speculate that the nature of the relationship a follower has with the leader may contribute either positively or negatively to the follower's own leadership relationship with others in the organization. They propose a framework that relates leader–member exchange at one level in the organization to the next level in the organization. They outline four possible types of relationships: *waterfalls*, where LMX at the higher level is positively related to LMX at the next lower level; *snowballs*, where LMX at the higher level is less than the lower level; *brick walls*, where LMX at the higher level is independent of the lower level; and *scuzzballs*, where LMX at the higher level is poor, and the lower level is either better, the same, or worse. Understanding the effects of these different types of relationships is important for motivating leaders to invest in relationship development.

In chapter 9, Jonathan Cox, Craig Pearce, and Henry Sims, Jr., examine leadership development by providing a new leader behavior typology that expands upon the concept of transformational–transactional leadership (Bass, 1985; Bass & Avolio, 1993). This new typology includes directive and empowering leader behavior. They argue that the benefits of leader behavior typologies, as many leadership development specialists know, are to help diagnose participants' preferred leadership strategies and to provide a quick guide to appropriate behavior. The authors discuss the historical roots of types of leadership, the behaviors associated with each, and the conditions under which each is appropriate. They also introduce the important concept of *shared leadership*, a recent conceptualization of leadership that explicitly emphasizes lateral influence among peers (Pearce, 2002; Pearce & Conger, 2003).

To conclude this section, Chester Schriesheim provides a provocative critique of the shortcomings of various theories of leadership with respect to leadership development, and he outlines six reasons why leadership research is irrelevant for leadership development. No leadership theory is spared examination in his overview. He traces the contributions of various theories, pointing out why they have not contributed as much to leadership development as they might have. His criticisms range from the inaccessible language used by leadership researchers, to the overreliance on the use of statistical significance, to the lack of consideration of the leader's motivation to expend effort to manage team members effectively. The chapter provides very important warnings for researchers not only for developing and testing theories and techniques of leadership development but also for translating these concepts to practice and to leadership practitioners.

Nearly all attention to organizational leadership development focuses on existing organizational leaders or preparing current workers for future leadership positions in the company. Yet organizations expect that those entering the workforce have some leadership aptitude; it is often used as a hiring criterion. Little attention has been given to leadership development prior to organizational entry. The next section focuses on this, examining leadership development in higher education. In chapter 11, Roya Ayman, Susan Adams, Erica Hartman, and Bruce Fisher look broadly at the type of leadership education provided in today's institutes of higher learning. These programs are specifically designed to enhance students' leadership capacity and potential and are often popular because they have direct relevance to the roles that students will fill in organizations. Colleges and universities have a long history of developing young leaders, and there is much that organizations can learn from their programs. Taking a slightly different perspective, Ron Riggio, Joanne Ciulla, and Georgia Sorenson summarize the unique features of leadership development programs in liberal arts schools. This model of developing future leaders is concerned not only with leadership skill development but also with issues of ethical leadership, good citizenship, social responsibility, and the meaning of leadership, which can serve as a guide—a sort of moral compass—for organizational leadership development programs.

The concluding chapter by Michael Mumford and Greg Manley ties together a number of themes from the preceding chapters and sets an important research agenda for leadership development. In introducing this chapter, the major question of "how can we go about developing more effective leaders?" is answered by focusing on issues such as how leaders' careers unfold over time, what skills are needed by people occupying leadership roles (as well as how these skills change as people move through different roles), and finally, how the acquisition of these skills is influenced by broader developmental processes.

We would like to express our appreciation to all those who have contributed to the 2001 conference and to the book. We thank the conference sponsors, Henry R. Kravis and the Vincent de Roulet family. Claremont McKenna College administration and staff have also provided support for this project, as well as the staff of the Kravis Leadership Institute, especially Lynda Mulhall, Assistant Director, and Sandy Counts, who have been instrumental in bringing the Kravis-de Roulet Conference together and facilitating the editing of this book. Annie Lee, Yoon Mi Kim, Kathyrn Gilmore, and Rachel Rosenfeld deserve special thanks for their work as editorial assistants throughout the project. Also, we thank Anne Duffy and her superb editorial group at Lawrence Erlbaum Associates.

REFERENCES

Bass, B. M. (1985). Leadership and performance beyond expectations. New York: The Free Press.
Bass, B. M., & Avolio, B. J. (1993). Transformational leadership: A response to critiques. In M. M. Chemers & R. Ayman (Eds.), *Leadership theory and research: Perspective and directions* (pp. 49–80). New York: Academic Press.
Buckingham, M., & Clifton, D. O. (2001). *Now, discover your strengths.* New York: The Free Press.
Cascio, W. (1995). Whither industrial and organizational psychology in a changing world of work? *American Psychologist, 50,* 928–934.
Conger, J. A., & Benjamin, B. (1999). *Building leaders: How successful companies develop the next generation.* San Francisco: Jossey-Bass.
Day, D. V. (2000). Leadership development: A review in context. *The Leadership Quarterly: Yearly Review of Leadership, 11,* 581–613.
Delahoussaye, M. (2001). Leadership in the 21st century. *Training, 8*(9), 60–72.
Giber, D., Carter, L., & Goldsmith, M. (2000). *Best practices in leadership development handbook.* San Francisco: Jossey-Bass/Pfeiffer.
Graen, G. B., & Scandura, T. (1987). Toward a psychology of dyadic organizing. In B. Staw & L. L. Cummings (Eds.), *Research in organizational behavior* (Vol. 9, pp. 175–208). Greenwich, CT: JAI Press.
Graen, G. B., & Uhl-Bien, M. (1995). Relationship-based approach to leadership: Development of leader-member exchange (LMX) theory of leadership over 25 years: Applying a multi-level multi-domain perspective. *The Leadership Quarterly, 6*(2), 219–247.
McCauley, C., Moxley, R., Van Velsor, E. (2000). Our view of leadership development. In C. McCauley, R. Moxley, & E. Van Velsor (Eds.), *The handbook of leadership development* (pp. 1–25). San Francisco: Jossey-Bass.
Pearce, C. L. (2002). Más allá del liderazgo heroico: Como el buen vino, el liderazgo es algo para ser compartido. *Revista de Empresa, 1*(2), 53–64.
Pearce, C. L., & Conger, J. A. (Eds.). (2003). *Shared leadership: Reframing the hows and whys of leadership.* Thousand Oaks, CA: Sage.
Riggio, R. E., Murphy, S. E., & Pirozzolo, F. (2002). *Multiple intelligences and leadership.* Mahwah, NJ: Lawrence Erlbaum Associates.
Zaccaro, S. J., & Klimoski, R. J. (2001). *The nature of organizational leadership: Understanding the performance imperatives confronting today's leaders.* San Francisco: Jossey-Bass.

I
Setting the Stage

1

Leadership Development: Understanding the Process

David V. Day
Pennsylvania State University

Patricia M. G. O'Connor
Center for Creative Leadership

The purpose of this chapter is to summarize what researchers and theorists—and scientists and practitioners—know about the process of leadership development. This has proved to be a daunting task because relatively little is known about the *process* of leadership development. A relevant question to ask (and one that is addressed in this chapter) is why is this the case? Why is it that we know so little about the process of leadership development, and what needs to be done to redress this oversight? One could argue that practice is to blame, given that the majority of leadership development efforts are designed around and evaluated through discrete events without much opportunity for understanding and implementing long-term, systemic approaches. Given the lack of empirical evidence to support the proposition that systemic approaches yield significantly greater returns to organizations, it is difficult to argue for a long-term, systemic strategy for leadership development. However, a practical emphasis on short-term, discrete events is an obstacle to better understanding the process of leadership development. Another reason for the gap in knowledge regarding process is that leadership development has not received much serious scientific attention. This is a puzzling state of affairs when one considers the critical role that leadership plays in organizations and the broader society.

WANTED: A SCIENCE
OF LEADERSHIP DEVELOPMENT

A hallmark of science is the scientific method. Knowledge is created or discovered from the results of carefully designed and tightly controlled experiments. Participants are randomly assigned to experimental and control conditions, key variables are manipulated, and relevant outcomes are measured. Any subsequent differences between groups in terms of outcomes can be causally linked to the manipulated variables. This type of true experiment is the gold standard of science, but it does not serve the study of leadership development particularly well. This is because leadership is a highly contextual construct that emerges through a complex interaction of leaders, followers, and situations (Fiedler, 1996). Furthermore, the most potent forces for leadership development occur in the context of ongoing work and not in formal classroom settings (McCall, Lombardo, & Morrison, 1988). Indeed, the ongoing work context serves as a catalyst for both leadership and development. Much of the richness provided by situational work contexts is what contributes to meaningful experience. Most true experiments strive to control those very "extraneous" situational forces that are most important for leadership development.

It is possible, albeit difficult, to study leadership development scientifically (see Dvir, Eden, Avolio, & Shamir, 2002, for a recent example). Thus, opportunities abound for advancing a science of leadership development. Instead of true experiments, researchers can and do use quasi-experimental methods, correlational designs, and qualitative approaches to the study of leadership development. Unfortunately, even these less rigorous scientific methods are used infrequently. What has developed over the years is a greater attention to the practice of leadership development than to its scientific study. Even an often cited handbook on the topic of leadership development (McCauley, Moxley, & Van Velsor, 1998) does not include much mention of rigorous scientific research. There is much sound advice on various programs and practices to promote leadership development, but little of it is grounded in an empirically based, scientific foundation. This underscores the observation that the practice of leadership development is far ahead of its scientific understanding (Day, 2000). A science of leadership development is needed if we are ever going to understand the process. To that end, this chapter discusses three areas of opportunity for advancing the science of leadership development: (a) development of theory, (b) advancement of multidimensional perspectives, and (c) application of sophisticated measures and models of change.

DEVELOPMENT OF THEORY

In addition to the scientific method, another hallmark of science is theory testing. Unfortunately, there are few extant theories of leadership development to test scientifically. Put somewhat differently, before the leadership development process can be modeled effectively, the content of what is being developed needs to be better understood. There has been some progress in this area, but more theoretical work is needed. There are a few, isolated examples in the literature that provide hope in terms of being able to successfully build a science of leadership development. For example, recent empirical work on the motivation to lead proposed (and tested) a model in which leadership self-efficacy mediates the relationship between leader individual differences (cognitive ability, personality, values, previous leadership experience) and the motivation to assume leadership training, roles, and responsibilities (Chan & Drasgow, 2001). This study is exemplary in developing a theoretically grounded model that guided the study's design, data collection, analyses, and results interpretation.

Another recently published study is laudable in terms of its scientific rigor and its emphasis on follower development. In that study, researchers examined the effects of transformational leadership training on follower development in a longitudinal, randomized field experiment (Dvir et al., 2002). In addition to the rigorous design and longitudinal focus, an especially strong feature of the Dvir et al. study is the multifaceted nature of the development construct. Pre- and post-training measures were gathered from followers on seven developmental variables: (a) self-actualization, (b) extra effort, (c) internalization of organizational moral values, (d) collectivist orientation, (e) critical-independent thinking, (f) active engagement, and (g) self-efficacy. Results indicated significant treatment by occasion interactions for self-efficacy, critical-independent thinking, and extra effort. This is exactly the kind of study needed to build a sound leadership development science. It tests theoretically grounded hypotheses regarding how transformational leaders are thought to transform their followers, and in turn, transform organizations. Studies of this type contribute to a better understanding of how developing leaders contribute to organization development (Day, Zaccaro, & Halpin, 2004) and provide advancements toward understanding the process.

A final notable theoretical contribution to the understanding of leadership development—and one that will help especially with further criterion development efforts—is the Leaderplex model (Hooijberg, Hunt, & Dodge, 1997), which proposes to understand leadership complexity in the form of cognitive, social, and behavioral complexity. Complexity in this context does not necessarily mean more complicated. Instead, it can be thought of as a more sophisticated or integrated way of thinking, doing, and being. A fundamental question underlying this conceptualization pertains to the reasons for complexity as a developmental imperative for leaders. In short, complexity provides the resources (cognitive, social, behavioral) for generating numerous possible responses to a given situation. Individuals as well as organizations are healthy and thrive when they are capable of many responses to a given situation, and become brittle and vulnerable to changing conditions when they are uniform and specialized (Sale, 1982). Thus, as catalysts for creative and adaptive responses in challenging situations, these forms of complexity might be considered keys to the developmental process.

In addition to the process-based approaches of the aforementioned studies, a catalyst to theoretical development could be added by more intentionally connecting with the adult development literature. Much of the contemporary theory and research on adult development can be traced to the late 1960s, when developmental theorists challenged Piaget on his highest stage of formal operations. The gist of the challenge was that further cognitive development was possible beyond formal operations, and that some people continue throughout their lifespan to transform their thinking and meaning-making into more complex and inclusive ways of knowing (Cook-Greuter, 1999). Such theories are sometimes called post-Piagetian but are more frequently termed postformal or postconventional. They hold the greatest promise for advancing a science of leadership development, because they focus on how people make sense of their experiences in increasingly complex ways.

A particular nuance of many postformal theories has important implications for the conceptualization and measurement of leadership development. Specifically, it is assumed that "people can understand thinking at their own level or levels below their own, but not at levels above their own" (Loevinger, 1998a, p. 33). If this assumption is true, there is an inherent asymmetry in the development process in which those at higher levels of complexity can understand the thinking of those at lower levels (if motivated to do so), but those at lower levels cannot understand the thinking of those at higher developmental levels. This makes sense, but the implications of such an assumption for the field of leadership are profound. It may help explain why some people only recognize certain, relatively simple forms of behavior as leadership (e.g., initiating structure, setting direction, command and control), whereas others can also see leadership in more complex and collective forms of interaction (e.g., dialogue, cooperation, emergent understanding). Thus, the postformal approaches to adult development are very relevant for understanding leadership development, because the way in which leadership is constructed in the minds of people can vary from relatively straightforward and individualistic to highly complex, abstract, and collectivistic. Given that thinking is for doing (Fiske, 1992), how leadership is cognitively constructed influences not only how a leadership role is enacted (Drath, 2001) but also whether followers will allow a social influence process to occur (Lord & Maher, 1991). Following Loevinger's (1998a) thinking, if leadership can be thought about in complex ways, it can still be enacted in relatively simple forms. As mentioned, however, this process is asymmetrical. If leadership can only be constructed in simple and unsophisticated ways, it cannot be enacted in terms of more complex strategies. This provides a distinct limitation in terms of responding to complex challenges for which there are few, if any, known solutions in the group. In essence, when there are limited ways of thinking about leadership, there are limited strategies available to an individual, group, or organization for dealing with a given challenge. If the challenge is especially novel or complex, leadership strategies that have been successful in the past may not result in successful adaptation.

A fundamental paradox with regard to adult development is that laboratory research suggests there are robust age-related deficits in important cognitive attributes, such as creativity, flexibility, organization skills, logical deduction, abstract thinking, and problem solving (Craik & Salthouse, 1992). The paradox is that the majority of top-level positions in organizations are held by individuals in their 50s, 60s, and 70s. Assuming that these older adults are in these important positions because of their decision-making and problem-solving skills, how did these skills improve (rather than decline) with age? That is a key question addressed in the adult development literature, with clear relevance to understanding leadership development. It is encouraging to see Mumford and Manley (chap. 13, this volume) address the issue directly. A key point made by those (and other) authors (e.g., Tesluk & Jacobs, 1998) is that development is not a matter of mere experience; rather, it depends on how the experience is organized and interpreted in terms of underlying concepts or knowledge structures.

Experience is an effective means for prompting development, provided that it causes an individual to think about something (self, other, leadership) in a different—and usually more complex—way. This raises an important issue with regard to the type of developmental theory that would likely be most helpful to building a science of leadership development. Rather than focusing on the psychosocial tasks that are hypothesized to be indicative of various age groupings (e.g., Erickson, 1959; Levinson, Darrow, Klein, Levinson, & McKee, 1978) or on understanding of the microlevel cognitive and physiological changes associated with aging (Craik & Salthouse, 1992), those theories of adult development that focus on more holistic cognitive development and the changes that occur in adult thinking are likely to be most helpful to the scientific study of the leadership development process. Three specific theories of adult development show particular promise for advancing leadership development science. Each of these theories has its roots in constructivist developmental theory but also has corresponding measurement instruments and some foundation of empirical research. A brief summary of each theory follows.

Reflective Judgment

The reflective judgment model (Kitchener, 1983; Kitchener & King, 1990) describes a series of changes that occur in the way adults understand the process of knowing. Changes in reasoning are described by seven distinct sets of assumptions about knowledge and how it is acquired. Each successive stage is hypothesized to represent a more complex and effective form of justification, which provides a better means of evaluating and defending a point of view (Kitchener & King, 1990). An individual's level of reflective judgment is determined by means of a structured interview process in which a standard set of questions about four ill-structured problems are presented (Kitchener, 1986). Reliability estimates of the scoring procedures appear to be acceptable.

One especially intriguing aspect of this model is its connection to what some have termed the "meta-competencies" of adaptability and identity—two overarching characteristics that are thought to be important in helping leaders learn how to learn (Briscoe & Hall, 1999). Adaptability involves an individual's ability to identify qualities needed for future successful performance and to make the personal changes necessary to acquire those qualities and meet those needs. Identity refers to the ability to gather self-relevant feedback, form accurate self-perceptions, and change one's self-concept when needed. Adaptability and identity work in tandem in helping someone learn how to learn. Adaptability without identity can result in change just for the sake of change, without any self-direction. Identity without adaptability would be very self-aware inaction. A research question to pursue from this theoretical perspective might involve examining the posited linkages among more complex levels of reflective judgment and heightened cognitive and behavioral complexity, as well as enhanced adaptability and better integrated identity (ego).

Ego Development

Postformal and postautonomous ego development models (Cook-Greuter, 1990; 1999) assume that the content and structure of individuals' language production denote their level of conceptual competence. People function at a level that helps them to best organize and make sense of their experience; as such, conceptual complexity refers to the complexity and facility in using cognitive concepts in sense making. Level of functioning can be assessed using the Washington University Sentence Completion Test (Hy & Loevinger, 1996; Loevinger, 1998b), which consists of 36 sentence beginnings (e.g., "When I get mad . . . ."; "My father . . . .") that participants are allowed to finish in any manner. Because of the projective nature of this assessment protocol, scoring is based on both content and structure clues following guidelines developed by Loevinger (1998b). Each of the various states of ego development is thought to emerge from an interaction of thinking, doing, and being. Thus, linguistic data from cognitive, operative, and affective domains are used to gauge an individual's ego state. A research question to pursue from this theoretical perspective is whether a leader's ego state is related to the complexity of how leadership is constructed or enacted. Do those with more advanced ego states have a broader repertoire of leadership strategies at their disposal? If so, does this enhance their adaptability as leaders or contribute to more integrated leader identity?

Orders of Consciousness

The foundation of Kegan's (1982, 1994) constructivist developmental model of the "orders of consciousness" is based on the supposition that humans construct a subjective understanding of the world that shapes their experiences. Accordingly, two individuals can construct very different meanings from an identical event (e.g., leadership episode) depending on their respective developmental level. Individuals at higher orders of consciousness are able to use a greater number of knowledge principles to construct their experiences (differentiation) and make more interconnections among these principles (integration), resulting in a broader perspective on how things are interrelated (inclusiveness).

The notion of continuous growth and change is central to Kegan's (1982, 1994) framework. Individuals are thought to be continuously involved in a process of being embedded in a certain knowledge principle (i.e., way of knowing) and simultaneously attempting to "disembed" themselves from that principle to a higher order of consciousness (i.e., level of complexity). Transition to a higher order of consciousness occurs when individuals can free themselves from a principle that is held as "subject" to holding that same principle as "object." A principle that is subject is something that one sees with implicitly—it is so central to identity that it cannot be reflected on or acted on independently. An issue that is subject is so basic to functioning that one is unaware of it. A principle that is object is used to see through experience explicitly. It can be directly reflected on, taken control of, or otherwise operated on; it is distinct and differentiated from other principles. What is subject at a specific order of consciousness becomes object at the next higher order. What one sees with and takes for granted at one order becomes something one sees through and analyzes explicitly at the next.

The recommended measurement technique in Kegan's framework is the subject–object interview (Lahey et al., n.d.). Ten standardized questions are used to elicit verbal data on how the participant organizes intra- and interpersonal experiences. Interview protocols are scored according to 21 epistemological distinctions in which 5 gradations between each epistemology (or way of knowing) are possible. Interrater reliability estimates are purported to range from .75 to .90, and test–retest reliability was estimated to be .83.

Kegan's theoretical framework offers another way of conceptualizing leadership complexity. Specifically, how does a leader think about or construct leadership? What are the leadership principles that a leader holds as subject and as object? What kinds of experiences help a leader disembed from a principle that is held as subject? An example could be seen in terms of expanding a leader's perspective on the meaning of leadership from a historically traditional (and limited) personal dominance principle to include more sophisticated modes of leadership, such as interpersonal influence, or an even more complex or sophisticated principle based on relational dialogue (Drath, 2001). These are some important research questions that can be addressed from Kegan's (1994) theoretical framework and that will help researchers better understand the process of leadership development.

We are aware of one study, although still ongoing, that is investigating changes in developmental level and its relationship to leader effectiveness (Bullis, Lewis, Bartone, Forsythe, & Snook, 2002). The study participants are West Point cadets, who were interviewed as freshmen, sophomores, and seniors using the Lahey et al. (n.d.) subject–object interview protocol. Despite the relatively small sample size (between 22 and 53, depending on the variable), results suggest development across time and that developmental level is positively related to supervisor and peer ratings of leader performance. These findings are encouraging, but larger numbers of participants are needed to conduct the kinds of sophisticated modeling needed to draw stronger inferences about causality.

The preceding examples are not meant to be exhaustive in either their numbers or the level of detail provided. Rather, they serve as exemplars of relevant theories from the adult development literature with potential applicability to better understanding the process of leadership development. A possible limitation with theories from the adult development literature is that they focus exclusively on individual development. This is a reasonable constraint given that their intended purpose is to further understanding of how adults continue to develop throughout their lifespan. Leadership, however, is a multidimensional and a multilevel phenomenon. Indeed, some have argued that leadership development is always a multilevel development process (Avolio, 2004). The most basic (and traditional) level is the individual leader; the next highest level includes relationships with followers, peers, and superiors (i.e., dyads and group); an even higher level is the organizational systems level. Also, taking into account networked relationships and systems forces becomes critical for sustaining the self-regulation process and continuously advancing self-development. In short, comprehensive leadership development never occurs within just an individual leader.

ADVANCEMENT OF
MULTIDIMENSIONAL PERSPECTIVES

Recognizing the multidimensional nature of the phenomenon is important for advancing a leadership development science. Multidimensional in this context refers to three separate but interrelated domains of interest. First, the target of leadership development can be at or between various levels (i.e., individual, dyad, group, and organization). Second, development is concerned with enhancing and leveraging a variety of resources (e.g., human, social, and systems capital; O'Connor, 2002). Third, choices related to both leadership and development are embedded in a particular leadership construct or "knowledge principle" (e.g., personal, interpersonal, or relational; Drath, 2001). Figure 1.1 presents an overview of multidimensionality with regard to understanding the process of leadership development. The basic message from this figure is that scientists and practitioners should expand the lens of leadership beyond the traditional, personal, individual-leader approaches that have been emphasized historically in leadership development. Understanding the developmental resources that can be found in social and systems capital, and building more complex leadership constructs to include interpersonal and relational ways of thinking about leadership, are critical concerns in enhancing an understanding of the leadership development process. By expanding the definition of what

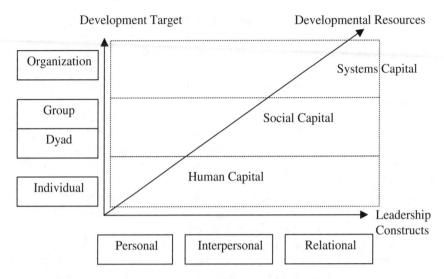

FIG. 1.1. Multidimensionality: Focal areas for understanding the process of leader(ship) development.

constitutes relevant leadership constructs and developmental resources, it becomes increasingly evident that leadership is a property of groups and organizations as opposed to solely individuals. By adopting such a multidimensional approach, one can better understand the nature of the leadership phenomenon as it is experienced in organizations and societies.

Previous work has articulated the importance of differentiating between leader development and leadership development (Day, 2000). The difference between these approaches is significant, because developing individual leaders does not necessarily translate into better leadership. This is because leader development emphasizes the acquisition or enhancement of intrapersonal (i.e., within-person) competencies, whereas leadership requires an interpersonal and relational (i.e., social) context—it is the dynamic interaction of leaders, followers, and situations. Developing an individual leader without regard for the social and systems influences brought to bear by followers and organizational forces (e.g., culture) will have at best only limited success in developing leadership. Conversely, focusing entirely on the social and organizational context without attending to individual development is likely to result in individuals feeling "in over their heads" when it comes to leadership (Kegan, 1994). Again, the overall result is limited in terms of impact. The ideal approach is to design comprehensive strategies that link individuals, groups, and organizations as well as leverage human, social, and systems capital.

Perhaps the biggest impediments to advancing a multidimensional perspective on development are fundamental differences in the various meanings of the leadership construct (i.e., knowledge principle). Most approaches to the study and the practice of leadership draw from a personal construct perspective, which assumes that leadership happens when a leader expresses leadership toward followers. The locus of leadership in this approach is with the individual leader who acts on (expresses leadership toward) followers (e.g., "Great Man" theories). Because of the belief that leadership is mainly a personal attribute, better leadership is thought to result by developing the knowledge, skills, and abilities (i.e., human capital) of individual leaders. Addressing this form of capital or developmental resource probably best constitutes what has been termed leader development, which builds on a foundation of individual competences, such as self-awareness, self-regulation, and self-motivation (Day, 2000). The overall development strategy is designed to help an individual leader engage in healthy attitude and identity development, to build a more sophisticated model of self, and to use that model of self to perform effectively across a myriad of organizational roles (Hall & Seibert, 1992), including formal and informal leadership roles. The unfortunate result has been a single-minded concern with human capital development of the individual leader. This emphasis is not wrong; rather, it is limited in terms of its ultimate effectiveness (Drath, 2001).

From the personal construct approach, leadership is resident within the individual leader. The social and systems contexts are thought to be relatively less important concerns. However, a comprehensive science of leadership development requires a perspective that tests not only a broader array of relevant dimensions but also, more importantly, the interrelationships between those dimensions. In doing so, the richness of a scientific study will more closely approximate the richness of the phenomenon it seeks to understand. Such a comprehensive approach should also provide for more sophisticated cognitive, behavioral, and social resources and thus be less limited in terms of leadership effectiveness.

Another prevalent construct holds that leadership is primarily an interpersonal process that is concerned primarily with negotiating influence (Hollander, 1964). Leadership is equated with interacting with others in ways that are socially intelligent, influential, persuasive, or instrumental. According to this leadership perspective, leaders act *with* followers rather than act *on* them. Development is concerned with helping individuals to gain those necessary interpersonal skills needed to be influential and effective in interpersonal contexts. Although this perspective recognizes leadership development as embedded in a process, it is limited to a particular type of process called influence.

By themselves, such developmental strategies do not fully develop leadership. This is because the developmental focus is primarily on an individual leader without sufficient attention to followers and the situation. Thus, there can be no leadership without some attention to the interpersonal or organizational context in which leadership occurs. Relevant to the present discussion is that it is difficult to understand or even recognize the process of development when the leadership phenomenon is assumed to be limited to the attributes of individuals.

Research recently conducted on the types of development needs that organizations request from external providers suggests that the majority of those needs could be classified as leader development issues (Jefferson, 2002). The emphasis is primarily on enhancing the knowledge, skills, and abilities of individual leaders (i.e., human capital). Relatively few organizations frame their requests with what the authors would term leadership development needs (i.e., enhancing the aggregate social capital of the organization or building its overall systems capital). One reason for this may be that organizational stakeholders cannot ask for leadership development if the only way in which leadership is constructed is as an individual attribute. Such findings may be indicative of a pervasive tendency to construct leadership in relatively simplistic terms. As noted previously, this precludes the ability to also construct it in complex ways. An organization's collective mindset about the construct of leadership may be one of the most important drivers or restrainers to developing a more complex and systemic approach to thinking about and enacting leadership.

Although there is much work to be done to further understand the more developmentally complex processes of leader development, limiting study solely to leaders runs the risk of grossly oversimplifying the leadership phenomenon. Leadership is inherently part of a dynamic, social environment (Fiedler, 1996; Salancik, Calder, Rowland, Leblebici, & Conway, 1975). Constructs embedded solely in a personal or even interpersonal perspective limit the reach of leadership development mainly to understanding individual competencies. Leadership in modern organizations is increasingly characterized by emergent and ambiguous, rather than predictable and prescribed, contexts. A more inclusive perspective on leadership may open fruitful venues for the scientific study of its development and better prepare all individuals to address the increasingly complex challenges of leadership. For example, a relational construct recognizes leadership as a social process in which influence, dialogue, and sensemaking are based in an interpersonal context. This developmental approach assumes that leadership is created and merges as people engage in work processes that require building, sustaining, and managing their interpersonal relationships (Drath, 2001).

Another impediment to advancing a multidimensional perspective on development pertains to the assumptions of what resources are leveraged and developed in leadership development. As discussed earlier, studies have traditionally focused on leader development, with components of human capital as the primary variables of interest. A basic axiom from the change management literature, however, is that sending a changed person back to an unchanged system is an exercise in futility. Nonetheless, leader development efforts that focus mainly on developing human capital rarely acknowledge the role the broader organizational context plays in developing leadership. A key to understanding the process is in bridging individual leader development with collective efforts at leadership development. This requires a multidimensional focus of study. To this end, recent advances in theory and research that move beyond a single-domain focus (e.g., Klein & Kozlowski, 2000) provide a great opportunity for developing a comprehensive leadership development science.

In addition to being concerned with understanding the process of developing personal and interpersonal competence, a comprehensive science of leadership development must also address social processes and organizational systems (Salancik et al., 1975). We propose that leadership development also involves enhancing the social capital in organizations—those networked connections among individuals that promote cooperation, mutual trust, and respect in creating organizational value (Burt, 1992; Tsai & Ghoshal, 1998; Uhl-Bien, Graen, & Scandura, 2000). As noted earlier, organizations are healthy and thrive when they are capable of many responses to a given situation. Lack of social connectivity can result in a handful of individuals trying to determine the best leadership response for an entire organization. Leveraging social capital provides a venue for development and makes a broader repertoire of leadership choices available to the organization.

There has been significant research into the identification and measurement of social networks (e.g., Burt, 1992) as well as the role of networks in individual effectiveness (e.g., job performance and career advancement; Sparrowe, Liden, Wayne, & Kraimer, 2001), but there has been no empirical work to date that has focused on an explicit relationship between networks and leadership development. This offers a major research opportunity for advancing the science of leadership development. For example, do certain sizes or types of networks promote more or less complex approaches to leadership? In what ways can social networks provide the developmental continuity and support often missing in more event-based approaches? How do social networks influence identity development and adaptability of leaders? To what degree can social networks be prescribed? Or must they emerge?

Organizational systems provide much of the support for human and social capital to develop. As such, these systems can profoundly influence the amount and type of individual, group, and organizational change that are central to development. As illustrated in Fig. 1.1, bridging leader development with leadership development requires attention to the developmental resources embedded in all forms of capital: human, social, and systems. All three components of assessment, challenge, and support that contribute to a developmental experience (Van Velsor, McCauley, & Moxley, 1998) can be embedded in an organization's formal and informal systems. This is perhaps best expressed in the statement that the state-of-the-art in development is helping leaders learn more effectively from their work, rather than taking them away from their work to learn (Moxley & O'Connor Wilson, 1998). In this manner, a science of leadership development needs to understand systems capital development not simply as a means of support or a force that provides challenging situations. Instead, there are opportunities to explore systems capital as a component of leadership, as integral as human or social capital (O'Connor & Quinn, 2003).

An organization's formal work systems and its informal belief systems have both been recognized as sources of systems capital (O'Connor, 2002). This form of capital is expressed in deeply ingrained organizational routines that organizational members engage in while addressing the responsibilities of leadership. These routines are important because they drive choices related to which form of leadership (personal, interpersonal, or relational) is expressed, who participates in leadership, what aspects of leadership are considered "developable," and what outcomes of leadership are considered valuable. Thus systems are not a force to control for when conducting leadership development research; rather, the systems themselves are targets for scientific inquiry. Although there have been previous investigations into the influence of formal work system design on the implementation of strategy and attainment of operational goals (e.g., high-performance work systems; Becker & Huselid, 1998) and the importance of leaders gaining insight into the informal systems at play within their organization (e.g., aspects of culture; Schein, 1996), there has been no empirical work to date explicitly investigating the role of systems in leadership and development. For example, to what degree do belief systems influence how leadership is understood in an organization? What types of systems promote more or less complex approaches to leadership? Is systems impact on leadership development level specific (i.e., individual, dyad, group, or organization)? What aspects of systems design promote collective developmental experiences in the context of ongoing work?

It should be noted that a multidimensional perspective also recognizes leadership as an outcome and not just as an input. As such, a primary purpose of development efforts is to draw leadership out of individuals, groups, and organizations (McCauley, 2000). Whereas leadership as an outcome of social processes and effective systems design was recognized decades ago (Salancik et al., 1975), the science continues to explore the phenomenon primarily as an attribute that is added to a person, group, or organization. Recognizing leadership as an outcome holds numerous implications for scientific investigation, the most significant of which may be measurement and modeling.

APPLICATION OF SOPHISTICATED MODELING APPROACHES TO CHANGE

At its core, development of any sort involves change—both a quantitative and qualitative change in state. The construct of change, however, has been historically difficult to measure reliably (Cronbach & Furby, 1971), particularly as the unit of analysis takes on a more multidimensional nature. Advances in methodological techniques such as latent growth modeling and random coefficients modeling have demonstrated how change can be modeled with better precision and offer exciting possibilities for modeling changes associated with leadership development. Although it is beyond the scope of the present chapter to review these techniques in detail, excellent introductions are provided by Bliese and Ployhart (2002); Hox

(2000); Lance, Vandenberg, and Self (2000); as well as by Ployhart, Holtz, and Bliese (2002).

Sophisticated modeling procedures such as latent growth modeling, random coefficient modeling, and hierarchical linear modeling allow researchers to estimate both within-person change over time (growth and development) as well as between-person effects on development (individual differences). Individual linear as well as curvilinear growth trajectories can be fit to the data, and these trajectories—both slopes and intercepts—can then be modeled using between-person predictors. In this manner, hypothesized similarities in growth curves can be tested statistically. This type of research approach can help answer important questions regarding how individual leaders develop over time, what are the kinds of practices that promote leader development, and what are the kinds of aggregate systems forces that drive or restrain leader development.

The notion of conceptualizing and modeling leader development as a form of complexity (e.g., Day & Lance, 2004) represents an additional opportunity for building a science of leadership development. However, much work needs to be done in terms of how to measure the core components of leadership complexity. There are no universally agreed-upon measures of complexity, and there is little agreement about whether complexity can be assessed directly or whether it is best to separately measure its components (e.g., differentiation and integration). Furthermore, no previous work on adult development has modeled longitudinally key concepts such as complexity using these state-of-the-art techniques.

There is also a pervasive need to measure complexity in context. Measures must be designed to assess constructs in work-related situations that challenge or otherwise enhance cognitive and behavioral complexity. Some possible measurement examples include the Role Concept Repertoire Test (Kelly, 1955) to estimate cognitive complexity in interpersonal perception domains; the Washington University Sentence Completion Test (Hy & Loevinger, 1996; Loevinger, 1998b) to estimate an individual's level of ego development, which could include aspects and cognitive, social, and behavioral complexity; the subject–object interview (Lahey, Souvaine, Kegan, Goodman, & Felix, n.d.) to assess an individual's principle of meaning coherence, which could be construed as cognitive complexity; social network analysis to measure the structure of an individual's social relationships as an indicator of social complexity; and 360-degree leadership ratings to measure others' perceptions of a leader's level of behavioral complexity. These examples are just a few of the many possible measures that could be used in leader development research. There is a distinct need for a comprehensive taxonomy of complexity measures as well as for additional empirical studies to assess their adequacy (i.e., construct validity) in leadership domains.

A final theory-related factor that has been an impediment to establishing a leadership development science is an overemphasis on leader performance at the apparent expense of addressing leader development as a worthwhile criterion construct. There is apparently a strongly held assumption among researchers that more highly developed leaders generally demonstrate better job performance. Although this is a potentially interesting hypothesis to test, it does little to advance a better understanding of development. It is entirely possible that performance could be improved with little or no leader development having occurred. It is also possible that leader development occurs with no subsequent improvement in job performance (at least immediately). These are all testable research hypotheses, but they require a much better understanding of the criterion of leadership development. Issues that need to be addressed in developing appropriate criteria include a comprehensive approach to how to conceptualize and operationalize the constructs of leader development and leadership development.

SUMMARY AND CONCLUSIONS

It might be disheartening to contemplate how relatively little we know right now about the process of leadership development, especially from a scientific perspective. Rather than dwell on what is missing, however, it is preferable in many ways to focus on the opportunities ahead. Understanding the process of leadership development first requires greater attention to both theory building and theory testing. A science of leadership development is needed that is firmly grounded in sound theory and rigorous empirical tests. There are recent efforts that provide shining examples of what a science of leadership development might be (e.g., Chan & Drasgow, 2001; Dvir et al., 2002), but there are plentiful remaining opportunities to contribute to both theory and research. Despite decades of scientific work in the area of leadership, the individual, social, and organizational processes that support leadership development are only beginning to be seriously considered. Furthermore, the timing might be just right. As discussed earlier, recent methodological advances in areas such as longitudinal growth modeling have immense potential for making important contributions to the advancement of the science of leadership development.

In addition to the lofty goals of advancing science, there are other important reasons why the area of leadership development is worthy of greater attention from the scientific community. Historically, leadership has been one of the most potent forces for good—or evil—in society. Within the corporate sector, the financial collapse of several high-flying organizations has been directly traced to failures in leadership among those who were entrusted with the firm's reputation and well-being. This underscores the proposition that ethics and leadership are inherently intertwined. The development of leadership most certainly includes the development of a sound ethical foundation. Leadership involves acting with (or on) other people; therefore, issues of goodness, fairness, and justice (i.e., ethics) are vitally important aspects of the process to understand. Through the development of a leadership science it may be possible not only to better understand the process, but also to intervene and shape the process in constructive ways.

REFERENCES

Avolio, B. J. (2004). Examining the full range model of leadership: Looking back to transform forward. In D. V. Day, S. J. Zaccaro, & S. M. Halpin (Eds.), *Leader development for transforming organizations*. Mahwah, NJ: Lawrence Erlbaum Associates, Inc.

Becker, B. E., & Huselid, M. A. (1998). High performance work systems and firm performance: A synthesis of research and managerial implications. *Research in Personnel and Human Resources Journal, 16*, 53–101.

Bliese, P. D., & Ployhart, R. E. (2002). Growth modeling using random coefficient models: Model building, testing and illustrations. *Organizational Research Methods, 5*, 362–388.

Briscoe, J. P., & Hall, D. T. (1999). Grooming and picking leaders using competency frameworks: Do they work? An alternative approach and new guidelines for practice. *Organizational Dynamics, 28*, 37–52.

Bullis, R. C., Lewis, P., Bartone, P., Forsythe, G. B., & Snook, S. A. (2002, April). *A longitudinal study of Kegan developmental level and leader effectiveness.* Paper presented at the 17th Annual Conference of the Society for Industrial and Organizational Psychology, Toronto, Canada.

Burt, R. S. (1992). *Structural holes: The social structure of competition.* Cambridge, MA: Harvard University.

Chan, K-Y., & Drasgow, F. (2001). Toward a theory of individual differences and leadership: Understanding motivation to lead. *Journal of Applied Psychology, 86*, 481–498.

Cook-Greuter, S. R. (1990). Maps for living: Ego-development stages from symbiosis to conscious universal embeddedness. In M. L. Commons, C. Armon, L. Kohlberg, F. A. Richards, T. A. Grotzer, & J. D. Sinnott (Eds.), *Adult development: Models and methods in the study of adolescent and adult thought* (Vol. 2, pp. 79–103). New York: Praeger.

Cook-Greuter, S. R. (1999). *Postautonomous ego development: A study of its nature and measurement.* Unpublished doctoral dissertation, Harvard University, Cambridge, MA.

Craik, F. I. M., & Salthouse, T. A. (Eds.). (1992). *The handbook of aging and cognition.* Hillsdale, NJ: Lawrence Erlbaum Associates, Inc.

Cronbach, L. J., & Furby, L. (1971). How should we measure "change"—Or should we? *Psychological Bulletin, 74*, 68–80.

Day, D. V. (2000). Leadership development: A review in context. *Leadership Quarterly, 11*, 581–613.

Day, D. V. (April, 2001). *Understanding systems forces for sustainable leadership capacity.* Paper presented at the 16th Annual Conference of the Society for Industrial and Organizational Psychology, San Diego, CA.

Day, D. V., & Lance, C. E. (2004). Understanding the development of leadership complexity through latent growth modeling. In D. V. Day, S. J. Zaccaro, & S. M. Halpin (Eds.), *Leader development for transforming organizations*. Mahwah, NJ: Lawrence Erlbaum Associates, Inc.

Day, D. V., Zaccaro, S. J., & Halpin, S. M. (Eds.). (2004). *Leader development for transforming organizations*. Mahwah, NJ: Lawrence Erlbaum Associates, Inc.

Drath, W. (2001). *The deep blue sea: Rethinking the source of leadership.* San Francisco: Jossey-Bass.

Dvir, T., Eden, D., Avolio, B. J., & Shamir, B. (2002). Impact of transformational leadership on follower development and performance: A field experiment. *Academy of Management Journal, 45*, 735–744.

Erickson, E. H. (1959). *Identity and the life cycle.* New York: International Universities.

Fiedler, F. E. (1996). Research on leadership selection and training: One view of the future. *Administrative Science Quarterly, 41*, 241–250.

Fiske, S. T. (1992). Thinking is for doing: Portraits of social cognition from daguerreotype to laserphoto. *Journal of Personality and Social Psychology, 63*, 877–889.

Hall, D. T., & Seibert, K. W. (1992). Strategic management development: Linking organizational strategy, succession planning, and managerial learning. In D. H. Montross & C. J. Shinkman (Eds.), *Career development: Theory and practice* (pp. 255–275). Springfield, IL: Charles C Thomas.

Hollander, E. P. (1964). *Leaders, groups, and influence*. New York: Oxford University Press.

Hooijberg, R., Hunt, J. G., & Dodge, G. E. (1997). Leadership complexity and development of the Leaderplex model. *Journal of Management, 23*, 375–408.

Hox, J. J. (2000). Multilevel analyses of grouped and longitudinal data. In T. D. Little, K. U. Schnabel, & B. Jurgen (Eds.), *Modeling longitudinal and multilevel data: Practical issues, applied approaches, and specific examples* (pp. 15–32). Mahwah, NJ: Lawrence Erlbaum Associates, Inc.

Hy, L. X., & Loevinger, J. (1996). *Measuring ego development* (2nd ed.). Mahwah, NJ: Lawrence Erlbaum Associates, Inc.

Jefferson, T., Jr. (2002). *An analysis of organizational needs for leadership development*. Unpublished master's thesis, Pennsylvania State University, University Park.

Kegan, R. (1982). *The evolving self: Problem and process in human development*. Cambridge, MA: Harvard University.

Kegan, R. (1994). *In over our heads: The mental demands of modern life*. Cambridge, MA: Harvard University.

Kelly, G. (1955). *The psychology of personal constructs*. New York: Norton.

Kitchener, K. S. (1983). Cognition, metacognition, and epistemic knowledge: A three-level model of cognitive processing. *Human Development, 4*, 222–232.

Kitchener, K. S. (1986). The reflective judgment model: Characteristics, evidence, and measurement. In R. A. Mines & K. S. Kitchener (Eds.), *Cognitive development in young adults*. New York: Praeger.

Kitchener, K. S., & King, P. M. (1990). The Reflective Judgment model: Ten years of research. In M. L. Commons, C. Armon, L. Kohlberg, F. A. Richards, T. A. Grotzer, & J. D. Sinnott (Eds.), *Adult development: Models and methods in the study of adolescent and adult thought* (Vol. 2, pp. 63–78). New York: Praeger.

Klein, K. J., & Kozlowski, S. W. J. (Eds). (2000). *Multilevel theory, research, and methods in organizations: Foundations, extensions, and new directions*. San Francisco: Jossey-Bass.

Lahey, L., Souvaine, E., Kegan, R., Goodman, R., & Felix, S. (n.d.). *A guide to the subject-object interview: Its administration and interpretation*. Cambridge, MA: Harvard University Graduate School of Education.

Lance, C. E., Vandenberg, R. J., & Self, R. M. (2000). Latent growth models of individual change: The case of newcomer adjustment. *Organizational Behavior and Human Decision Processes, 83*, 107–140.

Levinson, D. J., Darrow, C. N., Klein, E. B., Levinson, M. H., & McKee, B. (1978). *The seasons of a man's life*. New York: Knopf.

Loevinger, J. (1998a). Reliability and validity of the SCT. In J. Loevinger (Ed.), *Technical foundations for measuring ego development: The Washington University Sentence Completion Test* (pp. 29–39). Mahwah, NJ: Lawrence Erlbaum Associates, Inc.

Loevinger, J. (Ed.). (1998b). *Technical foundations for measuring ego development: The Washington University Sentence Completion Test*. Mahwah, NJ: Lawrence Erlbaum Associates, Inc.

Lord, R. G., & Maher, K. J. (1991). *Leadership and information processing: Linking perceptions and performance*. Boston, MA: Unwin Hyman.

McCall, M. W., Lombardo, M. M., & Morrison, A. M. (1988). *The lessons of experience: How successful executives develop on the job*. Lexington, MA: Lexington Books.

McCauley, C. D. (2000, April). *A systemic approach to leadership development*. Paper presented at the 15th Annual Conference of the Society for Industrial and Organizational Psychology, New Orleans, LA.

McCauley, C. D., Moxley, R. S., & Van Velsor, E. (Eds.). (1998). *The Center for Creative Leadership handbook of leadership development*. San Francisco: Jossey-Bass.

Moxley, R. S., & O'Connor Wilson, P. (1998). A systems approach to leadership development. In C. D. McCauley, R. S. Moxley, & E. Van Velsor (Eds.), *The Center for Creative Leadership handbook of leadership development* (pp. 217–241). San Francisco: Jossey-Bass.

O'Connor, P. M. G. (2002, April). *Building sustainable leadership capacity*. Paper presented at the Conference Board Annual Leadership Development Conference, New York.

O'Connor, P. M. G., & Quinn, L. (2003). Organizational capacity for leadership. In C. D. McCauley & E. Van Velsor (Eds.), *The Center for Creative Leadership handbook of leadership development* (2nd ed.). San Francisco: Jossey-Bass.

Ployhart, R. E., Holtz, B. C., & Bliese, P. D. (2002). Longitudinal data analysis: Applications of random coefficients modeling to leadership research. *Leadership Quarterly, 13*, 455–486.

Salancik, G. R., Calder, B. J., Rowland, K. M., Leblebici, H., & Conway, M. (1975). Leadership as an outcome of social structure and process: A multidimensional analysis. In J. G. Hunt & L. L. Larson (Eds.), *Leadership frontiers* (pp. 81–101). Kent, OH: Kent State University.

Sale, K. (1982). *Human scale* (2nd ed.). New York: Putnam.

Schein, E. (1996). *Organizational culture and leadership* (2nd ed.). San Francisco: Jossey-Bass.

Sparrowe, R. T., Liden, R. C., Wayne, S. J., & Kraimer, M. L. (2001). Social networks and the performance of individuals and groups. *Academy of Management Journal, 44*, 316–325.

Tesluk, P. E., & Jacobs, R. R. (1998). Toward an integrated model of work experience. *Personnel Psychology, 51*, 321–355.

Tsai, W., & Ghoshal, S. (1998). Social capital and value creation: The role of intrafirm networks. *Academy of Management Journal, 41*, 464–476.

Uhl-Bien, M., Graen, G. B., & Scandura, T. A. (2000). Implications of leader-member exchange (LMX) for strategic human resource management systems: Relationships as social capital for competitive advantage. *Research in Personnel and Human Resources Management, 18*, 137–185.

Van Velsor, E., McCauley, C. D., & Moxley, R. S. (1998). Our view of leadership development. In C. D. McCauley, R. S. Moxley, & E. Van Velsor (Eds.), *The Center for Creative Leadership handbook of leadership development* (pp. 1–25). San Francisco: Jossey-Bass.

2

Foundations for a Theory of Leadership

Edwin A. Locke
University of Maryland (Emeritus)

I believe that many people have been disappointed by the attempts to develop leadership theories in Industrial/Organizational Psychology and Organizational Behavior. Most of the theories developed to date are (a) theories of supervision rather than of leadership, (b) theories that are very narrow in their focus, and (c) theories that are so esoteric that one cannot make sense of them. What would be required to do better?

The first requirement for building a leadership theory that helps to develop leaders is to provide a definition of the concept. I was profoundly shocked some years ago when a prominent leadership theorist wrote an entire book on the subject but refused to define what he was writing about. I would define leadership as *the process of inducing others to pursue a common goal* (from Locke & Associates, 1999).

There are many implications of this definition. First, because leadership is a process, leaders must take actions; it is not just a matter of holding a position. Second, leaders (as opposed to dictators) must influence people through persuasion and inducements; they cannot use physical coercion. (The military is a possible exception in the short term, but soldiers are free to volunteer or not and to rejoin or not rejoin when their term is up.) Third, leaders have to get other people to follow them. Leadership is a concept of relationship: If there are no followers, there are no leaders (and vice versa). Fourth, organizations exist for a purpose, so leadership must be goal directed. This means that leaders must know where they are going, that is, what they want to accomplish. Although organizations may have multiple goals, it is important that they have one, central organizing purpose—thus, goals must be organized in a hierarchy leading to one end. Fifth, the leader must get everyone in the organization to work together toward the common goal or purpose. Without a common goal, you will have different parts of the organization working at cross-purposes, that is, organizational anarchy. Unity of purpose requires communication, coordination, cooperation, and inducements.

The second requirement for building a viable theory of leadership is the specification of the domain of action involved. For example, we can distinguish: business, political, nonprofit (including volunteer and educational institutions), and military leadership. Although, given the previously cited definition, there are elements in common among leaders in all of these contexts; there are also profound differences. Military leadership relies heavily on command and control, whereas the leaders of volunteer organizations require more grassroots support. Integrity is critical in business leadership, else employees and customers will not cooperate, whereas in politics (sadly) integrity appears to be a block to getting elected and staying in office. Furthermore, the outcome measures—or ultimate goals—are vastly different across domains. For the military, the bottom line is winning the war; for nonprofit organizations it may be cultural influence. The ultimate standard for business organizations is making a profit, whereas for politicians it seems to be getting reelected.

All this implies that, in addition to the goals, the traits and actions required for success, however defined, are likely to be very different in the different domains. Thus, generalization across domains is highly suspect. For example, a charismatic personality (as contrasted with having a clear vision, which is a content rather than a style issue; Kirkpatrick & Locke, 1996) may be highly beneficial, if not obligatory, in politics, but there is no evidence that it is critical to business success.

The third requirement for building a leadership theory is to identify the core tasks of leadership that are entailed by the domain in question. I begin this chapter by focusing on the importance of vision, followed by a focus on core values. The chapter ends with a summary of the traits, skills, abilities, and actions that are necessary to implement an organizational vision. In what follows, I confine myself to the leadership of profit-making organizations and leave the issue of generalization to additional domains to others.

VISION

Broadly speaking, the core tasks of a profit-making leader are to formulate a vision for the organization and to ensure that it gets implemented so as to make money. So let us begin with vision. This has been a rather overused concept in the literature, so it is essential to define clearly what one means by it. By vision I mean *seeing the future potential of a product, market, technology, invention, or competitive strategy* (definition based on Locke, 2000). Some might call this a business model, although that term sounds a bit static. It means seeing what will work to make the organizational profitable in the long term.

It is very hard to be visionary, so it is not surprising that very few people are good at it. The reason is that when envisioning you are not dealing with the present but with the future—something that does not yet exist. You are not dealing with an actuality but rather with a potentiality. Thus, envisioning involves an act of imagination. This does not mean that anything goes, however. Envisioning something impossible like time travel is worse than useless. A successful visionary projects into the future based on what is known; he tries to figure out, based on partial knowledge, what would really work, if it were tried.

What do business people actually do when they envision? We know very little about how visionary leaders come up with their ideas—obviously many of the connections they make come from the subconscious, the storehouse of our knowledge. However, we can, in part, infer the mental process based on the actions leaders actually take.

Here are 20 examples:

- Extrapolate a current trend. Consider the Internet. If it can be used to gather information, then maybe it can be used to sell products and services (e.g., eBay, Amazon). Although the Internet craze did not turn out to be the boon many expected, some companies have been successful at it (eBay).
- Make analogies from other industries. Henry Ford did not invent the ideas of mass marketing and the assembly line, but he was the first to apply them to the automobile industry. Before Henry Ford, automobiles had been viewed mainly as high-priced, custom-made, luxury items. His vision was to make a car that almost anyone could afford.
- Do some things that other people are already doing, but do them better (e.g., add quality). For example, reverse what Henry Ford did, by taking something, like coffee, that had been considered a low-cost item, and make it into more of a luxury item (Starbucks). Or make cars like lots of others are doing but improve their quality (Toyota).
- Do some things that other people are already doing, but do them more cheaply. Sam Walton (Wal-Mart) did not invent discount retailing, but he did it better than anyone else.
- Satisfy an expressed but unmet need—such as low-power chips, long-life batteries, or low-fat meals.
- Satisfy an unarticulated need or desire (the Minivan, the SUV, Xerography).
- Increase the size (Giant Coke, the jumbo jet, the VW Minibus).
- Increase the scale (McDonald's, grow from 1 store to 28,000 stores).

- Decrease the size (the VW Beetle, the Motorola Star Tac, the PC).
- Find a substitute product (electricity instead of gas—Thomas Edison).
- Save people time; increase speed (ATM machines, net shopping, express check-in and check-out at hotels, jet planes).
- Improve health (fitness clubs, diet programs, water filters, vitamin and herbal supplements).
- Enhance comfort (ergonomic desk chairs, high-tech mattresses).
- Increase convenience (airline shuttle buses, shopping malls, cell phones, Post-it notes, Palm Pilot, digital cameras, full-service banking).
- Reduce physical effort (household appliances, suitcases with wheels, forklifts).
- Enhance choice (Blockbuster, multiple types of toothpaste, food courts, multiplex theaters).
- Improve reliability and speed together (DSL, optic cable).
- Find uses for a new discovery (bacteria that eat oil; sonar to find fish, MRI, plastics).
- Facilitate wealth creation (stock-brokers, financial planners).
- Specialize (Bed, Bath & Beyond, Circuit City).

It is clear from this brief—and by no means exhaustive—list that there is almost no limit to what an imaginative businessperson can envision. There is no formula that can be applied regarding how to come up with business ideas that will work, because, as noted, what is envisioned has either never been done before or not been done in the same way as others have done it. However, people could be trained, I believe, to think along the lines noted previously. For example, how can we make it less costly? How can we move faster? How can we make it more convenient? How can we improve quality?

I do not want to make visionary leadership sound easier than it is. Millions of people come up with bright ideas for new business ventures everyday. Very few of those actually do something about it, and fewer still actually make their ideas succeed in generating profits. Consider the sad story of PSINet, a provider of Internet services to 100,000 businesses in 27 countries. Its CEO was considered a "brilliant" person. He grew the company mainly by scores of acquisitions paid for with debt, but he forgot one small detail: revenue. Eventually, a cash drain virtually bankrupted the company and cost the CEO his job. Visions do not work unless they produce cash flow.

A key aspect of vision for established companies is being able to divorce the future from the past. It is well known that companies that have been very successful in the past find it very difficult to change their strategies when confronted by major changes in the market—as IBM, Kodak, Xerox, GM, and others found out (Audia, Locke, & Smith, 2000). It is easy to assume that what worked in the past will always work and to dismiss the significance of market changes even as one's profits are plunging. This is happening today in the high-technology industry (e.g., Cisco). People who were once visionary can become very unvisionary due to both overconfidence and the failure to monitor the environment. Henry Ford, for example, who was brilliant in conceiving the Model-T, lost his dominant position to GM and almost bankrupted the company later, because he failed to change with the times. Contrast Ford with Tom Watson, Jr., who took IBM into the electronic age at the very time that they were making record profits from mechanical business machines (Locke, 2000).

The most visionary business leaders—Jack Welch of GE is one of them—anticipate market changes and adapt their own strategies before disaster strikes. This, as noted earlier, is very hard to do, because how do you know whether the trends you observe are critical? And if you do get a profit drop, how do you know if it is just a temporary blip or the harbinger of a sea change?

Three cognitive processes may be critical here: (a) to look outward at the environment rather than inward at the company—see what competitors are doing and what customers are looking for; (b) to look at current and future trends rather than focusing on what happened in the past (including past greatness); and (c) to take negative information regarding one's current strategy seriously rather than dismissing it and focusing only on the positive (Audia et al., 2000). This last process will involve not only problem solving but also problem finding, specifically finding problems that do not yet exist but which might occur. It will also involve encouraging constructive conflict and disagreement within the company, so that old ways of thinking can be questioned and, if necessary, modified.

These antidotes themselves have dangers. Looking too hard at competitors might put the company on a copycat treadmill and miss the fact that the competitors may be going down the wrong path. Changing too fast in the face of a drop in profits might lead one to abandon a strategy that actually still works but just needs adjustment. Focusing too much on negatives can demoralize the employees and prevent all risk taking. Constructive conflict may easily become destructive and lead to organizational anarchy.

All this is the reason why leadership is an art and not an exact science. It is also the reason why leadership is necessary. Those who claim that de-layering technology (e.g., e-mail) and empowerment (self-leadership) will do away with the need for organizational leadership are, in my opinion, very badly mistaken. An organization must be guided by a single mind, driven by a single vision. This is true regardless of how much input executives and managers have into the vision. When all is said and done, the top leader has to decide, "This is it." In the end, everyone must support the same strategy and the same values, and no one can ensure that this is done except the top person.

This does not mean that leaders should be authoritarian, that is, overcontrolling and overbearing, about every issue. Not utilizing the intelligence and knowledge of one's subordinates is a sure road to disaster. But the alternative is not to delegate everything. Delegation must be within certain constraints—the core purpose, vision, and values of the organization. People who reject these constraints must be terminated, or the organization is at risk. Let us now consider the issue of core values.

CORE VALUES

The ultimate goal of every profit-making organization is to make money. CEOs can pontificate all they want about serving mankind, but if they do not make money, their organization does not continue to exist. And if they do not make a reasonable rate of return, the CEO will be fired. CEOs who have mixed or contradictory goals will not function effectively. Consider, for example, a company that owns several unprofitable plants that are draining the company's resources. If the CEO feels so sorry for the employees that he or she keeps the plants open as a welfare gesture, then the whole company will eventually be at risk. Or if a CEO feels guilty about making profits and gives them all away rather than investing in new plants and equipment, the same result will ensue.

It does not follow that the focus should be on maximizing short-term profits. Successful CEOs cannot focus exclusively on either the short term or the long term—they must focus on both. Too much of a short-term focus (e.g., paying below market wages, thereby losing many key employees; skimping on quality) can destroy a company in the long run. Too much of a long-term focus (e.g., abandoning all the organization's current product lines) may cause so much short-term damage that there is no long run. To quote Jack Welch (Crainer, 1999, p. 52), "Anybody can manage short. Anybody can manage long. Balancing those two things is what management is about."

However, making a profit, even though it is the organization's ultimate goal, cannot be the organization's core value. Why not? Because this would imply that it would not matter how the organization made its money. Lying, cheating, stealing, cutting corners, producing trashy products would all be okay as long as they could "get away with it." This would be the worst kind of pragmatism—doing whatever seems to work at the moment. Ironically, this "practical" philosophy, in the end, does not work at all.

An organization, like an individual, needs a moral code and for the same reason: to guide its choices and actions so that it will be successful in the real world (Locke, 2000). Consider, by way of example, the code of values of BB&T, a very successful regional banking company in the eastern United States. Their values include: Fact-Based Decision Making (reality), Reason (objectivity), Independent Thinking, Productivity, Honesty, Integrity, Justice, Pride, Teamwork, and Self-Esteem.

BB&T considers these virtues to be the *means* to profits. Consider honesty (Locke & Woiceshyn, 1995). If a business does not treat its customers honestly, it will not keep them for long. The same is true with respect to employees, suppliers, and investors. Other core values that we see successful companies promote include: Innovation, Quality, Speed, Customer Service, and (Low) Cost. In addition, organizations may also have core values pertaining to how employees are to be treated, for example, Respect for the Individual and Fair Treatment (an aspect of the virtue of justice).

Note that I did not mention diversity. This is a very pernicious concept—in part, because people often do not say what they mean by it and, in part, because of what people do mean by it when they say it. If it refers to diversity of outlook due to variations in experience and functional specialty, this may be beneficial as a means of making better decisions. On the other hand, if it refers to diversity of demographic characteristics as an end in itself, I believe it is detrimental. What an effective organization should look for when hiring employees, over and above company-specific requirements such as industry experience or knowledge of a particular language, are:

- Character (honesty, integrity, etc.)
- Competence (job knowledge and skills, management skills, ability to learn, etc.)
- Motivation and personality (conscientiousness, commitment, energy, etc.)

Observe that none of these qualities are unique to any age, gender, racial, or ethnic group. Fairness and objectivity would demand that hiring and rewards (e.g., promotions, raises) be given on the basis of individual merit, not group membership. Individualism, not demographic diversity, should be the core value in relation to the selection and rewarding of employees.

Formulating the vision and developing core values are only the beginning stages of developing a successful company. The next, and very difficult, task is to implement the vision in reality so as to make a profit.

IMPLEMENTING THE VISION

Current charismatic theories of leadership acknowledge the importance of the leader's ability to implement the organization's vision (cf. Conger & Kanungo, 1987). However, many of these theories do not delineate the means by which this occurs nor the leader's specific role in making it happen. I divide the requirements for implementation into three categories: leader and manager traits, skills and abilities, and actions.

Traits

Not everyone is capable of being a successful business leader. Here are some of the relevant traits (some of the material in the following is based on Locke, 2000).

- Independence. The persons at the top stand alone. It is their vision that directs the enterprise. They do not follow orders; they give them. They have the final responsibility for the success of the organization. In the end, no matter how many people they consult, they must rely on themselves. A dependent conformist has no chance in such a job. Independence does not mean refusing to listen to good advice, but rather deciding for oneself whether the advice is good.
- Self-confidence. Independence and self-confidence are interdependent. People cannot make independent decisions if they do not trust their own judgment. People who rely on their own judgment become more confident in the process. I think there are two interrelated types of confidence: general confidence in being able to handle life's challenges (general self-esteem) and specific confidence or self-efficacy (Bandura, 1997), which involves the belief that one has specific skills (e.g., sales, marketing, finance, team building, technology, etc.). Self-confidence is also necessary in the realm of hiring. Great CEOs hire great people, some of whom know more than they do about certain business issues. If CEOs cannot judge who is great or if they are too insecure to hire smart people, including people who will disagree and argue with them, then any chance for successful growth is stifled. It is not the case, however, that the more confidence the better. Overconfidence, especially arrogance, can be as disastrous as underconfidence; it played a big role in the PSINet failure discussed earlier, as it has in many business failures. Overconfidence is confidence divorced from reality. I believe that it stems from the lack of the next trait: rationality.
- Rationality. This means, first and foremost, taking facts seriously. It means not substituting emotions (wishes, hopes, etc.) for actual knowledge. For example, you cannot run a business without cash flow, as PSINet discovered. Compare PSINet to eBay, one of the few dot-com success stories. CEO Meg Whitman (Q & A, 2001, p. 87) says, "From the beginning we focused on profitability, returns-based investment, and on growing revenue faster than costs." It means you cannot assume what worked in the past will always work. It means you cannot ignore your competition. It means you cannot make bad news go away by evading it. It means that you do not take actions (e.g., reducing quality) without knowing their consequences. It means you do not seek effects (e.g., sales) without understanding their causes (e.g., good products). It means looking at all the facts, not just at the ones you like.
- An active mind. Capitalism is a dynamic system; old businesses die off and new ones takes their place. Competitors appear out of nowhere to take away your customers. New products, technology, processes, and services are constantly being offered. A successful CEO must be constantly asking questions, gaining new knowledge, finding problems, looking for threats, and taking steps to improve products and lower costs. Mental passivity means drifting along, repeating the actions of the past without thinking of how to improve.

This only works if the environment remains static and unchanging—which it never does in a free economy.

- Drive. Drive means ambition, the desire to attain something great or important. It means setting high standards and goals for performance, growth, quality, cost reductions, and every other outcome that will foster profitability. It means energy, dynamism, and stamina—long hours, a fast pace, and initiative. It means tenacity—not giving up when things go badly, persisting in the face of failure and setbacks, unless the facts clearly indicate that a new course of action is mandatory.

- Egoistic passion. It is critical that the CEOs love their work, personally, selfishly, and passionately. Loving just the money is not enough (you only get paid once or twice a month); they must love the doing, the means of making the money. Egoism is not egocentrism (narcissism). Narcissists are self-absorbed and are focused on getting attention and adulation. One cannot run a successful business, however, by focusing all one's thoughts on oneself and looking in the mirror. Successful CEOs, the rational egoists, are focused on reality—what is needed to make the business work. What they love is not seeing their picture in the paper but rather achievement—getting the work done.

- Virtue. I discussed virtue in relation to the core values of an organization. But an organization cannot stand for values and virtues that the CEO does not stand for personally, both in word and in deed. These include (see Locke, 2000) independence, rationality (both discussed previously), honesty (Locke & Woiceshyn, 1995), integrity, and justice. CEOs are role models for everyone below them; CEOs' core values will be inferred not only from their words but also from their actions. For example, CEOs' honesty will be judged on the basis of whether they tell the truth and whether they engage in or condone dishonest practices. Their integrity will be judged based on whether they act in accordance with their professed convictions. Their sense of justice will be inferred from whom they reward and punish and how. There must be total consonance between the core values of the organization and the values and virtues of the CEO. This must also be extended to managers at every level below the CEO level if the organization is to have a coherent philosophy.

Observe that I did not include charisma in this list. As noted earlier, I do not think profit-making organizations need to be headed by charismatic personalities—people who can arouse emotions to a fever pitch and attract followers who think they are god-like. Nor did I include the latest fad, "emotional intelligence." That term gradually has been expanded to include everything but the kitchen sink; thus, it has lost all coherent meaning. Its original meaning pertained mainly to skill at introspection; this, of course, is an important skill for living, but business leaders have never been known to be particularly good at it. Secondarily, it meant sensitivity to others as a consequence of being aware of one's own feelings and emotions.

Again, successful business leaders have virtually never been described as sensitive, though it is helpful if they are not totally clueless about how they affect people (e.g., they have to be able to sustain morale and keep employees from leaving). I also did not include competitiveness as a separate trait, although a case could be made for it. All private-sector businesses, unless they have government subsidies or legal protection from the free market, must compete to be successful. However, I choose to regard competitiveness as an aspect of drive.

Knowledge, Skills, and Abilities

Nothing is more demoralizing to employees than CEOs who do not know what they are doing. This is not just a matter of having a clear vision, though that is important; it is a matter of having a vision that works, which will make the company financially successful. (Sometimes this is called a strategic vision, or a business model.) In some, but not all jobs, the CEO's technical and/or industry knowledge is critical. In other cases marketing or financial skills might be most important. Sometimes it is an issue of being able to identify good managers and giving them responsibility. At other times it is a matter of knowing how to allocate resources. But the bottom line is: The CEO must know what to do to make money. This is what vision is all about.

The intellectual aspect of leadership has been more neglected in the literature than any other topic—which is ironic, because it is arguably the most important. It is true that modern scholars have talked at length about "intellectual capital," but few have noted that the single-most important (though not the sole) source of such capital is the mind of the CEO! Being motivated and being able to motivate others are important but will not do any good unless the CEO is doing and getting others to do the right thing. Being highly motivated to do the wrong thing will harm the organization faster and more profoundly than not being motivated. Contrast, for example, a passive CEO who bumbles along using an increasingly outdated strategy but one who still brings in net income with a human dynamo who takes the company in a totally new direction that is completely the wrong one. An example is William Agee who took an old-line construction firm, Morrison Knudsen, into the railcar business. This and other management errors bankrupted the company.

Strategic errors often are the result of CEOs trying to apply a skill that they possess in a context where it is not applicable. It is almost axiomatic that marketing people find marketing solutions to business problems, whereas finance people find financial solutions, and production people find production solutions. They use what has worked for them in the past without regard to the present situation. Consider "Chainsaw" Al Dunlap. Downsizing had worked for him at Scott Paper, so he tried it again at Sunbeam; but it backfired there and virtually destroyed the company, not to mention his reputation and career. It is natural for people who cannot understand the whole to focus on a part, a part that they can understand and feel confident about.

This error results from paradoxical combination of over- and underconfidence—overconfidence in the efficacy of a familiar and previously successful strategy and underconfidence in being able to master or develop a new but unfamiliar strategy. It's the "one-size-fits-all" mentality. Lack of ability aside, mental laziness may be a motive for this error in some cases, but I think more often it is due to impatience—wanting to get fast results.

What skill is required to avoid this trap? Primarily, it is inductive reasoning. This involves the ability to look at and grasp the whole picture, which may mean examining hundreds or thousands of concrete facts and observations, to dismiss many of them as unimportant, and to integrate rest into a small number of core conclusions and principles; namely, what does this all add up to? What do we need to do? One's previous knowledge, of course, comes into play, but it must come into play in the context of the present circumstances. For example, CEOs may know from previous jobs that customer service is important, but exactly how it applies to their new job depends upon the circumstances of the new company. In summary, the facts have to be organized into a coherent structure that includes grasping cause-and-effect relationships.

Note that inductive reasoning involves *simplification*—more specifically, turning complexity into simplicity by imposing order on seeming chaos. (Note that simplicity is one of Jack Welch's core leadership principles.) This requires *essentializing*, that is, figuring out what is most fundamental—what other things most depend on. Inductive reasoning also involves *prioritizing*—identifying what has to be done before any other outcomes can be achieved. Are we in the right business? Are we making the right products? Are competitors answering customer needs better? Is there a quality problem? A speed problem? A cost problem? Are we using our employees' abilities fully? Do we have the right people in the right jobs? Is the organizational structure right? Is there enough cash flow? What should we fix first? What is most essential? What fix is a precondition for other fixes?

Deductive thinking is also required. Given what I have discovered, how should I apply this knowledge, and my prior knowledge, to the present situation? If costs are too high, how should I go about lowering them? If I do not have the right people in key jobs, what qualities do I need, and how shall I find people who have them?

All of this is very hard mental work and requires intelligence and logical thinking. Some CEOs simply cannot see the forest for the trees—the job is simply over their heads. The level of complexity is too great. So they bluster and make demands on subordinates and use familiar strategies, but they never get to the real heart of the problem because they do not know what it is. There may be a lack of creative imagination as well. I suspect that more CEOs fail because they are not intellectually up to the demands of their job than any other single factor.

Worse yet, CEOs often do not know that they cannot handle the job cognitively, because their self-esteem is based on always being right and always being in control of things. It would be a humiliating admission to say, "I can't do this," so they convince themselves that they can do it and engage in a whirlwind of desperate, uncoordinated actions, none of which is the right one. They substitute action for thinking. When things begin to go sour, they lash out at their critics and then isolate themselves so that they will not have to hear the bad news. All this makes them progressively less able to fix what is really wrong with the organization.

CEOs are more likely to acquire specific skills if they are generally able and intelligent. Consider decision making. If they are good inductive and deductive thinkers, they will make better decisions, because they will be better able to see the total picture and the consequences of choosing various alternatives. They will be better problem solvers, because they will be better able to frame problems and see various paths to the solution. They will also be better at planning, because they will be able to anticipate the future and know what is required to deal with it. Consider what Herb Kelleher, the brilliant CEO of Southwest Airlines (Booker, 2001, p. 70), said: "The way I've always approached things is to be prepared for all possible scenarios of what might happen. I usually come up with four or five different scenarios." This method of thinking helped Southwest to be the only major carrier that never lost money.

It must be stressed that raw intelligence (the ability to grasp abstractions) alone is not enough. It must be associated with an active, creative mind that is able to formulate a viable vision from facts that create only confusion in the minds of others.

This is not to deny that formal training can facilitate the development of these skills, but typically they are acquired (or sometimes not acquired) on the job. Exposing managers to specific types of experiences is useful and important. However, the more able CEOs are usually able to profit more from experience and to learn from their mistakes. Here again, inductive reasoning ability is critical. Experience is messy—hundreds and thousands of things happen day after day, year after year. There are lags between actions and consequences. Most events have multiple causes and effects. To profit from experience, leaders have to sort all this out—what are the most important things I have learned? What works and what does not? What's the best way to get X done? How do I get knowledge I can trust?

People skills (e.g., conflict management, morale building) are also acquirable on the job, but I believe many of them are mainly a matter of personality. Domineering authoritarians will not acquire people skills for the same reason that they are authoritarians in the first place; for example, they have a desperate need for power and are oblivious to everything else. Listening is perhaps the most learnable skill; able CEOs have a lot to say and a lot of energy, so it is easy for them to overwhelm subordinates. Over time or with training, they can learn that many subordinates have a lot to offer if given the chance to talk. The best CEOs (e.g., the late Sam Walton of Wal-Mart and Roberto Goizueta of Coca-Cola) spend a lot of time asking questions of others with the explicit purpose of draining them of everything they know. This is a good sign of an active mind at work.

The capacity to evaluate both managers and employees is another critical leadership skill. It is generally believed that more able leaders are more likely to pick able subordinates than less able leaders are. People tend to be attracted to people like themselves, which is beneficial if one is an able leader, but not helpful if one is not. Furthermore, the most able leaders are best able to recognize talent when they see it. I have certainly seen this in the academic realm—the better scholars seem to be much better judges of who are good scholars and what is good work than the less-than-better scholars. In fact, the ability of a manager to spot ability in others may in itself be a sign of leadership potential.

Business leaders have to communicate, but they do not have to be great public speakers, although this skill is certainly acquirable. However, the more glib a CEO is, the more suspicious I become. Many second-rate CEOs are great wordsmiths and can mesmerize an audience with visions of profits to come. They can also come up with brilliantly nuanced expositions as to why their bottom line is looking so bad, why all the problems are not their fault, and why everything will be fine if they can only borrow another $100 million. I find more credible those CEOs who do not try to put on a show, who come across as sincere, and who stick to the facts and do not make endless excuses.

There are numerous ways to communicate—speeches, e-mails, meetings, announcements, videos, letters, and symbolic gestures. Many leaders think frequent face-to-face meetings are critical because they are the richest form of communication. Taking action itself is also a form of communication; for example, if you get to work at 6:00 a.m., this sends a very different message than if you arrive at 10:30 a.m. (golf clubs in tow). Who you promote is a form of communication; namely, this is the kind of person who will get ahead here. Great leaders get their message across in some form.

Actions

Aside from formulating a vision and delineating core values, there are seven categories of action that leaders need to engage in. I am assuming that the basic competitive strategy—as an aspect of the vision—has already been identified.

- Setting an agenda (Kotter, 1982). This is basically a list of things to be done and follows the process of inductive thinking. It specifies what needs to get done in order of priority. Here are things that need to get done (see Locke & Associates, 1999).
- Structuring. Over the last 2 decades hundreds of large, bureaucratic businesses have delayed, downsized, and outsourced, often, though not always, to their benefit. Organizations are becoming more horizontal, and e-mail systems and various types of teams are fostering communication in every direction. However, every business is unique, so there are no formulas for deciding on the best structure, and most companies are constantly restructuring. For example, companies are always trying to get the right balance between centralization and decentralization. This is hard because there are advantages and

disadvantages to both. Structuring is always a work in progress in a dynamic company, and it is critical to organizational success, because it regulates authority relationships and affects communication and coordination. Contrary to the claim of some egalitarian gurus, however, there will never be a total elimination of the pyramid of authority, because, as noted earlier, the actions of the organization must be coordinated around a single vision.

- Selection and training. An organization can be worse than its employees, due to poor leadership, but it cannot be better. Great organizations have to select (and keep) great people. The best organizations (e.g., GE, Microsoft) spend an inordinate amount of time finding and developing outstanding employees. Then they teach them the organization's vision and core values. Finally, they train them in the specific skills they need to perform their jobs. In the best companies, employees are constantly being trained so that they possess the most up-to-date skills. Large companies even have their own "universities," where the CEO and top managers are regular teachers. The other side of this coin is that the best companies constantly winnow out those who do not have what it takes (e.g., the "C" managers at GE).
- Motivating. Motivating employees is a critical part of the leader's job. There are many different facets of employee motivation. Motivating may begin with inspiring the employees with the company's vision—getting them excited about what the company does and why it is important.

  Formal authority also plays a role. Given the hierarchy and the fact that employees are paid for their work, asking the employees to do things is considered fully legitimate. Employees naturally want to please their bosses, and defiance of authority is normally viewed as insubordination and could lead to termination. Formal authority will be most effective when the person giving the order or making the request is viewed as competent and trustworthy.

  Leaders can also motivate subordinates through serving as role models. Most revealing is how leaders spend their time. For example, if customer service is important, how often is the CEO seen talking to customers? If innovation is important, how much time do they spend talking to R&D people and announcing new products? Another giveaway is what items the leader puts on meeting agendas; for example, is customer service, quality, innovation, etc. the focus of every meeting? Another is how they allocate financial resources: Who gets money for investments? Another, as noted earlier, is who gets promoted? Finally, leaders serve as role models based on how they treat people; an abusive, belittling, screaming leader sends a very different message about appropriate behavior than one who is polite and considerate.

  Building employee self-confidence is another key task of the leader. This is especially important if the company has been doing poorly or is in a turnaround mode. Employees may have become demoralized by previous, poor-quality leaders, downsizing, and the lack of raises and/or net losses.

Training itself raises self-confidence; so do expressions of confidence by the leader, especially if accompanied by a new vision or plan for making the company successful in the future. Demoralized employees can be helped by making sure they get some "small wins" early on.

Empowerment (Conger, 2000) has probably received more attention than any other technique as a means of motivating subordinates, and it does have much to recommend it. Basically, it involves pushing responsibility down to lower levels so that decisions can be made without having to wade through multiple layers of bureaucracy. Empowerment gives people "ownership" of their function and the ability to fully utilize their knowledge and judgment. Empowering subordinates is an expression of confidence in them and makes it easy to evaluate their work because they are entirely responsible for it.

Empowerment, however, is not a universal panacea. It will not work unless the employee is fully competent and motivated to take responsibility. Furthermore, some things cannot be delegated, for example, the company vision and strategy and ethical standards. Furthermore, responsibility means accountability, so employees must take the blame if they do not get results.

How does one get results? By setting goals. Goals that are both specific and difficult (Latham, 2000) are most successful in getting high performance. It is a common procedure for the CEO or top management to set the overall goals for the company and for divisions, for example, a 15% ROA, a 10% increase in sales or profits. Successful CEOs are quite demanding in what they expect of top subordinates (e.g., Jack Welch). Goals that seem impossible can even be motivating if they push people to develop new, creative strategies for getting the job done.

For goals to be effective, people need feedback so they can track progress in relation to the goal and make the necessary adjustments in effort or strategy if they are below target. For goals to work, people have to be committed to them. The key determinants of commitment are confidence in being able to reach or approach it and belief that the goal is important.

There are several ways that a leader can make subordinates feel the goal is important (Locke & Latham, 1990). Tie it to the vision. Give reasons why it will benefit the company and the employee. Frame it as an opportunity for self-development. Present it as a challenge. Make the commitment public. Tie it to rewards.

Developing an effective reward system is very important and very difficult. Consider the issue of goals and rewards. Certainly anticipated rewards enhance goal commitment (Locke & Latham 1990). However, if you reward people only if they reach the goals, subordinates will be highly motivated to convince the leader to set easy goals (while pretending that they are hard) that will lead to low performance. If the goals are ultimately set at a very difficult level, subordinates may be motivated to fudge the figures or take other shortcuts (Jensen, 2001) so that they can be sure of getting the reward. They may also become demoralized if they see that the goal cannot be reached (Lee, Locke, & Phan, 1997).

The problem then is: How do you get the performance benefit of high goals and the commitment benefits of monetary rewards? There are several possibilities, but there have been no comparative studies to show which method is best. One procedure is to use goals to motivate people, but to reward according to performance (Jensen, 2001; Locke & Latham, 1990). Thus, a person who had a goal of say a 30% increase in sales and attained 20% would still get a reward, even though the goal was not reached, and would get a bigger reward than a person who set a goal of a 5% increase in sales and attained 6%, even though the goal was exceeded. One consideration here would be whether the company would set a minimum goal below which performance would be considered unsatisfactory. As noted earlier, most CEOs do set such minimums.

Another procedure would be to have a tiered system with multiple goal levels and different amounts of bonus attached to each. Thus, trying for a very hard goal but attaining only a lower one would still yield some reward.

Incentive reward systems have to be designed very carefully, because it is very easy to reward a person for doing the wrong thing. Not only does performance have to be measured in some way, but also the organization has to be very clear about what it wants, for example, quantity, quality, sales, ROI, ROA, teamwork, etc. And there must be controls, as well as core values, to prevent or at least reduce the probability of cheating and shortcutting. All rewards do not have to be monetary; people also value recognition. Even empowerment can be used as a reward.

Leaders also must build employee morale. However, I believe that if there is a clear vision that is working (the company is doing well) and the other motivation techniques (empowerment, confidence-building, rewards, etc.) are used effectively, morale will routinely be high.

- Information management. This involves information gathering and information dissemination. The leader must be an information vacuum, gathering it from many different sources, both inside and outside the company. This includes face-to-face contact (which, as noted earlier, is probably the most important and effective type of communication), question asking, e-mail, meetings, experts, databases, financial reports, reading, etc. The leader must be accessible and a good listener and must have a large network of contacts.

  On the other side of this coin, the leader needs to ensure that information of all types is widely disseminated within the company (e.g., through computer networks, teams, training programs, speeches, etc.). At the same time, it is critical not to have information overload, for example, reams of printouts that nobody could or even wants to read.

- Team building. There are three reasons why teams are needed in organizations. First, a group of people can usually get more done than one person working alone. Second, a team has more potential knowledge available than does a single individual. Third, teams are needed to ensure adequate communication and coordination among people, especially those in different functions, project teams, or departments. One of the first tasks of a CEO is to build an outstanding top management team, staffed by people who have all the skills needed at the top level, especially skills not possessed by the CEO. But teams have to be built all the way down to the bottom of the organization, because coordination is required at every level as well as between levels. Team building requires team-management skills and rules of conduct (e.g., no personal attacks).

* Promoting change. Under capitalism, as noted, there is constant change. Technology becomes outdated; consumer tastes change; new competitors spring up not just from within the country but from without; suppliers go out of business; new products and services are created; the economy goes through cycles; financing becomes easier or harder to get; stockholders raise their expectations. Nothing stays the same; to remain static is to die.

The leader has to constantly promote change; usually this involves changing the vision and then setting goals to bring the vision into reality. It requires getting subordinates to buy into change by convincing them that it is necessary and, especially, making their rewards contingent on their commitment to change.

It is critical not to go through the procedure of "flavor of the month"—every month a new initiative that simply withers on the vine and makes employees cynical. In the 20 years that Jack Welch ran GE, there were only four or five major, companywide change initiatives: work-out (getting employee input); boundary-lessness and best practices; use of the Internet (ebusiness); Six Sigma for quality and digitization (Globalization was pushed all along). However, they were all pushed relentlessly through all parts of the company, and all contributed to the company's success.

CONCLUSION

Considering the many complex actions described previously, it should be clear why, to paraphrase Kermit the Frog, it is not easy being a successful business leader. It is cognitively demanding; it is emotionally demanding; it is physically demanding. The job is never-ending, and there is no time for rest. No wonder there are so few good leaders around.

I have no opinion on the degree to which leadership is formally trainable. Most of the traits that I mentioned are developed early, and some portion of cognitive ability is innate. Knowledge and skill are gained through experience, but traits even affect the acquisition of business skills (Baum, Locke, & Smith, 2001). Experience is certainly critical to effective leadership, but we know very little about who profits the most from experience or how people process their experiences. What is critical, I believe, is to help potential leaders conceptualize their experiences in the form of inductively arrived at leadership principles and to help them understand how to apply these principles effectively in diverse settings. Some leaders do this naturally, but others could benefit from explicit instruction. We know very little about the best way to do this.

To build a valid theory of business leadership, we will need to study the aspects of leadership that I have noted here and look at how the various traits, skills, and competencies develop; how they affect each other; and how they relate to success.

ACKNOWLEDGMENT

The author would like to thank Robert Baum for his helpful comments on this manuscript.

REFERENCES

Audia, G., Locke, E. A., & Smith, K. G. (2000). The paradox of success: An archival and a laboratory study of strategic persistence following a radical environmental change. *Academy of Management Journal, 43*, 837–853.

Bandura, A. (1997). *Self-efficacy: The exercise of control.* New York: Freeman.

Baum, J. R., Locke, E. A., & Smith, K. G. (2001). A multi–dimensional model venture growth. *Academy of Management Journal, 44*, 292–303.

Booker, K. (2001). The chairman of the board looks back. *Fortune*, May 28, pp. 63ff.

Conger, J. A. (2000). Motivate performance through empowerment. In E. A. Locke (Ed.), *Handbook of principles of organizational behavior* (pp. 137–149). Oxford, England: Blackwell.

Conger, J. A., & Kanungo, R. (1987). Toward a behavioral theory of charismatic leadership in organizational settings. *Academy of Management Review, 12*, 637–647.

Crainer, S. (1999). *Business the Jack Welch way.* New York: AMACOM.

Jensen, M. (2001). *Paying people to lie: The truth about the budgeting process.* Unpublished manuscript, The Monitor Group and Harvard Business School Cambridge, MA.

Kirkpatrick, S. A., & Locke, E. A. (1996). Direct and indirect effects of three core charismatic leadership components on performance and attitudes. *Journal of Applied Psychology, 81*, 36–51.

Kotter, J. (1982). *The general managers.* New York: Free Press.

Latham, G. P. (2000). Motivate employee performance through goal setting. In E. A. Locke (Ed.), *Handbook of principles of organizational behavior* (pp. 107–119). Oxford, England: Blackwell.

Lee, T. W., Locke, E. A., & Phan, S. H. (1997). Explaining the assigned goal-incentive interaction: The role of self-efficacy and personal goals. *Journal of Management, 23*, 541–559.

Locke, E. A. (2000). *The prime movers: Traits of the great wealth creators.* New York: AMACOM.

Locke, E. A., & Latham, G. P. (1990). *A theory of goal setting and task performance.* Englewood Cliffs, NJ: Prentice-Hall.

Locke, E. A., & Woiceshyn, J. (1995). Why businessmen should be honest: The argument from rational egoism. *Journal of Organizational Behavior, 16*, 405–414.

Locke, E. A., & Associates (1999). *The essence of leadership.* New York: Lexington.

Q & A with Meg Whitman (2001). *Worth*, May 2001, p. 87.

II

Leadership Development
Challenges

3

Placing the "E" in E-Leadership: Minor Tweak or Fundamental Change

Bruce J. Avolio
Gallup Leadership Institute Department of Management, University of Nebraska, Lincoln

Surinder Kahai
Center for Leadership Studies and School of Management, Binghamton University

A fundamental question must be addressed at the outset, and that is whether e-leadership is different from leadership itself, and if so, in what ways. In this chapter, we examine how advanced information technology (AIT) influences and is being influenced by leadership. We propose that the effects of AIT emerge from their interaction with organizational structures of which leadership systems are a part in any organization. We pool relevant results and suggestions from a diverse array of literature to provide recommendations for developing a research agenda for exploring e-leadership at individual, team, and strategic levels.

We begin with a basic premise that underlies our reactions to an article published by Christopher Hoenig on September 1, 2000, in the Chief Information Officer (CIO) entitled, "Lose the E." Our premise is that we completely agree with his view that the focus on people is still as fundamental to leadership today as it was yesterday and will be tomorrow. However, leadership styles or behaviors may need to change, or simply will change, as they are displayed through electronic media. Over the last decade, we have found, in our own research on e-leadership, that the outcomes of leadership styles mediated through technology can be different from the outcomes in a face-to-face context employing the same leadership styles (Avolio, Kahai, & Dodge, 2000). To the degree that these differences legitimately exist, throwing out the "e" prematurely before fully examining its implications

49

would be a big mistake. We offer some support for retaining the "e" in e-leadership, while keeping in mind that e-leadership is part of the broader domain of the science and practice of leadership.

ORGANIZATIONAL LIFE IN TRANSITION

The global economy is going through a major transition, which fundamentally changes the way organizations now build new markets and relate to their stakeholders. At the center of this transformation is AIT, which has enabled completely new ways of working and creating value in both the "physical world" as well as the "virtual world" (Rayport & Sviokla, 1995; Schlosser, 2002). Today more and more people communicate at a distance through the Internet, video conferences, chat rooms, desktop net meetings, and groupware systems such as Lotus Notes. For example, 61% of Americans have now used handheld devices for communicating with each other (Schlosser, 2002). Yet, there has been relatively little investigation into how these handheld devices are changing the way people work and the way they are led in organizations. These changes may require a significant adaptation on the part of the leadership in organizations to the new emerging realities of the marketplace, while also continuing to evolve and remain productive within the "old world order."

How should leaders manage these new emerging relationships, build trust and identification, clarify expectations, and reprimand people through electronic media for maximum positive impact? Unfortunately, we do not know the answer to any of these questions, even though many project leaders are working through these issues every day in organizations throughout the world. Rapid advances in technology systems are clearly ahead of the impact we know they will have on the social systems within our organizations. And to the extent that leadership is a significant component of the social system in any organization or community, we should probably retain the "e" in our models and investigations of leadership to learn how to nurture and develop it for maximum positive effect. Moreover, as noted by Orlikowski (2000), "what is relevant to both academics and practitioners, is the use of the technology not the technology itself."

Information technology has challenged leaders to be more responsive to their followers, who oftentimes have information before their leader on the very initiative the leader is promoting. Today, contact with leaders and followers is expected to be 24/7. The U.S. military is one example where wide accessibility to information has changed the way senior leaders must now lead their followers. In today's military context, all levels in this command and control system have greater access to alternative and conflicting sources of information. Managing the rapid dissemination of information throughout the military is having profound consequences for the study and practice of leadership. Indeed, military leaders may brief their staff in the early morning, only to be contradicted by one of the many news sources that are disseminating information on the Web by lunchtime. The inconsistent information once received causes soldiers on the ground to question whether they have the latest details relevant to the mission that can potentially erode trust in the command system.

To accommodate some of the ongoing changes, the military command system has moved toward interpreting orders based on "intent" as opposed to simply "following an officer's directive." Military officers are now trained to talk to their soldiers about the "commander's intent" underlying the order, realizing in today's dynamic military environment the conditions in which they are leading will change even before the order is executed. Such leaders are saying "follow my intent, by understanding what it is, and then stay within its boundaries." Of course, what is happening in the military is also occurring in every organization where employees operate in a dynamic field in which they need to be aware of their leader's intent, while at the same time having the flexibility to make independent decisions at the point of contact with their customers.

The way leaders arrive at decisions and implement them is going through profound changes today with the increasing use of information technology. Today leaders can listen in on a chat discussion with a community of customers and communicate what they have learned to an entire global workforce within the same day. They can reinforce the vision of the organization and its core values through daily messages to the whole organization. Moreover, the connection runs both ways, offering each employee the opportunity to have direct contact with the CEO either synchronously or asynchronously. Such direct contact was unheard of even a decade ago. Now, both customers and employees have more direct contact with senior leaders, who must either manage those contacts electronically or risk being seen as "remote" or "disconnected." Imagine how powerful it is to articulate a vision in an organization with 17,000 employees and then to reinforce that vision daily with supporting messages from senior leaders, with the release of examples that support the vision over time, and with constant reminders of how the vision will provide the guiding path for the organization's future.

The interconnections made possible by information technology are already transforming our institutions and organizations, requiring that we dramatically alter how we study and develop leadership. For example, candidates for political leadership positions have at least four avenues for connecting with their constituency. They can meet them face to face or they can present to them via television or via a reporter's interview. Today, they can also use the Internet to broadcast information to and interact with a broader audience. How such leaders use "e" in their leadership to reach out undoubtedly has an impact on fundamental facets of leadership, including managing their public image, perceived responsiveness, building of networks and coalitions, gathering pulse data, etc.

TURNING TO THE DARK SIDE

It is possible that some very dangerous leaders will realize the powers associated with information technology to broaden their reach to a larger audience of potential followers. Having information is still power in organizations, but how it is gathered, translated, manipulated, and disseminated has fundamentally changed. The "e-charismatic leader" may have far greater opportunity to lure unsuspecting followers into cults and clans that do no good, except for the leader. Consider how quickly viruses are disseminated today as a consequence of the growing presence of networks within and between organizations. Now consider such leaders spreading their virus, and we believe you will appreciate our concerns for the unethical charismatic leader. Rapid dissemination of bogus information to serve the purposes of an unethical leader, who now has morphed into an unethical e-leader, will not simply go away. Being immoral or unethical has not changed, but the leader's ability to influence a broader range of unsuspecting followers has certainly changed today. We must hold onto the "e", so we can extend what we have already learned about impression management and rhetoric in face-to-face situations and apply that knowledge to interactions mediated through technology focusing on the full range of potential unethical to ethical leaders.

WHAT DO WE KNOW SO FAR
ABOUT E-LEADERSHIP?

Past leadership research has not focused on issues confronting the leadership in organizations where work is mediated by AIT. There is no work examining how leaders influence followers at a distance or vice versa through ubiquitous wireless technology. This paper begins to address the gap in the literature concerning how AIT is and will affect the way we study and practice leadership in organizations. The central purpose of this paper is to develop a broad conceptual framework primarily based on DeSanctis and Poole's (1994) Adaptive Structuration Theory (AST) as well as on Orlikowski and Iacono's (2001) ensemble view of technology, which discusses technology as it is embedded in the broader social context including culture, as starting points for guiding future research on e-leadership. According to both conceptual models, the effects of AIT emerge from their interaction with organizational structures of which leadership is a part. Furthermore, organizational structures, including leadership, may themselves transform as a result of interactions with AIT. We will use an AST-based framework to pool relevant results and suggestions from a diverse array of literature to provide recommendations for developing a research agenda on e-leadership.

First of all, we need to examine e-leadership "in context," so as not to pursue another avenue of leadership research where leader–follower relationships are studied in a vacuum (House & Aditya, 1997). In the case of e-leadership the context not only matters but also is a part of the construct being studied. Accordingly, we begin our analysis of e-leadership by examining the context in which this leadership process is emerging and then by defining what e-leadership represents. We end this paper by offering some guidance and direction for future research.

AIT AND E-LEADERSHIP

AIT is defined as tools, techniques, and knowledge that enable multiparty participation in organizational and interorganizational activities through sophisticated collection, processing, management, retrieval, transmission, and display of data and knowledge (DeSanctis & Poole, 1994). AIT includes, but is not restricted to, e-mail systems, message boards, groupware, group support systems (GSS), knowledge management systems, executive information systems, wireless communication devices, and collaborative supply-chain management systems. The use of these technologies, or technology practice (Willoughby, 1990), can help leaders scan, plan, decide, disseminate, and control information if they are fully appropriated and utilized.

Key opportunities for organizations in an AIT-enabled economy, are real-time information availability, greater knowledge sharing, including with stakeholders such as customers, and the use of this information and knowledge to build totally "customized" relationships. However, these customized relationships are putting tremendous pressure on organizations and their leaders to be more responsive to their stakeholders and on leaders to be more responsive to their followers anytime and anywhere. Accompanying these dramatic changes is the global nature of organizational relationships fueled by the ease with which information exchange is enabled across national borders and cultures (Avolio, Kahai, Dum Dum, & Sivasubramaniam, 2000; Drucker, 1993). Consequently, we have greater access to everyone, we are dealing with more complex work teams, and we are required to do work faster and at a higher level of quality.

Rapid turnover in markets has led to more work being done in temporary project teams, which are often transnational (Earley & Mosakowski, 2000). These project teams are oftentimes virtually configured, where individuals work at a distance from each other in different countries, cultures, and organizations (Avolio, Kahai, Dum Dum, et al., 2000; Lipnack & Stamps, 1997; O'Mahoney & Barley, 1999). Project team members, especially virtual teams, are likely to communicate via AIT, enabling asynchronous, synchronous, one-to-one, or one-to-many communication. Leaders display "tele- or e-leadership" when they communicate with other members of a virtual team over electronic media (Shamir & Ben-Ari, 1999). Also, according to Shamir (1997), rather than being bestowed upon a single individual, leadership now is being "shared" by team members creating opportunities for observing virtual *collective leadership or shared leadership*.

Leaders will need to play a more proactive role in creating the social structures that foster the implementation of AIT, which has quickly become an integral component for improving organizational effectiveness as well as survival in a global e-based economy. We use the term e-leadership to incorporate the new emerging context for examining leadership. E-leadership embraces the view that the primary aim of leadership is to produce change at the individual, group, organizational, or interorganizational level through social influence processes. **E-leadership is defined as a social influence process mediated by AIT to produce a change in attitudes, emotions, thinking, behavior, and/or performance with individuals, groups, and/or organizations.** E-leadership can occur at any hierarchical level in an organization and can involve from one-to-one interactions on up to one-to-many interactions within and across large units and organizations. It may be either associated with one individual or shared by several individuals as its locus changes over time. In other words, when a virtual team begins interacting, e-leadership may be an individual-level construct. Over time, if the team becomes more cohesive and trust develops, the leadership may emerge at the group level as shared or collective leadership.

The traditional sociotechnical systems approach (STSA) as it has come to be known, assumes that organizations are made up of social systems (consisting of people and the relationships among them) that use technology (consisting of tools, techniques, and knowledge) to produce goods or services (valued by customers who are part of the organization's external environment). According to STSA, organizational effectiveness is determined by how well the social and technical systems are designed to align with each other and with the external environment.

A major difference between the earlier focus on sociotechnical systems and our discussion of e-leadership is that we believe there is much less independence between the social and technical systems than was described by Trist (1993). Trist argued that although sociotechnical systems are correlative, they are still independent. We believe that AIT and social systems in which AIT are developed and used influence each other reciprocally (Orlikowski, 1992), resulting in Orlikowski and Iacono's (2001) recommendation to examine technology and organizational change based on the "ensemble" view of technology, which considers technology as being embedded in social structures, such as an organization's culture.

According to Weick (1990), technology is both a cause and a consequence of structures in organizations. Orlikowski (1992) uses the term "interpretive flexibility" to describe the recursive relationship between AIT and the organizational context in which it was developed and used. AIT is not viewed as some fixed object with fixed effects but rather as something that offers various possibilities for creation and interpretation. Organizational members, especially leaders, play a major role in the creation and interpretation of AIT. The *interpretation* of an AIT determines how it is used, what it can do, and ultimately its contribution to organizational performance. And its interpretation is based in part upon the context that technology is embedded.

Orlikowski, Yates, Okamura, and Fujimoto, (1995) related technology-use mediation to "genres" of an organization. The genres are somewhat analogous to what cognitive psychologists have referred to as "scripts," which serve as organizing structures or logic for shaping an organization's interactions. The authors illustrate the recursive relationship between AIT and social systems by describing how the introduction of new communication technology can lead to the enactment of modified or new genres within the new communication medium and how the interaction within the new medium can also be shaped by genres that exist prior to the introduction of new technology.

For example, Schlosser (2002) reported, in an initial field study of the use of wireless communication technology, that users adapted the way they expressed messages to others, their social etiquette, and their ways of doing business. Schlosser suggested that "wireless handheld may influence the way that employees interact with their direct supervisors" (p. 421).

For the purposes of this chapter, we will adapt a theoretical framework for examining e-leadership, based on AST, in order to help explain how technology and organizational structures influence each other in creating a new organizational leadership system. AST forms the basis for our description of the coevolution of e-leadership and technology in organizations. This framework clearly spells out the sources of structures that influence technology use and how technology interacts with those sources. It also helps to identify the relevance of leadership in the "emergent" interplay between technology and organizational structures.

ADAPTIVE STRUCTURATION THEORY

Based on earlier work by Giddens (1979), AST was created to explain the process through which people incorporate AIT into their work. According to AST, although an AIT's interpretation is influenced by the context in which it is used or embedded, it also has the ability to modify or alter that context. Depending on their work context, users of AIT adapt, resist, or reject technology, frequently leading to impacts that were not designed or intended by engineers. The actions of users (i.e., adaptation, resistance, or rejection), or the impacts of their actions, in turn, can lead to modification of the work context in which the technology is used. AST recognizes the coevolutionary relationship between technology and organizational social processes/context (Yates, Orlikowski, & Okamura, 1999).

According to AST, human action is guided by structures, which are defined as rules and resources that serve as templates for planning and accomplishing tasks (DeSanctis & Poole, 1994). Structures are provided by an AIT and a work group's internal system, task, and environment. Structures emerge when a work group acts on structures and produces new information that serves to structure subsequent interaction. These various sources of structure can be thought of as defining the context, in a way not so dissimilar to the way we say a leader "provides meaning to our work and context."

AIT comes bundled with structures that its developers build into its design. Developers build new structures as well as consider existing structures from non-technology sources, such as organizational hierarchies, knowledge, and standard operating procedures. The structures of an AIT have been described in two ways: the *structural features* and the *spirit* of those features (DeSanctis & Poole, 1994).

The *structural features* of an AIT refer to its actual design characteristics that govern how information is gathered, manipulated, and managed by users. The *spirit* of the structural features refers to the intent or purpose underlying the features. The spirit indicates the normative framework for interpreting and using a set of structural features, that is, how the features ought to be interpreted and used. According to DeSanctis and Poole (1994), when considering structural features of an AIT, one is concerned with questions such as "What does the system look like?" or "What modules does it contain?" (p. 127). When considering the spirit of an AIT, one is concerned with questions such as "What kind of goals are being promoted by this technology?" or "What kind of values are being supported?" The notion of AIT's spirit is akin to a leader's intent or underlying motives. For example, the spirit of a groupware system is to promote collaboration, just as the spirit of a participative leader is also to promote inclusion and collaboration.

In addition to AIT, a group's task and environment also provide certain structures and boundaries on interactions. The content and constraints of a task act as resources and rules that guide the accomplishment of that task. For instance, for the task of developing an AIT application, the user requirements and budgetary limits act as resources and rules for task participants. Likewise, the internal organizational environment's climate, culture, standard operating procedures, and history may act as rules and resources that guide organizational members' actions, as may the characteristics of the external environment such as economic climate, regulation, interorganizational relationships, competition, technological possibilities, turbulence, and crises.

During the use of AIT, users interpret the structures based on their various sources. Bringing these structures into action is defined as the *appropriation* of structures. The appropriation of structures and its outcomes reaffirm existing structures, modify existing structures, or give rise to totally new structures. As structures from AIT, the task, and the environment are *appropriated*, the information and outcomes generated by their appropriation becomes a further source of structures that emerge and come into play over time. Thus, in addition to structures provided by the AIT and a group's task and environment, new "emergent" structures may also channel a group's interactions. DeSanctis and Poole (1994) say the following, for instance, about technology structures and their use:

> So, there are structures in technology, on the one hand, and structures in action, on the other. The two are continually intertwined; there is a recursive relationship between technology and action, each iteratively shaping the other. (p. 125)

The repeated appropriation of information technology generates or transforms social structures, which over time can become a newly formed organizational system of interactions. For example, the use of an Electronic Brainstorming tool can create a structure for interaction that becomes a culture for promoting innovative ideas, even when members interact face to face. Scott, Quinn, Timmerman, and Garrett (1998) showed that groups, who used a groupware system over time, went from working with a norm of equality of input, which was more consistent with the system's spirit, to one based on hierarchical norms that evolved within the group. They speculated that as groups became more comfortable allowing for everyone to provide input, a hierarchy based on expertise emerged that enhanced the group's interactions, which went beyond the designer's original intent for leveling group members' idea generation.

Poole and DeSanctis (1990) suggest that irrespective of the features that are designed into an AIT, users mediate its effects by adapting it to their needs, resisting it, or refusing to use it. A group's internal system may be defined by a variety of factors including members' style of interacting, norms for behavior, their degree of knowledge and experience with the structures characterizing the technology, perceptions of others' knowledge of structure, and agreement on which structures should be appropriated (DeSanctis & Poole, 1994).

Modifications to AST

We propose certain modifications to AST for use as a broad conceptual framework to guide future work examining e-leadership. First, we expand the characterizations of a group's internal system by including the style of leadership in the group and also how group members relate to one another (e.g., as peers or in some hierarchical fashion). Corresponding to member's knowledge about AIT, perceptions of others' knowledge about AIT, and agreement on which AIT structures to appropriate, we employ the following more general characteristics that are not specific to an AIT: members' expertise, perceptions of others and the group, and shared mental models. We could also expand this list to include, for example, a variety of other characteristics such as identification with the group and diversity of membership, experience, and backgrounds.

Second, unlike DeSanctis and Poole (1994), who consider a group's internal system as influencing the appropriation of structures but not as a source of structures, we consider a group's internal system as being a source of structures. For example, the style of a group's leader is likely to channel a group's thinking and hence serve as a source of structures for subsequent appropriations of information technology (Kahai, Sosik, & Avolio, 1997; Sosik, Avolio, & Kahai, 1997). Likewise, shared mental models, members' expertise, perceptions of others and the group, diversity in the group, and identification with the group are likely to structure a group's thinking, interaction, and ultimately its process, structures, and outcomes. All of these must be considered as potentially relevant to the structures that emerge with the insertion of AIT.

RELEVANCE OF LEADERSHIP WITHIN
THE AST FRAMEWORK

Leadership can be viewed as a system embedded within a larger social organizational system, and it includes the implicit models in people's heads regarding how they should influence or be influenced by others at the same level, below them, or above them (Lord & Maher, 1991). Leadership systems also include the quality of dyadic interactions and relationships (Graen & Uhl-Bien, 1995), the collective leadership characterizing group interactions (Sivasubramaniam, Murry, Avolio, & Jung, 2002), and ultimately the leadership culture that characterizes an organization system or larger collective (House & Aditya, 1997). The leadership system encompasses both individual as well as collective leadership behavior within and across levels of the organization (Avolio, 1999). As such, a leadership system can be viewed as a source of structures that guide action, including the appropriation of AIT, within the AST framework (Kahai et al., 1997).

Leadership and Adaptation
to New Technology

The leadership system in an organization is oftentimes characterized by its "spirit" or intent. For instance, the spirit of a participative leadership system is to increase involvement of organizational members in decision making by fostering openness in communication and collaboration among organizational members. Consistency between the leadership's spirit and the spirit of the AIT is relevant to its appropriation and will likely predict how successful or unsuccessful new technology will be in an organization.

Consider Vandenbosch and Ginzberg's (1997) study on the insertion of a groupware system into an organization called Lotus Notes. The spirit of Lotus Notes is to increase collaboration among office workers. Yet, groups who did not collaborate prior to the introduction of a collaborative information technology failed to collaborate after the new technology was introduced. Vandenbosch and Ginzberg (1997) indicated that

> ... these systems more often reinforce existing structures and practices than they introduce new ones. The notion of information technology as the spearhead for change in organizations is in most cases, just not applicable. (p. 7)

Vandenbosch and Ginzberg (1997) noted that groupware systems such as Lotus Notes are likely to enhance collaboration in organizations that have an inherently collaborative culture. In cultures where the culture is a "strong force" and noncollaborative, it is unlikely that technology-practice will have a sustainable impact on group dynamics. Similarly, Marshall (1995) argued that to collaborate there must be appropriate leadership, culture, and support systems in place prior to the insertion of new technology.

We take the position here that the successful appropriation of AIT is tied to the type of leadership and cultural system in which it is inserted and embedded over time. Leadership will likely be the spearhead for adaptive change, where it prepares the system to coevolve with the use of new technology.

Then what specific role does leadership play when enabling AIT appropriations, which then result in successful adaptation? According to AST, the nature of AIT appropriations is likely to be influenced by a group's internal system, which is defined in terms of the group's style of interacting, member expertise, shared mental models, diversity, and identification. For instance, Kahai et al. (1997) reported that group members were more supportive of each other using a groupware system for interaction when the leader was more *participative* versus *directive*.

Not only can leadership promote successful adaptations to change; it is also possible for leadership to restrict new information technology use to such a point that it has little, if any, impact on the preexisting social–cultural system within an organization. For instance, autocratic leadership may repel the best attempts at collaboration enabled by a groupware system designed for collaboration, if the leaders interpret a more open system of exchange as leading to less control over their followers.

TECHNOLOGY'S EFFECT ON LEADERSHIP

Thus far, we have presented the role of leadership in how the social system appropriates AIT and adapts to it over time. We now present the effects of technology more explicitly on leadership. The effect of AIT on enabling e-leadership will in part depend on the perception and actual qualities of the AIT system, experiences members of the organization have had with prior technology, the legacy technology system that already exists, as well as the range of functions and processes provided by new technology.

Taking the extreme possibility as a case in point, consider how AIT can impact a closed and autocratic organizational system. In this type of organization, the leaders are rarely challenged when setting the mission or standard operating procedures. Leaders may have an implicit model of followers as passive, dependent, and nonconfrontational. With the introduction of AIT, access to a broader array of information can challenge preexisting beliefs of what constitutes "followership," as well as what constitutes a full range of appropriate leadership behavior. New technology can enable relationships to exist within and between networks where greater levels of collaboration can "spontaneously" emerge. Access to new information and development of knowledge can transform what was once considered acceptable and unacceptable behaviors by followers, as well as by leaders, resulting in a rethinking of how each should work together to accomplish their goals and those of their organization. However, it is also likely that to sustain such transformative change will require more than simply inserting new technology.

Summary

In summary, successful implementation and integration of AIT will typically require a transformation in the leadership system to accommodate and to complement its insertion in the organization. As argued previously, the leadership system that exists during AIT's introduction is likely to influence AIT's effects on people in that organization. Unfortunately, we do not know much either theoretically or empirically about these phenomena, as noted by Dodge, Webb, and Christ (1999):

> There are many gaps in our knowledge of the effects and consequences of digitization. We could find very few references to cite when it comes to the likely consequences of digitization on management and leadership, per se. (p. 31)

Effects of Group Leaders in Groupware Environments

Prior research in the area of GSS indicates what impact the presence or absence of leadership can have on teams interacting in a GSS environment. Furthermore, as demonstrated by the interaction effect of anonymity and leadership observed by George, Easton, Nunamaker, and Northcroft (1990), leadership has the potential to interact with structural features of a GSS that may affect appropriation of those features and the subsequent structural characteristics that provide the boundaries for a group's interactions. This supports our earlier point about examining the interaction between the leadership and the technical systems in terms of their optimal integration and impact on performance. However, in the absence of any systematic manipulation of leadership in most prior research on AIT and leadership (Fjermestad & Hiltz, 1999), it is not yet possible to generalize or derive any practical prescriptions for leadership in these computer-mediated environments. Since most studies have not controlled for nor measured leadership behavior directly, it is not clear what were the nature and level of leadership behavior displayed. Specifically, assigning, electing, or designating a leader may not have resulted in a consistent style of leadership displayed by the leaders and perceived by participants. This was the typical approach used to study leadership in the GSS literature.

There are some interesting questions that can be posed regarding the effects of AIT on the people interactions in organizations. For example, can "AIT structures" substitute for "leadership structures"? Leadership substitutes are characteristics of the context in which leadership is exercised, "which render relationship and/or task-oriented leadership not only impossible but also unnecessary" (Kerr & Jermier, 1978). Ho and Raman (1991) suggested that the provision of a process structure by a GSS in the form of a normative set of steps to follow (define problem, define selection criteria, define alternatives, etc.) could have made leadership redundant in their investigation.

Generally, there has not been enough research examining the specific features of the AIT systems and their linkages to leadership style to come to any firm conclusions. The linkage between the AIT system and the leadership system remains an area ripe for exploration.

Preliminary Studies of the Effects of Group Leadership in AIT Settings

Kahai et al. (1997) argued that participative leadership would be more consistent than directive leadership with the "participative spirit" of a GSS and, therefore, would lead to greater group member input in the form of solution proposals, critical remarks, and supportive remarks. However, they found that for a creativity task in which participants provided input anonymously, the number of solution proposals and critical comments generated was similar to that for directive and participative leadership. They suggested that in the presence of anonymity, control aspects of directive leadership could have been ignored by group members. Going back to our earlier comments about autocratic leadership, it is possible that technology use can alter the dynamic between leaders and followers, when its users are protected by anonymity.

Sosik et al. (1997) examined the mediating link between facilitator leadership styles and their effect on group processes such as potency and group performance. The styles compared included *transformational* versus *transactional* leadership (Avolio, 1999; Bass, 1998; Bass & Avolio, 1994). Both leadership styles had a positive effect on group potency, which in turn had a positive impact on the groups' performance. Sosik et al. (1997) reported that anonymity affected the impact of leadership style on performance differentially depending on whether the group was using the technology to brainstorm (divergent task) or to complete a report (convergent task). Transformational leadership had a greater positive impact on the collective performance of the group when group members were anonymous and the task was an *integrative* versus a *brainstorming* task. Transformational leaders are typically described as motivating the collective performance of their groups, and the authors speculated that the anonymous condition could have highlighted the need for such leadership (Bass, 1998).

Transformational leadership may also limit social loafing by getting all members to work for the good of the group, as was shown in a recent study by Kahai, Sosik, and Avolio (2000), also conducted within a GSS context. In this study, transactional leaders led groups that produced better reports working under identified conditions in which individual rewards could be assigned for performance. Groups led by transformational leaders performed better under anonymous and group reward conditions, where social loafing would have been expected to reduce performance, but performance actually increased.

Sosik, Kahai, and Avolio (1998a) examined the impact of the transformational facilitator leadership style on group creativity in a GSS context. Transformational leaders were described by Bass (1985) as being intellectually stimulating in the sense that they challenge old assumptions and help followers reframe how they think about problems. This style of facilitator leadership was expected to enhance group performance engaged in electronic brainstorming and measured in terms of ideational fluency, flexibility, originality, and elaboration (Torrance, 1965). They reported that transformational leadership impacted positively on levels of elaboration and originality of groups interacting via electronic brainstorming. Anonymity impacted positively on the flexibility of thinking in the groups, but not on other measures of creativity. Groups in the identified transformational condition demonstrated higher flexibility than groups in the identified nontransformational condition. Leadership effects were eliminated under the anonymous condition. As noted earlier, this may be due to the system substituting for leadership, because anonymity may provide a context in which flexibility of thinking is already encouraged.

Sosik, Avolio, and Kahai (1998b) also examined the impact of leadership style, anonymity, and interactions in a group decision support system on creative output. Their results provided some contradictory evidence to the results presented here. Specifically, when examining the separate components of transformational leadership, the authors found that intellectual stimulation and individualized consideration each had a negative impact on group creativity. Transactional goal setting and inspiring leadership both had a positive impact on group creativity. They suggested that it is possible that participants may have perceived the facilitator's intellectual stimulation as being critical or judicial, resulting in group members' curbing their input or being more cautious in generating ideas. Such judicial thinking can result in less creative output during brainstorming (Stein, 1975). Another alternative explanation is that by being perceived as critical of members' ideas, the intellectually stimulating leader may have been seen as violating the "spirit" of a group decision support system (DeSanctis & Poole, 1994).

The limited base of research on the impact of leadership style in GSS contexts suggests that style indeed does make a difference. Furthermore, anonymity interacts with the transformational and transactional leadership styles to influence group process and/or outcomes. These results lead to the following questions. How does leadership style interact with group history in terms of its impact on group process and performance? Does consistency of a leader's style with the AIT's spirit matter for group performance? Do AIT features influence how a leadership style is perceived? How do characteristics of the context, such as the task, moderate the effects of different leadership styles?

Summary

The work reviewed previously can be seen as focusing on the effects of leadership behaviors on the appropriation of technology, technology-practice, and a group's process and outcomes. The appropriation of technology, group process, and outcomes in turn can influence the structures under which a group operates, including the structures provided by a leader. However, to our knowledge, there has been no work on how the structures that result from the appropriation of technology and a group's process and outcomes influence leadership. For instance, what is the impact of the appropriation of collaborative groupware technology on a directive leader's behavior over time, or at least the perceptions of that behavior? Under what conditions do the group's appropriations of various structures lead to a change in leadership style? How does it change the follower's style? Future work must now examine the dialectic interplay between leadership as a source of structures and how leadership affects and is affected by the structures arising from the appropriation of technology.

CONCLUSIONS AND IMPLICATIONS FOR FUTURE WORK ON E-LEADERSHIP

Much of our discussion about the integration of computer-mediated technology in organizations and its impact on leadership suggests that we must examine the patterns that emerge over a period of time in the social systems when a new technology is introduced (Fulk, 1993). In our discussion, we have assumed that we are examining emergent social systems created over time through a complex interplay of various technical and human leadership system processes. For instance, some leaders can observe how others use technology to open up communication channels and challenge "old" ways of thinking in their organizations. Through observation, they learn that these changes in behavior can be effective for stimulating innovation, trust building, and enhanced commitment. Thus, they begin to role model those behaviors and create a new structure for interaction, which substitutes for older forms of interaction over time. These emergent systems are represented not only in terms of behaviors but also in the way people construe meaning from their interactions (Bandura, 1986; Fulk, 1993). Hence, technology becomes part of the social transformation in the organization and in turn part of leadership.

In contrast, another leader may view the appropriation of technology as a cost-efficient means of controlling employee behavior through constant monitoring of deviations from standards. The social system that emerges is likely to be quite different from the one that emerges with the first leader.

Technology itself does not reduce constraints on what is available information; rather it creates opportunities that can facilitate the reduction of such constraints, oftentimes increasing the discretion available to employees at all levels of organizations. However, as technology encounters power structures and strong cultures, its integration has become more complex and yet also more interesting. Perhaps the most important question now is "why" do people come together, as opposed to studying "how" they come together. The shift in question leads to an obvious need to study the social system in which technology is embedded and evolving over time, and at the heart of that social system is leadership. To do this requires that we define the level at which we intend to observe the interaction between technology and the human/social system, and at least for this moment, we would recommend the inclusion of at least four levels of analysis: individual, dyadic, group, and organizational.

Some Future Directions
for E-Leadership Research

With respect to future research on e-leadership, never has the context been more relevant to how we define leadership. If the context is in part the nature or "spirit" of technology, and technology is transforming the way leaders (teams) scan, interpret, and disseminate information, then "context" is integral to what constitutes leadership processes and systems in organizations. If this general assumption is accepted, then we must systematically examine how advanced information technology transforms the "traditional roles of leadership" at individual, dyadic, group, and organizational/systems levels.

Katz and Kahn (1978) described organizations as interconnected systems, in which changes in one part of the system can affect changes in other parts. We used AST in our discussion of e-leadership, in part, to demonstrate the importance of examining the interconnectedness of leadership and information technology systems within the larger organizational system. We have argued that organizational effectiveness is determined in part by how well social and technical systems are aligned with each other and the external environment.

With the introduction of e-leadership into the leadership literature, we must now examine how this construct should be conceptualized, measured, and analyzed using a multilevel framework. Going from the individual to the group and organizational levels, today a senior leadership team can communicate and disseminate information to all employees as often as they desire to communicate with them. How does this capability affect the leadership team's strategy for adapting to complexity and uncertainty in their environment? As the senior management team's leadership is mediated more through technology, how does it affect their credibility when articulating the organization's goals, strategy, and vision? How does AIT help the team to reinforce the organization's principles and values within and between various levels of analysis? What type of leadership team culture should be in place before going "e" in terms of widely disseminating information? As more and more strategic thinking, visions, goals, and messages are mediated through information technology, what impact will mediation have on direct and indirect followers operating at a distance? Will a closer alignment represented in the direct followers' views of the leadership team be more rapidly developed at subsequent levels by using AIT to disseminate and store key messages?

Alternatively, if employees at lower levels can access information as rapidly as their senior management team, will this have any effect on levels of alignment within both the overall organization and the "sense-making" function typically driven by an organization's leadership? Employees may access information that contradicts a strategic leadership directive with information that may not yet be available to the senior leadership team. How does the senior management team assure followers their message is authentic, if interactions occur primarily at a distance? With all good intentions, the senior leadership's directive may be seen as lacking in credibility, contributing to a lack of alignment around strategic goals and directions. Fundamentally, given broader access to information, how can the leadership of an organization best lead its followers, and how can the followers best influence their leaders?

The type of impact that information technology can have at a larger collective or organizational level can also be expected to emerge at unit and dyadic levels. Members of a team can reinforce the principles or agreements adopted by the team, by exchanging examples that support those principles, even if the team never meets face to face. The same is also true for two individuals who are interacting with each other via technology. The ability of the group to stay connected and informed about each other's work could have a positive impact on the group's level of cohesion, efficacy, and potency (Avolio, Kahai & Dodge et al., 2000). Yet, staying connected may also have a negative impact to the extent that information is rapidly transmitted about all of the problem areas in the group or that there is no down time for reflection. Moreover, Parasuraman and Simmers (2001) discussed the "double-edged sword" of technology, where increased availability and autonomy 24/7 resulted in higher work–family conflict and lower family satisfaction.

What we might observe at the group level can also be observed in the quality of relationships observed between a leader and his or her respective followers. Perhaps, it is now possible to develop high-quality relationships between leaders and followers at a more rapid pace, where leaders have the ability to have more frequent "virtual" contact with followers. Of course, just as high-quality relationships and even trust may be developed more quickly with the support of advanced information technology, so can poorer individual relationships be developed at an accelerated pace.

With the integration of AIT in organizations, the interpretation of distance between leaders and followers may also change. As we discussed earlier in reference to virtual teams and Shamir's work on both near and distance leaders, how one conceptualizes and measures e-leadership may change the way we view physical as well as social distance between leaders and followers.

How organizations gather, interpret, and disseminate information that impacts on strategic goals and plans will no doubt be affected by the use and integration of AIT. It is for these reasons that we have argued that e-leadership will transform our models of leadership, and ultimately the way they are measured and developed in organizations, even though many aspects of leadership will also remain the same. Leaders who are seen as more effective will still be more inspirational, caring, intellectually challenging, credible, honest, goal oriented, and stable. However, the "behavior" that results in their being seen as such will in many cases be mediated through AIT.

We have provided in the following some more specific themes that need to be explored in future research on e-leadership.

1. There is a need to examine how existing leadership styles and cultures embedded in a group and/or an organization affect the appropriation of advanced information technology systems.
2. There are several studies that have examined how leadership style and task type influence technology's impact on group interactions. We need to broaden the basis of inquiry to include tasks that have significant meaning to participants and also to vary the conditions under which those tasks are completed (e.g., stable versus unstable contexts). At the same time, we will need to vary leadership style to examine its interaction with task type, context, and the characteristics of technology.
3. Some preliminary research in computer-mediated contexts indicates that computer-mediated groups solve problems differently from those working face to face. For example, Lam (1997) reported that decision quality was higher in computer-mediated versus face-to-face groups when groups worked on tasks of increasing complexity. Computer-mediated groups spent more time analyzing the decision and discussing how to approach the task, assumptions, and so forth. In a face-to-face setting, the merits of each individual's proposal were not evaluated as extensively or as deeply as those in computer-mediated interactions. Critical comments here were directed toward analyzing the problem as opposed to being critical of one another. Future research needs to explore how introducing different styles of leadership may result in different patterns of problem-solving capacity in computer-mediated versus face-to-face groups.
4. As we focus on leadership style, we will need to take into consideration whether to examine the leadership style of an individual and/or the collective. In situations where teams already exist, it may be more appropriate to examine leadership *by* the team versus leadership *of* the team by a single individual (Sivasubramaniam et al., 2002). The impact of technology on a team's learning capacity at different points in its development remains a largely unexplored area (Saunders & Miranda, 1998).

5. Many of the groups that end up taking advantage of AIT are multicultural groups. There is a very slim base of research on how to best utilize technology within and between multicultural groups.

6. Gefen and Straub (1997) examined how men and women perceive the use of information technology, concluding that women tend to see communication tools such as e-mail as having much higher social presence. Thus, women may be more likely to appropriate such technology to build and sustain relationships in organizations. A key issue to consider here is how do men and women leaders appropriate new technology within and between different cultures? What impact does the appropriation have on emergent social systems? How does the emergence of these social systems impact subsequent interactions within and between different gender groups? Finally, do male versus female leaders use technology with followers in ways that are different, resulting in different social structures and interactions being formed?

7. The issue of "sense of presence" will become more relevant as emerging technologies involving video and auditory streaming hit the markets. In the near future, people will have a much broader range of channels with which to communicate with one another. Yet, we have little if any evidence in support of or against using broader band technologies to improve group dynamics or leadership performance. Broader band technologies may distract people from getting down to the specific task at hand. With most of the research on GSS systems discussed here, anonymity was protected since interactions were text based. One question that arises is whether the introduction of video and auditory cues will move us backwards in terms of the influence that stereotypes have had on social interactions in organizations. A related question concerns what are the implications for on-demand and spontaneous virtual communication in those groups working at a distance. Abel (1990) reported that having a continual audio–video cross-link enabled groups to build more cohesive teams. Instead of using less rich media, which can "remove" us from the person being interacted with, the newer media platforms bring us "virtually" in contact throughout the day with remote group members. How will this type of ubiquitous contact effect our interactions and expectations of each other as we work at a distance between leaders and followers?

In conclusion, there is a broad, new frontier opening up for research on leadership in the information environment that we have labeled e-leadership. We believe the field of leadership can directly benefit by exploring and testing existing leadership models and theories as they each apply to e-leadership. Advanced information technology will be inserted, and the information environment will evolve whether we study its impact on leadership or not. The question is not whether to study e-leadership but where now to start our research efforts.

REFERENCES

Abel, M. J. (1990). Experiences in an exploratory distributed organization. In J. Galegher, R. Kraut, & C. Agate (Eds.), *Intellectual team work: Social and technological foundations of cooperative work* (pp. 489–510). Hillside, NJ: Lawrence Erlbaum Associates, Inc.

Avolio, B. J. (1999). *Full leadership development: Building the vital forces in organizations.* Thousand Oaks, CA: Sage.

Avolio, B. J., Kahai, S., & Dodge, G. (2000). E-leadership and its implications for theory, research and practice. *Leadership Quarterly, 11,* 615–670.

Avolio, B. J., Kahai, S., Dum Dum, R., & Sivasubramaniam, N. (2000). Virtual teams: Implications for E-Leadership and team development. In M. London (Ed.), *How people evaluate others in organizations: Person perception and interpersonal judgement in I/O Psychology,* Mahway, NJ: Lawrence Erlbaum Associates, Inc.

Bandura, A. (1986). *Social foundations of creation and thought: A social cognitive view.* Englewood Cliffs, NJ: Prentice-Hall.

Bass, B. M. (1985). *Leadership and performance beyond expectations.* New York: Free Press.

Bass, B. M. (1998). *Transformational leadership: Industrial, military and educational impact.* NJ: Lawrence Erlbaum Associates, Inc.

Bass, B. M., & Avolio, B. J. (1994). *Improving organizational effectiveness through transformational leadership.* Thousand Oaks, CA: Sage.

DeSanctis, G., & Poole, M. S. (1994). Capturing the complexity in advanced technology use: Adaptive Structuration Theory. *Organization Science, 5,* 121–147.

Dodge, G. E., Webb, H. W., & Christ, R. E. (1999). *The impact of information technology on battle command: Lessons from management science and business.* U.S. Army Research Institute of the Behavioral Sciences Technical Report 1091.

Drucker, P. F. (1993). *Post-capitalist society.* New York: HarperBusiness.

Earley, P. C., & Mosakowski, E. (2000). Creating hybrid cultures: An empirical test of transnational team functioning. *Academy of Management Journal, 43,* 26–49.

Fjermestad, J., & Hiltz, S. R. (1999). An assessment of group support systems experimental research: Methodology and results. *Journal of Management Information Systems, 15,* 7–149.

Fulk, J. (1993). Social construction of communication technology. *Academy of Management Journal, 5,* 921–950.

Gefen, D., & Straub, D. W. (1997). Gender differences in the perception and use of e-mail: An extension to the technology acceptance model. *Management Information Systems Quarterly, 21,* 389–400.

George, J. F., Easton, G., Nunamaker, J. F., Jr., & Northcraft, G. (1990). A study of collaborative group work with and without computer-based support. *Information Systems Research, 1,* 394–415.

Giddens, A. (1979). *Central problems in social theory: Action, structure and contradiction in social analysis.* Berkeley: University of California Press.

Graen, G. B., & Uhl-Bien, M. (1995). Relationship based approach to leadership: Development of leader-member exchange (LMX) theory of leadership over 25 years. Applying a multi-level multi-domain perspective. *Leadership Quarterly, 68,* 219–247.

Ho, T. H., & Raman, K. S. (1991). The effect of GSS and elected leadership on small group meetings. *Journal of Management Information Systems, 8,* 109–133.

Hoenig, C. (2001). Lose the e. *CIO, 13(22),* 62–64.

House, R. J., & Aditya, R. W. (1997). The social science study of leadership: Quo Vadis? *Journal of Management, 23,* 409–473.

Kahai, S. S., Sosik, J. J., & Avolio, B. J. (1997). Effects of leadership style and problem structure on work group process and outcomes in an electronic meeting system environment. *Personnel Psychology, 50,* 121–146.

Kahai, S., Sosik, J., & Avolio, B. J. (2000). *Effects of leadership style, anonymity, and rewards in an electronic meeting system environment.* Working Paper, Center for Leadership Studies.

Katz, D., & Kahn, R. L. (1978). *The social psychology of organizations* (2nd ed.). New York: Wiley.

Kerr, S., & Jermier, J. M. (1978). Substitutes for leadership: Their meaning and measurement. *Organizational Behavior and Human Performance, 22,* 375–403.

Lam, S. S. V. (1997). The effects of group decision support on group communication and decision quality. *Journal of Management Information Systems, 13,* 193–215.

Lipnack, J., & Stamps, J. (1997). *Virtual teams: Reaching across space, time, and organizations with technology.* New York: Wiley.

Lord, R. G., & Maher, K. J. (1991). *Leadership and information processing: Linking perception and performance.* Boston: Unwin Hyman.

Marshall, E. M. (1995). The collaboration workplace. *Management Review,* 13–17.

O'Mahoney, S., & Barley, S. R. (1999). Do digital communications affect work and organization? The state of our knowledge. *Research in Organizational Behavior, 21,* 125–161.

Orlikowski, W. J. (1992). The duality of technology: Rethinking the concept of technology in organizations. *Organization Science, 3,* 398–427.

Orlikowski, W. J. (2000). Using technology and constituting structures: A practice lens for studying technology in organizations. *Organization Science, 11,* 404–428.

Orlikowski, W. J., & Iacono, C. S. (2001). Research commentary: Desperately seeking the "IT" in IT research—A call to organizations. *Information Systems Research, 12,* 121–134.

Orlikowski, W. J., Yates, J., Okamura, K., & Fujimoto, M. (1995). Shaping electronic communication: The meta-structuring of technology in the context in use. *Organization Science, 6,* 423–444.

Parasuraman, S., & Simmers, C. A. (2001). Type of employment, work-family conflict and well-being: A comparative study. *Journal of Organizational Behavior, 22,* 551–568.

Poole, M. S., & DeSanctis, G. (1990). Understanding the use of group decision support systems. The theory of adaptive structuration. In C. W. Steinfeld & J. Fulks (Eds.), *Organizational and communication technology* (pp. 173–193). Newbury Park, CA: Sage.

Rayport, J. F., & Sviokla, J. J. (1995). Exploiting the virtual value chain. *Harvard Business Review, 73,* 75–85.

Saunders, C., & Miranda, S. (1998). Information acquisition in group decision making. *Information and Management, 34,* 55–74.

Schlosser, F. K. (2002). So, how do people really use their handheld devices? An interactive study of wireless technology use. *Journal of Organizational Behavior, 23,* 401–424.

Scott, C. R., Quinn, L., Timmerman, C. F., & Garrett, D. M. (1998). Ironic uses of group communication technology: Evidence from meeting transcripts and interviews with group decision support users. *Communication Quarterly, 46,* 353–374.

Shamir, B. (1997). *Leadership in boundaryless organizations: Disposable or indisposable.* Unpublished manuscript, Hebrew University.

Shamir, B., & Ben-Ari, E. (1999). Leadership in an open army? Civilian connections, interorganizational frameworks, and changes in military leadership. In J. G. Hunt, G. E. Dodge, & L. Wong (Eds.), *Out of the box leadership: Transforming the 21st century Army and other top performing organizations.* CT: JAI Press.

Sivasubramaniam, N., Murry, W. D., Avolio, B. J., & Jung, D. I. (2002). A longitudinal model of the effects of team leadership and group potency on group performance. *Group & Organization Management, 27,* 66–97.

Sosik, J. J., Avolio, B. J., & Kahai, S. S. (1997). Effects of leadership style and anonymity and group potency and effectiveness in a group decision support system environment. *Journal of Applied Psychology, 82,* 89–103.

Sosik, J. J., Avolio, B. J., & Kahai, S. S. (1998a). Inspiring group creativity: Comparing anonymous and identified electronic brainstorming. *Small Group Research, 29,* 3–31.

Sosik, J. J., Kahai, S. S., & Avolio, B. J. (1998b). Transformational leadership and dimensions of creativity: Motivating idea generation in computer-mediated groups. *Creativity Research Journal, 11*, 111–121.

Stein, M. S. (1974). *Stimulating creativity*, (Volume 2). NY: Academic Press.

Torrance, E. P. (1965). *Rewarding creative behavior*. Englewood Cliffs, NJ: Prentice-Hall.

Trist, E. L. (1993). A socio-technical critique of scientific management. In E. Trist & H. Murray (Eds.), *The social engagement of social science: A Tavistock anthology* (pp. 580–598). Philadelphia, PA: University of Pennsylvania Press.

Vandenbosch, B., & Ginzberg, M. J. (1997). Lotus notes and collaboration: Plus ca change. *Journal of Management Information Systems, 13*, 65–81.

Weick, K. F. (1990). Technology as equivoque: Sense making in new techniques. In P. S. Goodman, L. S. Sproull & Associates (Eds.), *Technology and organizations* (pp. 1–44). San Francisco: Jossey-Bass.

Willoughby, K. W. (1990). *Technology choice: A critique of the appropriate technology movement*. Boulder, CO: Westview Press.

Yates, J., Orlikowski, W. J., & Okamura, K. (1999). Explicit and implicit structuring of genres in electronic communication: Reinforcement and change of social interaction. *Organization Science, 10*, 83–103.

4

Leadership Development in the Virtual Workplace

Gretchen M. Spreitzer
University of Michigan Business School

In an era of global integration, electronic connectivity, and network structures, the virtual workplace, where employees work remotely from one another, is becoming an important reality (Mohrman, 1998). Work is increasingly performed by geographically and organizationally disbursed teams and networks of employees who share accountability for a product, service, or task. A virtual workplace exploits complementary skills of its members to pursue common strategic objectives. Though periodic face-to-face interaction may occur, the bulk of the work in a virtual workplace is done while employees are physically separate.

The business rationale for a virtual workplace is compelling. A number of important advantages have been identified in the literature, including the following:

- *Boundarylessness.* Unrestrained interaction across geography, time, and organizational boundaries is becoming more important as organizations locate operations throughout the world to tap needed resources, to be close to customers, and to gain access to world markets (Mohrman, 1998). In places like Bangalore, India, U.S. companies are outsourcing their call centers for operations such as computer support.
- *Network organizations.* Companies can strip down their business to its essence to focus on where the greatest value creation lies; extraneous functions can

71

be eliminated through partnerships and newly supercharged forms of out-sourcing (Kirkpatrick, 2001). Cisco is on its way to doing this already—they partner or outsource virtually everything unrelated to systems integration.

- *Reduced real estate expenses.* Less office space is needed when employees work virtually.
- *Reduced cycle time for products and services.* Veriphone uses a so-called relay race of engineers across the world to develop software products faster than its competitors. Each works during normal business hours and then hands off their work to engineers in the next time zone (Cascio, 2000).
- *Increased customer service.* Because employees may be physically closer to the customer, they can better understand the needs and wants of customers.
- *Knowledge leverage.* When employees work virtually, there is greater op-portunity to leverage knowledge capability and best practices from different sources.
- *Global access to talent.* Because relocation is less important in a virtual system, companies have easier access to global markets for talent rather than primarily to their own hometown.
- *Environmental benefits.* With reduced commuting, fewer automobiles are on the road, requiring fewer natural resources and producing less pollution (Haywood, 1998).
- *Focus.* When employees work virtually, there is more opportunity for uninter-rupted thought and concentration (O'Mahoney & Barley, 1999). Employees are less likely to be distracted with conversations around the water cooler about sports teams or social lives (Froggatt, 2001).
- *Work–life balance.* When employees can have more control over the location and timing of their work, they have more flexibility to coordinate work and family responsibilities (Cascio, 2000).

Although all of these advantages are theoretically possible, anyone who has worked in a virtual environment will tell you it is not easy. Working in a virtual context requires a fundamental shift from a time when people worked largely in functional groupings side by side in the same location. Consequently, virtual work brings significant challenges to the workplace, including:

- significant setup costs associated with creating and maintaining distributed offices,
- loss of cost efficiencies due to the duplication of equipment in distributed offices,
- reduced identification and attachment to the organization,
- difficulties in cross-cultural coordination when employees work across na-tional borders,
- potential for burnout due to an inability to keep work and home life separate,

- and feelings of isolation that come from not working face to face with other employees (Cascio, 2000).

These disadvantages of the virtual organization can take away from the advantages that virtuality can bring to the workplace. How the transition to a virtual organization is implemented and the way virtual employees are cared for will determine to what extent the advantages of virtuality outweigh the disadvantages. Clearly the leadership of the virtual organization can make a large difference in minimizing the disadvantages that often accompany the virtual organization. The purpose of this paper is to examine conceptually the critical role that leadership can play in capturing the advantages of a virtual workplace while minimizing the potential disadvantages. Specifically, implications for leadership development in a virtual environment are addressed.

First, I define carefully what a virtual workplace is and discuss how it differs from a more traditional workplace. Then I identify the specific leadership characteristics necessary for success in a virtual environment and discuss their implications for leadership development. I draw from the growing body of research on the virtual organization and telecommuting as well as from my own research and experience with virtual work.

THE VIRTUAL WORKPLACE

A virtual organization is "a collection of geographically distributed, functionally and/or culturally diverse entities that are linked by electronic forms of communication and rely on lateral, dynamic relationships for coordination" (DeSanctis & Monge, 1998, p. 2). Employees are physically dispersed from one another, even across countries, and may be members of different organizations working toward a common goal. Often these distributed structures are exocentric, referring to a group whose primary work activities, interactions, and relationships are external in nature (Goodman & Wilson, 2000).

Particularly as organizations outsource a number of organizational functions, they often replace a traditional structure with an interorganizational network or virtual organization structure. The virtual organization emphasizes core capabilities and brings together the requisite set of employees to get work done effectively and efficiently. As a result, membership in a virtual team or organization may be more fluid than a traditional system, as membership will evolve according to changing task requirements (Townsend, DeMarie, & Hendrickson, 1998). The virtual structure itself may be either temporary, existing only to accomplish a specific task, or more permanent, used to address ongoing issues such as strategic planning.

Because virtual employees may be distributed across time zones, communication is just as likely to be asynchronous as it is to be synchronous in a virtual workplace. Employees working in a virtual workplace are assembled using a combination of telecommunications and information technologies to accomplish an organization task. At a mundane level, a virtual workplace might merely be an organization where some employees work at a remote location or telecommute but do occasionally meet face to face. Here employees are part of the same organization who work remotely (or telecommute) on a part-time basis (maybe 1 or 2 days a week).

A more complicated but increasingly common example of a virtual organization is one that makes use of a distributed team structure. A typical example of this type of virtual team is described in Mohrman (1998). This cross-functional team is a new product development group charged with developing a rugged land-based telescope that can send images throughout the world. The team has tight time and cost deadlines to meet that will determine the viability of the project. The team is composed of three subteams in three different locations. One subteam is located in Irvine, California, and works on software design. Another is based in Boston, Massachusetts, and works on hardware. A third is based in China and handles manufacturing and testing. The team is the product of an alliance of two firms: one North American based and one Chinese based.

Even if the whole team was located in one location, it would be difficult to manage. It is a cross-functional unit whose members have highly honed and distinct knowledge sets but who must work interdependently to be successful. All team members are not fully dedicated to this product development project; most have multiple projects on which they are working. Team members may receive conflicting directions not only from their functional heads but also from their respective organizations about the mission, purpose, and priorities of the team's efforts. Not only are the production engineers in another company, but also they are from another country in a completely different time zone with a substantially different culture. These differences can make the job of a leader particularly complicated.

LEADERSHIP CHARACTERISTICS REQUIRED IN A VIRTUAL WORKPLACE

Although many definitions of leadership have been offered throughout this volume, for this chapter, leadership is defined as the person who influences a group toward the attainment of the group's goals (Yukl, 1989). The type of leader I focus on is either the leader of a virtual team or one of a group of followers who works at a distance from the leader. Key findings from both research and best practices across many industries reveal that effective leadership from a distance includes the typical fundamentals for leading people in a traditional office environment (Thompsen, 2000). In fact, many of the contemporary management practices around employee involvement are particularly pertinent to a virtual environment, because they help employees to operate with more discretion and initiative. But these traditional capabilities are more difficult to develop, because interactions occur from a distance as though they were seen through a telescope—magnifying but also narrowing the leader's viewpoint. As an example, the leader may primarily interact with an employee through e-mail except during intensive periods of interaction in face-to-face meetings once every quarter. So the leader's viewpoint of the employee is narrow, because day-to-day behavior is observed only through the lens of e-mail. Yet it is magnified, because for a few days every quarter, interactions between the boss and subordinates are intensive during one-on-one visits to the home office.

In this section of the paper, we describe the key competencies for effective leadership in a virtual workplace. In particular, it is clear that virtual leaders need to (a) provide technological support and savvy, (b) possess effective communication skills, (c) be comfortable with empowering employees, and (d) build cohesiveness amidst individual differences.

Technological Support and Know-How

Compared to a more traditional work environment, in a virtual context, leaders must provide workers with the requisite technology to work remotely. The leader plays a key role in deciding the type and use of technology for the group. The leader, with the input of employees, will decide which technology the group should adopt. It is important that there be a standard technology so that it is compatible across different virtual workers. In organizations where many employees work semipermanently on a customer site, it may be impossible to send one e-mail to all employees, because each customer uses a different e-mail system that is not compatible with others. The compatibility problem is so complicated that some companies like the Ford Motor Company once, until the company entered its current financial crisis, provided free computers to employees for home use—a benefit to the company was that they have at least one mechanism for reaching employees virtually if their main work computer is not compatible.

Townsend et al. (1998) define three types of technology that will be critical for effective virtual work: (a) desktop videoconferencing, (b) collaborative software systems, and (c) Internet/Intranet systems. Each is briefly discussed in the following.

Desktop Videoconferencing. Although it is possible to work virtually without videoconferencing, this type of technology is an important substitute for regular face-to-face interactions in conventional work. Today desktop teleconferencing systems cost under $1,000 per station and can be added to almost any personal computer. Short of being there, this technology provides the best means for users to see each other's facial expressions and body language.

Collaborative Software Systems. Collaborative software systems allow users to simultaneously work on documents, analyze data, or sketch out ideas on shared whiteboards—almost like being physically proximate. They can also empower real-time group decision making and brainstorming—even offering the option of anonymity when desirable. In this way, this computer-mediated technology provides an important advantage not available in face-to-face interactions.

Internet/Intranet Systems. Finally, company Intranets and Internets provide virtual workers with the real-time information they need to do their work. Intranets are secure company Internet sites that disseminate employee information, offer training and tools, and provide a connective interface. They also allow employees to archive text, visual, audio, and numerical data. High-speed, DSL, or cable modem Internet connections are essential for employees to have the "feel" of their office computer systems at home. In the near future, it is likely that wireless connections will be the norm—so people can truly connect anytime anywhere—at speeds up to seven times the typical T1 connection (Gurley, 2001). These kinds of wi-fi networks are already installed at most universities and even Starbucks.

Because employees are linked together electronically, leaders of a virtual organization must be comfortable in working with and through technology themselves. Ideally, the leader will be a role model in the use of technology. The leader will, whether purposely or not, set norms about how technology will be used. (For example, how often should e-mail or voice mail be checked? What is a reasonable response time to an inquiry? Can e-mails be forwarded without permission?) It is also critical to inform employees about what is acceptable use of the technology. For example, can an office computer be used for personal business, such as e-mails to family or making purchases on the Web? What kinds of e-mail are appropriate to send to colleagues? (For example, are jokes ok?)

The leader must also allocate the appropriate training to make sure all virtual workers are proficient with the uses of these technologies. This type of training will likely need to be ongoing rather than a one-time event, because technology continues to evolve and reinvent itself at an ever-increasing rate.

Finally, it is important that whatever kind of information technology selected is secure so that employees feel free to communicate without their messages being intercepted. Moreover, connections to transfer data should be secure so that sensitive information can be passed without worry. If the organization plans to monitor any of their virtual interactions, employees should be notified of this in advance that this is occurring and for what purpose the monitoring is taking place (e.g., such as for training purposes). This is critical to avoid trust violations. In addition, covert monitoring may have legal implications (i.e., it is illegal to film or tape employees without notifying them ahead of time).

Implications for Leadership Development. Although an increasing percentage of the workforce is computer literate, a significant number of leaders are still uncomfortable with computers and other telecommunications technologies, because many are older and were educated before the age of personal computers. Remember that employees who are now only in their mid-30s were the first users of personal computers in higher education. Part of this problem will be obviated as computer and telecommunications technology becomes more user-friendly (Townsend et al., 1998). In the meantime, leaders without technological savvy will need special technological training and support to become proficient and comfortable with technology. This is critical, because if virtual leaders are not comfortable with or at the cutting edge of technology, then this will send an important message to employees that technology is not a valued tool.

Regardless, virtual technology can provide some important opportunities for leadership development. With the kinds of technologies in place for a virtual organization, new opportunities for the training and development of managers and executives are possible. Many companies are creating online or CD-based training and development programs that do not require employees to travel to a central location at a prescribed time. These development opportunities can be accessed when employees have short windows of time at their disposal—for instance, while they are either waiting at the airport to catch a delayed flight or in a hotel room after a day of meetings is over. The sophistication of these online and CD-based tools is high and can include assessments, simulations, interactive media, and real-time testing and feedback.

Having virtual technology in place can also augment other kinds of leadership development tools such as 360-degree assessments (see Atwater, Brett, & Waldman, chap. 5, this volume; Conger & Toegel, chap. 6, this volume). It is not necessary for employees to be physically proximate for these kinds of assessments, and the physical distance may even increase the perception of confidentiality/anonymity when the technology is in place and trusted. Many of the assessment procedures currently used in organizations are believed to be labor intensive and time consuming. But as people become more comfortable with the sophisticated technologies of the virtual organization, regular assessments become easy and efficient.

Communication Savvy

Because employees in a virtual workplace are connected remotely, communication is different from that in a traditional workplace in several important ways (Jarvenpaa & Leidner, 1998; London, 2002). First, virtual leaders typically have access to only "snapshots" of their employees in action through intermittent visits, memos, videoconferences, phone calls, voicemail, e-mail, and pager messages. Effective leaders need to be able to quickly and skillfully diagnose what is happening with this kind of limited information and then determine an appropriate course of action to assist their employees (Thompsen, 2000).

A second element missing in a virtual environment is the spontaneous interaction and informal learning that happens by chance in an organization, whether in the mailroom, by the water cooler, or passing in the hallway. These kinds of spontaneous interactions allow the leader to keep a pulse on what is happening in the organization. The leader cannot so easily see who is having difficulty with a task. Moreover, without these spontaneous social interactions, employees may feel more isolated and find it more difficult to develop close working relationships and friendships in the workplace (Cooper & Kurland, 2002). To counter the lack of spontaneous interaction, leaders must create alternatives for keeping a pulse on their people. This might be in the form of regular unplanned e-mails or phone calls, where the leader shares some tidbit or piece of organizational news and then inquires about how things are going.

Third, in a virtual environment largely dependent on e-mail, facial expression, gestures, and vocal inflections are more difficult to discern (Townsend et al., 1998). For example, without either visual or audio cues, it is more difficult to know when someone is either joking around or being sarcastic. Moreover, it is difficult to get a clear sense of the emotional content of a message that is often not obvious or even hidden within the communication (Thompsen, 2000). Thus, leaders have to be more careful when communicating virtually to avoid miscommunication. To aid in this endeavor, the leader must listen particularly carefully and verify their interpretation of communications when there is any ambiguity. The leader might include active listening (i.e., saying "this is what I am hearing you say ..."). The leader can also use and encourage others to use e-mail typography to communicate emotion.

Fourth, research has also shown that it takes longer and is more difficult to reach consensus using computer-mediated technology (O'Mahoney & Barley, 1999). This may be because computer-mediated technology produces a greater volume of information that makes closure more difficult. It may also be because positions stated in writing are perceived as more firm than when made verbally. Thus, leaders may need to allocate more time for decision making and carefully facilitate employee interactions to bridge potential conflict.

Although computer-mediated communication may bring with it some inherent problems, it also brings some advantages in communication that the leader can build on. First, when workers communicate only through electronic media, the distinctions among member's social status become less visible (Sproull & Kiesler, 1991), equalizing differences among employees. Racial and gender differences are not so obvious. And when collaborative software systems are used that allow for anonymity, then these differences may completely disappear. However, as computer-mediated technology comes closer to approximating face-to-face encounters (such as those in desktop videoconferencing), these equalizing effects of technology will diminish.

A second potential advantage is that employees who are shy or for whom English is a second language may be more comfortable communicating using computer-mediated technology. Here they can think through and have more time to craft their ideas before sharing them publicly. Research has shown that in a virtual environment, there is an opportunity for enhanced organizational democracy and greater participation in work and decision making (Bikson & Eveland, 1990).

And third, electronic communications can be asynchronous (i.e., not time dependent) giving people more temporal control over their work (Sproull & Kiesler, 1991). When I open my door to a knock or pick up a phone call, I am in a position where I must respond immediately, given the nature of the communication. With e-mail, I can manage my correspondence as my time and schedule permit. I can respond immediately, or if I am busy or feel that I need some time to cool down to an emotionally heated message, I can wait for a bit.

Implications for Leadership Development. In order for leaders to truly understand the implications of leading in a virtual environment, it is imperative for them to have experience working virtually themselves. This experience helps them to be able to put themselves in the shoes of their virtual employees to better understand the isolation and potential for misunderstanding that are characteristic of a virtual context. The best teacher in life is experience. So it is important for organizations to develop leaders by giving them virtual assignments, ideally as a member of a virtual team.

Moreover, organizations may want to offer training in computer-mediated communication. Training in the use of e-mail functions can help avoid embarrassing unintended exchanges that often occur when individuals "reply to all" when they only mean to reply to the sender. An understanding of e-mail topography can help leaders to infuse their messages with emotion. Leaders can also receive training in more sophisticated uses of computer technology to support group processes such as brainstorming, anonymous voting, and decision support systems so that they can have the full use of technology at their disposal (Kurland & Bailey, 2002).

Comfort With Employee Empowerment

In a traditional workplace, the leader can physically observe the behavior and performance of employees. In a virtual workplace, where employees work remotely, sometimes even across time zones, employees will need to be able to work independently without direct supervision. Because managers cannot see their subordinates in action, they will have a more difficult time knowing when an employee is having job-related problems and thus may not be in the position to provide accurate and constructive performance feedback (Kurland & Bailey, 1999). In a virtual context, leaders will need to empower employees to act with discretion, because it will not be visually possible for them to monitor their employees' every move.

Although traditional visual monitoring will not be possible in a virtual context, the technology for communication and archiving can facilitate a different kind of managerial monitoring. For example, managers could view archived recordings of virtual meetings to assess employee contributions and progress. However, this is a tradeoff, as this kind of monitoring for evaluation purposes may inhibit the free flow of communication due to concerns about privacy and system security. To counter this problem, the leader should establish a clear policy regarding communications privacy and then strictly adhere to that policy (Townsend et al., 1998). Over time, then, workers can realize that these communications arenas are a safe media within which to share ideas and concerns.

Moreover, with the asynchronous communication often used in a virtual environment, getting the leader's approval before an employee takes action will create an onerous delay, particularly when the two may be operating across time zones. Instead, virtual employees require the capability to act in empowered ways.

What can the leader do to support this kind of empowerment? First, leaders must provide employees access to the kind of information they would have in a traditional workplace to enable them to make good decisions independently. "Information technology makes distance less important in determining where decisions should be made by bringing information to decision makers wherever they are" (Malone, 1997, p. 28). Leaders can create information technologies to provide employee access to necessary information—information ranging from administrative data to information on their individual and firm performance. Today, many organizations are creating company portals and Intranets to provide all necessary organizational data to employees anywhere 24/7.

Second, employees need access to training and development, so they can develop the capabilities necessary for them to work independently. Often, in a virtual context, this can be done through technologies such as the Web, so that employees can have access to personal and professional development opportunities when and where it is convenient for them. This kind of virtual training saves travel costs and time. Helping virtual employees stay on the cutting edge of their skill set will increase their attachment to the firm, also a crucial factor in a virtual context (as we will discuss later).

Third, it will be important for leaders to reward employees based on the results they achieve rather than on effort, activity, or face time (Cascio, 2000). Kurland and Bailey (1999) suggest that managers monitor performance outcomes rather than the processes or behaviors that typically get noticed and measured. For example, a leader would not reward software engineers based on how, when, or where they wrote their code but rather on the quality and swiftness of their code writing. For many others types of employees (particularly in managerial or professional roles), monitoring and measuring performance are difficult; therefore, leaders need to be vigilant not to equate face time with performance. Leaders need to establish expectations about employee performance and the criteria for judging success.

Moreover, virtual employees may feel that when they are out of sight, they are out of the mind of the boss. The boss is less likely to notice the extra hours an employee is putting in when they are not visible in the workplace. They are less likely to see the good citizenship behaviors being exhibited. Research indicates that when individuals begin to telecommute (even just 1 day per week), they are evaluated less favorably by their boss, even when their output remained the same and their peers were comfortable with the arrangement (Perlow, 1997). Thus, leaders must ensure that adequate recognition and rewards are available to virtual workers. In addition, clear schedules must be established with institutionalized progress reports and interim deliverables so both the leader and the employees will know whether things are on track.

Fourth, empowerment cannot happen without the leader trusting employees (Spreitzer & Mishra, 1999). Trust forms the glue that holds relationships together across distance and time (Mayer, Davis, & Schoorman, 1995). The leader must trust that employees will perform rather than shirk, even when their behavior cannot be visually monitored (Jarvenpaa & Leidner, 1998). Without trust, leaders will be compelled to continually check up on employees to the point of smothering any employee initiative. The leader must get beyond the misconception that remote workers will have a greater tendency to shirk their work responsibilities because they cannot be visibly monitored (O'Mahoney & Barley, 1999). Research on this issue has indicated that with professionals, the opposite is likely to be true—professionals are willing to work *additional* hours at home to obtain more uninterrupted time for complex tasks (Perlow, 1997).

In addition, leaders must build the trust of their virtual followers (Avolio & Kahai, chap. 3, this volume). The leader can build the confidence of employees by letting them know that the leader believes in their capabilities and trusts them to determine the appropriate means for effective action. When mistakes are made, the leader must focus on helping employees learn from their mistakes rather than on punishing them.

Implications for Leadership Development. Because of the physical distance between the leader and the follower, it may be more difficult for leaders themselves to identify and develop the next generation of leaders. Without face-to-face interaction, it will be more difficult for the leader to see who is struggling in an assignment or who has specific potential or capabilities. It will be more difficult to identify high-potential employees in a virtual environment. Moreover, informal means of development may not be visible in a virtual context. For example, the type of vicarious learning that occurs when employees can observe the interactions of the leader with others may be constrained in a virtual context. Employees may not see the leader taking time to pull aside an employee for some informal coaching when interactions take place across the computer rather than in an office.

More specifically, Cooper and Kurland (2002) found that telecommuters miss three types of developmental opportunities typically available to co-located workers: (a) interpersonal networking with others in the organization, (b) informal learning that enahcnes work-related skills and information distribution, and (c) mentoring from colleagues and superiors. Therefore, leadership selection and development processes will have to be more deliberate in a virtual context to be effective. Formal mentors may need to be assigned because informal mentoring is much less likely to occur when people are not co-located. Moreover, knowledge management systems may need to be developed, because the informal knowledge networks may not be as obvious when coworkers are not co-located. In addition, it will be important to build training on effectiveness in a virtual setting into conventional development programs. For example, assessments might have a segment on management with remote subordinates.

Ability To Coalesce Differences To Create Cohesiveness

Leaders who guide virtual teams (as distinct from guiding a set of individual contributors) must also build cohesiveness among team members who bring important differences (be they functional, organizational, or cultural) (London, 2002). Leaders of virtual teams must create a sense of shared purpose or a mental model necessary for employees to work together in a coherent fashion. Creating a shared mental model can help overcome the feelings of isolation that often come from working remotely (Kurland & Bailey, 1999). Maznevski and Chudoba (2000) found that teams with shared expectations needed less interaction and information to make good decisions over time.

However, it is more difficult to build a sense of shared identity in a virtual environment than in a traditional one (Kurland & Bailey, 1999), because team members are less visibly connected to the organization. The usual corporate signs and symbols and the reception area, cafeteria, and mailroom, which are readily visible to on-site employees, are mostly invisible to virtual employees. The difficulty in creating a shared mental model may also lead to reduced loyalty or community on the part of the virtual employee.

How can a leader help a virtual team create a shared mental model? To begin with, the leader's initial interactions with virtual employees are crucial. A shared mental model is most easily built through face-to-face interactions. But even when teams can only interact virtually, they can begin their work together with a series of communications where members can learn more about the team, its mission, and its members (Cascio, 2000).

Early in their team's development, leaders need to develop a clear and inspiring vision of where the organization needs to go, making sure to provide a compelling logic for why this vision is the right one. A clear vision allows empowered team members to align their actions with the direction of the organization. Leaders want to ensure that virtual employees receive regular company newsletters, broadcasts of "all-hands" types of meetings, and have the opportunity for regular on-site visits to enmesh them in the organization's vision and culture.

The leader must also work with the virtual team to set norms to guide interactions. The leader must be a role model in establishing and adhering to ground rules, etiquette for interaction, and expectations for working. For example, the leader can be instrumental in setting norms about work schedules (must employees work a traditional schedule [e.g., 8 a.m.–6 p.m.] or do they have flexibility?) and appropriate response times (how soon are employees who work virtually expected to return phone calls or emails?). Establishing norms before virtual work begins is important for effective work and for the avoidance of misunderstandings.

Another way to help build a shared mental model is for the leader to help team members to understand the different competencies that each brings to the team effort. So that each member brings a crucial skill to the team, the leader must select employees based on their complementary capabilities and ensure that individual roles are clearly delineated to all employees. This is important for virtual employees to be able to work in a coordinated fashion, and for employees to realize the value and capability of their coworkers—to create a transitive memory that allows teams to work together effectively (Moreland, 1999).

A final consideration for the leader in building a shared mental model is the importance of having a sensitivity to individual differences (Thompsen, 2000). Because employees may be working across organizations and nations, it will be important for the leader to be sensitive to cultural differences, regardless of whether those differences are organizational or cultural. The leader may find that he or she must use different leadership styles with different employees, depending on individual needs (Spreitzer, Shapiro, & Von Glinow, 2002). There will also be the need to teach team members how each of their respective cultures differ and how they can use these differences to the team's advantage. Good conflict management skills will be important for dealing with the inevitable differences that will arise.

Implications for Leadership Development

One difficulty for leadership in the traditional workplace is that to give leaders the right kinds of developmental experiences they must be rotated across a variety of positions that are located in different functions, parts of the company, and even regions of the world. As a leader moves into general management positions, it is critical that the leader understand how the different parts and functions of the organizations work. But many people find these frequent moves hard on family and personal life. These transitions create significant stress, and in today's age of dual-career marriages, uprooting people every few years is increasingly prohibitive. When people can change jobs but not change locations by working virtually, then leaders can be given the variety of experiences that are so critical to their development without the dysfunctional side effects of moving.

In addition, for them to understand the real complexities of working across cultures, it is helpful for the leader to have had experience in an expatriate assignment or as part of a virtual team with members from different cultures. These kinds of international experience help develop many other leader capabilities that are important in traditional settings as well.

CONCLUDING THOUGHTS

Although this chapter focuses on issues of leadership development in a virtual context, it is also likely that the characteristics for selecting virtual leaders may differ from those of a traditional work environment. For example, a charismatic personality in a leader may be less important in a virtual context (see also Locke, chap. 2, this volume). It is not clear that the inspirational qualities and physical presence of a charismatic leader would translate well using computer-mediated technology. Other capabilities like public speaking ability or even attractiveness may also not be as important in a virtual context. That said, transformational leadership is still expected to be relevant in a virtual context (Bass, 1985). In fact, many of the dimensions of transformational leadership were implicit in the discussion of leadership capabilities in a virtual context, including the need for the leader to provide a vision, to role model appropriate behaviors, to provide individualized consideration to meet the varied needs of diverse employees, to provide the intellectual stimulation that comes with empowerment, and to create group goals that are the essential of a shared mental model.

Although a charismatic personality and public speaking ability are not likely to be as relevant in a virtual setting, there are likely to be other qualities pertinent to the selection of virtual leaders. Rosen, Furst, Blackburn, and Shapiro (2000), in a study of executives charged with creating and managing virtual teams in Fortune 500 companies, found that virtual leaders might be selected based on their liaison skills, diplomacy, and sensitivity to cultural differences. Followers in a virtual context might be selected based on their proactivity, willingness to take initiative, and ability to work without supervision.

Clearly, we are in the infancy of virtual work organizations and have much to learn as this form of organization evolves. This chapter provides some nascent direction to leaders in these emerging organizational forms.

ACKNOWLEDGMENTS

I thank the Marshall School of Business and the Center for Effective Organizations (CEO) for support of this research. I was fortunate to be able to build on related work by my colleagues at CEO, including Susan Cohen, David Finegold, Cristina

Gibson, and Sue Mohrman, as well as by my virtual colleagues Debra Shapiro and Mary Ann Von Glinow.

REFERENCES

Bass, B. (1985). *Leadership and performance beyond expectations.* New York: Free Press.
Bikson, T., & Eveland, J. D. (1990). The interplay of work group structures and computer support. In J. Galegher, R. Kraut, & C. Egido (Eds.), *Intellectual teamwork: Social and technological foundations of cooperative work* (pp. 245–290). Hillsdale, NJ: Lawrence Erlbaum Associates, Inc.
Cascio, W. F. (2000). Managing a virtual workplace. *The Academy of Management Executive, 14*(3), 81–90.
Cooper, C. D., & Kurland, N. B. (2002). Telecommuting, professional isolation, and employee development in public and private organizations. *Journal of Organizational Behavior, 23,* 511–532.
DeSanctis, G., & Monge, P. (1998). Communication processes for virtual organizations. *Journal of Computer-Mediated Communication, 3*(4), 1–12.
Froggatt, C. C. (2001). *Work naked: Eight essential principles for peak performance in the virtual workplace.* San Francisco: Jossey-Bass.
Goodman, P., & Wilson, J. (2000). Substitutes for socialization in exocentric teams. In M. Neale, B. Manx, & T. Griffith (Eds.), *Research in groups and teams* (Vol. 3, pp. 53–77). Oxford, England: Elsevier Science Ltd.
Gurley, J. W. (2001, March). Why wi-fi is the next big thing. *Fortune,* 184.
Haywood, M. (1998). *Managing virtual teams: Practical techniques for hi-tech project managers.* Boston: Artech House.
Jarvenpaa, S. L., & Leidner, D. E. (1998). Communication and trust in global virtual teams. *Journal of Computer-Mediated Communication, 3*(4), 13–46.
Kirkpatrick, D. (2001, March). From Davos, talk of death: The modern corporation on its last legs. *Fortune,* 180.
Kurland, N. B., & Bailey, D. E. (1999). When workers are here, there and everywhere: A discussion of the advantages and challenges of telework. *Organizational Dynamics, 28,* 53–68.
Kurland, N. B., & Bailey, D. E. (2002). A review of telework research: Findings, new directions, and lessons for the study of modern work. *Journal of Organizational Behavior, 23,* 383–400.
London, M. (2002). *Leadership development: Paths to self-insight and professional growth.* Mahwah, NJ: Lawrence Erlbaum Associates, Inc.
Malone, T. W. (1997). Is empowerment a fad? Control, decision-making and IT. *Sloan Management Review, 38,* 23–35.
Mayer, R., Davis, J., & Schoorman, D. (1995). *An integrative model of organizational trust. Academy of Management Review, 20*(3), 709–734.
Maznevski, M., & Chudoba, K. (2000). Bridging space over time: Global virtual team dynamics and effectiveness. *Organization Science, 11,* 473–492.
Mohrman, S. A. (1998). The contexts for geographically dispersed teams and networks. In C. Cooper, & D. Rousseau (Eds.), *Trends in organizational behavior* (pp. 63–80). New York: Wiley.
Moreland, R. L. (1999). Transactive memory: Learning who knows what in work groups and organizations. In L. Thompson, J. Levine, & D. Messick (Eds.), *Shared cognition in organizations: The management of knowledge* (pp. 3–31). Mahwah, NJ: Erlbaum.
O'Mahoney, S., & Barley, S. R. (1999). Do digital telecommunications affect work and organization? The state of our knowledge. *Research in Organizational Behavior, 21,* 125–161.
Perlow, L. (1997). *Finding time: How corporations, individuals, and families can benefit from new work practices.* New York: Cornell University.

Rosen, B., Furst, S., Blackburn, D., & Shapiro, D. (2000). *Is virtual the same as being there—Not really!* Presentation at the 2000 Meetings of the National Academy of Management, Toronto, Canada.

Spreitzer, G. M., & Mishra, A. K. (1999). Giving up control without losing control. *Group and Organization Management, 24*(2), 155–187.

Spreitzer, G. M., Shapiro, D. L., & Von Glinow, M. A. (2002). A model of trust building in transnational teams. In E. Mannix, M. Neale, & H. Sondak (Eds.), *Research on groups and teams* (Vol. 4, pp. 203–234). Greenwich, CT: JAI Press.

Sproull, L., & Kiesler, S. (1991). *Connections: New ways of working in the networked organization.* Cambridge, MA: MIT Press.

Thompsen, J. A. (2000). Effective leadership of virtual project teams. *Futurics, 24*(3/4), 85–91.

Townsend, A. M., DeMarie, S. M., & Hendrickson, A. R. (1998). Virtual teams: Technology and the workplace of the future. *Academy of Management Executive, 12*(3), 17–29.

Yukl, G. A. (1989). *Leadership in organizations* (2nd ed.). Englewood Cliffs, NJ: Prentice-Hall.

III

Leadership Development
Techniques

5

Understanding the Benefits and Risks of Multisource Feedback Within the Leadership Development Process

Leanne E. Atwater, Joan F. Brett,
and David Waldman
Arizona State University West
School of Management

Three-hundred-sixty-degree or multisource feedback, the process in which subordinates, peers, supervisors, and customers provide anonymous feedback to recipients, has grown in popularity over the past decade (Waldman & Atwater, 1998). The primary purpose of this feedback is leadership development. That is, feedback is provided confidentially to feedback recipients (usually managers or supervisors), and the expectation is that they will use it to make needed improvements. In July 1995, The *APA Monitor* published the following: "Anecdotal information indicates that these [360-degree] feedback methods heighten managers' awareness of their strengths and weaknesses; create an atmosphere of constructive dialogue; remove personal blind spots; and are a powerful incentive for change." In 1996, Antonioni reported that an estimated 25% of companies were using some type of upward or 360-degree feedback process. (Upward feedback is solicited from only one source, subordinates.) In fact, numerous studies have reported improvements in overall performance following 360 or upward feedback interventions (e.g., Atwater, Roush, & Fischthal, 1995; Reilly, Smither, & Vasilopoulos, 1996). So why would any organization not engage in a 360-degree intervention?

Although the use of 360-degree programs has increased in the 1990s, research during this time on multisource feedback has taken a number of twists and turns that suggest that positive results are not the only potential outcome. Research indicates that a variety of factors can impact the success of a feedback intervention. In this chapter, we review the pivotal studies, those that question the validity of the impact of feedback interventions, those addressing factors that influence change, and those that identify potential risks and negative effects. These studies are summarized in Table 5.1. Note that the studies shown in Table 5.1 are representative, rather than exhaustive, of the different categories that are displayed. We also integrate what we know about performance appraisal feedback that is relevant to multisource feedback processes and conclude by providing suggestions for practitioners as well as for future research.

BACKGROUND

The potential value of multisource feedback over the traditional superior-to-subordinate feedback process can be summarized as follows. First, feedback from constituencies other than supervisors may provide new information that captures complexities of an individual's performance in multiple roles. Second, feedback from multiple sources may reinforce and support the feedback provided from the supervisor, thus making it more salient and more difficult to discount as just one (perhaps biased) person's viewpoint. There are also assumptions about the process, including a belief that negative or discrepant feedback (differences between self- and other ratings) will create awareness of development needs and motivate individuals to change behaviors in order to raise their ratings and decrease self–other discrepancies. Although studies such as those presented at the top of Table 5.1 have suggested that this is sometimes the result, more recent studies have questioned the true impact of feedback on behavior change, and other research suggests that positive outcomes from feedback may not always result.

Kluger and DeNisi (1996), in their seminal piece on the impact of feedback on performance, cautioned that not all feedback interventions result in improvements. In their meta-analysis based largely on performance appraisal feedback, Kluger and DeNisi concluded that in over one third of the cases, feedback actually resulted in decreased performance. Similarly, Atwater, Waldman, Atwater, and Cartier (2000) found that improvement following upward feedback only resulted for 50% of the managers who received feedback. Although the purposes of performance appraisal feedback and upward feedback differ in that one is evaluative and the other is not, these results nevertheless suggest that there may be a myriad of factors that influence how individuals react to feedback. They also suggest who will improve following feedback and who will not.

Another assumption behind the use of multisource feedback is that individuals will be motivated to change their behavior when they receive information, from various sources, that they are not performing optimally. Because most multisource feedback is anonymous, feedback providers feel comfortable providing honest

TABLE 5.1

Research Trends in 360-Degree Feedback

Author(s)	Type of Organization	Rater Type (N of Leaders)	Key Findings
Impact of feedback on behavior and self-awareness			
Hegarty (1974)	University	Upward (56)	Significant positive change for supervisors receiving feedback compared to control group.
Atwater et al. (1995)	Naval Academy	Upward (978)	Leader behavior improves following feedback; overestimators get the most benefit from feedback.
Hazucha et al. (1993)	Utility company	Upward and peer (198)	Skill increases and higher self-coworker agreement years after receiving multisource feedback.
Smither et al. (1995)	Information management	Upward (238)	Managers with low or moderate scores improved.
Questioning the validity of change			
Atwater et al. (2000)	Police	Upward (110)	Study incorporated a control group; those receiving feedback did not improve significantly more than did survey-only group.
Reilly et al. (1996)	Telecommunications	Upward (238)	Performance improvements sustained over time, primarily managers whose initial feedback scores were low.
Walker & Smither (1999)	Regional bank	Upward (252)	Managers rated as low or moderate showed improvements over 5 years—effects beyond regression to the mean.
Self–other agreement			
Atwater & Yammarino (1992)	Naval officers	Upward (158)	Performance best for those with self-ratings in agreement with subordinate ratings.
Van Velsor et al. (1993)	Various	Upward (648)	Underraters are most effective; overraters are least effective.
Atwater et al. (1998)	Various	Upward (1460)	Overraters are poorer performers; underraters are better performers.

(Continued)

91

TABLE 5.1
(Continued)

Author(s)	Type of Organization	Rater Type (N of Leaders)	Key Findings
Bottom-line results			
Bernardin et al. (1995)	Retail stores	Upward and peer	Feedback leads to improvements in both subordinate and peer ratings—but not in customer ratings or sales volume.
Smither & Walker (2001)	Banking	Upward (252)	Upward feedback scores correlated significantly with measures of customer loyalty, which translated into revenue enhancement.
Factors influencing responses to multisource feedback			
Atwater et al. (2000)	Police	Upward (110)	Feedback resulted in less impact for those who were highly cynical about the organization and those with negative reactions to the feedback process.
Goldsmith & Underhill (2001)	Various	Multisource (3,655)	Leaders who followed up with raters after receiving formal feedback improved more than those who did not.
Walker & Smither (1999)	Banking	Upward (252)	Holding feedback sessions with subs leads to more performance improvement; effects of feedback can be sustained over a number of years.
Unintended outcomes of the feedback process			
Kluger & DeNisi (1996)	Meta-analysis	—	Feedback may result in decreased performance; negative feedback discourages (rather than motivates) improvement.
Johnson & Ferstl (1999)	Accounting	Upward ($n > 2,000$)	Underraters show a performance decline following feedback.
Atwater et al. (2000)	Police	Upward (110)	Negative feedback was associated with reduced commitment to subordinates.
Brett & Atwater (2003)	MBA students	Multisource (125)	Negative feedback was related to anger and discouragement; negative reactions were associated with belief that feedback was not useful.

feedback. Anonymity combined with the tendency for self-raters to see themselves positively (Harris & Schaubroeck, 1988) results in many cases where feedback recipients receive feedback that is more negative than expected. Although one possibility is that this new awareness will motivate positive change, research on performance appraisal feedback suggests that when individuals receive negative feedback, they are often discouraged rather than motivated to improve (Kluger & DeNisi, 1996). Multisource feedback is generally not evaluative, but it is clearly possible that individuals will respond similarly to negative feedback regardless of its purpose. This may account, in part, for the fact that not all individuals react favorably to multisource feedback.

Impact of Feedback on Behavior and Self-Awareness

A number of studies have investigated the impact of upward or multisource feedback interventions on changes in self-awareness and behavior for feedback recipients. Earlier studies generally showed modest improvements in ratings following feedback provided by subordinates or by other sources when ratings collected prior to and following feedback are compared. Changes have also been noted in self-ratings following feedback. That is, self-ratings become more similar to others' ratings after feedback. For example, as early as 1974 before the term 360-degree feedback had been coined, Hegarty conducted a study with two groups of supervisors. In the experimental group, supervisors received survey feedback from their subordinates about their performance. The control group received no feedback. Following feedback to the experimental group, ratings were collected a second time in both groups, and the experimental group scored higher on performance as rated by subordinates than did the control group.

In a later study, Atwater et al. (1995) found improvements in subordinate ratings of leaders on measures of leader performance following feedback. Improvements were calculated as changes in ratings from Time 1 to Time 2. Similarly, Hazucha, Hezlett, and Schneider (1993) found improvements in managerial skills as evidenced by peers', subordinates', and superiors' ratings of change (i.e., ratings of whether skills deteriorated or improved). Smither et al. (1995) found that managers initially rated as moderate or low by their subordinates improved over a 6-month period. These studies as well as others (e.g., Atwater, Ostroff, Yammarino, & Fleenor, 1998; Atwater & Yammarino, 1992; Van Velsor, Taylor, & Leslie, 1993) have also demonstrated improved self-awareness as evidenced by self-ratings in greater agreement with ratings from others following feedback. For example, Atwater et al. (1995) investigated changes in self-ratings following feedback and found that those who were overraters (rated themselves high relative to their subordinates) lowered their self-ratings following feedback, whereas those who were underraters raised their self-ratings. They suggested that this was evidence that the feedback process impacts self-awareness as well as performance.

Questioning the Validity of Change

Although the studies mentioned previously provided support for using feedback from sources other than superiors to improve self-awareness and performance, researchers have raised challenges to the methodological approaches used to evaluate change (e.g., regression to the mean, response shift bias, and ceiling effects). Regression to the mean is a problem in any measure that has less than perfect reliability. For example, improved self-awareness as measured by the agreement between self- and other ratings may not be a result of true change; rather it may result from regression to the mean. Likewise, those with extremely high scores on the first set of ratings are more likely to score lower on the next set of measures regardless of actual performance. A number of studies have assessed change accounting for regression to the mean and shown changes beyond those that could be expected due to regression to the mean. These include Atwater et al. (1995), Reilly et al. (1996), Smither et al. (1995), Johnson and Ferstl (1999), and Walker and Smither (1999).

Ceiling effects may also mask behavior change for some managers. Those managers who received extremely high scores have less room for improvement than managers with much lower scores. An additional threat to the validity of 360-degree improvement is the response shift bias that occurs when using pre/post ratings of self and others (Martineau, 1998; Smither & Walker, 2001). Response shift bias obscures the true impact of 360-degree interventions on behavior change (alpha change). Beta change and gamma change capture two different processes behind response shift bias. In beta change, the respondent recalibrates the rating scale from Time 1 to Time 2. Hence, true changes in behavior may be obscured in the prepost assessment, because the individual's interpretation of the rating scale and/or expectations for the behavior have changed. For example, what was a 3 on a 1 to 7 scale in the rater's mind is now only a 2 (Smither & Walker, 2001). Gamma change reflects changes from Time 1 to Time 2 in the meaning of the construct measured. Pre- and posttest scores may not reflect actual change because the rater now interprets the construct differently. For example, the rater may have thought he/she was good at giving feedback, and as a result of meeting with subordinates, learns what they really expect. He/she now rates himself/herself lower on giving feedback because he/she understands it differently. Both beta and gamma change can mask improvements in behavior that have occurred as a result of the 360-degree intervention. Retrospective pretest ratings, retrospective change ratings, and ideal ratings are alternatives to eliminating response bias and ceiling effects (Martineau, 1998; Smither & Walker, 2001).

Given the concerns with the validity of the change measures used to assess improvements following feedback, attempts have been made to study feedback interventions in a more systematic way, and over time. For example, Reilly et al. (1996) followed 92 managers over 4 administrations of upward feedback for over $2\frac{1}{2}$ years. They concluded that a feedback program can result in sustained change over a relatively long period of time. However, it should be noted that even those who were just exposed to the survey process, and did not receive feedback, improved! Although this was not a systematic controlled experiment, it calls into question the value of feedback over merely sensitizing individuals to the desired behaviors that occur during the self-rating process. More recently, Atwater et al. (2000) conducted a controlled experiment and found no significant, positive changes for the group receiving feedback when compared to a group that merely completed surveys. This did not mean that no one improved, but when group means were compared, they were not significantly different. Perhaps, given Kluger and DeNisi's (1996) results (e.g., only one third of the individuals receiving performance appraisal feedback improved) expecting change that is dramatic enough to detect when all individuals are averaged together over a large number of behaviors is expecting too much. Walker and Smither (1999) studied a feedback process for 5 years and found that subordinate ratings of their supervisors improved over the 5-year upward feedback program, although no changes were evident in the first 2 years. They noted that managers who initially scored the lowest improved the most, and this effect could not be attributed solely to regression to the mean.

In summary, these recent studies suggest that perhaps the results of feedback interventions are not as dramatic as once believed, and/or the process may need to be repeated over time for effects to emerge. Alternatively, as advocated by Smither and Walker (2001) and by Goldsmith and Underhill (2001), change may need to be assessed more selectively, that is, in terms of assessing change relative to the goals managers set. Is it realistic to expect change on more than a few targeted dimensions? Most surveys include over 50 behavioral items. Improvement on 4 items may be significant in terms of behavior change but get lost when statistical assessments of change are made.

Self–Other Agreement

Comparisons of self- and other ratings provide another indicator of a manager's self-awareness and indicate blind spots. Conclusions generally have been that those who see themselves more similarly to the way they are seen by others are better performers. Church (1997) as well as Atwater and Yammarino (1992) found that those who were the highest performers were more likely than average performers to agree with other raters about their performance. Research by Van Velsor et al. (1993) supported this conclusion. In their study, managers who were most self-aware, and who had self- and other ratings that were most similar, were the highest performers.

Recently, the results of these studies have also been questioned based on the research methods used to study over- and underrating. For example, Atwater and Yammarino (1992), Van Velsor et al. (1993), as well as Fleenor, McCauley, and Brutus (1996) categorized individuals as over- or underraters based on the differences between self- and other ratings. This method has been criticized by Edwards (1995) for using difference score methods, and regression-based models have been advocated. In a 1998 study, Atwater et al. (1998) used regression models as advocated by Edwards to test the impact of self–other agreement on performance. The results supported the earlier conclusions that overraters were poorer performers than under- and in-agreement raters.

Whether these findings mean that feedback that allows one to adjust their self-ratings to be more in line with those of others will promote better performance has not been tested. In other words, being self-aware may be a characteristic that accompanies good performance but may not contribute to it.

Self–Other Agreement Across Cultures. Recent work by Atwater, Ostroff, Waldman, and Robie (2001) has looked at the issue of self–other agreement across cultures. Their findings suggest that although self–other disagreement (i.e., being an overrater) was related to poorer performance in the United States, being an overrater was particularly problematic in both France and Denmark. Overrating had no consequence for performance in Italy. The explanation provided was that cultural norms such as the tendency to value egalitarianism and humility in France and Denmark contributed to the performance problems overraters experienced in those countries. These results have implications for the administration of multi-source feedback across cultures and suggest that the impact of 360-degree feedback may vary as a function of cultural differences.

Bottom-Line Results

In addition to questioning the validity of the methods researchers used to assess change and the relevance of self–other agreement, practitioners have begun to ask about the extent to which improvements in a supervisor's ratings translated into bottom-line measures such as revenue or profits. Very few studies have investigated outcomes of multisource feedback other than changes in self- and other ratings, with two notable exceptions. Bernardin, Hagan, and Kane (1995) found improvement in subordinate and peer ratings following feedback, but no changes in customer ratings or sales volume. Smither and Walker (2001), however, correlated managers' upward feedback ratings with measures of customer loyalty in various branches of a bank. They then calculated the revenue that could be gained from customer loyalty and concluded that even a 1% change in customer loyalty could result in substantial increased revenue for the bank. This tentatively suggests that although changes may be more dramatic for interpersonal measures than for bottom-line measures, over time, changes in bottom-line measures may be realized. That is, as leadership improves, so too will other aspects of organizational performance, but the effects may occur further into the future.

Factors Influencing Responses to Multisource Feedback

There are a number of factors that can affect whether the feedback that accompanies a multisource feedback process will result in favorable versus unfavorable outcomes. These factors include characteristics of the feedback, such as the nature of the self–other discrepancy (i.e., how the individual rated him or herself relative to others' ratings), as well as other individual characteristics including degree of organizationally focused cynicism, the individual's goal orientation, and the attitudes that individuals have about multisource feedback in general. Reactions to the feedback, such as whether the feedback is seen as accurate or useful, as well as how individuals respond to the feedback (e.g., do they share feedback results with raters) are also important in ultimately determining favorable versus undesirable feedback outcomes. Each of these factors and their relevance is discussed in detail in the following.

Self–Other Discrepancies.   Brett and Atwater (2001) found that individuals who received feedback most discrepant with their own ratings (i.e., overraters) believed the feedback was less accurate and less useful. Further, these individuals were more likely to react negatively (e.g., with anger and discouragement) than those whose feedback was more in line with self-ratings. This suggests that the discrepancies may not motivate individuals to change in order to reduce discrepancies. Rather, individuals may simply discount negative feedback as inaccurate.

Organizational Cynicism.   Atwater et al. (2000) found that individuals who were most cynical about the organization (e.g., did not believe that positive change was possible in the organization and efforts to change were not worth the trouble) were less likely to improve their performance following feedback. The explanation given was that individuals who feel the organization is not ever going to improve also see no point in improving their own performance in that organization. In our experience, providing feedback reports to recipients in group feedback sessions, cynical individuals are much more likely to either discount the feedback or attribute the feedback to the organization's problems rather than to their own behavior. For example, we recently implemented upward feedback in a policing agency. Individuals professing more cynicism with regard to the potential for serious organizational change seemed less likely to want to use upward feedback results to make personal changes pertaining to their own behavior and leadership.

Recently we conducted a study (Atwater, Waldman, & Brett, 2000) to assess whether cynicism contributed to attitudes toward the feedback itself (i.e., its perceived accuracy or usefulness). Cynicism was unrelated to attitudes toward feedback. This suggests that although cynicism contributes to change, it is not because they see the feedback as less accurate or useful, but more likely they have little motivation to use it constructively.

Follow-up After Feedback. Clearly, what the feedback recipient does with his or her feedback data should influence behavior change. Goldsmith and Underhill (2001), for example, found that executives who followed up with raters after feedback, explaining what they had learned from the process, were more likely to show improvements in effectiveness than those who did not follow up. Eighty-six percent of the group that did follow up showed an increase in effectiveness, whereas only 67% of those who did not do follow up showed increases in effectiveness. For those who did not follow up, 26% had no change, and 7% were less effective. For those who did follow up, 14% showed no change, and only 2% showed a decrease in effectiveness. Walker and Smither (1999) also demonstrated the value of follow-up behavior. In their longitudinal study, they found that managers improved more in years when they discussed the pervious year's feedback with direct reports than in years when they did not discuss the previous year's feedback.

Attitudes and Reactions Toward the Feedback Process. Two recent studies (see Brett and Atwater 2001; Waldman et al., 1996) demonstrated that how individuals feel about the feedback process influences whether they are likely to change following feedback. Specifically, those who had the most positive attitudes about the process, for example, those who thought their feedback was sincere and helpful, showed more improvements following feedback. Understanding leaders' attitudes and reactions to multisource feedback is important, because theory and research suggest that the ways in which individuals react to feedback is a critical determinant of whether they will take actions to improve following feedback (Bannister, 1986; Ilgen, Fisher, & Taylor, 1979). Recently, research has demonstrated a number of factors that may contribute to these attitudes and reactions.

The sign of feedback has a strong and consistent effect on the valence of affect. For example, Podsakoff and Farh (1989) found that negative feedback induced frustration and dissatisfaction. This is consistent with the work of Brett and Atwater (2001) suggesting that negative feedback (in terms of low ratings from others, as well as self-ratings that were higher than those of others) results in negative reactions such as anger and discouragement. An illustrative comment from a feedback recipient who received low ratings was, "Next time instead of going through this process, why don't you just give our boss a chainsaw and let him perform open-heart surgery. I think it would feel better."

Facteau, Facteau, Schoel, Russell, and Poteet (1998) as well as Brett and Atwater (2001) found that higher ratings received from subordinates were associated with greater acceptance of the ratings and perceptions that the feedback was more useful. Or, in other words, low ratings were seen as less acceptable and less useful. In addition, Brett and Atwater (2001) found that the more self-ratings were inflated relative to other ratings, the less the feedback was seen as accurate or useful. Stone and Stone (1985) also found that those who received lower evaluations were less likely to believe it, suggesting that the worst performers may be the least likely to benefit from appraisal-related information.

The source of the feedback also figures into how individuals react to it. Brett and Atwater (2001) assessed participants' reactions to feedback from various sources. Although negative feedback from peers and superiors prompted negative reactions, participants did not experience anger, criticism, or other negative reactions when they received low ratings (or ratings that were lower than their self-ratings) from direct reports. Supervisors receiving feedback may expect, given various performance or interpersonal issues, that some subordinates would rate them lower or discrepant from their own ratings. Or alternatively, they may believe that low ratings from supervisors or peers can negatively impact them, whereas low ratings from subordinates will not. Regardless, feedback from direct reports appears not to influence reactions as much as feedback from supervisors and peers.

Summary. The findings summarized previously suggest that feedback delivery may need to be tailored to individual characteristics. Attitudes and reactions that individuals have about the feedback process, as well as their organizations, can come into play. Furthermore, whether feedback is positive or negative and its source also are relevant.

Unintended Outcomes of the Feedback Process

The research to date suggests that the premise behind multisource feedback, namely, that negative feedback will spur positive behavior change, is only one possible scenario. To be sure, we experienced a case where an individual who received upward feedback improved from an overall average score across 43 dimensions of about 2.8 to 4.8 (on a 1–5 scale) in the course of 9 months. And he had no changes in the members of his workgroup during that time. However, this result cannot be expected in all cases. Rather, research suggests that feedback, particularly negative feedback, provokes a variety of responses, not all of which are beneficial or desirable. As researchers have begun to study more of the subtleties of feedback interventions, cautions regarding potential risks have become evident. Risks such as negative reactions, reduced effort, dissatisfaction with raters, and decreased commitment to subordinates following feedback are discussed in this section.

Negative Reactions. Brett and Atwater (2001) found that low ratings and self-ratings that were higher than those of others resulted in negative reactions such as anger and discouragement. These individuals were not motivated to improve. Not surprisingly, these negative reactions were associated with perceptions that the feedback was not useful. Those receiving high ratings, however, did not show positive reactions nor motivation to improve.

Reduced Effort.   As far back as 1965, Meyer, Kay, and French reported that negative feedback (i.e., discussion of performance weaknesses) had a negative effect on goal achievement, whereas positive feedback had little effect one way or another. Those who received more than an average amount of criticism subsequently gave poorer performance and were less likely to achieve goals than those who received less criticism. Brett and Atwater (2001) found that those individuals who received negative multisource feedback found it to be less useful and were less development focused (as rated by a facilitator) than those who received more positive feedback. Although most of the negative effects of feedback result from low ratings or negative feedback, even positive ratings can produce undesired effects. Johnson and Ferstl (1999), for example, found underraters (those who received ratings from others that were higher than their own self-ratings) actually showed a performance decline following feedback, suggesting that the feedback that they were doing better than they expected allowed them to "slack off."

Decreased Satisfaction with Raters.   Research has demonstrated that individuals who receive negative appraisals from their supervisors are more dissatisfied with those supervisors as compared to those who receive more positive ratings (Baird, 1977). Similarly, in a recent study, Atwater, Waldman, and Brett (2000) found that feedback ratings influenced leader member exchange (LMX) and liking ratings supervisors made of their subordinates following feedback.[1] Specifically, ratings leaders received on an upward feedback instrument accounted for significant variance in LMX and liking ratings supervisors provided about their subordinates following feedback when prefeedback liking and LMX were controlled. That is, those who received positive feedback increased their liking and LMX toward subordinates, whereas those who received negative feedback decreased their LMX and liking toward subordinates following feedback.

Commitment.   Pearce and Porter (1996) found that after instituting a performance feedback process, those who received feedback that their performance was satisfactory (as opposed to higher ratings) showed a stable drop in organizational commitment following feedback. Atwater, Waldman, Atwater, et al. (2000) likewise showed that when supervisors received low ratings from their followers in an upward feedback intervention, they subsequently had lower commitment to their followers.

Summary.   Overall, the studies on upward feedback suggest that positive effects result for some of the people, some of the time. The studies do not indicate,

---

[1] A sample LMX item is "my supervisor understands my problems and needs."

however, that all individuals benefit from multisource feedback. In fact, as mentioned earlier, Atwater, Waldman, Atwater, et al. (2000) found that improvements resulted for only 50% of the upward feedback recipients. This suggests that some individuals likely "got worse" and others did not change, at least as evidenced by changes in ratings pre- and postfeedback. Some of the ways in which positive outcomes may be encouraged are provided in the next section.

MAXIMIZING THE BENEFITS/MINIMIZING THE RISKS

We are continuing to learn about multisource feedback and how it can be implemented to maximize the benefits. Based on the results presented earlier, as well as on our personal consulting experiences, we provide some suggestions for making multisource feedback interventions more successful.

1. Provide activities and training opportunities to increase individuals' self-awareness. Increased self-awareness should result in more accurate self-ratings, thereby minimizing the degree of self-rating inflation and the negative impact of overrating. We have found that merely cautioning self-raters about the tendency to overrate prior to the implementation of the multisource process has resulted in reduced self-rating inflation.

2. Conduct face-to-face orientations with all employees (either individually or in group sessions) that will be involved in the process. The orientations should describe how the process will be implemented and give employees a chance to ask questions. Confidentiality and anonymity can be assured. These sessions increase trust in the process and engender more positive attitudes toward the feedback process. It is also our recommendation that multisource feedback be introduced as a developmental process wherein only the feedback recipient sees his or her report. All information provided by raters should be provided anonymously (unless the recipient has only one superior, in which case the superior's identity is obviously known).

3. Train raters to provide honest and constructive feedback. Recipients are less likely to react negatively if they believe feedback is accurate. This is particularly important when open-ended comments about the individual's performance are included.

4. Assess the degree of organizational cynicism among employees prior to beginning a multisource feedback process. If cynicism is high, steps should be taken to reduce cynicism if the process is to be most successful. For example, in one organization in which we worked, cynicism was greatly reduced when a new leader was put in place, and individuals believed positive changes were now possible. Thus, a window of opportunity was created in which individuals might be more inclined to embrace feedback and personal change.

5. Measure individual characteristics of feedback recipients as part of the self-rating process. Specifically, characteristics such as goal orientation can be measured and scored. In most cases, we recommend that face-to-face feedback sessions be conducted by an outside facilitator who is not part of the organization. The facilitator can then use the data about the individual to customize feedback delivery. For example, they may need to work harder with those who have a performance prove goal orientation to get them to see the value of feedback.

6. Recognize that feedback, particularly negative feedback, can have negative effects. Assumptions that negative feedback is motivational, and should encourage individuals to set development goals, are overly simplistic. There may be a myriad of reactions to negative feedback for which facilitators or coaches should plan. This suggests that merely providing feedback and leaving individuals on their own to "fix" the problems is unrealistic. Follow-up coaching and encouragement are advisable. Relatedly, we should formally assess outcomes in addition to future multisource ratings. For example, do those who receive negative feedback tend to leave or transfer? Does feedback impact subsequent job satisfaction?

7. Provide structure for how to solicit follow-up feedback with feedback providers. This is optimally done in a group setting to minimize defensiveness and encourage participation. In our own experience, we encourage individuals to have a member of the group facilitate a group session. The supervisor meets with the group and shares his/her strengths and weaknesses. Then the supervisor leaves the group with a facilitator to identify specific strategies for his/her improvement. When ideas have been generated, the supervisor rejoins the group for discussion. This allows raters to provide additional feedback anonymously.

8. Integrate multisource feedback with other training and development efforts. Individuals who receive feedback that changes are needed, yet feel unable to make those changes without training or other types of assistance, will be frustrated and unmotivated.

9. Institutionalize multisource feedback as part of the organizational culture (Waldman & Atwater, 1998). It often takes multiple administrations for the results of feedback to be fully realized. Over time, individuals adapt to the process, and organizations tailor the process to fit their needs. Even if the process is not institutionalized, it should be repeated at least twice so that individuals can see the results of their efforts and any improvements they have made.

10. Be aware that lessons learned from studies conducted in the United States (which account for the vast majority to date) may not be applicable to countries with different cultural norms.

FUTURE RESEARCH

Research has clearly demonstrated that multisource feedback can be beneficial. Yet, much remains to be learned about how to optimize the process. The following are ideas for future research.

1. Many organizations use multisource feedback as a strategy to improve supervisor/manager performance. However, to date, no studies have explicitly compared whether multisource feedback really works better than traditional top-down feedback in changing behavior. Because multisource feedback is costly to organizations, we should have evidence that it actually improves performance or other organizational outcomes more than single-source feedback if the costs are to be justified. Studies need to compare single-source (supervisor) feedback with multisource feedback, assessing the outcomes of each.

2. Although we know that feedback can change individuals' self-ratings to be more in line with others' ratings, we do not know if these changes are accompanied by performance improvements. It would be interesting to compare the performance of individuals who had more similar self–other ratings prior to feedback with those whose self–other rating similarity followed feedback. Does the self–other rating similarity result from greater self-awareness and/or from behavior changes? Do those who become more accurate also improve their performance, or does the greater agreement merely indicate a desire to have fewer discrepancies in ratings?

3. As stressed earlier, research has demonstrated that negative ratings, even when provided only for developmental purposes such as in a multisource feedback intervention, can result in negative reactions such as anger or discouragement. What is not understood is how long these reactions last, whether there are individual difference variables that contribute to lasting versus fleeting reactions, and how these reactions may manifest themselves in other ways. For example, do those who experience negative reactions also develop lower job satisfaction? Do they take retaliatory action on the feedback providers? Do they have stronger intentions to turnover?

4. A better understanding of how feedback facilitators can tailor feedback reports, as well as their coaching activities to encourage positive outcomes for different individuals, is needed. For example, perhaps for some individuals (e.g., those with a performance-avoid goal orientation), feedback reports should not include any numbers, because such numbers may be seen as very negative. Instead, perhaps only written statements that summarize the data should be provided to those individuals.

5. We certainly need to investigate outcomes other than postfeedback ratings. To date, most of the research touting the benefits of multisource feedback has been based on postfeedback ratings, rather than on indicators of bottom-line performance. For example, how does multisource feedback impact sales, profits, or quality indicators? Perhaps a multisource feedback intervention could be designed, wherein comparable departments implemented the feedback process sequentially. That is, those that implemented it earlier could be compared on relevant performance indicators to those that have not yet implemented it.

6. Additional studies of the longitudinal impact of multisource feedback as it becomes institutionalized in organizations are needed. For example, do the advantages of multisource feedback diminish over time to a point where it is no longer cost effective to spend organizational resources on the process? Do individuals revert to old habits if the process is discontinued?

7. Additional studies of multisource feedback processes and their outcomes are needed. As companies become increasingly global and multinational, questions grow concerning how to best implement these processes in cultures outside the United States.

CONCLUSIONS

We have attempted to integrate the most recent research results on the topic of multisource feedback with what we have learned over the years about performance feedback in general. Clearly, there is more to be learned. However, we believe that this review and set of recommendations represent the state of the art at this time. We hope it gives practitioners new ideas about how to continue to improve the multisource feedback process in their organizations. We also hope it gives feedback providers/facilitators ideas about how to individualize the feedback process. In addition, we have attempted to provide "food for thought" for researchers concerning ideas for future research.

ACKNOWLEDGMENT

The contents of this chapter were adapted from a paper entitled Understanding and Optimizing Multisource Feedback by L. Atwater, J. Brett and D. Waldman published in *Human Resource Management Journal*, 2002, 41(2), 198–208. This material is used by permission of John Wiley & Sons Inc.

REFERENCES

Antonioni, D. (1996). Designing an effective 360-degree appraisal feedback process. *Organizational Dynamics, 25,* 24–38.
Atwater, L., Ostroff, C., Waldman, D., Robie, C., & Johnson, K. (2001). *Self-other agreement: How much does it matter across cultures.* Working Paper.
Atwater, L., Ostroff, C., Yammarino, F., & Fleenor, J. (1998). Self-other agreement: Does it really matter? *Personnel Psychology, 51,* 577–598.
Atwater, L. A., Roush, P., & Fischthal, A. (1995). The influence of upward feedback on self- and follower ratings of leadership. *Personnel Psychology, 48,* 35–60.
Atwater, L. A., Waldman, D., Atwater, D., & Cartier (2000). An upward feedback field experiment. Supervisors' cynicism, follow-up and commitment to subordinates. *Personnel Psychology, 53,* 275–297.
Atwater, L., Waldman, D., & Brett, J. (2000). *The effect of upward feedback on Leader Member Exchange (LMX) and liking relationships.* Working paper.
Atwater, L., Waldman, D. A., & Brett, J. (2002). Understanding and optimizing multisource feedback. *Human Resource Management 41*(2), 193–208.

Atwater, L., & Yammarino, F. (1992). Does self-other agreement on leadership perceptions moderate the validity of leadership and performance predictions? *Personnel Psychology, 45*, 141–164.

Baird, L. (1977). Self and superior ratings of performance: As related to self-esteem and satisfaction with supervision. *Academy of Management Journal, 20*, 291–300.

Bannister, B. (1986). Performance outcome feedback and attributional feedback: Interactive effects on recipient responses. *Journal of Applied Psychology, 71*, 2, 203–210.

Bernardin, J., Hagan, C., & Kane, J. (1995, May). The effects of a 360 degree appraisal system on managerial performance: No matter how cynical I get, I can't keep up. In W. W. Tornow (Chair), *Upward feedback: The ups and downs of it*. Symposium conducted at the 10th annual conference of the Society for Industrial and Organizational Psychology, Orlando, FL.

Brett, J., & Atwater, L. (2001). 360 degree feedback: Accuracy, reactions and perceptions of usefulness. *Journal of Applied Psychology, 86*, 930–942.

Church, A. (1997). Do you see what I see? An exploration of congruence in ratings from multiple perspectives. *Journal of Applied Social Psychology, 27*, 11, 983–1020.

Edwards, J. (1995). Alternatives to difference scores as dependent variables in the study of congruence in organizational research. *Organizational Behavior and Human Decision Processes, 64*, 307–324.

Facteau, C. L., Facteau, J. D., Schoel, L. C., Russell, J. A., & Poteet, M. (1998). Reactions of leaders to 360-degree feedback from subordinates and peers. *Leadership Quarterly, 9*, 427–448.

Fleenor, J. W., McCauley, C. D., & Brutus, S. (1996). Self-other rating agreement and leader effectiveness. *Leadership Quarterly, 7*(4), 487–506.

Goldsmith, M., & Underhill, B. (2001). Multi-source feedback for executive development. In D. Bracken, C. Timmreck, & A. Church (Eds.), *The handbook of multi-source feedback*. Jossey-Bass: San Francisco.

Harris, M., & Schaubroeck, J. (1988). A meta-analysis of self-supervisor, self-peer and peer-supervisor ratings. *Personnel Psychology, 41*, 43–61.

Hazucha, J., Hezlett, S., & Schneider, R. (1993). The impact of 360-degree feedback on management skills development. *Human Resource Management, 32*, 23, 353–372.

Hegarty, W. (1974). Using subordinate ratings to elicit behavioral changes in supervisors. *Journal of Applied Psychology, 59*, 764–766.

Ilgen, D. R., Fisher, C. D., & Taylor, M. S. (1979). Consequences of individual feedback on behavior in organizations. *Journal of Applied Psychology, 64*, 349–371.

Johnson, J. W., & Ferstl, K. L. (1999). The effects of interrater and self-other agreement on performance improvement following upward feedback. *Personnel Psychology, 52*, 271–303.

Kluger, A. N., & DeNisi, A. (1996). The effects of feedback interventions on performance: A historical review, a meta-analysis, and a preliminary feedback theory. *Psychological Bulletin, 119*, 254–284.

Martineau, J. (1998). Using 360-degree surveys to assess change. In W. Tornow, M. London, & CCL Associates (Eds.), *Maximizing the value of 360-degree feedback*. Greensboro, NC: Center for Creative Leadership.

Meyer, H., Kay, E., & French, J. (1965). Effects of threat in a performance appraisal interview. *Journal of Applied Psychology, 49*, 311–317.

Podsakoff, P. M., & Farh, J. L. (1989). Effects of feedback sign and credibility on goal setting and task performance. *Organizational Behavior and Human Decision Processes, 44*, 45–67.

Pearce, J. L., & Porter, L. W. (1986). Employee responses to formal performance appraisal feedback. *Journal of Applied Psychology, 71*, 211–218.

Reilly, R. R., Smither, J. W., & Vasilopoulos, N. L. (1996). A longitudinal study of upward feedback. *Personnel Psychology, 49*, 599–612.

Smither, J., London, M., Vasilopoulos, N., Reilly, R., Millsap, R., & Salvemini, N. (1995). An examination of the effects of an upward feedback program over time. *Personnel Psychology, 48*, 1–34.

Smither, J., & Walker, A. G. (2001). Measuring the impact of multi-source feedback. In D. Bracken, C. Timmreck, & A. Church (Eds.), *The handbook of multi-source feedback.* Jossey-Bass: San Francisco.

Stone, D., & Stone, E. (1985). The effects of feedback consistency and feedback favorability on self-perceived task competence and perceived feedback accuracy. *Organizational Behavior and Human Decision Processes, 36,* 167–185.

Taylor, M. S., Fisher, C. D., & Ilgen, D. R. (1984). Individuals' reactions to performance feedback in organizations: A control theory perspective. In K. M. Rowland, & G. R. Ferris (Eds.), *Research in personnel and human resources management* (pp. 81–124). Greenwich, CT: JAI Press.

Waldman, D., & Atwater, L. E. (1998). *The power of 360° feedback: How to leverage performance evaluations for top productivity.* Houston, TX: Gulf Publishing.

Waldman, D., Atwater, L., Clement, D., & Atwater, D. (1996, August). *Attitudinal and behavioral outcomes of an upward feedback process.* Paper presented at the National Meeting Academy of Management, Cincinnati, OH.

Walker, A., & Smither, J. (1999). A five-year study of upward feedback: What managers do with their results matters. *Personnel Psychology, 52,* 393–423.

Van Velsor, E., Taylor, S., & Leslie, J. (1993). An examination of the relationships among self-perception accuracy, self-awareness, gender and leader effectiveness. *Human Resource Management, 32*(2–3), 249–264.

6

Action Learning and Multirater Feedback: Pathways to Leadership Development?

Jay A. Conger and Ginka Toegel
London Business School

Over the past decade, leadership development has become a major concern for many organizations. Although a variety of approaches have been employed to facilitate the development needs of managers, two of the most popular have been multirater feedback and action learning (Conger & Xin, 2000). For example, in the last decade, multirater or 360-degree feedback has evolved from "a nice-to-have technique" to a "must-have tool" (Atwater, Brett, & Waldman, chap. 5, this volume; Church & Bracken, 1997). Using surveys with ranking scales, information from relevant organizational others, such as direct reports, peers, superiors, or customers, is fed back to the focal manager together with his or her self-ratings. Through feedback and increased self-awareness, it is assumed that managers can improve their leadership effectiveness. Action-learning formats are more complex and involve company-based projects that serve as the learning vehicle. Unlike traditional classrooms in which learning may be removed from the day-to-day experiences of participants, action-learning programs send managers out to the field where they grapple with important challenges or opportunities specific to their organizations. In teams, participants learn to apply analytical tools and formal knowledge to these specific challenges. Because the experience is grounded in actual organizational issues, learning is viewed as far more useful and therefore more appealing. The action-learning experiences push participants to develop skills and worldviews that prepare them for expanded leadership roles back on the job.

In this chapter, we argue that despite their popularity neither of these two approaches has been deployed properly to facilitate leadership development. Specifically, we show that in most cases these interventions fail to realize their full potential as development experiences. Indeed, although many practitioners see them as important pathways to leadership development, we believe that they oftentimes prove to be expensive and time-consuming dead ends. On the other hand, we are not pessimistic about their potential. We do believe that they hold the possibility of accelerating the development of leadership capabilities in many managers. To supplement our critique, we offer proposals that can enhance the effectiveness of both interventions.

ACTION LEARNING: SHORTCOMINGS AND OPPORTUNITIES

Action learning typically describes educational approaches where managers learn using issues from their own companies. These formats involve a continuous process of learning and reflection, built around working groups of colleagues, more often with the aim of getting work-related initiatives accomplished. Most experiences therefore share the following characteristics: (a) an emphasis on learning by doing, (b) conducted in teams, (c) addressing company issues, (d) with participants placed into problem-solving roles, and (e) where team decisions are required and formalized into presentations (Dotlich & Noel, 1998; Noel & Charan, 1988). For example, a typical action-learning project might involve participants in conducting a team-based field investigation of new markets for company products. The learning outcome would result in a presentation containing findings and recommendations to company senior management. For instance, at General Electric, programs are built around consulting projects provided by the company's business units, seeking ideas in return for their cooperation. The company's locomotive division has had teams investigate markets for leasing train engines. The European Plastics division has had teams assess the division's overall strategy and marketing plans for plastic applications for automobile bodies. In the more elaborate action-learning programs, managers might be sent off to foreign countries where they conduct market surveys, meet government officials, interview potential clients, and immerse themselves in culture and language courses.

The stages of an action-learning experience are fairly standardized. Typically, after receiving project assignments and reviewing background materials, action-learning teams travel to the headquarters of their assigned businesses—domestic or foreign—to perform further diagnostic research. They have access to key managers and can review essential financial and marketing information as well as visit the field and customers. As their findings and recommendations progress and materialize into drafts, these drafts are reviewed by outside consultants who identify gaps in the analyses and assist in mapping out strategies for overcoming internal resistance to the team's recommendations. The conclusion of their efforts results in presentations to a senior group of executives from the business units concerned. In follow-up sessions, participants also have opportunities to learn about the successes or problems that their recommendations have encountered as they were implemented by the businesses. In this way, participants learn firsthand about the implementation challenges facing their ideas and draw important post-project lessons. Presumably many of these situations demand and in turn develop leadership skills.

The Advantages of Action Learning

These learning experiences have become enormously popular in the corporate world. Within a decade, they have gone from being relatively rare to common features of many in-company leadership programs (Conger & Xin, 2000). Their popularity has been driven in large part by two forces. The first is a strong desire on the part of companies to see their investments in education produce tangible outcomes. Learning experiences therefore revolve around projects that address key issues facing the company either today or in its future. Oftentimes these projects can translate into company initiatives that grow markets, cut costs, streamline operations, redesign the organization, and build leadership talent.

The second force favoring action learning is a growing appreciation for the learning requirements of adults. Advances in the fields of adult education and cognitive psychology over the last 2 decades have substantially increased our knowledge of how adults best learn. Specifically, research has shown that adults are most motivated for learning when it is immediately relevant to their lives. Participants are able to test the utility of frameworks and techniques on tangible problems and to see for themselves what can be usefully applied (Garrison, 1992; Hayes, 1993).

Moreover, research in adult learning confirms the power of action-learning experiences when it comes to developing complex skills such as leadership. For example, we know from studies in cognitive psychology that knowledge comes in essentially two forms. One form is procedural knowledge; the other is declarative knowledge (Clark, 1992). Procedural knowledge involves tasks that can be accomplished through standardized formulas and step-by-step learning. Thus, for example, accounting techniques and financial formulas are forms of procedural knowledge—in other words, they are tasks that can be accomplished according to a clear set of procedures.

The ability to develop principles and concepts to explain complex events is at the heart of declarative knowledge. For example, in a business context, we use declarative knowledge when we are in a leadership capacity—for example, leading individuals through organizational change or formulating a strategic vision. These are complex situations with many contingencies, and no one situation is likely to be identical to the next. Step-by-step techniques and formulas are of little use. Rather, one must detect patterns, make creative connections, and formulate in-the-moment theories of action.

How people learn procedural knowledge is fairly well understood (Clark, 1992). Behavioral psychology has taught us that traditional training methods are best suited for procedural knowledge—applying knowledge in practice sessions spread over time and using corrective feedback and appropriate incentives to direct and motivate learning (VanLehn, 1996). In contrast, learning declarative knowledge requires developing a set of concepts and principles that permits creative connections to be drawn between events. The ability to create and use appropriate analogies to connect several domains of knowledge is particularly important to the process. The more frequently individuals can successfully link events that are seemingly unrelated—but actually similar—to the new problems they are addressing, the more they will be able to produce creative solutions. In essence, action-learning instructional formats achieve this outcome by presenting learners with complex situations that parallel events they will encounter in their work. As such, action learning is an ideal pedagogy for declarative knowledge.

When and Why Action-Learning Formats Fail at Leadership Development

Despite the appeal of these learning experiences, many fail to truly develop leadership capability. The reasons are numerous, but most are the product of design flaws or content issues. In the following, we describe the more common flaws in these programs when it comes to leadership development.

1. *A singular learning experience.* From a design standpoint, the most obvious flaw is the fact that the learning in these programs is often based on a *one-time* experience—in other words, a single program. To truly develop declarative knowledge, learners require repeated or multiple exposures (Clark, 1992). Individuals need these multiple experiences to begin developing a reliable repertoire of principles and a valid conceptual understanding of what they are experiencing. Yet, the vast majority of programs are built around the assumption that a single action-learning experience is sufficient to build declarative knowledge in subjects as complex as leading change or formulating strategic vision.

To enhance action learning's potential for leadership development, programs would need to ensure the following steps. The first would be to make certain that participants move from their action-learning programs directly to job assignments that build upon program lessons and in turn perpetuate the learning process. By not doing so, the learning process stops prematurely. Second, organizations would ideally involve participants in multiple-action learning programs that build upon the lessons of the *prior* program—in essence reinforcing learning and increasing the number of case experiences to enhance the acquisition of declarative knowledge.

2. *Weak links between the project and leadership challenges.* From the standpoint of leadership development, it seems obvious to argue that the projects must have an explicit connection to leadership. Yet in many cases, the connection that is drawn is implicit at best. For example, exploring market opportunities in India not only entails lessons about national economics, government affairs, and consumer behavior but also lessons about the challenge of leading in a cross-cultural context along with the leadership skills of building a new enterprise in a foreign land. It is often assumed that participants will learn about leadership "along the way" (Conger & Benjamin, 1999). We feel that program designers must be far more conscientious about drawing direct learning links to the leadership dimensions of an action-learning project. For example, programs need to carefully identify the specific leadership challenges associated with each project, to create supporting educational experiences, and then to make leadership recommendations an explicit part of the project findings delivered by the action-learning teams. For example, in an action-learning project designed to explore new venture opportunities, there would be classroom sessions about entrepreneurial or new venture leadership capabilities, feedback to participants about their own capabilities in this regard, and then project recommendations that identify the specific leadership challenges of the venture and suggested actions.

3. *Few real opportunities for reflective learning.* One of the advantages of action-learning environments is that they remove participants from the day-to-day demands of their work and provide what would otherwise be rare time for reflective learning (Davis & Hogarth, 1992). At the same time, part of their attraction is that they are task based—in other words, they are all about achieving important projects by a certain deadline. As a result, the accomplishment of the task can potentially overwhelm the process of learning. Without reflection and feedback, action learning, however, would be no different from a normal day on the job. Feedback is essential, because managers receive so little direct feedback on their own performance and learning (Kolb & Kolb, 2001). At the same time, an individual's personal interpretation of feedback can be ambiguous, and sometimes actually the *wrong* lessons can be learned from experiences (Davis & Hogarth, 1992). Therefore, it is essential that active and disciplined feedback be provided by objective sources (Davis & Hogarth, 1992). Coaches, facilitators, company managers, and teammates are all sources of useful feedback in action-learning experiences. They can also foster and reinforce reflective learning in how they structure sessions with participants. For example, a good facilitator employs feedback techniques that promote discussion and reflection. They use questions and discussions rather than statements and lectures to guide learning.

Reflective learning opportunities should be staged with regular frequency (see Day, chap. 1, this volume, for more on reflective learning). Often in programs, structured reflection on important lessons learned during the program is conducted on the final day (Conger & Benjamin, 1999). This is a serious mistake. Instead there should be daily opportunities where participants reflect on lessons learned to that point in the program. This type of daily reflection has two advantages. One, it forces participants to reflect more directly on immediate moments and events; therefore, learning tends to be richer and to occur more around specific incidents. This fits with what we know about research on feedback—it is most useful to learners when focused on recent events. End-of-program reflections miss the smaller moments of learning and can overlook events and stages that in hindsight appear to be far fewer and far less memorable. We also know that in looking back retrospectively we often distort our perceptions of an experience. The more reflections are tied to immediate events, the lower the likelihood of distortion. Second, by instituting daily reflection, a program is modeling what we hope managers will learn to do for themselves—to reflect on their actions and decisions on a day-by-day basis.

How can a program be structured to ensure that critical reflection actually occurs on a regular basis? There are several approaches that action-learning experts recommend. For example, Dotlich and Noel (1998) recommend the following. One is to pair team members up with one another to provide one-on-one feedback. Each participant might be asked to give the other a single behavioral change, say around leadership, that they wish to have made as an outcome of the program. Another device is to have participants write observations about each other on Post-it notes and then place them on a wall for all to read. Their observations are shaped by the question posed: "Describe what you think your team member should do more of, less of, or continue as is." Names are not attached to the Post-its, but members choose the one that they feel most applies to them. In turn, participants ask for examples of their behavior and its effects and solicit general feedback. Journals or daily diaries can also be used as sources of reflection and learning. Finally, it is helpful at regular intervals to schedule team meetings where time is devoted solely to providing group process feedback around leadership and team dynamics. Ideally, a facilitator should moderate these sessions to ensure maximum impact.

4. *Limited emphasis placed on team solutions and team learning.* A critical lesson we have learned is that team dynamics can significantly affect the quality of project outcomes and learning (Conger & Benjamin, 1999). In general, teams that develop strong norms around candor and diversity of perspectives produce more insightful and more creative project recommendations and have deeper learning experiences. In contrast, in teams where one individual or a single functional perspective dominates, the group tends to produce

outcomes that are far less innovative and insightful. In addition, facilitators can play an important role by encouraging team norms that support openness of ideas, shared leadership, and constructive confrontation. But most importantly, teams should not have participants who are "experts" on the issue being addressed. Otherwise there is a strong tendency to defer to those individuals, and as a result, both team and individual learning can be drastically minimized—if it occurs at all. Instead with no experts on hand, groups are more likely to identify and debate a wider range of ideas and solutions.

Team dynamics are of course strongly influenced by the composition of the team and the selection process (Jackson et al., 1991). Though it is extremely difficult to control a team's chemistry in advance, there are certain membership guidelines that may increase the probability of greater team performance and learning. First of all, it is extremely helpful to know beforehand how highly motivated potential participants are. In the ideal case, we would naturally pick only those who are motivated and who see themselves wishing to develop their leadership potential rather than simply to hone their expertise in a particular technique (Revans, 1980). Given the expense of these programs, action learning is best employed for the development of high potentials—in other words, the organization's next generation of senior leaders. Selection criteria should reflect the project's goals. For example, if the program has an objective of broadening cross-functional perspectives, then it is important that the mix of participants represent multiple functions. If the objective is to instill a cross-cultural perspective, then team members should be drawn from different cultures. If a goal of the program is to facilitate change across multiple organizational levels, then it is advisable to have team members selected from different levels. Finally, selection criteria should always keep in mind the person's career stage and developmental needs. This should be a foremost concern. Is this action-learning program a good opportunity to accelerate their learning in preparation for leadership roles in the near future? Will the person's next promotion most likely allow them to build further upon the learnings from the program? These questions should strongly drive the selection process.

5. *Poor follow-up on project outcomes.* Some projects have a better probability of being implemented by a business unit. As a result, they are more attractive for ensuring deeper learning among participants, because the leadership and organizational issues related to implementation challenges can also be examined. It could even be argued that the execution phase is where most of the real learning occurs.

Yet, often when action-learning projects end, they quite literally *end*. There is an assumption that sufficient learning has taken place during the program itself and that it will be self-sustaining. Nothing could be further from the truth. Like any form of training, action-learning programs need mechanisms to ensure the transfer of learning back to the workplace. For example, participants might be promoted or moved to positions where they are directly responsible for the initiatives proposed by the action-learning teams. Or they might receive ongoing briefings from those who are implementing their ideas. Yet, many programs do not either involve their participants in the implementation phase or hold post-implementation debriefings with action-learning teams. In the ideal case, programs would be structured to ensure that participants be involved in implementation. If such steps are not feasible, participants could be kept informed of the implementation through debriefings staggered over the implementation life of an initiative. These debriefing sessions would allow participants to see how the implementation process unfolded, including a review of unexpected obstacles and the leadership challenges that were faced and how these were tackled.

In summary, action learning holds great promise in accelerating the development of leadership talent within organizations. Yet, in many cases, its potential remains simply that—potential. We feel very strongly that programs need to focus more rigorously on the leadership aspects of projects and to ensure that the educational experiences and follow-up activities facilitate deeper and more lasting learning. In addition, embedded in many of these programs is another popular leadership development intervention—multirater feedback. Here also we find that current approaches have important shortfalls. In the section to follow, we examine these and propose solutions that can enhance the effectiveness of these feedback approaches in developing leadership talent.

MULTIRATER FEEDBACK: SHORTCOMINGS AND OPPORTUNITIES

At the core of multisource feedback is the cognitive process of self-reflection, which increases our self-awareness (Church, 1994; Tornow, 1993; Yammarino & Atwater, 1993). It is triggered by the comparison of ratings from different sources (direct reports, supervisors, peers, customers, etc.) to self-evaluations. Why do managers need this comparison? Accurate self-perception is crucial for effective leadership. Supervisors' behavior is guided by their own leadership scheme, and multisource feedback ensures that the latter is more precise (London & Smither, 1995). Unfortunately, our own perceptions of our accomplishments are not reliable enough, because "self-ratings (be they of behaviors, personality, or skills) suffer from inflation, unreliability, and bias" (Yammarino & Atwater, 1997, p. 36). On average, our self-ratings are 0.3 SD higher than those provided by others, and this tendency is consistent over time (Nilsen & Campbell, 1993). For example, only 2% of school seniors rated themselves as below average in leadership abilities (Gilovich, 1991). Therefore, leadership development is contingent on discovering the discrepancies among self- and other ratings. Focal managers need valid and accurate feedback in order to modify their behavior to accommodate the expectations of relevant others.

The philosophy that we need multiple perspectives in feedback is not new. More than 3 decades ago, Lawler (1967) advanced the idea that no single organizational perspective can provide the information necessary to evaluate a person's effectiveness. One specific source would reflect a particular context depending on his or her position in the organizational hierarchy (Ferris & Judge, 1991). Different organizational roles activate different value systems; hence, expectations of effectiveness depend on the eye of the beholder (Salam, Cox, & Sims, 1997). The picture that emerges as a result of multisource feedback is like a patchwork with pieces of various colors and shapes, some of them brighter and more regular than others. Because of the uniqueness of perspectives, disagreement is almost programmed. Supervisors, for example, rate "encouraging independent action" as negatively related to performance, whereas direct reports consider it to be positively related to performance (Salam et al., 1997). The interesting point with multisource feedback is that differences of opinions are desired and valued. Therefore, contradictory data are not regarded as errors, but as useful information (Tornow, 1993). In addition, managers' responsiveness to feedback and the way they handle discrepancies can influence constituent opinions about them. When expectations of others conflict with their own, managers, for example, have four different strategies for responding (Tsui, Ashford, Clair, & Xin, 1995). First, they can change their own behavior, for example, exert more effort. Second, they can try to influence expectations of others. Third, they can seek to explain to others their behavior, for example, provide rationales for their actions. Finally, they can avoid the feeling of discrepancy by ignoring dissatisfied constituencies. Managers are considered to be responsive mainly when they change their behavior and invest extra effort to meet others' expectations—the first strategy described previously (Tsui et al., 1995). Therefore, management development is a successful strategy for leaders. However, the self is a construction, something about which we make inferences (Baumeister, 1998), and managers need to know in what way their behavior must be modified. Multirater feedback can play a vital role here because it increases self-knowledge. The latter leads to adaptive benefits improving the person–environment fit. In that sense, "self-digest" that contains useful information about the self is a means, not an end (Higgins, 1996).

The Advantages of 360-Degree Feedback

Multisource feedback gives a much *more precise picture* of leaders' strengths and weaknesses. In modern organizations, it is not always easy to provide the right feedback that leaders need for their development. Flatter organizational structures are accompanied by an increased span of control. Often, managers do not have enough knowledge or personal observations to assess the job performance of their direct reports. Many organizations have a matrix structure where employees report to different people in the hierarchy. All these factors lead to a high degree of role and expectations ambiguity. Information from multiple sources yields more reliable, and therefore, more meaningful data for the ratee (Church & Bracken, 1997). Despite discrepancies, multisource feedback is accurate because we grant every individual source the right to observe and judge the focal manager from his or her own perspective. In addition, feedback in 360-degree programs is given anonymously, which makes it more honest.

Multisource feedback also *reduces defensiveness* of ratees, because the data are perceived to be much more objective and constructive. There is still a probability that ratees will ignore or deny some aspects of the feedback or that they will focus only on the highest ratings or attribute the lowest ones to external factors (London, Smither, & Adsit, 1997). These cases, however, are not predominant, especially when leaders feel accountable to a coach, and they both can work together on a development plan.

At the same time, leaders experience pressure to please their constituencies. It is, however, almost an impossible task to satisfy everyone around them. If they challenge the formal system, for example, they will get higher ratings from their direct reports but lower ones from their bosses (Salam et al., 1997). Multisource feedback broadens the horizon and demonstrates vividly the complex nature of leaders' social roles. It makes leaders' *expectations much more realistic*, giving evidence that sometimes a well-intended change in behavior will not necessarily be followed by improved ratings across all constituencies.

When and Why 360-Degree Feedback Fails at Leadership Development

It seems that the more powerful the instrument, the more sensitive it is to different issues of design and application. Multisource feedback is a complex system involving a target individual and information about him or her from many stakeholders. Serious problems emerge when we try either to reduce it to a quantitative tool or to stretch it to universal purposes. Multirater feedback is also sensitive to the cultural context in which it is embedded and is vulnerable because it stirs emotions.

Multisource Feedback for Appraisal Purposes. The most common use of multirater feedback is for development (Bracken, 1994), but eventually, some companies extend its application to include administrative decisions such as annual performance appraisals, promotions, pay, etc. (London & Smither, 1995). This coupling has a negative impact on the effectiveness of multisource feedback for enhancing leader's development. Maxine Dalton from the Center for Creative Leadership in Greensboro, NC, argues that feedback is provided primarily to encourage behavioral change. "If you are using 360 for appraisal, you really are violating the most basic condition for change that a person feel psychologically safe" (Filipczak, Hequet, Lee, Picard, & Stamps, 1996, p. 25). Therefore, it is not surprising that employees have a more positive attitude toward multisource feedback when it is used for development and not for administration (Bettenhausen & Fedor, 1997; Westerman & Rosse, 1997). Some institutions, such as the Center for Creative Leadership that create 360-degree systems, go even one step further: they restrict the use of their multisource feedback instruments only to development.

As argued earlier, leadership development starts with self-awareness. However, the construction of self-knowledge is a cognitive process that can be driven by three different motives. The *appraisal motive*, for example, reflects the need of an individual for accurate feedback from others; the *self-enhancement motive* encourages people to seek favorable information about themselves; the *consistency motive* is a quest for evidence that confirms what people already know about themselves. Research shows that self-enhancement is the strongest motive when we pursue self-knowledge. It is followed by consistency, and unfortunately, the appraisal motive comes last (Sedikides, 1993). These findings point out that there is a strong and deeply rooted self-enhancement orientation in our social behavior (Baumeister, 1998). When the goal of multisource feedback is administrative decisions, we can expect that the self-enhancement motive will be strengthened because it leads to rewards in terms of promotions, pay increase, etc. In this case, thinking well of oneself and inflating one's view of self will become even more desired. As a result, "positive illusions" about the self may be fostered (Baumeister, 1998; Taylor, 1989; Taylor & Brown, 1988). The impact that self-deception processes have on our behavior is well documented. People try to minimize the time spent on processing critical feedback (Baumeister & Cairns, 1992), they selectively forget negative feedback (Crary, 1966); they compare themselves against less successful others under ego threats (Crocker & Major, 1989), or they create a sense of uniqueness of their abilities (Marks, 1984). Thus, using feedback for appraisal is counterproductive, because it strengthens our natural tendency to look for favorable information and weakens the appraisal motive or the need to look for accurate information from others.

There is another argument in favor of decoupling the purposes. If the goal of 360-degree systems is appraisal, leaders might feel inclined to decrease discrepancies between self- and other ratings through impression management techniques without changing their real behavior. Self-presentation refers to our tactics to convey information about ourselves to others. One of the motives that drive our inclination to manipulate others' opinion of ourselves is the *strategic self-presentation*. It is instrumental, because "the task of impressing others is a strategy for achieving ulterior goals" (Baumeister, 1998, p. 704), for example, promotions, pay increase, etc. There are different forms of self-presentation (Jones & Pittman, 1982): *ingratiation* (emphasizing appealing traits in order to be liked), *self-promotion* (getting respect after convincing others of one's competence), or *exemplification* (showing one's moral virtues). When feedback is used for appraisal, the focal leaders can aim either at real behavioral change or at manipulating the impression of themselves through self-presentation. Research shows that "if the goal is to secure rewards from the other person, then one tries to present oneself as closely as possible to the other person's values and preferences" (Baumeister, 1998, p. 705). Self-presentation might be perceived as an easier way to achieve the goal of favorable feedback. In other words, the focus of attention will be shifted from behavior change, which requires serious cognitive effort, to self-presentation through well-designed manipulation of target raters.

In addition, when used for administrative purposes, multisource feedback data become the property of the organization, not of the individual (Lepsinger & Lucia, 1997). Development, however, is best served when ratees own entirely the information gathered and when they have discretion over whether to share the data with others. This contradiction is another major caveat of the coupling of developmental and appraisal purposes.

The idea to kill two birds with one stone by coupling might seem rational in the majority of cases, but in multisource feedback it is definitely not a good idea to annex appraisal to the developmental purpose. This practice not only distracts cognitive energy from the process of development and channels it into self-presentation strategies but also changes the definition of the situation and therefore the motivation of focal leaders in how they process and use feedback.

Emphasis on the Quantitative and Not on the Qualitative Aspects of Multisource Feedback. The greatest benefit of 360-degree systems is that information comes from unique perspectives. Every rater provides rich data from his or her own organizational point of view. As already argued, multiple sources reflect different values and expectations, and therefore disagreement is almost inevitable. Attitudes toward these discrepancies differ in two camps. One of them endorses the quantitative view; the other endorses the qualitative view. The first group conceptualizes multisource feedback as a quantitative method and is driven by a wish to minimize disagreements among raters. Consequently, its "validity" is mechanistically boosted either by discarding all ratings that are more than 20% different from the rest of the raters or by sanctioning respondents who produce ratings inconsistent with others (see Edwards & Ewen, 1996). In other words, the more agreement captured, the more accurate the assessment. From this point of view, any disagreement is considered to be a rater error and therefore undesirable. On the other side, proponents of the second camp view 360-degree mainly as a qualitative instrument and try to capture or even increase rater variance. In this case, the underlying assumption is that differences in rater views reflect legitimate differences in the perceptions of the observer. The potential of multisource feedback as a development tool is strongly restricted if "accuracy" (the minimizing of disagreements) wins over variation. It gets even worse, when feedback from different sources gets aggregated, because averaging conceals important variation. First, there are method effects (Conway, 1996); that is, bosses evaluate differently from peers, who assess differently from direct reports, etc. In addition to the method effects, there is an *idiosyncratic rating tendency* of individual raters (Mount, Judge,

Scullen, Sytsman, & Hezlett, 1998). This means that assessment from each rater, regardless of level, captures unique variance, and these are different enough to constitute a separate method. The implication is that information should be displayed separately for each one of the raters (Mount et al., 1998). This will enable the focal individual to examine the patterns. The latter is of crucial importance when leaders try to determine their strengths and weaknesses. The widespread practice of aggregating ratings within or across rating levels is inappropriate because it reduces the construct validity of the ratings (Mount et al., 1998). The only exception is at the supervisor level where validity does not decrease as a result of aggregation (Mount et al., 1998; Viswesvaran, Schmidt, & Ones, 1996). An inference can be made: In order to draw conclusions about the development needs of leaders, data analysis should move from the quantitative, statistical comparison of averages and standard deviations to the discussion of response patterns and written comments and examples.

Wrong Focus of the Feedback Intervention.   Changes in self-esteem can be accompanied by a strong emotional response (Baumeister, 1998). According to the feedback intervention theory of DeNisi and Kluger (2000), our behavior is regulated by a comparison of the received feedback with a goal or a standard. These goals or standards are arranged hierarchically by importance for the individual. The highest is the *self-level*, where gaps between our standard and the feedback we receive makes us question our self-concept. A leader, for example, who finds it difficult to be sensitive to other people's problems but is told that this is one of the most essential elements of good leadership, might begin to question his/her self-identity when confronted with negative feedback. The second level of goals and standards is the *task level*, where discrepancies between feedback and goals make us work harder. Managers could focus, for example, on achieving certain concrete goals, such as delegating a certain percentage of tasks to direct reports, reducing the number of e-mails, and increasing face-to-face communication. The third one is the *task-learning level*. It includes goals and standards that are related to the details involved in the execution of a certain task. The problem is that attention in this case might be distracted to specific details of our performance at the expense of actual accomplishments. If leaders, for example, decide to improve their communications with direct reports, they could try to create the perfect system of formal one-to-one meetings with all direct reports. Neglecting different informal opportunities and group formats, they will be less effective because attention will shift to the detail.

Since attention is a scarce resource (Simon, 1997), behavior will be regulated only by those feedback-standard gaps that receive sufficient attention. Therefore, feedback interventions change the locus of attention. When the latter is focused on the task, we try to narrow the gap between actual and goal performance. But when attention shifts to the self, we start questioning who we really are. In this case, strong affective reactions, such as disappointment or despair, might occur. As a result, subsequent performance may well suffer.

Festinger (1954) suggests that people compare themselves to others, and if the latter outperform them, then they may experience negative feelings. If the ability that is being compared is closely related to one's self-concept, negative feedback could produce a strong reaction. For example, an individual who works in advertising will be much more affected by a low rating on creativity than another who works in logistics, because originality and innovation are dominant elements in the self-concept of leaders in advertising. Threatening the ego of feedback recipients is counterproductive because of the strong emotions that are evoked. Concerns over self-esteem can lead to emotional distress. When self-evaluation is favorable but the evaluation from other people is unfavorable, the individual can experience "threatened egotism," which is a blow to the ego (Baumeister, 1998). It can produce high-order irrationality and impair the adaptive function of the self. Shame, for example, can be extremely shattering leading to social withdrawal or anger (Tangney, Burggraf, & Wagner, 1995). Embarrassment or perceived loss of other's esteem (Modigliani, 1971) is another consequence when dealing with unfavorable comparison with others. Therefore, if a feedback intervention moves to the self-level, developmental goals might be displaced by a need to cope with strong emotions and with an identity crisis. Consequently, the best strategy to assist leaders' development is to focus multisource feedback only on the *task* level.

One type of ratees, labeled as "overraters," however, is inclined to move the intervention to the self-level. For example, Atwater, Ostroff, Yammarino, and Fleenor (1998) distinguish between overraters (self-ratings are higher than those of others), underraters (self-ratings are lower than those of others), in-agreement/good raters (both, self- and other ratings are favorable), and in-agreement/poor (both, self- and other ratings are unfavorable). They suggest that management effectiveness is highest in the case of in-agreement/good raters and in that for underraters, but it is lowest for overraters (see London & Smither, 1995). The case with overraters requires special attention because of the potential danger to move the feedback intervention to the self-level. As we have argued, this is a counterproductive strategy.

Biases and Failure To Train Raters.   Feedback ratings are judgments and therefore can be subjected to different cognitive biases (Salam et al., 1997). It is well known that we are selective about what we notice, learn, remember, or infer (Markus & Zajonc, 1985). Many studies give evidence that our social perception can be self-centered and self-biased. According to the self-image bias, people judge others, using mainly traits on which they themselves rank high (Lewicki, 1984). When we construct category prototypes, like a "good leader," we tend to emphasize our own traits (Dunning, Perie, & Story, 1991). Information referring to the self is processed in a special way because of its high importance. Two good examples of this are the actor–observer bias, when we make dispositional inferences about others (Jones & Nisbett, 1971), and the self-reference effect, which suggests that people process more thoroughly and remember better information pertaining to the self (Rogers, Kuiper, & Kirker, 1977). Since ownership is a form of self-reference (Baumeister, 1998), feedback will have a special status if the ratee owns it. As Kahneman, Knetsch, and Thaler (1990) argue, things gain in value merely by being owned, and this effect might extend to seemingly trivial things (Baumeister, 1998). We can infer that if our goal is development, ownership of multisource feedback by the ratee is crucial. In order to reduce the probability of biased judgments, informants must be trained to recognize and avoid them. In addition, feedback items should reflect aspects of behavior that are salient to the rater. Because direct reports, peers, and supervisors observe different facets of the focal individual's performance, they should be subgrouped according to their level in the organization and asked to provide information only on dimensions that are appropriate to their level (Furnham & Stringfield, 1998). The best strategy is to customize the instrument for each of these using different "master lists" with behavioral descriptions that are relevant for the particular referent group. This approach suggests that raters can select items and individualize the feedback survey (Westerman & Rosse, 1997). In order to be appointed as raters, employees must have had observations on the focal individual for at least 4 months (Yukl & Lepsinger, 1995). The size of the rater group should enable a multifaceted view of the focal individual. Raters should be made aware of errors and biases such as leniency, harshness, central tendency, range restriction, halo effect, friendship bias, etc. Open-ended comments need even more attention in terms of achieving constructiveness and of an orientation on behaviors (Atwater & Waldman, 1998). Ratees also must be trained in how to select respondents in order to leverage diversity, how to share and analyze feedback, and how to develop a personal action plan.

The structure of the survey can influence raters' errors and biases. In the traditional form, the open questions are at the end. There are two important reasons why we should instead place them at the beginning of the survey. First, it is necessary to minimize the effect of response fatigue on the quality of information. Open questions are of special importance, and raters should give them adequate attention and time. By coming at the end when respondent fatigue is setting in, raters give little thought and attention to qualitative questions. Second, asking the open questions at the beginning will make it possible to elicit employees' opinions without "priming" them through the closed questions.

Insensitivity to Cultural Readiness and Lack of Coaching.   Multisource feedback cannot initiate leadership development in organizations that lack a climate of trust. As Snader (1997, p. 4) puts it: "You say assessment; they see a cutback." For example, in a period of downsizing, it is difficult to believe that the goal of multisource feedback is developmental and that it will be used for the benefit of the target manager and not against him/her. In itself, multisource feedback does not solve problems; it only surfaces them. A fit between the feedback system and the organizational culture is essential. Leadership development will remain largely rhetorical if there is no alignment and consistency between survey items and strategic competencies throughout all human resources functions and if there is no commitment of senior and middle management and guarantee of confidentiality and anonymity. People must believe that their view truly counts.

For multisource feedback to cause behavioral change, a leader's participation in it should be voluntary. Any pressure against their will is demotivating. Moreover, the higher the perceived costs of seeking feedback, the less inclined managers are to make use of it (Funderburg & Levy, 1997). Therefore, 360-degree programs should not demand substantial time investment from both ratees and raters. It is counterproductive to overwhelm leaders with data from extensive surveys and leave them to do the sense-making on their own. Coaching is a major factor for success. Trained facilitators can be of great help to the focal individual (Nemeroff & Cosentino, 1979). Especially when data are contradictory, they facilitate the sense-making process, provide a safe environment to deal with strong emotions after unexpected negative feedback, and assist the leader in prioritizing the behaviors that are in most need of improvement. The developmental effectiveness of feedback depends on goal setting (Locke & Latham, 1990). Leadership enhancement is questionable if multisource feedback stops at the level of interpretation without setting specific improvement goals. London and Beatty (1993) suggest that the crucial factor for performance betterment is the subsequent follow-up of the action plan. Accountability and recognition for accomplishments can shift the ratees' interest to their personal development process (Antonioni, 1996). Therefore, if multisource feedback is perceived as a single event, not as an enduring system in the organization, developmental effects will be strongly impaired.

CONCLUSION

Although achieving great popularity as leadership development tools, action-learning and multirater feedback have yet to realize their full potential. We believe that both have been poorly deployed to date. For example, although grounded in real company issues, action-learning formats may fail to provide the multiple learning experiences necessary to develop complex knowledge. Moreover, inadequate opportunities to reflect on learnings, poor facilitation, and a failure to follow up on project outcomes can seriously hamper the real potential of these learning interventions to develop leadership talent. Similarly, multirater feedback has the potential to solicit rich information that can stimulate leadership development. Compared to traditional feedback systems, it provides a more precise picture of the target individual, reduces defensiveness, and can lead to a high degree of personal satisfaction. Yet, its impact falls short when we try to stretch its use and couple different purposes, emphasize mainly its quantitative aspects and neglect the qualitative ones, focus the feedback intervention on the self- and not on the task level, or conceptualize it as a single event rather than as an enduring system. Both of these interventions require far more attention and thoughtful application if they are to realize their potential to develop leadership talent for organizations.

REFERENCES

Antonioni, D. (1996). Designing an effective 360-degree appraisal feedback process. *Organizational Dynamics, 25*(2), 24–38.

Atwater, L., Ostroff, C., Yammarino, F., & Fleenor, J. (1998). Self-other agreement: Does it really matter? *Personnel Psychology, 51*(3), 577–598.

Atwater, L., & Waldman, D. (1998). Accountability in 360-degree feedback. *HRMagazine, 43*(6), 96–104.

Baumeister, R. (1998). The self. In D. Gilbert, S. Fiske, & G. Lindzey (Eds.), *The handbook of social psychology* (pp. 680–740). Boston, MA: McGraw-Hill.

Baumeister, R., & Cairns, K. (1992). Repression and self-presentation: When audiences interfere with self-deceptive strategies. *Journal of Personality and Social Psychology, 62*, 851–862.

Bettenhausen, K., & Fedor, D. (1997). Peer and upward appraisals: A comparison of their benefits and problems. *Group & Organization Management, 22*(2), 236–263.

Bracken, D. (1994). Straight talk about multirater feedback. *Training & Development, 48*(9), 44.

Church, A. (1994). Managerial self-awareness in high performing individuals and organizations. *Dissertation Abstracts International, 55*-OSB, 2028.

Church, A., & Bracken, D. (1997). Advancing the state of the art of 360-degree feedback. *Group & Organization Management, 22*(2), 149–161.

Clark, R. (1992). How the cognitive sciences are shaping the profession. In H. Stolovitch & J. Keeps (Eds.), *Handbook of human performance technology* (pp. 688–700). San Francisco: Jossey-Bass.

Conger, J., & Benjamin, B. (1999). *Building leaders: How corporations are developing the next generation.* San Francisco: Jossey-Bass.

Conger, J., & Xin, K. (2000). Executive education in the 21st century. *Journal of Management Education, 24*(1), 73–101.

Conway, J. (1996). Analysis and design of multitrait-multirater performance appraisal studies. *Journal of Management, 22*, 139–162.

Crary, W. (1966). Reactions to incongruent self-experiences. *Journal of Consulting Psychology, 30*, 246–252.

Crocker, J., & Major, B. (1989). Social stigma and self-esteem: The self-protective properties of stigma. *Psychological Review, 96*, 608–630.

Davis, H. L., & Hogarth, R. M. (1992). Rethinking management education: A view from Chicago. In *The University of Chicago, Graduate School of Business, Selected Papers, no. 72.*

DeNisi, A., & Kluger, A. (2000). Feedback effectiveness: Can 360-degree appraisals be improved? *Academy of Management Executive, 14*(1), 129–139.

Dotlich, D., & Noel, J. (1998). *Action learning.* San Francisco: Jossey-Bass.

Dunning, D., Perie, M., & Story, A. (1991). Self-serving prototypes of social categories. *Journal of Personality and Social Psychology, 61*, 957–968.

Edwards, M., & Ewen, A. (1996). *360 degree feedback: The powerful new model for employee assessment & performance improvement.* New York: AMACOM.

Ferris, G., & Judge, T. (1991). Personnel/human resource management: A political influence perspective. *Journal of Management, 17*, 447–488.

Festinger, L. (1954). A theory of social comparison processes. *Human Relations, 7*, 117–140.

Filipczak, B., Hequet, M., Lee, C., Picard, M., & Stamps, D. (1996). 360 degree feedback: Will the circle be broken? *Training, 33*(10), 24–25.

Funderburg, S., & Levy, P. (1997). The influence of individual and contextual variables on 360-degree feedback system. *Group & Organization Management, 22*(2), 210–235.

Furnham, A., & Stringfield, P. (1998). Congruence in job-performance ratings: A study of 360 degree feedback examining self, manager, peers, and consulting ratings. *Human Relations, 51*(4), 517–530.

124   CONGER AND TOEGEL

Garrison, D. R. (1992). Critical thinking and self-directed learning in adult education: An analysis of responsibility and control issues. *Adult Education Quarterly, 42*(3), 136–148.

Gilovich, T. (1991). *How we know what isn't so.* New York: Free Press.

Hayes, E. (1993). Current perspectives on teaching adults. *Adult Education Quarterly, 43*(3), 173–186.

Higgins, E. (1996). The "self-digest": Self-knowledge serving self-regulatory functions. *Journal of Personality and Social Psychology, 71*, 1,062–1,083.

Jackson, S. E., Brett, J. F., Sessa, V. I., Cooper, D. M., Julin, J. A., & Peyronnin, K. (1991). Some differences make a difference: Individual dissimilarity and group heterogeneity as correlates of recruitment, promotions, and turnover. *Journal of Applied Psychology, 76*(5), 675.

Jones, E., & Nisbett, R. (1971). *The actor and the observer: Divergent perceptions of the causes of behavior.* Morristown, NJ: General Learning Press.

Jones, E., & Pittman, T. (1982). Toward a general theory of strategic self-presentation. In J. Suls (Ed.), *Psychological perspectives on the self* (pp. 231–262). Hillsdale, NJ: Lawrence Erlbaum Associates, Inc.

Kahneman, D., Knetsch, J., & Thaler, R. (1990). Experimental tests of the endowment effect and the Coase theorem. *Journal of Political Economy, 98*, 1,325–1,348.

Kolb, A., & Kolb, D. A. (2001). *Experiential learning theory bibliography 1971–2001.* Boston, MA: McBer & Company.

Lawler, E. (1967). The multitrait-multirater approach to measuring managerial job performance. *Journal of Applied Psychology, 51*, 369–381.

Lepsinger, R., & Lucia, A. (1997). 360-degree feedback and performance appraisal. *Training, 34*(9), 62–70.

Lewicki, P. (1984). Self-schema and social information processing. *Journal of Personality and Social Psychology, 47*, 1,177–1,190.

Locke, E., & Latham, G. (1990). *A theory of goal setting and task performance.* Englewood Cliffs, NJ: Prentice-Hall.

London, M., & Beatty, R. (1993). 360-degree feedback as a competitive advantage. *Human Resource Management, 32*(2,3), 353–372.

London, M., & Smither, J. (1995). Can multi-source feedback change perceptions of goal accomplishment, self-evaluations, and performance-related outcomes? Theory-based applications and directions for research. *Personnel Psychology, 48*(4), 803–839.

London, M., Smither, J., & Adsit, D. (1997). Accountability: The Achilles' heel of multisource feedback. *Group & Organization Management, 22*(2), 162–184.

Marks, G. (1984). Thinking one's abilities are unique and one's opinions are common. *Personality and Social Psychology Bulletin, 10*, 203–208.

Markus, H., & Zajonc, R. (1985). The cognitive perspective in social psychology. In G. Lindzey & E. Aronson (Eds.), *Handbook of social psychology* (pp. 137–230). New York: Random House.

Modigliani, A. (1971). Embarrassment, facework, and eye contact: Testing a theory of embarrassment. *Journal of Personality and Social Psychology, 17*, 15–24.

Mount, M., Judge, T., Scullen, S., Sytsman, M., & Hezlett, S. (1998). Trait, rater and level effects in 360-degree performance ratings. *Personnel Psychology, 51*(3), 557–576.

Nemeroff, W., & Cosentino, J. (1979). Utilizing feedback and goal-setting to increase performance appraisal interviewer skills of appraisees. *Academy of Management Journal, 22*, 566–576.

Nilsen, D., & Campbell, D. (1993). Self-observer rating discrepancies—once an overrater, always an overrater? *Human Resource Management, 32*, 265–281

Noel, J., & Charan, R. (1988). Leadership development at GE's Crotonville. *Human Resources Management, 27*(4), 433–447.

Revans, R. W. (1980). *Action Learning.* London: Blond & Briggs.

Rogers, T., Kuiper, N., & Kirker, W. (1977). Self-reference and the encoding of personal information. *Journal of Personality and Social Psychology, 35*, 677–688.

Salam, S., Cox, J., & Sims, H. (1997). In the eye of the beholder: How leadership relates to 360-degree performance ratings. *Group & Organization Management, 22*(2), 185–209.

Sedikides, C. (1993). Assessment, enhancement, and verification determinants of the self-evaluation process. *Journal of Personality and Social Psychology, 65,* 317–338.

Simon, H. (1997). *Administrative behaviour. A study of decision-making processes in administrative organizations.* New York: The Free Press.

Snader, J. (1997). Misusing feedback. *Executive Excellence, 14*(8), 4.

Tangney, J., Burggraf, S., & Wagner, P. (1995). Shame-proneness, guilt-proneness, and psychological symptoms. In J. Tangney & K. Fischer (Eds.), *The self-conscious emotions* (pp. 343–367). New York: Guilford.

Taylor, S. (1989). *Positive illusions: Creative self-deception and the healthy mind.* New York: Basic Books.

Taylor, S., & Brown, J. (1988). Illusion and well-being: A social psychological perspective on mental health. *Psychological Bulletin, 103,* 193–210.

Tornow, W. (1993). Perceptions or reality: Is multi-perspective measurement a means or an end? *Human Resource Management, 32*(2,3), 221–229.

Tsui, A., Ashford, S., Clair, L., & Xin, K. (1995). Dealing with discrepant expectations: Response strategies and managerial effectiveness. *Academy of Management Journal, 38*(6), 1,515–1,543.

VanLehn, K. (1996). Cognitive skills acquisition. *Annual Review of Psychology, 47,* 513–539.

Viswesvaran, C., Schmidt, F., & Ones, D. (1996). Comparative analysis of the reliability of job performance ratings. *Journal of Applied Psychology, 81*(5), 557–574.

Westerman, J., & Rosse, J. (1997). Reducing the threat of rater nonparticipation in 360-degree feedback systems: An exploratory examination of antecedents to participation in upward ratings. *Group & Organization Management, 22*(2), 288–309.

Yammarino, F., & Atwater, L. (1993). Understanding self-perception accuracy: Implications for human resource management. *Human Resource Management, 32*(2,3), 231–247.

Yammarino, F., & Atwater, L. (1997). Do managers see themselves as others see them? Implications of self-other rating agreement for human resources management. *Organizational Dynamics, 25*(4), 35–45.

Yukl, G., & Lepsinger, R. (1995). How to get the most out of 360 degree feedback. *Training, 32*(12), 45.

IV

Leadership Development Theory

7

Relationship Development as a Key Ingredient for Leadership Development

Mary Uhl-Bien
University of Central Florida

Although interpersonal relationships have always held importance within the organizational literature (Blau, 1964; Follett, 1941), a focus on relational perspectives is recently experiencing renewed interest in organizational behavior and leadership research (Brass & Krackhardt, 1999; Day, 2000; Nahapiet & Ghoshal, 1998; Uhl-Bien, Graen, & Scandura, 2000). According to Hunt and Dodge (2001), relational perspectives are at the forefront of emerging leadership thrusts. A relational focus is one that "moves beyond unidirectional or even reciprocal leader–follower relationships to one that recognizes leadership wherever it occurs, is not restricted to a single or even small set of formal or informal leaders, and in its strongest form, functions as a dynamic system embedding leadership, environmental, and organizational aspects" (Hunt & Dodge, 2001, p. 448). Such perspectives allow for broader and more dynamic views of leadership than traditional approaches, which focus primarily on the formal leader and supervisory behavior (Yukl, 1998).

A relational approach presents a wealth of opportunities for research and practice on leadership development (Day, 2000). Relationships are generators of social capital that take human capital and transform it into a competitive advantage (Nahapiet & Ghoshal, 1998). Despite this, we do not yet know how to systematically facilitate the growth of work relationships in organizations (Uhl-Bien et al., 2000). As noted by Day (2000; and Day & O'Conner, chap. 1, this volume), a problem with leadership development to date is that the majority of work has emphasized *leader* rather than *leadership development*. Whereas leader development focuses on developing the formal leader, primarily through training individual-based knowledge, skills, and abilities associated with formal leadership roles, leadership development focuses on building and using interpersonal competence. This approach views leadership as a complex interaction between leaders and social and organizational environments (Fiedler, 1996; Salancik, Calder, Rowland, Leblebici, & Conway, 1975). Leadership development increases understanding of how to use social (i.e., relational) systems to build commitment among members of a community of practice (Wenger, 1998). Using such an approach, both individual and relational lenses are important concerns.

An area of research that speaks directly to leadership development, as defined by Day (2000), is Leader–Member Exchange (LMX) theory (Graen & Uhl-Bien, 1995; Liden, Sparrowe, & Wayne, 1997; Uhl-Bien et al., 2000). Researchers working with this leadership model have been investigating the value of developing effective work relationships between managers and subordinates for the past 30 years (Dansereau, Graen, & Haga, 1975; Graen, 1976; Graen, Novak, & Sommerkamp, 1982; Graen & Scandura, 1987; Graen & Uhl-Bien, 1991a, 1991b). During this time, LMX has shown the value of high-quality relationships and the problems associated with lower quality relationships (Gerstner & Day, 1997).

Although LMX offers evidence to support the value of relational approaches to leadership, many questions still remain about key issues related to leadership development. In particular, a question that needs to be addressed in LMX research is: what leads to development of higher and lower quality work relationships (e.g., antecedents to LMX)? Although past research has investigated antecedents to LMX, a clear picture of what these are and how they operate still has not emerged. Focused investigations addressing how leadership relationships form and evolve will help generate a clearer framework for relationship development that would enhance the contribution LMX can make not only to leadership development (Day, 2000; Drath & Palus, 1994) but also to work on social capital more generally.

The purpose of this chapter is to discuss how LMX research can speak to theory, research, and practice on leadership development. The chapter begins by briefly reviewing the value of relationships from a social capital perspective and then defines leadership relative to relationships. This lays the groundwork for new ideas regarding relationship development in the workplace. In particular, in contrast to hierarchical and leader-dominated perspectives on relational differentiation, I argue that the goal and responsibility of leadership should be to work to develop effective relationships more broadly with interdependent others, rather than with only a group of "trusted assistants" (e.g., Dansereau, Graen, & Haga, 1975). Drawing from the foundations established by Day (2000) and Drath (1998; Drath & Palus, 1994), I also argue that leadership development needs to be considered (a) beyond hierarchical notions of manager–subordinate relationships, (b) as the responsibility of both members of the dyad (rather than leader-controlled), and (c) with allowance for more variability in what is considered a high-quality, or effective, relationship (rather than assuming universal attributes of high-quality relationships, House & Aditya, 1997). Finally, to help spark new advancements in addressing the question of how LMX develops, I introduce notions of *implicit relational theories* (borrowing from work on implicit leadership theories), *relational favorability* (e.g., interpersonal and situational), and *relational skills* (e.g., distinct from interpersonal skills). These are used to offer specific implications for leadership development. As such, this chapter is meant to spark interest among LMX and relational leadership researchers in the study and practice of leadership development.

MAKING THE CASE FOR RELATIONSHIPS: THE VALUE OF SOCIAL CAPITAL

As organizations continue to face challenges and demands from external environments, effective work relationships will no longer be an option but a critical source of competitive advantage (Bouty, 2000; Brass & Krackhardt, 1999; Drath, 1998; McCall, 1998; Uhl-Bien et al., 2000). This is largely due to the social capital that effective relationships generate. Social capital is derived through the social structure of the organization and facilitates the actions of individuals within the larger organizational framework (Nahapiet & Ghoshal, 1998). This capital generates resources through networks of mutual acquaintance and recognition (Uhl-Bien et al., 2000; Whitener, 2000). In contrast to human capital, which is a quality of individuals (e.g., KSAs: knowledge, skills, and abilities), social capital is a quality created among people. Social capital comes from the assets created and leveraged from interpersonal relationships developed through a history of interactions among individuals (Bordieu, 1986). Therefore, we cannot consider employees' knowledge, skills, and abilities as human capital until we recognize that their contributions to firm performance depend on how they interact with one another through interpersonal relationships.

Despite this, as a theoretical domain in the management literature, interpersonal work relationships have not received as much attention as they should (Nahapiet & Ghoshal, 1998; Uhl-Bien et al., 2000). Interpersonal relationships are often considered as variables in management research, but work relationships have not emerged as a dominant field of inquiry in organizational behavior study (Graen & Uhl-Bien, 1995; Hollander & Offermann, 1990). In the human resource (HR) literature, relationships have hardly been mentioned at all. For example, Schuler and MacMillan (1984) argued that companies that systematically plan with their human resources in mind are most likely to gain a competitive advantage by having "the right people at the right place in the right time" to produce quality products efficiently. This focus on individuals, however, does not address the fact that within organizations people do not act in isolation. To more accurately reflect leadership and HR functioning, we must realign our focus toward the "right people at the right place in the right time *with the right relationships.*"

The value of a relational focus is shown by research examining the positive benefits of high-quality manager–subordinate relationships on work-related outcomes. Mayfield and Mayfield (1996) showed that performance is about 20% higher and satisfaction about 50% higher for subordinates who have higher quality relationships with their supervisors than subordinates with lower quality relationships. More importantly, low-quality relationships can present tremendous costs to organizations (Gerstner & Day, 1997), with employees in lower quality relationships tending to quit after approximately 12 months, costing the organization training and recruitment expenses (Mayfield & Mayfield, 1998). Employees in higher quality relationship move on for promotions within the same firm.

A focus on relationships, therefore, represents a largely untapped opportunity to improve firm performance. To understand how to capitalize on this opportunity, we must first understand what leadership is and how it is linked to relationships.

HERE WE GO AGAIN ... WHAT IS LEADERSHIP?

Although a vast number of leadership definitions have been offered over the years (Yukl, 1998), there appear to be two common denominators among these definitions: change and influence. Leadership is about managing change; it differs from management in that management is about coping with complexity (Kotter, 2001). According to Kotter (2001), the function of leadership is to produce change. Leadership behaviors involve looking for patterns, relationships, and linkages that help explain events in the environment, and then using these to develop and act upon visions and strategies for how to create change. Leadership involves generating ideas for change (e.g., analyzing, recommending, creating vision) and acting successfully to get others to follow (e.g., motivating, inspiring, persuading). Being a leader means being a risk taker, from the standpoint of both making decisions in an ambiguous situation (e.g., one risks being wrong) and taking a public stand (e.g., the risk of speaking out, going against status quo).

Leadership also involves influence. Katz and Kahn (1978) defined leadership as the incremental influence that gets people to go above and beyond mechanical compliance with routine directives of the organization. This perspective emphasizes personal power rather than position power (Etzioni, 1961), such that followers are intrinsically motivated (Steers, Porter, & Bigley, 1996) and perform extra-role behaviors (Organ, 1988). The intent of this influence is to get people not just to comply with directives but also to act in ways not specified by their formal roles. Thus leaders differ from managers in that they gain personal influence with others to get them to do more than they would otherwise (i.e., to *create change*).

Combining these two perspectives means that leadership is using influence to create change. Thus influence is the essence of leadership (Yukl, 1998), as is creating change (as change results from the use of influence) (Kotter, 2001). Contrary to a previous view that influence is a characteristic that a leader (i.e., manager) may or may not have (Yukl, 1998), the perspective presented here suggests that perhaps we should consider it as a defining element of leadership. When individuals engage in the use of influence to create change, they are engaging in leadership.

Assumption 1. Leadership occurs when individuals use influence to create change.

The value of this definition is that it views leadership as a behavior, not as a formal role. In this way, we gain a broader perspective of leadership and of how to develop leaders. By using this definition *anyone* may act as a leader, not just those in formal roles, *when they use leadership behaviors* (i.e., behaviors that use influence to create change) (Day, 2000; Drath, 1998; Drath & Palus, 1994). In other words, those individuals we typically consider followers (e.g., subordinates) may act as leaders even when in a subordinate role.

This perspective helps alleviate problems in the literature of using the terms leader and manager interchangeably, which assumes that by studying managers we are studying leaders, since managers are those in formal roles that require leadership. Similarly, it addresses problems of confounding the terms follower and subordinate, which assumes that followers are subordinate (e.g., subordinate is a hierarchical term suggesting subordination, and followers are not always subordinate). Such terminology limits thinking about what leadership (and followership) is and can be within organizations. This thinking also contributes to limited conceptualizations about leadership development that focus on those in formal managerial roles or those targeted to take on such roles in the future. By thinking of leadership as a behavior, not a formal role, it extends the capability for leadership behaviors to *all* organizational members and calls for a change in how we approach leadership development, which then should focus beyond managers or future managers to include all organizational members. Moreover, such a transition in LMX theory would take it from managerial leadership theory to relational leadership theory.

Assumption 2. Leadership is a behavior, not a formal role (therefore, individuals not in formal roles are leaders when they use leadership behaviors).

RELATIONSHIPS AS GENERATORS OF LEADERSHIP INFLUENCE

Leadership is engaging in behaviors that create change, and creating change requires influence. To be leaders, therefore, individuals need to have and effectively use influence (Hollander, 1985; Mintzberg, 1983). Influence is the power to affect others: the ability to produce outcomes due to some personal characteristic that gets others to follow (Pfeffer, 1992; Yukl, 1998). (Note, influence as defined here, is *not* force.)

By definition, influence is inherently interpersonal. Influence takes place within the context of interpersonal relationships. According to relational leadership theories, influence comes from relationships (Brower, Schoorman, & Tan, 2000; Graen & Uhl-Bien, 1995; Hollander & Offermann, 1990). Relational perspectives in leadership view leadership as generated through mutual influence that results from the development of trust, respect, and obligation among dyad members (Drath, 1998; Graen & Uhl-Bien, 1995; Uhl-Bien et al., 2000).

LMX theory describes this influence as being created through stages of relationship building (Graen, 1976; Graen & Scandura, 1987; Graen & Uhl-Bien, 1995; Uhl-Bien et al., 2000). Individuals begin at a "stranger" stage, get to know one another through testing processes, and as a result of the testing process, either progress to an advanced stage of leadership development (e.g., partnership) or remain at lower levels of relationship development (e.g., acquaintance or stranger) (for a detailed discussion of this, see Graen & Uhl-Bien, 1991a, 1991b, 1995; Uhl-Bien et al., 2000).

Those who attain more advanced stages of relationship building—and thus develop more effective relationships with interdependent others (e.g., managers and other higher-ups, subordinates, peers, clients, external constituents)—are able to more effectively perform their roles. More effective, or high-quality, leader–member exchanges are described as *leadership* rather than as *supervisory* relationships (Dansereau et al., 1975). High-quality relationships are considered mature partnerships based on respect, trust, and mutual obligation for one another (Graen & Uhl-Bien, 1995). These relationships go beyond the formal contract and generate personal power (i.e., influence given by the other), rather than position power or authority (Yukl, 1998). They are also characterized by willing followership, meaning employees are driven by intrinsic as opposed to extrinsic motivation (Steers et al., 1996). As a result, dyad partners (i.e., individuals engaged in an exchange) act because they *want* to, not because they have to. Research on LMX shows that more effectively developed relationships have significant and positive associations with performance, organizational commitment, employee citizenship behavior (i.e., extra-role behavior), job satisfaction, delegation and participation in decision making, and enhanced career development opportunities (for reviews, see Gerstner & Day, 1997; Graen & Uhl-Bien, 1995; Liden, Sparrowe, & Wayne, 1997). These relationships are negatively related to turnover, job problems, and role conflict and ambiguity (Dunegan, Uhl-Bien, & Duchon, 1992; Graen & Ginsburgh, 1977).

The benefits of high-quality relationships come from relational resources (Nahapiet & Ghoshal, 1998) they create. Such resources include durable obligations (e.g., arising from feelings of gratitude, respect, and friendship), network contacts and connections (including privileged access to information and opportunities, social status, and reputation of influential others), and the ability to have open information exchanges with those around them (Nahapiet & Ghoshal, 1998).

Relationships that do not develop so well are considered lower quality. These relationships are not as beneficial for the individuals involved or for the organization as a whole (Gerstner & Day, 1997; Liden et al., 1997). Lower quality relationships are described as contractually defined, formal exchanges based on limited trust and in-role interactions (Uhl-Bien et al., 2000). These types of relationships generate management rather than leadership. They are characterized by lack of mutual respect, formal downward communications, little mutual understanding, limited support and commitment for one another, and no mutual obligation (i.e., a "stranger" relationship) (Graen & Uhl-Bien, 1991a). Findings have shown that lower quality relationships are negatively related to satisfaction, organizational citizenship behaviors, and commitment, and are positively related to turnover (Gerstner & Day, 1997). Uhl-Bien and Maslyn (2003) recently found evidence of an even more extreme case of low-quality relationship, which is characterized by negative reciprocity, or an exchange of injuries (e.g., negative social exchange, Ruehlman & Karoly, 1991).

Thus, based on relational leadership theory, effective relationships may generate mutual influence and understanding that allow leaders to more effectively perform their roles.

Assumption 3. Leadership influence to create change is enabled by effective relationships.

Yet, despite the value of high-quality relationships for organizations, not all relationships are high quality. Given the findings from LMX theory, we know that low-quality relationships are not beneficial in terms of many aspects of organizational functioning, so they are not desirable in organizations, but they still are prevalent (Gerstner & Day, 1997). Moreover, in some cases we may even have negative, or dysfunctional relationships (Uhl-Bien & Maslyn, in press). Why is this, and what can we do about it? (See also Cogliser & Scandura, chap. 8, this volume, for additional implications of various types of LMX.)

BEYOND LMX DIFFERENTIATION

The LMX literature says that LMX differentiation, in which leaders have higher quality relationships with some subordinates and lower quality relationships with others, occurs because leaders do not have time (or the need) to generate high-quality relationships with everyone (Dansereau et al., 1975; Liden et al., 1997). Therefore, they develop a group of trusted assistants to help them perform the work of the unit. These trusted assistants would supposedly be the best or most reliable employees in the unit.

Twenty years after the inception of the theory, Graen and Uhl-Bien (1995) argued that the creation of "in-groups" and "out-groups" within work units is not beneficial, and that instead leaders should strive to develop high-quality relationships with *all* subordinates. They do this by "making the offer" of high-quality relationships to all and then through testing processes, different quality relationships result (Uhl-Bien et al., 2000). This perspective allows for the fact that all relationships may not (and likely will not) reach high quality, but at least the dyad members both take part in how the relationship develops (rather than the leader determining who will be the trusted assistants) and have the opportunity to create a high-quality relationship.

This perspective also recognizes that a focus on differentiation rather than on high-quality relationships offered to all creates tremendous opportunity for *lost potential* in organizations. As noted by Organ (1990), when individuals are not fully committed (or are dissatisfied), they will withdraw discretionary behaviors that benefit others or the organization (e.g., helping, altruism, civic behaviors). These discretionary behaviors are beneficial to the organization (Organ, 1988; Konovsky & Pugh, 1994), and as a result, much attention has been given in the literature to determining when and how individuals engage in these behaviors (Lambert, 2000; Organ & Ryan, 1995; Van Dyne, Graham, & Dienesch, 1994).

Instead of LMX differentiation, therefore, our goal should be for individuals to strive to have influence with one another (and with higher-ups). With the support of a relationship, individuals are freer to open up and provide one another with more accurate and complete information (Avolio, 1999) so they can provide the "real" information (the "real" story). This goes both ways: with a good relationship comes reduced filtering (holding back) of information, both up and down the hierarchy (Fairhurst & Sarr, 1996). It allows individuals to share with one another the hard truth. Too many leaders do not have good information, and too many hold back in being truthful with their subordinates (Fairhurst & Sarr, 1996). If we extend this beyond managers to leaders more broadly, then we can argue that organizational members need to be comfortable with providing information to one another, and this comes with having effective work relationships (Avolio, 1999).

Remembering that effective leaders are defined as those who use influence to create change, individuals' abilities to be effective leaders are directly related to their ability to have influence in the organization. Since effective work relationships can extend individuals' influence networks (Brass & Krackhardt, 1999), those who have more effective relationships with others will likely have more opportunity to gain and use influence (Hollander & Offermann, 1990). Therefore, leadership effectiveness is likely enhanced by the ability to build effective work relationships with a broader range of interdependent others (Avolio, 1999).

Proposition 1a. Leadership effectiveness is enhanced by the individual's ability to build effective work relationships with interdependent others.

Moreover, given the benefits of high-quality relationships and the lost potential (Organ, 1990) or harm of low-quality relationships (Uhl-Bien & Maslyn, in press), more effective work situations are those with leader/managers who develop more high-quality relationships or fewer low-quality relationships.

Proposition 1b. More effective leaders are those who are able to build relationships with a wider range of others (rather than with only a select few).

A NEW TWIST ON
RELATIONSHIP DEVELOPMENT

Both of the approaches (described previously) regarding LMX differentiation are highly manager driven: The "leader" is the primary responsible party for the quality of the relationship, either by selecting the trusted cadre (Dansereau et al., 1975) or by making offers to all (Graen & Uhl-Bien, 1995; Uhl-Bien et al., 2000). The notion of leader control seems to be an assumption throughout LMX and leadership research (Yukl, 1998). As noted by Lord and Emrich (2001), the leadership literature often assumes that causality (for leadership) originates in a leader, but this is likely an oversimplification, because leadership processes always involve an interaction of leader, subordinate, and contextual qualities.

Recently, Maslyn and Uhl-Bien (2001) considered manager–subordinate relationship development from the standpoint of investigating who put effort into the relationship development: the manager or the subordinate. Consistent with reciprocity and social-exchange perspectives (Gouldner, 1960; Homans, 1958), the findings showed that *own* effort in relationship development was not significant, but *other* effort was highly significant. In other words, both parties were responsible for relationship development through the amount of effort that each perceived the other to have put into the relationship (e.g., norm of reciprocity, Gouldner, 1960). Moreover, these findings were consistent across managers and subordinates. This suggests that perhaps we need to rethink some traditional notions about how relationships develop to focus more generally on the roles and responsibilities of both dyad members in relationship building.

We may also need to rethink commonly accepted conceptualizations about what constitutes a high-quality relationship. In a criticism of LMX theory, House and Aditya (1997) stated that high-quality relationships have been identified in the literature as having trust, respect, mutual obligation (loyalty) and influence, and wide latitude for discretion. House and Aditya (1997) pointed out, however, that these may not be universal attributes of high-quality relationships. In other words, ideas about what is considered to be a high-quality relationship may, and likely will, vary according to the members of the relationship. Moreover, it suggests that we need to more carefully consider the antecedents to relationship development relative to what each dyad member wants from the relationship.

Implicit Relational Theories

Taken together, and combined with new perspectives to be discussed here, these ideas present some very interesting possibilities regarding how we may view the development of managerial relationships in the workplace. First, considering relationship development specifically, it is possible that some relationships are easier, more "natural" to form than others. For example, in some relationships individuals may "hit it off" from the beginning, for whatever reason. This could be because they have complementary personalities, common values, congruent perspectives or interpersonal styles, similar backgrounds, and so on, such that the relationship gets off to a good start and just keeps going, with neither member really thinking about or consciously managing the process. Other relationships, however, may be much harder to develop due to personality differences, style differences, incongruent values, and so on, that make it more difficult for dyad members to build the relational components necessary for higher quality relationships. These relationships that are less compatible and require more effort to develop may be the ones that result in lower quality relationships. In contrast, those that are easier to develop may become the higher quality relationships.

Extending this logic, it is possible that LMX differentiation may be related to what I will term *relational favorability*, or the extent to which conditions are favorable or unfavorable for the development of the relationship. This could include a wide range of variables, such as personality characteristics, value congruence, job/organization fit, task characteristics, unit size, demographics, etc. Although LMX literature has attempted to identify antecedents to LMX relationships (Bauer & Green, 1996; Duchon, Green, & Taber, 1986; Phillips & Bedeian, 1994; Wayne & Ferris, 1990), we still know little about what leads to higher and lower LMX and, with the exception of work on relational demography (Bauer & Green, 1996; Duchon et al., 1986; Green, Anderson, & Shivers, 1996), this line of investigation has not taken on a strong relational focus.

To advance understanding of relational leadership theory and leadership development, more work needs to be conducted investigating issues regarding relational favorability. Specifically, we need to better understand both interpersonal (i.e., relational) and contextual situations that foster effective relationships and interpersonal and contextual situations that work against them.

Taking the concept of relational favorability one step further, it is possible that relational favorability from an interpersonal standpoint (versus a contextual or work environment standpoint) may be associated with implicit relational theories. The concept of implicit leadership theories (ILTs) has had a strong presence in the leadership literature (Eden & Leviatan, 1975; Gioia & Sims, 1985; Lord, Foti, &

DeVader, 1984; Offermann, Kennedy, & Wirtz, 1994), but the concept of an implicit *relational* theory has not been considered.

ILTs examine the extent to which followers recognize leaders based on their fit with leadership prototypes that followers hold (Lord & Emrich, 2001; Lord & Maher, 1991). Prototypes are expectations about patterns of traits, skills, and behaviors of leaders and are developed and refined over time as a result of experiences with leaders and social–cultural influences (Rush, Thomas, & Lord, 1977). Once someone matches the follower's prototype (e.g., is labeled an effective or ineffective leader), subsequent information is filtered through the ILT, to the extent that followers may have difficulty determining actual behaviors from the behaviors associated with the ILT. Leaders who do things inconsistently with follower prototypes would be considered less favorably than those who conform to the ILT, and these perceptions would then affect subsequent attitudes and behaviors of the follower.

The ILT cognitive approach has contributed greatly to our understanding of how followers perceive and react to leaders (Lord & Emrich, 2001). Though this approach addresses interactions and cognitive behavioral interpretations that occur between a follower (subordinate) and a leader (manager), it does not address *relationships*. The distinction between an ILT and an implicit *relational* theory (IRT), therefore, would be that the latter focuses specifically on relationships: *what are the prototypes individuals hold regarding work relationships?* An IRT would be the beliefs and assumptions about the characteristics of effective relationships (distinguishing between work and personal relationships). This is a broader perspective, because IRT allows for schemas addressing a broader set of roles beyond the leader role (e.g., relationships with followers, coworkers, higher-ups, etc.). For example, individuals might hold global implicit relational schemas for professional or work relationships and then hold more specific implicit relational schemas that would address different types of relationships (e.g., with managers, subordinates, coworkers, higher-ups, etc.).

Therefore, it can be argued that just as individuals hold ILTs, they also hold IRTs, which consist of prototypical traits and behaviors that they expect relational partners to demonstrate. When dyad partners exhibit these prototypes, interpersonal favorability is higher, and relationship development to more advanced stages of relationship building is facilitated. Examination of IRTs and how they are associated with concepts of relational favorability may help provide the next step in advancing understanding about leadership relationship development.

Proposition 2. Individuals have *relationship prototypes* that are part of their implicit relational theories for their work relationships.

Proposition 3. If a dyad partner matches an individual's relational prototype, interpersonal relational favorability is higher and the relationship will be more likely to develop into a higher quality relationship. Conversely, if a dyad partner does not match an individual's relational prototype, interpersonal relational favorability is lower and the relationship will be less likely to develop into a higher quality relationship.

Relational Skills

The propositions just presented may not hold for all individuals, however. It may be that some individuals are able to develop effective work relationships even in situations of relational "unfavorability." Moreover, some individuals may be able to manage their implicit relational schemas such that, in situations of high need for relationship development (e.g., high interdependency), they may be able to develop effective relationships, even with those who do not initially match their prototypical relational schemas. For these individuals, they may be able to modify their cognitive representation of what constitutes a high-quality relationship to meet their situational needs, realizing that effective work relationships are necessary for personal success in organizations.

Such individuals could be considered to be higher in *relational skills*. In contrast to interpersonal, or social, skills (the ability to interact effectively with others), relational skills can be identified as the skills necessary to build effective and lasting work relationships (with a variety of people and across varying task situations). The distinction between interpersonal or social and relational skills is in their focus. Interpersonal and social skills focus on interacting to present a good image of oneself, being able to persuade and influence the other person to meet one's interpersonal goals. Relational skills focus specifically on actions taken in the context of a relationship with the objective of building effective relationships that are mutually beneficial and enduring. Although the distinction may seem subtle, I believe it offers a critical and valuable addition to leadership development literature. This value lies in the explicit distinction between those who are able to make themselves look good in interactions (high interpersonal and social skills) and those who understand the qualities necessary to build effective work relationships (high relational skills).

Relational skills comprise components of emotional intelligence (EI) (Goleman, 1995) and social skills (Riggio, 1986; Riggio & Zimmerman, 1991). However, they differ in that relational skills focus specifically on relationship building, whereas social skills and EI approaches do not fully address this. Because of this, they single out specific dimensions of social skills and EI that address relationship building, as well as add dimensions not previously described in those literatures, particularly testing processes and reciprocity (Gouldner, 1960; Uhl-Bien et al., 2000).

For example, social skills are the skills involved in the basic sending, receiving, and controlling of information relative to emotional-nonverbal and social-verbal domains (Riggio, 1986; Riggio & Zimmerman, 1991). Emotional intelligence is "the ability to monitor one's own and others' feelings and emotions, to discriminate among them and to use this information to guide one's thinking and actions"

(Salovey & Mayer, 1990, p. 189). It reflects a composite of distinct emotional rea-soning abilities: perceiving emotions (understanding and interpreting the meaning of various emotional states and their relation to other sensory experiences), under-standing emotions (interpreting how basic emotions are blended to form complex emotions, whether various emotional reactions are likely in given social settings), and regulating emotions (controlling emotions in oneself and in others) (Goleman, 1995; Mayer & Salovey, 1997). Although both address interpersonal skills, as can be seen by these definitions, neither explicitly describes the processes and objectives of relationship building.

Relational skills fill in the gaps left in these approaches by addressing the skills necessary to establish and maintain effective interpersonal relationships with others. (I focus here on work relationships.) Relational skills include character-istics such as: (a) an understanding of the testing process in relationship build-ing (reciprocity) (Uhl-Bien et al., 2000; Uhl-Bien & Maslyn, in press); (b) social skills, since they address self-presentation and dyadic communication skills neces-sary for relationship building (e.g., emotional expressivity, emotional sensitivity, emotional control, social expressivity, social sensitivity, social control, Riggio, 1986; Riggio & Zimmerman, 1991); (c) relational self-management skills (self-correcting behavior, ability to accept negative feedback from a dyad partner and use it to adapt accordingly, taking blame/accepting responsibility for failed actions in the relationship); and (d) relational feedback giving (effectiveness in addressing difficult/sensitive issues in a way that the other will listen; not avoiding difficult subjects with the other).

Relational skills may also involve awareness of one's implicit relational schemas and the ability to manage the potential inhibiting effects of these schemas. For example, one's implicit relational schema may include affect (i.e., liking) as a critical aspect of an effective relationship. To develop effective work relationships, however, affect may not really be a critical component (Graen & Uhl-Bien, 1995). In other words, it is not likely that individuals will always (or often) *like* the people with whom they work (Uhl-Bien et al., 2000). For individuals high in relational skills they may recognize the need to develop high-quality relationships even with those they do not like, and manage/adjust their schema to disregard or downplay the lack of affect and its mismatch with their relational prototype. This may subsequently involve their making adjustments to their schema to reduce affect as a necessary prototype. Those lower in relational skills may not understand the effect their relational schema is having on them and, therefore, they perceive the dyad partner as not a good match and engage in behaviors that would not lead to development of a higher quality relationship (potentially without ever realizing what happened).

Because building relationships is a complicated (and sometimes treacherous) process, some people may understand how to better navigate the many stages of relationship development, whereas others are not as aware of these processes. Consistent with the previous suggestions, individuals lower in relational skills would likely be those who can develop effective relationships in situations that are favorable to relationship building (and match their implicit schema), whereas individuals higher in relational skills would be able to read the signs of the various stages of relationship development and make necessary adjustments to ensure that high-quality relationships result.

This discussion suggests two propositions regarding relational skills and relationship development. The first is a main effect of relational skills, proposing that individuals higher in relational skills will be generally more effective at relationship building across a variety of situations and with various types of others. The second is a moderator effect of the relationship predicted in Proposition 3. Specifically, an individual's relational skills may moderate the relationship between prototype match and quality of relationship development.

Proposition 4.   Individuals higher in relational skills will be more effective at relationship building (and demonstrate a record of more effective relationship building) than individuals lower in relational skills.

Proposition 5.   Relational skills will moderate the relationship between prototype match and quality of relationship development, such that individuals higher in relational skills will be more likely to develop high-quality relationships even in situations of relational "unfavorability" than individuals lower in relational skills.

In summary, the arguments presented in this paper suggest that effective leadership involves generating effective relationships with interdependent others. Individuals who know how to build relationships are considered high in relational skills. They use these skills to develop high-quality relationships with those with whom they interact and understand that effective relationships with others produce positive relational resources. These relational resources increase their ability to influence others to create change. In such a way, leadership is not reserved for those in formal leadership roles but may be exhibited by any individual who works to use influence to create change.

IMPLICATIONS FOR LEADERSHIP DEVELOPMENT: A FOCUS ON RELATIONSHIP BUILDING

Thinking of leadership in this way creates a range of possibilities for *leadership* development (as contrasted with leader development, Day, 2000; Day & O'Connor, chap. 1, this volume). The main contribution of the viewpoint presented here is in the suggestion that, consistent with Day (2000) and Drath (1998; Drath & Palus, 1994), leadership development should not be reserved for those in managerial positions (or those *targeted* for managerial positions) but should be offered to *all* organizational members. Leadership development activities should focus on demonstrating to individuals how they may generate influence to create positive change. In this way, organizational members should understand that leadership is a behavior, not a role, and therefore can be exhibited regardless of the position one occupies.

This perspective allows for a broader view of leadership development activities because it recognizes leadership wherever it occurs and is not restricted to formal leaders. It focuses on leadership at the dyadic level as a two-way influence process between dyad members. This new way of thinking recognizes that leaders are only as good as their followers—there is no leadership without followers who allow leaders to influence them. In this way, a much-needed emphasis is placed on the critical role of "followers" (e.g., subordinates) in the leadership process. To advance theory and practice regarding these issues, future research needs to investigate questions including, how can subordinates help their leaders be more effective (i.e., what is effective "followership")? How can subordinates demonstrate leadership in follower roles? How should leadership development opportunities be tailored differently to individuals in subordinate roles versus those in formal leadership roles?

The views presented here also address issues related to relationship building. Relationships were argued to be beneficial for enabling leaders to have influence, such that individuals better at developing relationships will have greater opportunity to demonstrate leadership influence. Therefore, knowledge of relationship building should enhance leadership efforts within organizations. For leadership development, this means that individuals need to be trained on how to build relationships. An explicit focus on relational skills, rather than a more general focus on interpersonal/social skills or emotional intelligence, could greatly enhance leadership development efforts.

This chapter also has several important implications for LMX theory. An assumption of LMX theory has been that leaders manage relationship building processes by either identifying those with whom they will develop high LMX or making offers to all subordinates to provide opportunities for high LMX. This chapter suggests a more active role of followers in this process. Followers who more proactively manage their relationship development (by understanding relationship-building processes) may be more effective at generating high-quality relationships. In this way, relationship development is the responsibility of both managers and subordinates. Given the benefits of high-quality relationships and costs of low-quality relationships, organizations that focus development efforts on relationship building may benefit from a higher number of effective work relationships.

The introduction of concepts of relational favorability and implicit relational theories are offered to the LMX literature to address critical questions that remain about antecedents to LMX. Although we have studied LMX for almost 30 years, we still know very little about what contributes to the development of high- and low-quality relationships. Examining these issues from the standpoint of relational favorability can help us identify factors that facilitate or detract from effective relationship development. Relational favorability should be considered from the standpoint of interpersonal favorability (e.g., relational/interpersonal characteristics) and of situational/contextual characteristics (e.g., task situation, person–job fit, person–organization fit, organizational change context, etc.). Examination of implicit relational schemas can help identify variables that individuals consider important in work relationships and how these variables affect individuals' attitudes and behaviors during relationship development.

Finally, as far as implications for research more generally, this paper makes several critical assumptions that need to be examined in future research. The first is that by training individuals in relationship building and influence skills, they will be able to develop a broader range of high-quality relationships. It is assumed that these skills can be identified and that they are trainable. The second is that effective leaders are those who are able to develop a broader range of relationships. Leadership effectiveness is assumed to come in these cases from relational resources generated by the relationships. The third is that having more high-quality relationships will enhance organizational capabilities. Consistent with social capital perspectives, high-quality leadership relationships should help transform human capital into social capital for the organization. Although these arguments make intuitive sense and are supported by leadership literature, their validity and value for organizational effectiveness and leadership development need to be examined.

CONCLUSION

Day's (2000) distinction between leader development and leadership development was a critical first step in focusing much-needed attention on the role of relationship building for leadership development. This chapter builds on the ideas presented by Day (2000) by specifically addressing how relational leadership and LMX theory can contribute to research and practice on leadership development. Although the work presented here does not pretend to fully address the entire depth or complexity of thinking on leadership needed to design, evaluate, and improve leadership development efforts for the present and future (Day, 2000; Day & O'Connor, this volume), it does provide new perspectives and ideas to initiate efforts for building a framework for leadership development. Moreover, it identifies new directions for LMX theorists in the hopes that future research will work to better address the critical question regarding relationship building: What causes some relationships to develop better than others? By answering this question, LMX will be able to make a more valuable contribution to leadership development and to relational leadership theory.

REFERENCES

Avolio, B. (1999). *Full leadership development: Building the vital forces in organizations.* Thousand Oaks, CA: Sage.

Bauer, T., & Green, S. (1996). Development of leader-member exchange: A longitudinal test. *Academy of Management Journal, 39*(6), 1538–1567.

Blau, P. (1964). *Exchange and power in social life.* New York: Wiley.

Bordieu, P. (1986). The forms of capital. In J. G. Richardson (Ed.), *Handbook of theory and research for the sociology of education* (pp. 241–258). New York: Greenwood.

Bouty, I. (2000). Interpersonal and interaction influences on informal resource exchanges between R&D researchers across organizational boundaries. *Academy of Management Journal, 43,* 50–65.

Brass, D. J., & Krackhardt, D. (1999). The social capital of 21st century leaders. In J. G. Hunt, G. E. Dodge, & L. Wong (Eds.),*Out-of-the box leadership. Transforming the 21st century army and other top performing organizations* (pp. 179–194). Greenwich, CT: JAI Press.

Brower, H. H., Schoorman, F. D., & Tan, H. H. (2000). A model of relational leadership: The integration of trust and leader-member exchange. *Leadership Quarterly, 11,* 227–250.

Dansereau, F., Graen, G., & Haga, W. (1975). A vertical dyad linkage approach to leadership in formal organizations. *Organizational Behavior and Human Performance, 13,* 46–78.

Day, D. V. (2000). Leadership development: A review in context. *Leadership Quarterly, 11*(4), 581–613.

Drath, W. H. (1998). Approaching the future of leadership development. In C. D. McCauley, R. S. Moxley, & E. Van Velsor (Eds.), *The center for creative leadership handbook of leadership development* (pp. 403–432). San Francisco: Jossey-Bass.

Drath, W., & Palus, C. (1994). *Making common sense: Leadership as meaning-making in a community of practice.* Greensboro, NC: Center for Creative Leadership.

Duchon, D., Green, S. G., & Taber, T. D. (1986). Vertical dyad linkage: A longitudinal assessment of antecedents, measures, and consequences. *Journal of Applied Psychology, 71,* 56–60.

Dunegan, K. J., Uhl-Bien, M., & Duchon, D. (1992). *Task-level climate and LMX as interactive predictors of performance.* Paper presented at the Academy of Management annual meeting, Las Vegas, NV.

Eden, D., & Leviatan, U. (1975). Implicit leadership theory as a determinant of the factor structure underlying supervisory behavior scales. *Journal of Applied Psychology, 60,* 736–741.

Etzioni, A. (1961). *A comparative analysis of complex organizations.* New York: The Free Press.

Fairhurst, G. T., & Sarr, R. A. (1996). *The art of framing: Managing the language of leadership.* San Francisco: Jossey-Bass.

Fiedler, F. E. (1996). Research on leadership selection and training: One view of the future. *Administrative Science Quarterly, 41,* 241–250.

Follett, M. P. (1941). In H. S. Metcalf, and L. Urwick, (Eds.), *Dynamic administration: The collected papers of Mary Parker Follett.* New York: Harper & Row.

Gerstner, C. R., & Day, D. V. (1997). A meta-analytic review of leader-member exchange theory: Constructs and issues. *Journal of Applied Psychology, 82*(6), 827–844.

Gioia, D. A., & Sims, H. P., Jr. (1985). On avoiding the influence of implicit leadership theories in leader behavior descriptions. *Journal of Educational and Psychological Measurement, 45,* 217–237.

Goleman, D. (1995). *Emotional intelligence: Why it can matter more than IQ.* New York: Bantam Books.

Gouldner, A. W. (1960). The norm of reciprocity: A preliminary statement. *American Sociological Review, 25,* 161–177.

Graen, G. B. (1976). Role making processes within complex organizations. In M. D. Dunnette (Ed.), *Handbook of industrial and organizational psychology* (pp. 1201–1245). Chicago: Rand-McNally.

Graen, G. B., & Ginsburgh, S. (1977). Job resignation as a function of role orientation and leader acceptance: A longitudinal investigation of organizational assimilation. *Organizational Behavior and Human Performance*, 19, 1–17.

Graen, G., Novak, M., & Sommerkamp, P. (1982). The effects of leader-member exchange and job design on productivity and satisfaction: Testing a dual attachment model. *Organizational Behavior and Human Performance*, 30, 109–131.

Graen, G. B., & Scandura, T. (1987). Toward a psychology of dyadic organizing. In B. Staw and L. L. Cummings (Eds.), *Research in organizational behavior* (Vol. 9, pp. 175–208). Greenwich, CT: JAI Press.

Graen, G., & Uhl-Bien, M. (1991a). The transformation of professionals into self-managing and partially self-designing contributors: Toward a theory of leadership-making. *Journal of Management Systems*, 3(3), 33–48.

Graen, G. B., & Uhl-Bien, M. (1991b). Partnership-making applies equally well to teammate-sponsor, teammate-competence network, and teammate-teammate relationships. *Journal of Management Systems*, 3(3), 49–54.

Graen, G. B., & Uhl-Bien, M. (1995). Relationship-based approach to leadership: Development of leader-member exchange (LMX) theory of leadership over 25 years: Applying a multi-level multi-domain perspective. *The Leadership Quarterly*, 6(2), 219–247.

Green, S. G., Anderson, S. E., & Shivers, S. L. (1996). An examination of organizational constraints on leader-member exchange. *Organizational Behavior and Human Decision Processes*, 66, 203–214.

Hollander, E. P. (1985). Leadership and power. In G. Lindzey & E. Aronson (Eds.), *The handbook of social psychology* (3rd ed., pp. 485–537). New York: Random House.

Hollander, E. P., & Offermann, L. R. (1990). Power and leadership in organizations: Relationships in transition. *American Psychologist*, 45(2), 179–189.

Homans, G. C. (1958). Social behavior as exchange. *American Journal of Sociology*, 63, 597–606.

House, R. J., & Aditya, R. (1997). The social scientific study of leadership: Quo vidis? *Journal of Management*, 23, 409–474.

Hunt, J. G., & Dodge, G. E. (2001). Leadership déjà vu all over again. *Leadership Quarterly*, 11(4), 435–458.

Katz, D., & Kahn, R. L. (1978). *The social psychology of organizations* (2nd ed.). New York: Wiley.

Konovsky, M., & Pugh, S. (1994). Citizenship behavior and social exchange. *Academy of Management Journal*, 37, 656–669.

Kotter, J. (2001, December). What leaders really do. *Harvard Business Review*, 85–96.

Lambert, S. J. (2000). Added benefits: The link between work-life benefits and organizational citizenship behavior. *Academy of Management Journal*, 43(5), 801–815.

Liden, R. C., Sparrowe, R. T., & Wayne, S. J. (1997). Leader-member exchange theory: The past and potential for the future. In G. R. Ferris & K. M. Rowland (Eds.), *Research in personnel and human resources management* (Vol. 15, pp. 47–119). Greenwich, CT: JAI Press.

Lord, R., & Emrich, C. (2001). Thinking outside the box by looking inside the box: Extending the cognitive revolution in leadership research. *Leadership Quarterly*, 11(4), 551–579.

Lord, R., Foti, R., & DeVader, C. (1984). A test of leadership categorization theory: Internal structure, information processing, and leadership perceptions. *Organizational Behavior and Human Performance*, 34, 343–378.

Lord, R., & Maher, K. (1991). *Leadership and information processing: Linking perceptions and performance*. Boston: Unwin-Hyman.

Mayer, J. D., & Salovey, P. (1997). What is emotional intelligence? In P. Salovey & D. J. Sluyter (Eds.), *Emotional development and emotional intelligence* (pp. 3–31). New York: Basic Books.

Maslyn, J., & Uhl-Bien, M. (2001). Leader-member exchange and its dimensions: Effects of self and other effort on relationship quality. *Journal of Applied Psychology*, 86(4), 697–708.

Mayfield, M., & Mayfield, J. (1996). A test of the moderating effects of job autonomy on LMX outcomes: A meta-analysis with performance and job satisfaction. *Proceedings of the 38th Annual Meeting of the Southwest Academy of Management*, 251–255.

Mayfield, J., & Mayfield, M. (1998). Increasing worker outcomes by improving leader follower relations. *The Journal of Leadership Studies, 5*(1), 72–81.

McCall, M. W. (1998). *High flyers: Developing the next generation of leaders.* Boston: Harvard Business School Press.

Mintzberg, H. (1983). *Power in and around organizations.* Englewood Cliffs, NJ: Prentice-Hall.

Nahapiet, J., & Ghoshal, S. (1998). Social capital, intellectual capital, and the organizational advantage. *Academy of Management Review, 23*(2), 242–266.

Offermann, L., Kennedy, J., & Wirtz, P. (1994). Implicit leadership theories: Content, structure, and generalizability. *Leadership Quarterly, 5*, 43–58.

Organ, D. W. (1988). *Organizational citizenship behavior: The good soldier syndrome.* Lexington, MA: Lexington Books.

Organ, D. W. (1990). The subtle significance of job satisfaction. *Clinical Laboratory Management Review, 4*(1), 94–98.

Organ, D. W., & Ryan, K. (1995). A meta-analytic review of attitudinal and dispositional predictors of OCB. *Personnel Psychology, 48*(4), 775–802.

Pfeffer, J. (1992). *Managing with power: Power and influence in organizations.* Boston: Harvard Business School Press.

Phillips, A. S., & Bedeian, A. G. (1994). Leader-follower exchange quality: The role of personal and interpersonal attributes. *Academy of Management Journal, 37*, 990–1001.

Riggio, R. (1986). Assessment of basic social skills. *Journal of Personality and Social Psychology, 51*(3), 649–660.

Riggio, R., & Zimmerman, J. (1991). Social skills and interpersonal relationships: Influences on social support and support seeking. *Advances in Personal Relationships, 2*, 133–155.

Ruehlman, L. S., & Karoly, P. (1991). With a little flak from my friends: Development and preliminary validation of the Test of Negative Social Exchange (TENSE). *Psychological Assessment, 3*, 97–104.

Rush, M., Thomas, J., & Lord, R. (1977). Implicit leadership theory: A potential threat to the validity of leadership behavior questionnaires. *Organizational Behavior and Human Performance, 20*, 93–110.

Salancik, G., Calder, B., Rowland, K., Leblebici, H., & Conway, M. (1975). Leadership as an outcome of social structure and process: A multidimensional analysis. In J. G. Hunt & L. L. Larson (Eds.), *Leadership frontiers* (pp. 81–101). Kent, OH: Kent State University.

Salovey, P., & Mayer, J. D. (1990). Emotional intelligence. *Imagination, Cognition, and Personality, 9*, 185–211.

Schuler, R., & MacMillan, I. C. (1984). Gaining competitive advantage through human resource management practices. *Human Resource Management, 23*(3), 241–255.

Steers, R., Porter, L., & Bigley, G. (1996). *Motivation and leadership at work.* New York: McGraw-Hill.

Uhl-Bien, M., Graen, G., & Scandura, T. (2000). Implications of leader-member exchange (LMX) for strategic human resource management systems: Relationships as social capital for competitive advantage. In G. R. Ferris (Ed.), *Research in personnel and human resources management* (Vol. 18, pp. 137–185). Greenwich, CT: JAI Press.

Uhl-Bien, M., & Maslyn, J. (in press). Reciprocity in manager-subordinate relationships: Components, configurations and outcomes. Journal of Management.

Van Dyne, L., Graham, J. W., & Dienesch, R. M. (1994). Organizational citizenship behavior: Construct definition, measurement, and validation. *Academy of Management Journal, 37*(4), 765–802.

Wayne, S. J., & Ferris, G. R. (1990). Influence tactics, affect, and exchange quality in supervisor-subordinate dyads. *Journal of Applied Psychology, 75*, 487–499.

Wenger, E. (1998). *Communities in practice: Learning, meaning, and identity.* Cambridge, UK: Cambridge University.

Whitener, E. (2000, August). *The processes of building social capital in organizations: The integrating role of trust.* Paper presented at the Academy of Management Annual Meeting, Toronto, Canada.

Yukl, G. A. (1998). *Leadership in organizations (4th ed.).* Upper Saddle River, NJ: Prentice-Hall.

8

Waterfalls, Snowballs, Brick Walls, and Scuzzballs: Does Leader–Member Exchange Up the Line Influence Leader Development?

Claudia C. Cogliser
University of Oklahoma

Terri A. Scandura
University of Miami

Organizations today are facing a looming leadership crisis. A combination of factors—massive retirements (both from large-scale hiring during the Eisenhower years and younger executives who are retiring early due to money gained from stock options and investments), lack of planning for executive succession, elimination of middle-management positions—have resulted in statistically fewer people available for top-management slots (Caudron, 1999; Marshall-Mies et al., 2000; Schafer, 2001). Executive succession has been shown to account for up to 40% of the variance in organizational performance (Day & Lord, 1988). Companies now have to compete in an aggressive market for qualified individuals who have the appropriate leadership skill mix. Some have suggested that the only effective means to combat this crisis is by growing and developing the needed talent from within the organization (Caudron, 1999). Yet, getting the right persons groomed for executive leadership positions is no easy task. The example of the problems experienced by Xerox under Richard Thoman is a poignant reminder of the importance of having the right pool of talent *within* the firm. In a sense, the Xerox executive succession system failed because they had to hire someone from outside the company who did not fit the organizational culture. Yet leadership development programs targeting internal leadership talent may not be a panacea or even a palliative for today's leadership crisis. *Training & Development* journal recently reported on the state of leadership and executive development programs:

> The disparate experiences [of leadership development programs] we described have some things in common, and they illustrate some of the flaws in current leadership development. Everyone running those programs was doing what seemed best at the time. They used the latest teaching and learning methods. They wanted to make a difference in the lives of the participants. The executives from the client companies that sponsored the activities believed in the importance of developing their key people. They willingly spent money and gave participants time off from work. The immediate results were some new ideas, a broadened perspective, new ways of framing problems, and some new tools.
>
> The ultimate outcomes of those programs also had much in common. There was no evidence of permanent improvement or that the participants were better leaders in the end—and that ostensibly, was the purpose for which the programs were given. (Zenger, Ulrich, & Smallwood, 2000, p. 22)

Despite this gloomy forecast, we believe that a focus on relationship development between supervisors and subordinates can have an impact on the extent to which subordinates can develop high-quality relationships with their own subordinates, an essential leadership skill. Our focus in this paper uses the leader–member exchange (LMX) framework, whose basic premise is that variation occurs in the quality of the relationship between a leader and each of his or her direct reports, such that the leader might have a high-quality relationship with one subordinate and a poor relationship with another, rather than adopting similar behaviors or a leadership style across subordinates. A high-quality exchange is characterized by positive leadership processes that are indicative of a social exchange, such as increased subordinate job latitude and influence in decision making, more open and honest subordinate communication with the supervisor, and greater trust and loyalty among dyad members (Cogliser & Schriesheim, 2000; Duchon, Green, & Taber, 1986; Scandura, Graen, & Novak, 1986; Settoon, Bennett, & Liden, 1996; see also, Uhl-Bien, chap. 7, this volume). Low-quality LMX relationships are more economic or transactional in nature, and dyadic behaviors rarely progress beyond what is specified in the employment contract. With regard to leadership development, those subordinates interested in leadership development receive it as part of the relationship contract. Those that are not interested in becoming leaders do not receive leadership development as part of their psychological contract and receive a different allocation of on-the-job training.

The purpose of our paper is to develop a framework that explores whether the relationship behavior of a leader influences the leadership relationship behavior of his or her followers. Our paper raises several questions. Does a subordinate who has a high-quality exchange with his or her boss then go on to develop high-quality exchanges with his or her own subordinates? That is, does LMX cascade like a waterfall throughout the hierarchical levels of the organization? If one has a good relationship with one's superior, does that person work to develop an even better relationship with his or her own subordinates? What types of LMX relationships develop when one has an extremely poor LMX relationship with his or her boss ("toxic leadership")—better ones? Worse ones? Or instead, is the relationship with one's boss independent of the relationships that are developed among followers? The development of our leadership similarity framework follows in the next section.

Research Support for Cascade Effects at Different Hierarchical Levels

Likert (1961) proposed that effective organizations have units that are tied together, through "linking-pin" positions, where members in these organizations become more aware of problems at lower levels in the system and coordinate activities efficiently through accurate flows of information, influence, and resources among the units involved. The persons occupying these linking-pin positions are integrated members in two or more groups and play the role of both supervisor and subordinate. Graen and his colleagues explored the effectiveness of the LMX relationship between incumbents of linking-pin positions and their supervisors and the behavior, attitudes, and treatment of lower level members (Graen, Cashman, Ginsburgh, & Schiemann, 1977). They found that the quality of LMX of the linking-pin incumbent was related to the quality of working life of the followers who reported to the linking pin. When subordinates develop high-quality exchanges with their bosses, they receive greater influence, latitude, support, and attention from their bosses, and they experience a more desirable situation overall. These researchers continued by pointing out that the quality of members in a higher dyad (hierarchically) contributed to the quality of life of members in hierarchically lower dyads. We used this linking-pin concept to build our conceptualization of LMX at one level influencing LMX at a different level.

We found support in the broader leadership literature for the fact that followers' behaviors or attitudes are positively associated with their supervisor's leadership behaviors or attitudes over time. Stogdill (1955) found that participatory leadership at higher levels in the organization was related to its being practiced at lower levels in the organizational hierarchy. Bowers and Seashore (1966) demonstrated that followers' attitudes and behaviors—their emphasis on goals and interaction facilitation—were positively related to the extent to which their supervisors exhibited similar behaviors and attitudes. Michaelson (1973) found that the values of upper-level supervisors accounted for more variance in lower level supervisor's behavior than did the lower level supervisor's own values. Ouchi and Maguire (1975) found the superiors and followers used similar control methods for dealing with subordinates. Misumi (1985) discovered that both supervisors and subordinates within the same unit adopted similar leadership styles with their followers.

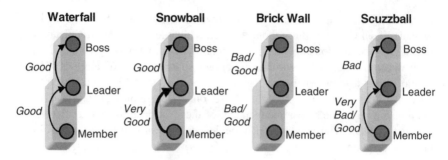

FIG. 8.1. Linking-pin dyads and nature of relationship of LMX between member and leader and between leader and boss.

Bass, Waldman, Avolio, and Bebb (1987) found that transformational leadership behavior at one level was related to similar behavior at the next lower level. Bass (1990) pointed out that these findings suggested that followers tend to emulate or model the leadership behavior and attitudes they see displayed by their supervisors, lending support for the waterfall effect of leadership. An alternative explanation provided was that hierarchically lower supervisors are self-selected, selected by the next level manager, or organizationally selected so that they will be compatible with their superiors.

We located only one published LMX study that discussed the effect of leader LMX behavior on subordinates' leadership behaviors. Graen and Cashman (1975) highlighted the importance of the leader's providing cues for subordinate behaviors. They found that subordinates enlarged their interests to match more closely those of their leader and that followers attempted to increase esteem in the eyes of their leader through ingratiation. The mechanism for this is consistent with the Dansereau et al. (1998) model of individualized leadership, which asserts that leaders influence particular subordinates by reinforcing these subordinates' sense of self-worth.

As shown in Fig. 8.1, we believed there could be four types of relationships when comparing the LMX of a hierarchically superior dyad and the LMX of the dyad directly below. We have characterized these relationships as (a) Waterfalls, (b) Snowballs, (c) Brick Walls, and (d) Scuzzballs.[1]

Waterfalls. Viewing leadership phenomena as a waterfall has alternatively been labeled "falling dominoes" or "cascading leadership" (Bass et al., 1987); the basic premise from an LMX perspective is that your relationship with your boss may lead you to have similar types of relationships with your own subordinates.

---

[1] The authors wish to thank Ed Locke for his contribution of "Scuzzballs" to our title and theoretical framework. He used this term during the 11th Annual Kravis deRoulet Leadership Conference at Claremont McKenna College in March 2001, and we felt it superbly portrayed a leader displaying toxic leadership behaviors.

Our research question is thus: If you have high LMX with your boss, do you develop similarly high LMX relationships with your subordinates? Bass (1990) proposed that subordinates are converted into effective leaders when dedication, caring, and participation of their charismatic leader (who has many overlapping behaviors and attitudes with high LMX superiors) cascades down through successive hierarchical levels. High LMX leaders can raise self-esteem and confidence in followers, who are inclined to identify with the high LMX superior. Another viewpoint is that the relationship-oriented high-level leader proposes changes either in the unit or the organization, and lower level managers tend to adopt leadership behaviors and attitudes that support the high-level manager's vision (Tichy & Ulrich, 1984). This is increasingly important, as many organizations today have had to undergo shifts in their vision and wide-scale organizational change.

How is it that LMX at one level could influence LMX at another? A recent survey may provide some answers. In 1998, a benchmarking study of best practices in leadership development identified six organizations as having a strong or innovative leadership development process: Arthur Andersen, General Electric, Hewlett-Packard, Johnson & Johnson, Shell International, and The World Bank (Fulmer & Wagner, 1999). One of the study's findings was that best-practices partners used action learning with their members, whereby they developed leaders internally, preparing them to make critical decisions, equipping them with the necessary skills, qualities, and techniques to apply knowledge in ambiguous situations. This is similar to the process of role making, whereby high LMX subordinates are given increased latitude to make decisions, choices and more critical job assignments, and other developmental activities with increased influence (Graen & Scandura, 1987). It is clear from the empirical research that LMX is positively related with performance and career success (Scandura & Schriesheim, 1994; Wakabayashi, Graen, Graen, & Graen, 1988). What we want to examine is whether or not these LMX development processes cascade throughout the organization like a waterfall. Thus, we are examining LMX from a systems perspective, or what Graen and Uhl-Bien (1995) described as Stage 4 in the development of LMX theory—the expansion of dyadic LMX partnerships to group and network levels. Following from Graen and Scandura (1987), who proposed that LMX should not be viewed as independent dyads but rather as a system of interdependent dyadic relationships, this recent stage of LMX research focuses on how these differentiated dyadic relationships form a larger network assembly that constitutes the leadership structure within the organization.

Snowballs.   Another viewpoint on the relationship between LMX at one level and another is what we have labeled "Snowballs." Along the lines of the waterfall effect, we wondered if perhaps subordinates realized the value of high-quality LMX relationships and enhanced their role-making process with their own subordinates. We speculated that the positive relationship a person has with his or her supervisor could enhance or develop leadership and relationship skills such that this person would be encouraged to develop an even higher quality exchange with his or her followers—"the snowball builds as it rolls downhill." In this situation, subordinates may augment their LMX relationship rather than merely mirror their leaders' behavior.

Conversely, one might expect the "snowball" to get smaller as it rolls downhill, whereby relationship-building behaviors are constrained as supervisors move down the hierarchy. Taylor and Bowers (1972) proposed that supervisors who are higher in the organization have considerable latitude in their functioning, whereas supervisors who are hierarchically lower in the organization have their policies and procedures spelled out for them, and the latitude with which they can operate gets smaller. It is this concept of negotiating latitude that distinguishes high-quality exchanges from lower ones (e.g., Dansereau, Graen, & Haga, 1975). Although organizational climate variables have been positively related to LMX (Cogliser & Schriesheim, 2000), the relationship between climate and LMX at higher versus lower levels in the organization has been untested. However, Franklin (1973) found that the effect of climate on leadership behavior increases at lower levels in the organizational hierarchy, because climate is more constraining because of the emphasis on rules, policies, and procedures at lower levels in the organization.

Brick Walls. We also considered that LMX relationships at a higher hierarchical level might be independent of those at a lower level. It doesn't matter how good or bad the LMX is with your boss, it has no effect on the liking, trust, respect, and loyalty you develop with your subordinates. Essentially, LMX hits a brick wall rather than cascades down the waterfall. In this instance, relationships operate independently of one another, and there is little influence on the lower dyad.

Support for this concept is drawn from the individualized leadership model of Dansereau and his colleagues (Dansereau et al., 1998), which suggests that individuals will form a relationship with one person totally independent of relationships that person has with others. The fact that the relationship may be similar to or different from another is totally dependent on how the focal individual (a supervisor) views the other person in the dyad (a follower). The individualized leadership model draws its strength from its focus on individual differences of subordinates, rather than from either differences *between* groups of subordinates (the traditional view of leadership or "average leadership style" [ALS] approach) or differences *within* groups of subordinates (the vertical dyad linkage [VDL] or LMX approach). Following the individualized leadership conception, subordinates are independent, unique individuals (Dansereau et al., 1998), and the relationship that develops between them is not from a superior's tendency to evaluate subordinates as a group (ALS), or to contrast followers relative to each other (VDL or LMX), but is based on the superior's subjective appraisal of the subordinate's performance. Thus, the relationship that the particular supervisor has with his or her superior is irrelevant to or independent of the relationships that he or she develops with subordinates.

Scuzzballs. Last, we wanted to explore the effect of "toxic" leadership at different levels—we wanted to explore the type of relationships that would develop if your boss were a "Scuzzball." We had three competing alternatives that might result from this type of LMX relationship. First, we thought subordinates might want to compensate for the harmful LMX with their boss and thus cultivate good relationships with their own followers, resulting in a negative relationship between LMX at one level and LMX at the next lower level. Although research generally supports the notion that leaders serve as models for their subordinates, some research has found that subordinates tended to model only those superiors they saw as more competent and successful (Weiss, 1977), and those who displayed initiation and consideration in their leadership behavior (Adler, 1982). Thus, a supervisor who displays dysfunctional behavior might elicit a contradictory behavior style in followers when that follower interacts with his or her subordinates. Bass (1990, p. 343) phrases this proposition uniquely: "If A kicks B, will B kick C or will B become solicitous of C after being kicked by A?" He proposes that a threatening boss may create a manager who rewards subordinates in exchange for their support against the threatening boss. Thus, strong leaders at one hierarchical level may alternate with weak leaders below them.

An alternative situation would be that followers would directly model their supervisors' behavior (similar to the waterfall effect described earlier) and would behave in a similarly dysfunctional manner (eliciting a positive relationship with LMX across levels). This modeling would be based in part on the concept of behavioral contagion (Wheeler, 1966), where a punitive, inappropriate or dysfunctional boss who exhibits the "dark side of leadership" (Conger, 1990), machiavellianism (Drory & Gluskinos, 1980), or narcissism (Kets de Vries & Miller, 1985), for example, could generate or reproduce a set of punitive, inappropriate, or dysfunctional subordinates, who then go on to be punitive, inappropriate, or dysfunctional supervisors themselves (Bass, 1990). Graen, Dansereau, and Minami (1972) found a dysfunctional consequence with several leadership styles. They found that a supervisor's initiating structure behavior moderated the relationship between consideration and subordinate performance. They stressed that leadership style *does* make a difference in organizations, but the difference was not so much how the leader acts, but how members interpret the behavior.

Finally, we propose the "kick the dog" syndrome, where subordinates in a toxic or extremely poor LMX relationship would behave in a fashion that is even worse to their followers. When a norm of reciprocity does not develop in the LMX dyad, subordinates have no say in decision making—they receive no influence, latitude, information, support, or attention from their supervisors—these subordinates are likely to be highly dissatisfied with many aspects of their job situation. Some support for this outcome can be found from research on punitive leadership. Day (1971) found that punitive supervision was significantly related to subordinates' aggressive feelings toward their coworkers as well as their supervisors. deCharms and Hamblin (1960) found that punitive supervisory behavior resulted in subordinates' increased tension and lower productivity. These findings are consistent with general psychological findings that severe punishment produces anxiety that is disruptive for followers (Bass, 1990).

HOW DO WE PASS DOWN A LEGACY
OF RELATIONSHIP DEVELOPMENT?

We believe that it is possible (as well as desirable) to maximize LMX relationships throughout the organization and to develop either the waterfall or the snowball effect among leaders and followers. There are several leadership practices that should enable cascading leadership effects.

Develop and Communicate a Vision

We believe that a boss needs to develop and communicate a vision that is consistent with that of the organization's. For example, the boss needs to understand that substantially different behaviors may be required to develop high-quality relationships in organizational cultures that do not emphasize individualistic or egalitarian values. He or she needs to ensure that his or her behavior is consistent with his or her vision and the values of the organization. Thus, leadership development should be incorporated into the organizational context and aligned with the strategy of the organization. The vision relating to the future direction of the organization is of primary importance, and any attempt to develop dyadic relationships must be consistent. Yet, this is where empirical research has demonstrated that leader development programs fail—when existing managerial practices do not support the content of the leadership training (e.g., Burke & Day, 1986; Sykes, 1962).

Communicate Values

We believe that the values espoused by the leader must be consistent with those of the organization and should be communicated clearly to the set of subordinates. We also propose that a subordinate's relationship with his/her boss is a mechanism to help the subordinate internalize those values and pass them on, since subordinates depend on their superiors as a prime source for behavioral cues (e.g., Graen & Cashman, 1975). If the focus of the dyad is on developing trust, respect, mutual obligation, and mutual loyalty, this should support core values of the organization regarding the nature of human relations (i.e., how people treat one another) (Schein, 1992).

Have a "Teachable" Point of View (Tichy, 1999)

Tichy and his colleagues (Barnett & Tichy, 2000; Tichy, 1999) have recently outlined a strategy for leadership development in organizations, and they stressed that leaders must be great teachers—that is, they should have a point of view that is uniquely developed and articulated to others in a way that motivates action and mobilizes resources. It is the leader's values, ideas, emotional energy, and edge that energize followers to act. Having a teachable point of view also creates greater loyalty, communicates an expectation of continual improvement, and creates a climate of open, direct, and candid communication among followers (Barnett & Tichy, 2000). Clawson (1979) found that followers learned a great deal from their supervisors when the supervisor was perceived as relations oriented, and if the subordinate respected and liked their bosses. In this study, more effective supervisors also considered themselves to be teachers and were involved in setting examples and providing clear feedback (Clawson, 1979). Each of these factors outlined by these scholars can all enhance LMX quality (Liden, Sparrowe, & Wayne, 1997) and increase the likelihood of high LMX cascading throughout the organization.

Model Behavior Consistently for Subordinates

Bosses need to "walk the walk" for leadership development to be effective (Weiss, 1977). A famous quotation from Einstein is "Setting an example is not the main means of influencing someone, it is the only means." The mentoring literature speaks to the importance of senior manager role models (Kram, 1985). Dedication, caring, and participation are multiplied outward from supervisors to their subordinates (Burns, 1978), but it appears only effective when the behavior is consistent (Misumi, 1985).

Transform Leadership Development From an Event Into a Process

Although there is some evidence for the efficacy of formal LMX development training programs (Graen, Liden, & Hoel, 1982; Scandura & Graen, 1984), we would rather see a continual emphasis on relationship development in organizations. We feel this will help create a culture of commitment and accountability and will continue to foster "home-grown" leaders, seen as most effective in a recent survey (Fulmer & Wagner, 1999).

The LMX model clearly has utility for its application to leadership development. Empirical studies have supported the relationship of high-quality exchanges with positive organizational outcomes, and the broader leadership literature supports the cascading or waterfall effect of the supervisor's leadership behavior impacting the subordinates. There is now a need to empirically test the research questions raised in this paper. It is our belief the findings will support our "waterfall" propositions, and we feel this bodes positively for organizations and their development of their leadership potential.

There is a clear need for methods that more effectively socialize junior managers for executive positions. Dyad-level coaching may be one of the most effective means for transmitting organizational culture, thereby promoting the organization's core values. We believe that dyad management development has not been utilized to the full extent possible to leverage the potential of the pool of executive talent. To avoid the leadership crisis many authors are now writing about, future research and practice on leadership should begin to explore the possible impact of cascading leadership effects.

REFERENCES

Adler, S. (1982). *Subordinate imitation of supervisor behavior: The role of supervisor power and subordinate self-esteem.* Paper presented at the International Congress of Applied Psychology, Edinburgh.

Barnett, C. K., & Tichy, N. M. (2000). Rapid-cycle CEO development: How new leaders learn to take charge.*Organizational Dynamics, 29,* 16–32.

Bass, B. M. (1990). *Bass & Stogdill's Handbook of leadership.* New York: The Free Press.

Bass, B. M., Waldman, D. A., Avolio, B. J., & Bebb, M. (1987). Transformational leadership and the falling dominoes effect. *Group & Organization Studies, 12,* 73–87.

Bowers, D. G., & Seashore, S. E. (1966). Predicting organizational effectiveness with a four-factor theory of leadership. *Administrative Science Quarterly, 11,* 238–263.

Burke, M. J., & Day, R. R. (1986). A cumulative study of training. *Journal of Applied Psychology, 71,* 232–265.

Burns, J. M. (1978). *Leadership.* New York: The Free Press.

Caudron, S. (1999). The looming leadership crisis. *Workforce, 78,* 72–75.

Clawson, J. G. (1979). *Superior-subordinate relationships in managerial development.* Unpublished D. B. A., Harvard University, Cambridge, MA.

Cogliser, C. C., & Schriesheim, C. A. (2000). Exploring work unit context and leader-member exchange: A multi-level perspective. *Journal of Organizational Behavior, 21*(5), 487–511.

Conger, J. A. (1990). The dark side of leadership. *Organizational Dynamics, Autumn,* 44–55.

Dansereau, F., Graen, G., & Haga, W. J. (1975). A vertical dyad linkage approach to leadership within formal organizations: A longitudinal investigation of the role making process. *Organizational Behavior & Human Decision Processes, 13,* 46–78.

Dansereau, F., Yammarino, F. J., Markham, S. E., Alutto, J. A., Newman, J., Dumas, M., et al. (1998). Individualized leadership: A new multiple-level approach. In F. Dansereau & F. J. Yammarino (Eds.), *Leadership: The multiple-level approaches* (Vol. 24, pp. 363–405). Stamford, CT: JAI Press.

Day, R. C. (1971). Some effects of combining close, punitive, and supportive styles of supervision. *Sociometry, 34,* 303–327.

Day, D. V., & Lord, R. G. (1988). Executive leadership and organizational performance: Suggestions for a new theory and methodology. *Journal of Management, 14,* 453–464.

deCharms, R., & Hamblin, R. I. (1960). *Structural factors and individual needs in group behavior.* St. Louis, MO: Washington University.

Drory, A., & Gluskinos, U. M. (1980). Machiavellianism and leadership. *Journal of Applied Psychology, 65*, 81–86.

Duchon, D., Green, S. G., & Taber, T. D. (1986). Vertical dyad linkage: A longitudinal assessment of antecedents, measures, and consequences. *Journal of Applied Psychology, 71*, 56–60.

Franklin, J. L. (1973). *A path analytic approach to describing causal relationships among social psychological variables in multi-level organizations.* Unpublished dissertation, University of Michigan, Ann Arbor.

Fulmer, R. M., & Wagner, S. (1999). Leadership: Lessons from the best. *Training & Development, 53*, 28–32.

Graen, G., & Cashman, J. F. (1975). A role-making model of leadership in formal organizations: A developmental approach. In J. G. Hunt & L. L. Larsen (Eds.), *Leadership Frontiers* (pp. 143–165). Kent, OH: Kent State University Press.

Graen, G., Cashman, J. F., Ginsburgh, S., & Schiemann, W. (1977). Effects of linking-pin quality on the quality of working life of lower participants. *Administrative Science Quarterly, 22*, 491–504.

Graen, G., Dansereau, F., & Minami, T. (1972). Dysfunctional leadership styles. *Organizational Behavior & Human Decision Processes, 7*, 216–236.

Graen, G. B., Liden, R. C., & Hoel, W. (1982). Role of leadership in the employee withdrawal process. *Journal of Applied Psychology, 67*, 868–872.

Graen, G. B., & Scandura, T. A. (1987). Toward a psychology of dyadic organizing (Vol. 9, pp. 175–208). Greenwich, CT: JAI Press.

Graen, G. B., & Uhl-Bien, M. (1995). Relationship-based approach to leadership: Development of leader-member exchange (LMX) theory of leadership over 25 years: Applying a multi-level multi-domain perspective. *Leadership Quarterly, 6*, 219–247.

Kets de Vries, M., & Miller, D. (1985). Narcissism and leadership: An object relations perspective. *Human Relations, 38*, 583–601.

Kram, K. E. (1985). Improving the mentoring process. *Training & Development Journal, 39*, 40–43.

Liden, R. C., Sparrowe, R. T., & Wayne, S. J. (1997). Leader-member exchange theory: The past and potential for the future. In G. R. Ferris (Ed.), *Research in personnel and human resources management* (Vol. 15, pp. 47–119). Greenwich, CT: JAI Press.

Likert, R. (1961). *New patterns of management.* New York: McGraw-Hill.

Marshall-Mies, J. C., Fleishman, E. A., Martin, J. A., Zaccaro, S. J., Baughman, W. A., & McGee, M. L. (2000). Development and evaluation of cognitive and metacognitive measures for predicting leadership potential. *Leadership Quarterly, 11*, 135–153.

Michaelson, L. K. (1973). *The effects of situational conditions and human values on leadership behavior in organizations: An empirical investigation.* Unpublished dissertation, University of Michigan, Ann Arbor.

Misumi, R. (1985). *Leadership in Japanese organizations.* New York: Harper & Row.

Ouchi, W. G., & Maguire, M. A. (1975). Operational control: two functions. *Administrative Science Quarterly, 20*, 559–569.

Scandura, T. A., & Graen, G. B. (1984). Moderating effects of initial leader-member exchange status on the effects of a leadership intervention. *Journal of Applied Science, 69*, 428–436.

Scandura, T. A., Graen, G. B., & Novak, M. A. (1986). When managers decide not to decide autocratically: An investigation of leader-member exchange and decision influence. *Journal of Applied Psychology, 71*(4), 579–584.

Scandura, T. A., & Schriesheim, C. A. (1994). Leader-member exchange and supervisor career mentoring as complementary concepts in leadership research. *Academy of Management Journal, 37*, 1588–1602.

Schafer, M. (2001). Developing leaders. *Software Magazine, December/January*, 61–64.

Schein, E. H. (1992). *Organizational culture and leadership* (2nd ed.). San Francisco: Jossey-Bass.

Settoon, R. P., Bennett, N., & Liden, R. C. (1996). Social exchange in organizations: Perceived organizational support, leader-member exchange, and employee reciprocity. *Journal of Applied Psychology, 81*, 219–227.

Stogdill, R. M. (1955). Interactions among superiors and subordinates. *Sociometry, 18*, 552–557.

Sykes, A. J. M. (1962). The effects of a supervisory training course in changing supervisors' perceptions and expectations of the role of management. *Human Relations, 15*, 227–243.

Taylor, J. C., & Bowers, D. G. (1972). *Survey of organizations*. Ann Arbor: Institute for Social Research.

Tichy, N. M. (1999). The teachable point of view: A primer. *Harvard Business Review, 77*, 76–88.

Tichy, N. M., & Ulrich, D. O. (1984). The leadership challenge—A call for the transformational leader. *Sloan Management Review, 26*, 59–68.

Wakabayashi, M., Graen, G., Graen, M., & Graen, M. (1988). Japanese management progress: Mobility into middle management. *Journal of Applied Psychology, 73*, 217–227.

Weiss, H. M. (1977). Subordinate imitation of supervisor behavior: The role of modeling in organizational socialization. *Organizational Behavior and Human Performance, 19*, 89–105.

Wheeler, L. (1966). Toward a theory of behavioral contagion. *Psychological Review, 73*, 179–192.

Zenger, J., Ulrich, D., & Smallwood, N. (2000). The new leadership development. *Training & Development, 54*, 22–27.

9

Toward a Broader Leadership Development Agenda: Extending the Traditional Transactional– Transformational Duality by Developing Directive, Empowering, and Shared Leadership Skills

Jonathan F. Cox
Center for the Study of Work Teams
University of North Texas

Craig L. Pearce
Peter F. Drucker School of Management
Claremont Graduate University

Henry P. Sims, Jr.
R. H. Smith School of Business
University of Maryland

Most leadership development efforts currently focus on transactional and transformational leadership and focus narrowly on individuals who occupy formal leadership positions or are being groomed to occupy such positions. In this chapter, we argue that the behavioral focus of leadership development should be expanded to include the development of *directive* and *empowering* leadership. We also argue that followers should be included in leadership development efforts to prepare them to exercise *shared leadership* (Pearce, 1997, 2002; Pearce & Conger, 2003) in certain team-based work contexts.

Leadership has long captured the interest of academicians, leadership-development practitioners, and the business community at large. The scale of this popular interest in leadership—what it is, where it comes from, how we develop and use it—is quickly apparent from the space devoted to the topic in any bookstore. In our daily lives, we often hear descriptions of an individual as an "X" type of leader. Indeed, most professionals would probably agree that developing a keen sense of different types of leaders, how they behave, and what they expect, is essential for success.

Even informal, conversational descriptions of leadership, at least implicitly, refer to clusters of behavior that seem (perhaps intuitively) consistent or related. For example, an employee's description of an "iron-fisted" boss might be intuitively supported by examples of his or her manager's insistence on strict obedience, intolerance of disagreement, inflexible enforcement of rules, and the like. Whether they are intuitive—based on personal experience—or formalized through controlled observation and research, these clusters or *types* of related behavior make it easier to size up leaders and make sense of patterns of leadership behavior. Two or more contrasting leadership types, in turn, form a *typology* (see Doty & Glick, 1994) of different kinds of leadership.

Descriptive typologies offer a guiding framework that is critical for implementing coherent leadership development efforts. The behavioral richness of the typologies guiding leadership development define and, in some cases, limit the leadership behaviors supported by development strategy and curriculum (Goleman, 2000). To prepare aspiring leaders with a more complete palette of behavioral options, we recommend extending leadership development beyond the limits of today's dominant *transactional–transformational* leadership typology, to include the time-tested directive and emerging empowering leadership types as well. To illustrate this broader leadership development agenda, in the next section we discuss the historical roots of the four types of leadership mentioned previously, the behaviors associated with each, and the conditions under which each is appropriate. We round out our discussion by introducing *shared leadership*, a recent conceptualization of leadership that explicitly emphasizes lateral influence among peers, in addition to upward and downward influence (Pearce, 2002; Pearce & Conger, 2003), and the task characteristics that call for its development.

TYPOLOGIES IN LEADERSHIP RESEARCH AND LEADERSHIP DEVELOPMENT

Organizational researchers are often interested in how particular approaches to leadership relate to individual, group, and organizational effectiveness. Most scholarly inquiries into leadership take the form of theories that relate leadership patterns to outcomes such as productivity, innovation, turnover, and the like. In research settings, then, leader behavior typologies supply the independent variable—the "cause" that the research hopes to relate to organizational "effect." In leadership development settings, leadership behavior typologies supply a useful shorthand that aids diagnosis of participants' preferred leadership strategies and simplifies description of other, perhaps more effective, alternatives. This is why leadership development professionals so often depend on typologies to guide their development efforts. Indeed, theories of leadership and the typologies they imply can be critical for orchestrating a coherent, internally consistent leadership selection, training, appraisal, and development strategy.

Given the importance of leadership in academic research and applied leadership development, it is critical that we develop leadership typologies that are as comprehensible and complete as possible (Goleman, 2000; Hunt, 1996, p. 170). As Yukl (1998) emphasized, it is imperative that we understand the range of leader behavior patterns and how these patterns affect leaders, followers, and the organizations they enact. Today's leadership development efforts rest largely on developing two types of leadership: transactional and transformational. We submit that this duality paints an incomplete developmental picture because it misses two additional leadership alternatives: The time-tested (but presently unfashionable) directive leadership approach and the empowering leadership approach. All four of these alternatives have been extensively researched and are useful and appropriate in certain situations.

If, as we believe, leadership is fundamentally a performing art, aspiring leaders must be prepared to move smoothly among the leadership roles they may be expected to play during their lives. These four approaches to leadership offer a far richer range of behavioral options for productive influence than the narrow transactional–transformational duality so popular today. The discussion that follows will briefly trace the historical roots of these four established approaches to leadership, sample the leader behaviors associated with each approach, and describe the conditions under which each is appropriate.

The Transactional–Transformational Typology

The dominant leadership model used in leadership development today is the transactional–transformational typology, the subject of much academic leadership research in recent years (e.g., Bass & Avolio, 1993; Brown & Lord, 1999; Conger, 1999). However, a revisionist movement in the research community now questions whether scholars are missing the potential of a broader range of leadership options by coalescing too narrowly on this two-factor typology. Yukl (1989) summarized this concern by observing that the transactional–transformational typology "is fast becoming a two factor theory of leadership processes, which is an unwarranted oversimplification of a complex phenomenon" (p. 212). Bass and Avolio (1993) also called for a more comprehensive view of leadership by inviting "critics and supporters to join in the effort to shape a theory and model of leadership that captures a broader array of leadership behaviors and attributes than previously studied" (p. 76).

We urge leadership development professionals to join this challenge by extending their work beyond the reductionism of today's two-factor transactor–transformer typology. Doing so will offer aspiring leaders an array of behavioral options that capture more of what is new in leadership research, as well as some forgotten wisdom from the past.

A Four-Factor Alternative

We propose a more comprehensive leadership typology based on years of study of the leadership literature, as well as our own empirical research. Recently, we completed an analysis of several leadership types that spanned multiple independent research studies (Pearce et al., 2003). This analysis produced a four-factor typology of empirically distinct approaches to leadership that confirmed and extended several recent attempts to produce a more comprehensive inventory of leader behaviors (e.g., Bass, 1985; Bass & Avolio, 1993; Cox, 1994; Cox & Sims, 1996; Manz & Sims, 1991). It also builds on the work of Yukl (1987, 1989, 1998) and on that of Quinn and associates (Quinn, 1988; Quinn, Faerman, Thompson, & McGrath, 1990). The typology that emerged from our research includes the four leadership types mentioned previously in the introduction: (a) directive, (b) transactional, (c) transformational, and (d) empowering. Each type builds on a substantial base of past leadership research, theory, and tradition. Historical contributions to the model are summarized in Table 9.1. Table 9.2 lists the behaviors associated with each type and the situations in which each type of behavior is likely to be most effective. Table 9.3 compares our typology to the typologies of Quinn and colleagues (e.g., Quinn et al., 1990) and Yukl (1998).

In the following sections, we describe the four types of leadership from our historical analysis of the leadership literature. Our discussion parallels Tables 9.1, 9.2, and 9.3 by describing the theoretical roots of each type, their relationship to other typologies, the behaviors associated with each type, and the circumstances that make each type situationally appropriate.

Directive Leadership.   The first distinct type of leadership identified in our work, *directive leadership*, describes leadership that primarily relies on *position power* or *legitimate power* and may also include *coercive power* (cf., French & Raven, 1959). This approach influences follower behavior through directive behaviors such as issuing commands, assigning goals, intimidation, and reprimand.

The roots of directive leadership lie in so-called *theory* X *management* (e.g., McGregor, 1960), *initiating structure* behavior as documented in the Ohio State leadership studies (e.g., Fleishman, 1953; Halpin & Winer, 1957; Schriesheim, House, & Kerr, 1976), *task-oriented leadership* identified in the

TABLE 9.1
Theoretical and Research Bases of the Historically Derived Model
of Leadership Types

Leadership Type	Theoretical and Research Bases
Directive leadership	Theory X leadership (McGregor, 1960) Initiating structure from Ohio State studies (e.g., Fleishman, 1953) Task-oriented behavior from Michigan studies (e.g., Katz et al., 1950) Punishment research (e.g., Arvey & Ivancevitch, 1980)
Transactional leadership	Expectancy theory (e.g., Vroom, 1964) Path–goal theory (e.g., House, 1971) Equity theory (e.g., Adams, 1963) Exchange theory (e.g., Homans, 1961) Reinforcement theory (e.g., Luthans & Kreitner, 1985; Sims, 1977; Thorndike, 1911) Reward research (Podsakoff, Todor, & Skov, 1982)
Transformational leadership	Sociology of charisma (e.g., Weber, 1946) Charismatic leadership theory (e.g., House, 1977) Transformational leadership (e.g., Bass, 1985; Burns, 1978)
Empowering leadership	Behavioral self-management (e.g., Thorenson & Mahoney, 1974) Social cognitive theory (e.g., Bandura, 1986) Cognitive behavior modification (e.g., Meichenbaum, 1977) Participative management and participative goal-setting research (e.g., Likert, 1961, 1967; Locke & Latham, 1990) Mentoring research (e.g., Ensher & Murphy, 1997; Zey, 1988)

Michigan studies (e.g., Katz, Maccoby, & Morse, 1950; Likert, 1961, 1967), and more recent research on *punishment* (e.g., Arvey & Ivancevitch, 1980; Ball, 1991; Ball, Sims, & Trevino, 1994; Kazdin, 1975; Korukonda & Hunt, 1989; Podsakoff, Todor, & Skov, 1982; Sims, 1980). This leadership type is similar to what Quinn and associates call *consolidation orientation* (e.g., Quinn et al., 1990).

Directive leadership is presently out of fashion in much leadership development work, perhaps because it seems "old school," not in keeping with the expectations of today's workforce, or insufficient for the demands of knowledge work in an environment of rapid and discontinuous change (e.g., Carnevale, 1991). Directive leadership also may have fallen out of favor because of the wide range of behavior, some of it distasteful, that it can involve. We certainly agree that the directive approach is not, in itself, sufficient to meet contemporary leadership challenges. However, consistent with our position that effective leadership requires a range of situationally appropriate behaviors, we feel that *no single type of leadership will be sufficient to meet all leadership challenges.* Further, we contend that leadership can be directive without necessarily being abusive, threatening, or coercive.

TABLE 9.2
Representative Behaviors and Situational Demands for Four Leader Strategies

Leader Strategy	Representative Behaviors	Situational Demands
Directive leadership	Issuing commands Assigning goals Engaging in intimidation Dispensing reprimand	Early in group life Crisis situations Subordinates are new to tasks Consensus is difficult to obtain and subordinates likely to follow leader
Transactional leadership	Providing personal rewards Providing material rewards Monitoring performance	Need to set expectations for rewards Need to assess performance Need to dispense rewards for performance
Transformational leadership	Providing vision Expressing idealism Using inspirational communication Challenging the status quo	Need to unify group around long-term purpose Need to change course of action
Empowering leadership	Encouraging self-leadership Encouraging teamwork Encouraging self-development	Need to tap the knowledge of followers Need to develop new leaders

We can all think of times when we wish our leaders could help us make sense of ambiguous or unusually difficult challenges by setting a course and issuing well-meaning directives to coordinate best-guess attempts at productive action. Directive leadership, appropriately delivered, may well be appreciated by followers under these circumstances and may even be mission-critical. From a leadership development perspective, building appropriate capabilities in directive leadership can help aspiring leaders maintain a necessary short-term focus on task performance and forward movement. Research has demonstrated that directive leadership can be very effective in focusing attention on short-term and long-term goals (Weldon & Yun, 2000). As such, directive leadership can be appropriate: (a) early in the life of a group, (b) in crisis situations where fast action is required, (c) when followers are new to their tasks, and (d) in ambiguous situations where clear consensus is impossible and the group is likely to follow the leader. Because these leadership demands are often encountered in the workplace, building skills in appropriate directive leadership adds significantly to the aspiring leader's palette of behavioral options. In essence, directive leadership is an extension to the monitoring behavior that has been classified as part of transactional leadership.

Transactional Leadership. A second type of leadership that emerged from our research, *transactional leadership*, is consistent with the transactional–transformational leadership typology currently in favor. This type of leadership

TABLE 9.3

Comparison of the Quinn and Colleagues and Yukl Typologies with Our Typology

Current Study Typology	Quinn and Colleagues Typology				Yukl Typology
	Consolidation Orientation	Output Maximization Orientation	Change Orientation	HR Development Orientation	
Directive					
Issuing commands	Receiving & organizing information	Taking initiative			Organizing
Assigning goals	Evaluating routine information	Goal setting			Problem solving
Engaging in intimidation	Responding to routine information				Clarifying roles & objectives
Dispensing reprimands	Organizing				Informing
	Controlling				
Transactional					
Monitoring performance		Motivating others	Negotiating agreement & commitment		Recognizing
Providing personal rewards					Rewarding
Providing material rewards					Monitoring
Transformational					
Providing vision	Planning		Building & maintaining a power base		Planning
Expressing idealism			Negotiating & selling ideas		Motivating & inspiring
Using inspirational communication			Living with change		Networking
Challenging the status quo			Creative thinking		
			Managing change		

(Continued)

TABLE 9.3
(Continued)

Current Study Typology	Quinn and Colleagues Typology				Yukl Typology
	Consolidation Orientation	Output Maximization Orientation	Change Orientation	HR Development Orientation	
Empowering 　Encouraging self-leadership 　Encouraging teamwork 　Encouraging self-development		Delegating effectively		Understanding self & others Interpersonal communication Developing subordinates Teambuilding Participative decision making Conflict management	Consulting Delegating Supporting Developing & mentoring Managing conflict & team building
Behaviors not contained in our typology		Personal productivity & motivation Time & stress management			

168

includes behaviors such as monitoring performance, providing contingent personal rewards, and providing contingent material rewards. The bases of this type of leadership lie in expectancy theory (Vroom, 1964), path–goal theory (House, 1971; House & Dessler, 1974; House & Mitchell, 1974), exchange/equity theory (Adams, 1963; Homans, 1958, 1961), and reinforcement theory (Luthans & Kreitner, 1985; Scott & Podsakoff, 1982; Sims, 1977; Thorndike, 1911). Transactional leadership is somewhat similar to what Quinn and associates termed *output maximization orientation* (Quinn et al., 1990).

Developing appropriate transactional leadership skills is important because it equips aspiring leaders with the ability to provide feedback, signal appropriate behavior, align action and motivation with organizational goals, and promote equity and fairness. This type of leader behavior, appropriate in most situations on an ongoing basis, forms the backdrop for what most leadership development professionals would consider rational, effective maintenance leadership. For example, early in the life of a group, transactional leadership aids coordination by setting expectations, clarifying needed performance and behavior, and clarifying reward contingencies. Over time, transactional behavior can be used to leverage performance monitoring and send signals that enable continuous coordination and adjustment of individual behavior to achieve organizational objectives.

Transformational Leadership. The third distinct leadership type identified in our analysis, *transformational leadership*, is again consistent with today's dominant transactional–transformational typology. However, there is some conceptual confusion about what constitutes transformational leadership (Bryman, 1992). In general, transformational leadership behavior includes providing a unifying vision, expressing idealism, using inspirational communication, and challenging the status quo. The theoretical bases of the transformational type are drawn from the sociology of charisma (Trice & Beyer, 1986; Weber, 1924/1947), charismatic leadership theory (Brown & Lord, 1999; Conger, 1999; House, 1977, 1999; House & Shamir, 1993; House, Howell, Shamir, Smith, & Spangler, 1993; Riggio, 1987; Wofford, 1999; Yukl & Howell, 1999), and transformational leadership theory (Avolio & Bass, 1988; Bass, 1985, 1990; Bass, Avolio, & Goodheim, 1987; Burns, 1978; Hater & Bass, 1988; Waldman, Bass, & Einstein, 1987; Yammarino & Bass, 1990). Transformational leadership is related to what Quinn and associates term *change orientation* (e.g., Quinn, 1988; Quinn et al., 1990).

Developing transformational leadership skills enables aspiring leaders to supply long-term vision that brings meaning to otherwise disconnected tasks and coordinates individual performance. To some extent, transformational leadership may also supply a healthy motivational counterbalance to the instrumental focus of transactional leadership by engaging followers on a basis that extends beyond parochial self-interest. Supplying vision, inspiration, and deeper meaning may also promote incremental contributions through effort "beyond the call of duty" (Burns, 1978).

Empowering Leadership. The fourth empirically distinct type of leadership identified in our research is *empowering leadership.* Our view of empowering leadership follows closely from Manz and Sims' (1990, 1991) conceptualization of *SuperLeadership.* Central to empowering leadership is its focus on preparing followers for self-direction and responsible autonomy by encouraging development of self-leadership skills. Empowering leaders, then, emphasize shifting employees "from dependence on external management to independence" (Manz & Sims, 1990, p. 68).

Note a key difference between this approach and our discussion so far. Until now, discussion has been leader-centric with an emphasis on what leaders supply to followers: Directive leaders provide clear guidance, transactors provide clear performance expectations and contingent rewards, and transformers supply vision and meaning. In contrast, empowering leaders focus on creating a context where followers have the skills necessary to navigate their careers and work roles relatively independently. The empowering leader, then, is "one who leads others to lead themselves" (Manz & Sims, 1990, p. 4). A broad range of empowering leadership behaviors are possible, including leader encouragement of follower self-leadership, teamwork, and self-development. The key, of course, is the leader's emphasis on helping followers build habits of work and thought that combine independent initiative and responsible engagement.

The historical bases of empowering leadership are found in behavioral self-management (e.g., Mahoney & Arnkoff, 1978; Manz & Sims, 1980, 1990; Thorenson & Mahoney, 1974), social cognitive theory (e.g., Bandura, 1986), cognitive behavior modification (e.g., Bandura, 1986; Manz & Sims, 1990; Meichenbaum, 1977), participative management and participative goal setting (e.g., Drucker, 1954; Erez & Arad, 1986; Likert, 1961, 1967; Locke & Latham, 1990), and mentoring research (e.g., Ensher & Murphy, 1997; Zey, 1988). Empowering leadership is related to what Quinn and associates term a *human resource development orientation* (e.g., Quinn et al., 1990).

Like transactional leadership, the empowering leadership type is a useful approach to maintenance leadership. However, leadership development efforts to build empowering leadership skills have the potential to help aspiring leaders dramatically expand their influence over time. Effectively practiced, empowering leadership enables leaders to leverage the energy, talent, and initiative of the whole organization through follower self-responsibility, self-management of daily work, and self-leadership toward new challenges (Cohen, Chang, & Ledford, 1997). Significantly, the empowering leader's strong emphasis on self-direction skill building among followers also has the potential to build enduring resilience and capability in the organization.

Summary. We identified four distinct types of leader behavior that we advocate for inclusion in leadership development efforts: (a) directive leadership, (b) transactional leadership, (c) transformational leadership, and (d) empowering leadership. In the next section we describe shared leadership and identify situations that would benefit from its development.

SHARED LEADERSHIP: A NEW FRONTIER IN LEADERSHIP RESEARCH AND DEVELOPMENT PRACTICE

When we think of leadership we typically think of one person projecting influence downward on followers; even the empowering leader influences downward with the objective of fostering greater autonomy, initiative, and self-management among followers. However, recent research demonstrates that it is possible for individuals to lead themselves, as a team, through a process of that is primarily laterally peer-based influence that we term shared leadership (Pearce, 1997, 2002; Pearce & Sims, 2000, 2002; Pearce & Conger, 2003). Shared leadership describes a situation in which all members of a team are fully engaged in the team's functioning and flexibly exercise leadership influence with their teammates on an as-needed basis. Shared leadership involves mutual influence processes between the members of teams where the agent and target of influence changes depending on the nature of the specific task of the team and the knowledge, skills, and abilities of team members. Early research evidence suggests that shared leadership may have an even greater influence on team effectiveness than on hierarchical, vertical leadership strategies (Pearce & Sims, 2002; Pearce, Yoo, & Alavi, 2003). However, the development of shared leadership is a topic that has not yet received much empirical attention.

Shared leadership is related to empowerment, a topic that has received considerable attention (e.g., Cohen et al., 1997; Conger & Kanungo, 1988; Pearce & Sims, 2002). The distribution of power is the central concept in the empowerment literature. The traditional model of organizational life emphasizes that power is vested in the top of the organization and that individuals' power decreases as one goes further down the hierarchy. With empowerment, however, the idea is the sharing of organizational power with front-line employees—those dealing with the day-to-day situations that require organizational decisions. We argue that empowerment of individuals is a necessary, but not sufficient, condition for the development of shared leadership.

Most theory and research on empowerment focuses on the empowerment of individuals (Conger & Kanungo, 1988). Recently, however, some scholars have extended empowerment research from individuals to the group level of analysis (Mohrman, Cohen, & Mohrman, 1995; Kirkman & Rosen, 1999). Thus, empowerment of teams is the next step toward the development of shared leadership. From a leadership development perspective, however, the central challenge is to ensure that empowered team members actually practice effective peer influence strategies required for shared leadership.

Research and development practice in support of self-managing work teams (SMWTs), occasionally described as self-directed teams (SDTs) or self-directed work teams (SDWTs), has made the greatest strides toward developing the work context and individual skills needed for shared leadership. However, although recognizing that team members can effectively assume roles and responsibilities that were once reserved for management, most SMWT research has retained the familiar focus on the role of the appointed vertical leader rather than that on the lateral influence strategies that are used by the team members themselves (e.g., Cohen et al., 1997; Kirkman & Rosen, 1999). Further, although recent work has recognized that team members can effectively exercise lateral influence, or shared leadership, in teams (e.g., Cox, Pearce, & Perry, 2003; Ensley, Pearson, & Pearce, 2003; Pearce, Perry, & Sims, 2001; Perry, Pearce, & Sims, 1999), attention is only now turning to the challenge of effectively developing shared leadership in organizationally appropriate circumstances. We argue that shared leadership is not a replacement for leadership from above and, further, is fully beneficial only in certain task contexts to be described below. However, our early work suggests that shared leadership can work in conjunction with more traditional vertical leadership approaches to provide a more robust, flexible, and dynamic leadership infrastructure.

When Should Shared Leadership Be Developed?

Shared leadership is not something that is universally applicable. In fact, developing shared leadership involves a significant up-front developmental investment and ongoing effort by team members to engage in leadership behavior and manage the team dynamics of lateral, downward, and upward influence. These costs, sometimes called *process losses* (see Steiner, 1976), must be offset by the benefits of shared leadership to justify development and maintenance of a shared leadership work context. Specifically, shared leadership is likely to be most beneficial in work contexts requiring extensive mutual adjustment, support, and accommodation among colleagues working on interdependent tasks. We propose five task characteristics that are likely to leverage the benefits of shared leadership, thus justifying a developmental and maintenance investment (see Table 9.4): (a) interdependence, (b) creativity, (c) complexity, (4) criticality, and (5) urgency.

Interdependence. Team members working under conditions of dynamic interdependence are likely to benefit from opportunities for real-time peer-based leadership. Interdependent tasks at once provide ready opportunity for peer influence and require team reliance on guidance by team members with specific expertise at various points in the production life cycle. Thus, the level of team member task interdependence is a factor to consider in the decision to develop shared leadership in the team.

TABLE 9.4
Team Task Characteristics and the Need for Developing Shared Leadership

Task Characteristic	Need for Developing Shared Leadership
Interdependence	The greater the interdependence between the tasks of the members of the team, the greater the need for developing shared leadership in the team
Creativity	The more creative and novel the task of the team, the greater the need for developing shared leadership in the team
Complexity	The more complex the task of the team, the less likely that any single member of the team will be able to effectively lead the team through to task completion, and thus the greater the need for developing shared leadership in the team
Criticality	The more mission-critical the task of the team to the organization, the more important it is that the team be successful, and thus the greater the need for developing shared leadership in the team
Urgency	The more urgent the task, the greater the need for shared leadership.

Creativity.   Another important task characteristic to consider in the decision to develop shared leadership is the amount of creativity required of a team. In general, creative team tasks require divergent inputs from multiple individuals. To the extent that shared leadership enables input from widely across the team, it seems likely that shared leadership would support greater information search, debate, and generation of novel solutions to unique problems. Thus, if the team task requires a great deal of creativity, it is likely that the developmental investment in shared leadership would pay greater dividends.

Complexity.   Complex tasks also suggest that teams will benefit from development of shared leadership capability. Extremely routine tasks diminish the need for any type of leadership, vertical or shared, because the simplicity of the task itself supplies a structured work context requiring very little external influence or coordination (e.g., Kerr & Jermier, 1978). However, more complex tasks are likely to increase interdependence (see previous discussion) although decreasing the likelihood that any one individual has all of the knowledge, skills, and abilities required for task completion.

Criticality.   In general, tasks that are organizationally critical are more likely to benefit from shared leadership. For mission-critical tasks where the consequences of failure can be disastrous, shared leadership brings broader collective intellectual resources to bear that can provide a potential buffer between success and failure. Thus, the criticality of the team's task is also related to the need to develop shared leadership.

Urgency. Urgent tasks are also likely to benefit from shared leadership. For example, strategy formulation and implementation in high-velocity environments would benefit from the energy, personal investment, and accountability likely to result from collegial give and take in teams that share leadership. Eisenhardt, Kahwajy, and Bourgeois (1997), for example, found that top-management teams in the high-velocity, high-technology industry characterized by shared leadership types of team dynamics—broad, intense, and sometimes divergent input from all members—made quicker and better strategic decisions than teams dominated hierarchically by the CEO. Thus, urgent team tasks may also suggest shared leadership development as a beneficial investment.

CONCLUSION

We believe that leadership is, above all, a performing art with a range of leadership roles that must be filled in different situations. Oftentimes a single leader is called upon to fill these many varied roles. Shared leadership offers an attractive, though not cost free, alternative. Shared leadership has the potential to enable real-time lateral influence among front-line peers, thus enhancing coordination while enabling individuals with task-relevant expertise to provide leadership on a flexible, as-needed basis. Of course, these significant benefits must be weighed against the cost of broadly developing shared leadership skills and supporting shared leadership over time. We hope that the task characteristics highlighted previously will provide leadership development practitioners with touchstones to guide developmental decisions.

Any single approach to leadership will likely be insufficient to meet changing leadership demands over time (Goleman, 2000). To endure successfully, leaders must be prepared to navigate smooth, rapid transitions across a range of leader behaviors in response to situational demands, as well as navigate smooth transitions between leadership and followership. We recognize this as a significant challenge, a challenge shared by leaders and the professionals charged with developing leadership capability. From a development perspective, this challenge requires that development strategy, infrastructure, and curricula be designed to include an array of leader behavior options.

We urge leadership development professionals to portray a range of leader behavior options and build the knowledge, experience, and confidence to apply them. Just as important, we urge a broader perspective about who may benefit from leadership development. We have presented a four-factor typology of leadership behavior in hopes that it will broaden perspectives about what constitutes appropriate leadership and will encourage leadership development professionals to build a broader range of behavioral options into their development efforts. Unfortunately, today's emphasis on the transactional–transformational typology unnecessarily limits these options (Yukl, 1998), thus denying aspiring leaders the benefit of past leadership wisdom (i.e., directive leadership) while failing to prepare them with leadership capabilities that have been explored in more recent research (i.e., empowering leadership). In constructing our typology, our empirical research has demonstrated that both directive leadership and empowering leadership exist as independent leadership types. These findings suggestively integrate the past and present of leadership research as a guide for leadership development efforts. At the same time, past work on self-managing teams and our own current research on shared leadership suggest that most, if not all, organizational members—such as formally appointed leaders—may benefit from leadership development (Pearce & Conger, 2003; Pearce et al., in press; Pearce & Sims, 2002).

Conceptually, our discussion builds a case for distinguishing among directive, transactional, transformational, and empowering leadership types. Directive leadership includes behaviors associated with the leader providing structure and issuing directives on how work is to be done. Transactional leadership focuses on establishing the conditions of the exchange relationship between the leader and the follower. Transformational leadership defines and sustains vision, elicits inspiration from followers, and stimulates change. Finally, empowering leadership emphasizes developing followers as empowered self-leaders capable of initiative, creativity, and independent action.

Each type of leadership has compelling advantages and is appropriate for certain situations. Directive leadership, appropriately delivered, is both necessary and appreciated when the path forward is unclear, as is often the case early in team life, or in times of crisis. Transactional leadership is a rational, broadly acceptable approach to maintaining ongoing operations, enhancing perceived equity and meritocracy, coordinating effort, and linking individual motivation to organizational goals. Transformational leadership, like the directive type, engages followers in times of crisis. However, it also has the potential to provide longer range engagement around vision and purpose during times of significant change or extended uncertainty. Like the transactional type, transformational leadership also links individuals to the organization. However, it complements transactional leadership by engaging the aspirations, not just the parochial interests, of followers. Empowering leadership, a more recently identified type whose distinctness has only recently been confirmed in empirical research (Pearce et al., 2003), is another maintenance approach that complements transactional leadership. However, its explicit focus on fostering independence and building self-leadership capability among followers has additional potential to extend the indirect influence of leaders and expand organizational capability.

Certainly, each leadership type contributes significantly to the behavioral repertoire of effective leaders—be they formal leaders or, in the case of shared leadership, informal leaders. Just as certainly, considered individually, each type is insufficient to meet the range of challenges that today's leaders are likely to face over time. We hope that our discussion, tables, and reference list stimulate thought and offer a useful resource guide to those considering a more comprehensive leadership development offering.

REFERENCES

Adams, J. S. (1963). Wage inequities, productivity and work quality. *Industrial Relations, 3*, 916.

Arvey, R. D., & Ivancevitch, J. M. (1980). Punishment in organizations: A review, propositions, and research suggestions. *Academy of Management Review, 5*, 123–132.

Avolio, B. J., & Bass, B. M. (1988). Transformational leadership, charisma, and beyond. In J. G. Hunt, B. R. Baliga, H. P. Dachler, & C. A. Schreisheim (Eds.), *Emerging leadership vistas: International leadership symposium series*, vol. 8 (pp. 29–49). Lexington, MA: Lexington.

Ball, G. A. (1991). *Outcomes of punishment incidents: The role of subordinate perceptions, individual differences, and leader behavior.* Ph.D. dissertation, The Pennsylvania State University.

Ball, G. A., Sims, H. P., & Trevino, L. K. (1994). Just and unjust punishment: Influences on subordinate performance and citizenship. *Academy of Management Journal, 37*, 299–322.

Bandura, A. (1986). *Social foundations of thought and action: A social cognitive theory.* Englewood Cliffs, NJ: Prentice-Hall.

Bass, B. M. (1985). *Leadership and performance beyond expectations.* New York: The Free Press.

Bass, B. M. (1990). *Bass & Stogdill's handbook of leadership: Theory, research and managerial applications* (3rd ed.). New York: The Free Press.

Bass, B. M., & Avolio, B. J. (1993). Transformational leadership: A response to critiques. In M. M. Chemers and R. Ayman (Eds.), *Leadership theory and research: Perspective and directions* (pp. 49–80). New York: Academic Press.

Bass, B. M., Avolio, B. J., & Goodheim, L. (1987). Biography and the assessment of transformational leadership at the world-class level. *Journal of Management, 13*, 7–19.

Brown, D. J., & Lord, R. G. (1999). The utility of experimental research in the study of transformational/charismatic leadership. *Leadership Quarterly, 10*, 531–540.

Bryman, A. (1992). *Charisma and leadership in organizations.* Newbury Park, CA: Sage.

Burns, J. M. (1978). *Leadership.* New York: Harper & Row.

Carnevale, A. (1991). *America and the new economy.* San Francisco: Jossey-Bass.

Cohen, S. G., Chang, L., & Ledford, G. E. (1997). A hierarchical construct of self-management leadership and its relationship to quality of work life and perceived group effectiveness. *Personnel Psychology, 50*, 275–308.

Conger, J. A. (1999). Charismatic and transformational leadership in organizations: An insider's perspective on these developing streams of research. *Leadership Quarterly, 10*, 145–170.

Conger, J. A., & Kanungo, R. N. (1988). The empowerment process: Integrating theory and practice. *Academy of Management Review, 13*, 639–652.

Cox, J. F. (1994). The effects of superleadership training on leader behavior, subordinate self-leadership behavior, and subordinate citizenship. *Dissertation Abstracts International, 55*, 10B (UMI No. 9507927).

Cox, J. F., Pearce, C. L., & Perry, M. L. (2003). Toward a model of shared leadership and distributed influence in the innovation process: How shared leadership can enhance new product development team dynamics and effectiveness. In C. L. Pearce & J. A. Conger (Eds.), *Shared leadership: Reframing the hows and whys of leadership* (pp. 48–76). Thousand Oaks, CA: Sage.

Cox, J. F., & Sims, H. P., Jr. (1996). Leadership and team citizenship behavior: A model and measures. In M. M. Beyerlein, D. A. Johnson, & S. T. Beyerlein (Eds.), *Advances in interdisciplinary studies of work teams: Team Leadership* (pp. 1–41). Greenwich, CT: JAI Press.

Doty, D. H., & Glick, W. H. (1994). Typologies as a unique form of theory building: Toward improved understanding and modeling. *Academy of Management Review, 19*, 230–251.

Drucker, P. F. (1954). *The practice of management.* New York: Harper & Row.

Eisenhardt, K. M., Kahwajy, J. L., & Bourgeois, L. J., III. (1997). How management teams can have a good fight. *Harvard Business Review, 75*(4), 77–85.

Ensher, E. A., & Murphy, S. E. (1997). The impact of race, gender, perceived similarity, and contact on mentor relationships. *Journal of Vocational Behavior, 50,* 460–481.

Ensley, M. D., Pearson, A., & Pearce, C. L. (2003). Top management team process, shared leadership and new venture performance: A theoretical model and research agenda. *Human Resource Management Review, 13*(6), 1–18.

Erez, M., & Arad, R. (1986). Participative goal-setting: Social, motivational, and cognitive factors. *Journal of Applied Psychology, 71,* 591–597.

Fleishman. E. A. (1953). The description of supervisory behavior. *Personnel Psychology, 37,* 1–6.

French, J. R. P., & Raven, B. (1959). The bases of social power. In D. Cartwright (Ed.), *Studies in social power.* Ann Arbor: University of Michigan, Institute for Social Research.

Goleman, D. (2000). Leadership that gets results. *Harvard Business Review, 78,* 78–90.

Halpin, A. W., & Winer, B. J. (1957). A factorial study of the leader behavior descriptions. In R. M. Stogdill & E. A. Coons (Eds.), *Leader behavior: Its description and measurement.* Columbus: Ohio State University, Bureau of Business Research.

Hater, J. J., & Bass, B. M. (1988). Superiors' evaluations and subordinates' perceptions of transformational and transactional leadership. *Journal of Applied Psychology, 73,* 695–702.

Homans, G. C. (1958). Social behavior as exchange. *American Journal of Sociology,* 597–606.

Homans, G. C. (1961). *Social behavior: Its elementary forms.* New York: Harcourt, Brace.

House, R. J. (1971). A path goal theory of leader effectiveness. *Administrative Science Quarterly, 16,* 321–338.

House, R. J. (1977). A 1976 theory of charismatic leadership. In J. G. Hunt & L. L. Larson (Eds.), *Leadership: The cutting edge.* Carbondale, IL: Southern Illinois University Press.

House, R. J. (1999). Weber and the neo-charismatic leadership paradigm: A response to Beyer. *Leadership Quarterly, 10,* 563–575.

House, R. J., & Dessler, G. (1974). The path goal theory of leadership: Some post hoc and a priori tests. In J. G. Hunt & L. L. Larson (Eds.), *Contingency approaches to leadership.* Carbondale: Southern Illinois University Press.

House, R. J., Howell, J. M., Shamir, B., Smith, B., & Spangler, W. D. (1993). *Charismatic leadership: A 1993 theory and five empirical tests.* Unpublished manuscript.

House, R. J., & Mitchell, T. R. (1974). Path-goal theory of leadership. *Journal of Contemporary Business, 3,* 81–97.

House, R. J., & Shamir, B. (1993). Toward the integration of transformational, charismatic and visionary theories of leadership. In M. Chemers & R. Ayman (Eds.), *Leadership: Perspectives and research directions* (pp. 81–107). New York: Academic Press.

Hunt, J. G. (1996). *Leadership: A new synthesis.* Newbury Park, CA: Sage.

Katz, D., Maccoby, N., & Morse, N. (1950). *Productivity, supervision, and morale in an office situation.* Ann Arbor, MI: Institute for Social Research.

Kazdin, A. E. (1975). *Behavior modification in applied settings.* Homewood, IL: Dorsey.

Kerr, S., & Jermier, J. (1978). Substitutes for leadership: Their meaning and measurement. *Organizational Behavior and Human Performance, 22,* 374–403.

Kirkman, B. L., & Rosen, B. R. (1999). Beyond self-management: Antecedents and consequences of team empowerment. *Academy of Management Journal, 42,* 58–75.

Korukonda, A. R., & Hunt, J. G. (1989). Pat on the back vs. kick in the pants: An application of cognitive inference to the study of leader reward and punishment behaviors. *Group & Organization Studies, 14,* 299–324.

Likert, R. (1961). An emerging theory of organizations, leadership and management. In L. Petrullo & B. M. Bass (Eds.), *Leadership and interpersonal behavior.* New York: Holt, Reinhart & Winston.

Likert, R. (1967). *The human organization*. New York: McGraw-Hill.

Locke, E. A., & Latham, G. P. (1990). *A theory of goal setting and task performance*. Englewood Cliffs, NJ: Prentice-Hall.

Luthans, F., & Kreitner, R. (1985). *Organizational behavior modification and beyond*. Glenview, IL: Scott, Foresman.

Mahoney, M. J., & Arnkoff, D. B. (1978). Cognitive and self control therapies. In S. L. Garfield & A. E. Borgin (Eds.), *Handbook of psychotherapy and therapy change* (pp. 689–722). New York: Wiley.

Manz, C. C., & Sims, H. P., Jr., (1980). Self-management as a substitute for leadership: A social learning theory perspective. *Academy of Management Review, 5*, 361–367.

Manz, C. C., & Sims, H. P., Jr. (1990). *SuperLeadership*. New York: Berkeley Books.

Manz, C. C., & Sims, H. P., Jr. (1991). SuperLeadership: Beyond the myth of heroic leadership. *Organizational Dynamics*, 18–35.

McGregor, D. (1960). *The human side of enterprise*. New York: McGraw-Hill.

Meichenbaum, D. (1977). *Cognitive-behavior modification: An integrative approach*. New York: Plenum Press.

Mohrman, S. A., Cohen, S. G., & Mohrman, A. M., Jr. (1995). *Designing team-based organizations: New forms for knowledge work*. San Francisco: Jossey-Bass.

Pearce, C. L. (1997). *The determinants of change management team effectiveness: A longitudinal investigation*. Unpublished doctoral dissertation. University of Maryland, College Park.

Pearce, C. L. (2002). Más allá del liderazgo heroico: Como el buen vino, el liderazgo es algo para ser compartido. *Revista de Empresa, 1*(2), 53–64.

Pearce, C. L., & Conger, J. A. (Eds.) (2003). *Shared leadership: Reframing the hows and whys of leadership*. Thousand Oaks, CA: Sage.

Pearce, C. L., Perry, M. L., & Sims, H. P., Jr. (2001). Shared leadership: Relationship management to improve NPO effectiveness. In T. D. Connors (Ed.), *The nonprofit handbook: Management* (pp. 624–641). New York: Wiley.

Pearce, C. L., & Sims, H. P., Jr. (2000). Shared leadership: Toward a multi-level theory of leadership. *Advances in interdisciplinary studies of work teams, 7*, 115–139.

Pearce, C. L., & Sims, H. P., Jr. (2002). Vertical versus shared leadership as predictors of the effectiveness of change management teams: An examination of aversive, directive, transactional, transformational, and empowering leader behaviors. *Group Dynamics: Theory, Research, and Practice, 6*, 172–197.

Pearce, C. A., Sims, H. P., Jr., Cox, J. F., Ball, G. A., Schnell, E., Smith, K. A., & Trevino, L. K. (2003). Transactors, transformers and beyond: A multi-method development of a typology of leadership. *Journal of Management Development*.

Pearce, C. L., Yoo, Y., & Alavi, M. (2003). Leadership, social work and virtual teams: The relative influence of vertical vs. shared leadership in the nonprofit sector. In R. Riggio & S. Smith-Orr (Eds.), *Improving leadership in nonprofit organizations*. San Francisco: Jossey-Bass.

Perry, M. L., Pearce, C. L., & Sims, H. P., Jr. (1999). Empowered selling teams: How shared leadership can contribute to selling team outcomes. *Journal of Personal Selling and Sales Management, 19*, 35–52.

Podsakoff, P. M., Todor, W. D., & Skov, R. (1982). Effect of leader contingent and noncontingent reward and punishment behaviors on subordinate performance and satisfaction. *Academy of Management Journal, 25*, 810–821.

Quinn, R. E. (1988). *Beyond rational management: Mastering the paradoxes and competing demands of high performance*. San Francisco, CA: Jossey-Bass.

Quinn, R. E., Faerman, S. R., Thompson, M. P., & McGrath, M. R. (1990). *Becoming a master manager*. New York: Wiley.

Riggio, R. E. (1987). *The charisma quotient: What it is, how to get it, how to use it*. New York: Dodd Mead.

Schriesheim, C. A., House, R. J., & Kerr, S. (1976). Leader initiating structure: A reconciliation of discrepant research results and some empirical tests. *Organizational Behavior and Human Performance, 15*, 197–221.

Scott, W. E., & Podsakoff, P. M. (1982). Leadership, supervision and behavioral control: Perspectives from an experimental analysis. In L. Frederickson (Ed.), *Handbook of organizational behavior management*. New York: Wiley.

Sims, H. P., Jr. (1977). The leader as manager of reinforcement contingencies: An empirical example and a model. In J. G. Hunt and L. L. Larson (Eds.), *Leadership: The cutting edge*. Carbondale: Southern Illinois University Press.

Sims, H. P., Jr. (1980). Further thoughts on punishment in organizations. *Academy of Management Review, 5*, 133–138.

Steiner, I. D. (1976). Task-performing groups. In J. W. Thibaut, Spence, & R. C. Carson (Eds.), *Contemporary topics in social psychology* (pp. 393–422). Morristown, NJ: General Learning Press.

Thorenson, E. E., & Mahoney, M. J. (1974). *Behavioral self-control*. Holt, Rinehart & Winston.

Thorndike, E. L. (1911). *Animal intelligence: Experimental studies*. New York: Macmillan.

Trice, H. M., & Beyer, J. M. (1986). Charisma and its routinization in two social movement organizations. *Research in Organizational Behavior, 8*, 113–164.

Vroom V. H. (1964). *Work and motivation*. New York: Wiley.

Waldman, D. A., Bass, B. M., & Einstein, W. O. (1987). Leadership and outcomes of performance appraisal process. *Journal of Occupational Psychology, 60*, 177–186.

Weber, M. (1924/1947). *The theory of social and economic organization* (T. Parsons, Trans.). New York: The Free Press.

Weldon, E., & Yun, S. (2000). The effects of proximal and distal goals on goal level, strategy development, and group performance. *Journal of Applied Behavioral Science, 36*, 336–344.

Wofford, J. C. (1999). Laboratory research on charismatic leadership: Fruitful or futile? *Leadership Quarterly, 10*, 523–530.

Yammarino, F. J., & Bass, B. M. (1990). Long-term forecasting of transformational leadership and its effects among naval officers. In K. E. Clark & M. B. Clark (Eds.), *Measures of Leadership* (pp. 151–170). West Orange, NJ: Leadership Library of America.

Yukl, G. A. (1987). *A new taxonomy for integrating diverse perspectives on managerial behavior*. Paper presented at the American Psychological Association meeting, New York.

Yukl, G. A. (1989). *Leadership in organizations* (2nd ed.). Englewood Cliffs, NJ: Prentice-Hall.

Yukl, G. A. (1998). *Leadership in organizations* (4th ed.). Englewood Cliffs, NJ: Prentice-Hall.

Yukl, G A., & Howell, J. M. (1999). Organizational and contextual influences on the emergence and effectiveness of charismatic leadership. *Leadership Quarterly, 10*, 257–284.

Zey, M. G. (1988). A mentor for all reasons. *Personnel Journal, 67*, 46–51.

10

Why Leadership Research Is Generally Irrelevant for Leadership Development

Chester A. Schriesheim
University of Miami

Let me preface my remarks with a brief autobiographical statement. I am a university professor who has been plying his trade as a research scientist and educator for what is now going on close to 3 decades. I have a good research record, and my teaching is consistently rated highly by my students. Thus, I have a real stake in maintaining the status quo—a system of higher education that treats scientific research and publication as the coin-of-the-realm for tenure, promotion, salary, and other key personnel decisions (with teaching and related activities being typically treated as secondary objectives). However, based upon my years of involvement in the extant system I cannot shake the nagging feeling that much of what we do as leadership researchers is not particularly relevant for the real-world development of managers in work organizations—despite the fact that these people are directly and indirectly footing the bill for our research. Thus, when I look at what my colleagues and I do as researchers and compare that to our teaching, training, and management development activities, I cannot help but believe that, in general (and with few exceptions), leadership research is largely irrelevant for leadership development.

Why is leadership research generally irrelevant for leadership development? In thinking about it, I have come up with six possible reasons or explanations. Let me briefly outline what they are and then come back and talk about each of them

181

in more detail. My purpose in doing this is not necessarily to get you to agree, but to get you to think about these ideas and the implications they might have for the way we do research, the way we publish our research, and the way we try to communicate our research to our brethren in the practice part of the profession (who actually might be able to use the "stuff"—the new knowledge—that we produce). I will not provide a heavy stream of literature citations but will use my own work and the work of others where it is relevant to the points that I wish to make.

Briefly, the six reasons are as follows. First, we don't speak the same language as managers. That is one of the reasons why leadership research is, in fact, irrelevant for leadership development. Second, we look for the wrong things. We look for statistical significance. Managers, in fact, look for something else. Third, our theories, despite all the effort that we put into their development and testing, are not clearly valid. Furthermore, their validity may not even matter. Fourth, many of our theories, models, and frameworks are highly complex. However, like all humans, managers have what is termed "bounded rationality" (limited short-term, information-handling capabilities). This means that highly complex approaches, although perhaps necessary to capture the details of the leadership process, are very unlikely to be used by managers in everyday settings. Fifth, our theories of leadership generally assume that the leader has the technical ability to make good decisions and provide sound direction to subordinates. This, of course, is an absurd assumption. Sixth and finally, leadership involves the personal investment of time, energy, and emotion in followers. Many managers are simply unwilling or unable to do so, or they define their jobs in a way that doesn't require such investments. Let me move on now and elaborate on each of these six themes.

DIFFERENCES IN LANGUAGE

The language difference between what we do as academics and what managers do as practitioners is important. We talk about things like constructs and latent variables. How many lay people know what these things are? Some do, or at least think they do (it would be interesting to see whether these conceptions fit with what has developed in the academic community—say, as presented in a standard research methodology textbook, such as Kerlinger & Lee, 2000). Academics also conceptualize in terms of things like independent variables, dependent variables, moderator variables, and intervening variables. We use structural models, fit coefficients, canonical correlations, chi-squares, and other "esoteria" in our work. This is stuff that simply is not natural. Doing academic research, in fact, is not a natural act. In educating our doctoral students, we have to teach them to think differently, talk differently, and communicate differently than they would otherwise. In fact, one of the very serious problems that we sometimes encounter with older beginning doctoral students is that their previous success in life often interferes with their learning our (i.e., researchers') way of thinking, writing, and speaking. I believe that this creates some very real and serious problems because, once in the traditional academic mind set, it becomes very difficult to communicate with other people. We teach that clarity and parsimony are desirable in our theories (cf. Filley, House, & Kerr, 1976), but we seem preoccupied with constructing the most obtuse and elaborate theories and models that we can build and with writing empirical papers that are understandable only to other researchers in the profession.

For me, one of my most humbling experiences was as a new assistant professor proudly presenting my mother with reprints of my best articles from several top-tier academic outlets (*Journal of Applied Psychology, Psychological Bulletin*, and *Academy of Management Journal*). She put them on the coffee table so that all the neighbors who came by would see them. And, after the papers had been there for a few months, I looked, and the pile hadn't been moved except possibly for dusting. I asked her, "Did you read my articles, mom?" and she kind of looked away. Then I asked, "What did you think about them?" and she looked the other way. Then I asked her, "What part of them didn't you understand?" and she said, "Well, I read the titles." Who are we talking to is an important issue. How are we talking to these folks? Are we really reaching the audience we would like to reach? I don't believe that this is the case, because most of us probably don't want to be irrelevant to everyone except other researchers and because our natural audience consists of managers or aspiring managers.

Managers speak a different language than do academic research scientists—they speak the language of action. They are typically most concerned about only observable things ("measured variables"—such as employee job performance) and they employ relatively simple ideas about causation. I think that they are also likely to use relatively simple cognitive maps. How else do you explain the success of the various leadership training programs that are out there teaching things like, "show high concern for people" and "show high concern for production" and you'll be successful—despite the accumulated leadership literature of 30 or 40 years showing that those basic conceptions are invalid and do not fit with the data that we have in hand (for examples of this research literature, see Kerr & Schriesheim, 1974; Kerr, Schriesheim, Murphy, & Stogdill, 1974). The reason that simplistic models are still the most commercially popular and most commercially viable approaches in this domain is because they satisfy the need for simple, understandable, and actionable answers to vexing problems. The question is how simple, understandable, and action oriented do we have to get? Current leadership research just doesn't give adequate consideration to these issues at all, and we'll consider this issue of theory complexity in another one of my six points. However, so as to not sound completely negative, let me provide a positive example of speaking the manager's language. Fred Fiedler, the godfather of modern leadership research, developed the contingency model of leadership (Fiedler, 1967). This has had the major and highly important effect of reorienting leadership thinking away from very static and non-contingent perspectives and toward recognizing the importance of the situation.

Surely, the contingency model is esoteric, and much of what has been written about it and many of the debates surrounding it have been highly academic in both content and language (e.g., Fiedler, 1977; Schriesheim & Kerr, 1977a, 1977b). However, Fiedler has clearly gone the next step—something that academics rarely do. He has translated the leadership knowledge embodied in his model into writings that are clear, written in English, and understandable to nonacademics (e.g., Fiedler & Chemers, 1984; Fiedler, Chemers, & Mahar, 1976). Furthermore, Fiedler's more lengthy applied works (e.g., Fiedler & Chemers, 1984; Fiedler et al., 1976) take managers step by step through the process of using the contingency model to improve their leadership effectiveness. Because of this, Fiedler's model can be said to speak to academics in the language of science and to students and managers in their language as well. It would clearly be good if more of us did the same.

DIFFERENCES IN GOALS/OBJECTIVES

Let me now talk about the difference between statistical significance and what managers really want. One of the tenets of science is that the null hypothesis (i.e., "no effect" or "no difference") cannot be proven (cf. Kerlinger & Lee, 2000). Perhaps as a consequence, even if exceptionally well designed and executed, and even if conceptually compelling, a study is usually not publishable if it does not obtain statistically significant findings. Since the academic world is typically a "publish or perish" place, this causes researchers to seek statistical significance in virtually all research endeavors.

Unfortunately, the quest for statistical significance has several dysfunctional side effects. As most of us who do research know, statistical significance is determined by a number of things, particularly effect size, error, and sample size. For example, here's an equation for whether a correlation coefficient (r) is statistically significant (N is the sample size; McNemar, 1969):

$$t = r(N - 1)^{1/2}.$$

Playing the devil's advocate, let me focus on the impact that sample size has on the t statistic of the previous equation (the magnitude of the t statistic determines whether or not a statistically significant finding is obtained). Simply put, a trivial relationship ($r = 0.02$) may be "statistically significant" if the sample size is large enough (in this case $\geq$ 10,000). The same phenomenon generally holds true for other statistical tests, so that we know that if we collect a large enough sample even trivial relationships will be "statistically significant" (and therefore potentially publishable).

I would also include as variants within this problem such things as opportunistic sampling—where we know that some samples are more likely to show a particular effect than others. Additionally, I would add things such as measuring lots of variables and correlating them all usually yields some statistically significant relationships. If we are desperate enough, we could pick (like plucking cherries off a tree) the significant results from among the many nonsignificant ones and report those findings. This will satisfy departments, deans, and tenure and promotion committees but it doesn't add much to the advancement of knowledge (since the "findings" are merely an artifact of the process that we have employed).

What do managers need? Henry Mintzberg (1982) wrote a piece many years ago titled, "If you're not serving Bill and Barbara, then you're not serving leadership." His argument was if you're not speaking to managers, then maybe you are doing the wrong stuff. I really didn't like his paper very much at the time it was written because it was contrary to my beliefs about the value of academic research—because Mintzberg was saying that if research can't be used by managers, then maybe we shouldn't be doing it. This may be too applied or too commercial a view of the research process, but it has been so wholly disregarded by virtually all of the academic community that it probably warrants reiteration and reconsideration. Mintzberg also went on and noted that what he believes managers found of value were works that provided "startling insight." Based on my experience in the years since Mintzberg's paper was published, I tend to agree with him about this. What would be a startling insight? One of the elements of something being startling is that it is counterintuitive, that it counters a prevailing wisdom or prevailing thought. Let me give you another positive example from the work of Fred Fiedler (1967). Embedded within his contingency model are a number of starling insights. One of them is the idea that managers may not change. Most of the stuff we teach assumes that if we instruct people in our theories or models, they will be (a) smart enough to know how to use them and (b) flexible enough to be able to alter their behavior in such a way as to do what the theory/model suggests. Part of Fiedler's original thesis (40 years ago) was that maybe this isn't the case. Maybe there are folks out there who can't or don't change and for whom leadership training may not be functional (or perhaps even dysfunctional). Again, this is heresy within the traditional leadership establishment, but it is a startling insight and worth considering. It is counterintuitive.

A startling insight may also involve nonsignificant findings as well as significant findings: not only what is but also what isn't. Another example that is one of the interesting findings of Fiedler's research (Fiedler, 1967; Fiedler & Chemers, 1984; Fiedler et al., 1976) is that there are situations where some leaders are not effective—just as there are situations where they are effective. And, knowing the situations where they are effective is important, but also knowing where they are not effective is important as well. That doesn't fit with the traditional research perspective that focuses on finding the "where they are effective," the statistical significance, if you will. However, the nonsignificant findings can be immensely informative and immensely useful in planning strategies for management development.

Not only are startling insights "startling," but they also have action implications. Managers ask, "What can I do about it?" "Is there some action I can take to deal with this?" Using Fiedler's work as an example, he proposed the very radical idea, still radical in many quarters today, that maybe we need to engineer the situation to fit the manager instead of trying to change the manager to fit the situation (cf. Fiedler & Chemers, 1984; Fiedler et al., 1976). Will that work for all managers? Is that a universal prescription? Perhaps not, but it would fit a subset of managers that aren't as diagnostically capable and/or as behaviorally flexible as others. Last, for an insight to be useful to managers, it has to deal with a problem or issue that managers feel is important. Much research is done looking at issues that are small and possibly important to the research community, but that doesn't necessarily mean that they have much importance or value for practice. Again, if you look at Fiedler's work, some of the things that he proposed were some very concrete ways that the situation could be changed (Fiedler & Chemers, 1984; Fiedler et al., 1976). For example, ways of improving the leader's relationship with subordinates, one of the central elements of the situational control or favorability aspect of his model, were suggested. Other things that have been discussed as actionable alternatives include ways of increasing or decreasing the leader's power or the type of clarity or structure that is inherent in subordinates' tasks.

LACK OF VALIDITY AND IRRELEVANCE OF VALIDITY FOR PRACTICE

The next element about which we were criticizing leadership research concerned whether our theories are valid or whether validity is needed in the first place. The research support for the validity of each of our extant major theories of leadership is, in general, mixed. For example, Bass's (1985) theory of transformational leadership is one of our most current and important theories of leadership and it is seen by many scholars as being fundamentally sound. However, others argue that it includes some aspects of leader behavior that are not appropriate and that it omits others that are important (e.g., House & Podsakoff, 1994). Additionally, the empirical evidence in support of the theory is mixed (Bycio, Hackett, & Allen, 1995; Lowe, Kroeck, & Sivasubramaniam, 1996; Yukl, 2002), and some have even faulted the measurement and data-analytic practices that have been employed in tests of the theory. This suggests that even those aspects of the theory that are considered supported by data may not really have valid support at all (e.g., Schriesheim, Castro, Zhou, & Yammarino, 2001; Tepper & Percy, 1994; Yammarino, Dionne, & Chun, 2002). Similarly, leader–member exchange theory (Graen & Uhl-Bien, 1995) is one of our premier leadership theories. However, it has been subjected to theoretical criticism since its inception (e.g., Cummings, 1975), and this continues to the present day (e.g., Dansereau & Yammarino, 1998). It is true that some aspects of the theory are touted as being supported by the accumulated empirical research evidence (Erdogan & Liden, 2002; Gerstner & Day, 1997). However, serious questions have been raised about the measurement and data-analytic practices that have been employed in this research as well (e.g., Schriesheim, Castro, & Cogliser, 1999; Schriesheim, Castro, & Yammarino, 2000). What this means, in practical terms, is that neither transformational leadership theory nor leader–member exchange theory can be said to be clearly valid. The same is true for all of the other extant leadership theories as well.

This might be bothersome, but there are some interesting and provocative writings arguing that scientific validity may not matter very much (if at all) in the real world. Here's why. If we are teaching people different theories, in part we're teaching them different thought processes. Therein may lay the benefit of much leadership training and development: stopping the habituated acts that managers may otherwise undertake and getting them to think and act in accord with the demands of the situation (which may be very unique and require a different type of behavior than that which they might otherwise have employed). Here's an interesting quote from some years ago by Rice and Kastenbaum (1983). They were talking about one particular training program, but I think the same may be said for others as well.

> The [X] training program may be effective even if the [X] model is totally lacking in validity. The program's success may derive from a general sensitizing of leaders to the possibility of changing their situation. Such sensitization could be a powerful and beneficial intervention even if the specific model suggestions are neither valid nor followed by leaders so trained. Another interpretation is that this training may be effective simply because it bolsters the confidence that leaders have after receiving their training. (Rice & Kastenbaum, 1983, p. 386)

What we are talking about here has been labeled different things, but what is suggested is that the scientific validity of our theories may be less important than we would like to believe. On the other hand, speaking the manager's language and providing startling insights may matter more, at least in terms of effects produced in the world of leadership practice.

EXCESSIVE INTRICACIES IN OUR THEORIES

Let me now talk about the nature of leadership theories, models, and approaches in terms of their detail. The fourth reason why leadership research is generally not relevant to leadership development is because, being human, managers are forgetful and also have what is called "bounded rationality." This is based upon the anatomy and physiology of the brain, and it involves, in part, a limited ability to store and manipulate (i.e., use) large amounts of information in short-term memory (for a readable summary of the key elements and concepts involved in "bounded rationality," see Behling & Schriesheim, 1976, chap. 2). If you look at most of the leadership frameworks, models, theories, and approaches that have been proposed, developed, tested, and taught over the last 25 or 30 years, they tend to be fairly complex. In fact, I believe that they are too complex for managers to be able to use them on a daily basis because they exceed the cognitive capabilities that managers and, in fact all of us, have (due to our bounded rationality and to other factors, such as forgetfulness).

Let me give you an example of a complex theory. Consider the "normative decision-making" or "leader participation" model of Vroom and Yetton (1973) and Vroom and Jago (1988). This model is commonly given considerable coverage in undergraduate- and graduate-level organizational behavior texts, in addition to being treated in detail in most leadership books. One of the basic premises underlying the model is that we need to teach people the distinction among seven different leadership decision-making styles. These vary from AI (extreme autocratic), where the leader makes decisions unilaterally using information that the leader has on hand, to DI (delegative), where the leader shares the problem with a subordinate, provides whatever information the leader has, tells the subordinate that he/she will support the subordinate's decision, and then lets the subordinate make the decision him or herself.

Next, there is a series of 8 diagnostic questions. They are lettered A through H. We answer these questions "yes" or "no" and work our way along a decision tree. One decision tree (there are several different trees) has 18 endpoints. Each of these 18 endpoints has a list of "feasible" leadership styles. They are listed for both group-based problems and individual problems. We then use some supplemental criterion (which might be the least time spent making the decision, subordinate development, or something else) to select the leadership decision-making style that best fits the situation as we have diagnosed it (by our answers to the 8 diagnostic questions).

Let's summarize. For the decision tree described previously, there are 7 leadership styles, 8 diagnostic questions, and 18 endpoints (each having one or more of the leadership styles as acceptable choices). Additionally, if binary answers (yes/no) seem too simplistic, there is also a computer program that is available where answers can be entered as decimal probabilities (e.g., 0.5). (This is based on treating a "yes" as meaning probability $= 1.0$ and a "no" as meaning probability $= 0.0$.)

How likely is it that the average manager or aspiring leader will be able to memorize this model (including the various decision trees) and remember the details longer than the quiz, final exam, or end of the course or training program? How likely is it that this person will stop and restudy the model (assuming that he/she has forgotten some aspect of it) before selecting a leadership decision-making style? Or, stop everything, go to his/her desk, sit down, call up, and use the computer program? From the discussions that I have had with managers and aspiring managers, my assessment is that most will simply not consider using the model because they cannot remember it or cannot keep all of its parts straight in

TABLE 10.1

The Behaviors of Charismatic and Transformational Leaders[a]

1. Articulate an attractive ideological vision
2. Selectively arouse pertinent follower motives
3. Display passion, self-sacrifice, and personal risk taking
4. Engage in role modeling
5. Show individualized support
6. Show self-confidence, determination, and persistence
7. Exhibit high-performance expectations for followers
8. Display confidence in followers' ability to achieve expectations
9. Engage in personal image building
10. Foster the acceptance of group goals
11. Communicate in an inspirational manner
12. Intellectual stimulation (encourage and provoke questioning)
13. Engage in and encourage innovative behavior
14. Engage in "frame alignment"
15. Show environmental sensitivity
16. Act as an external representative

[a]Based on Castro and Schriesheim's (1998) review of charismatic and transformational leader behavior (meant as a summary of the major behaviors purportedly displayed by charismatic and transformational leaders, according to major leadership scholars).

their heads. The few that might use the model typically tell me that they would use a simplified version that they can recall from memory and then employ. Typically, such a model would include only a few of the diagnostic questions and lead to only one or two leadership decision-making styles.

What's the point? The point is that I believe that leadership is a complex phenomenon and that, consequently, academics are likely to construct complex portrayals of the process. The problem is that such portrayals may be too complex to usefully serve the practice of leadership and leadership development. I've just chosen the Vroom and Yetton (1973) and Vroom and Jago (1988) model as but one illustration of this problem because it is one of the most flagrant examples. However, we are all guilty. As another example, consider the hot leadership area of "charismatic and transformational leadership." Go through the scientific research literature and you will come up with something like Table 10.1.

Table 10.1 presents the behaviors that charismatic and transformational leaders supposedly enact (Castro & Schriesheim, 1998). Can you do all of that? Can anyone do all of that? How are we going to train people to do all that stuff? Which of these behaviors are more important? Which of these behaviors are safest to ignore? I'm not convinced that charismatic and transformational leadership research is particularly bad about excessive detail. However, it is another illustration of the same point—that our research tends to be complex, but our minds tend to be reasonably simple. There seems to be a fundamental misfit here. We need to rethink what it is that we are teaching our managers and our students.

Probably one of the things that we need to examine is the suitability of skill training. First, identifying basic skills that are useful for people if they are going to be successful in this process we call leadership. Then, developing training segments that enhance people's ability to engage in those particular activities. I fear that this suggestion would cause all kinds of problems at most universities and therefore be greeted like the plague. Why is that? Because skill training belongs in the community college, or in technical schools, or (gasp!) in companies. I'm not exactly sure what the exact university reaction would be to such a proposal, but I wouldn't expect an open-armed embrace. We like our complex stuff. After all, it's what differentiates greater from lesser institutions and greater from lesser academics.

ASSUMED LEADER COMPETENCE

In an earlier draft of this work, I had entitled this section, "Assume is Spelled Ass-u-me." Maybe I should have kept that title. Anyway, many (if not most) of our theories of leadership implicitly assume that the leader has the technical ability to make good decisions and provide sound direction to subordinates. For example, House's initial (House, 1971) and revised (House, 1996) path–goal theory of leadership, as well as its intermediate versions (House & Mitchell, 1974), consider situations where it is desirable for the leader to provide subordinates with "task direction," "initiating structure," or "instrumental leadership." However, in these presentations it is assumed that the leader is technically competent or proficient and thereby gives the subordinate appropriate direction, guidance, and structure. What happens if this assumption is violated?

It is true that expert power (French & Raven, 1959) does not require the actual possession of knowledge, skill, and ability but only that that the target *perceives* that the person attempting to exercise expert power (the "agent") has these attributes. However, even with good impression management tactics it will eventually matter whether the agent actually has these attributes or not—Lincoln was probably right when he observed that you cannot fool all of the people all of the time. Thus, our assuming that leaders are technically proficient is, in practice, tantamount to ignoring the issue of leader ability and technical competence altogether, despite its potential importance.

How important is leader ability? We have known for a long time (cf. Campbell, Dunnette, Lawler, & Weick, 1970) that knowledge, skill, and ability are absolutely critical for job performance—at all levels of the organizational hierarchy. Although it is true that motivation "matters" (and more will be said about this later), sheer competence often swamps motivation as a performance determinant. If this is so (and it is!), then how can we ignore the leader's competence in our theories of leadership? This is simply inexcusable, but I think it can be explained, at least in part, by the politics of leadership.

What do I mean, "politics of leadership"? Just that leadership as a field has certain imbedded political processes. For example, leadership scholars avoid debating whether we should be studying and teaching something other than leadership. However, over the years I have come to believe that "followership" is important because although everyone may want to be a leader, everyone (except possibly the CEO) is, for sure, a follower of someone else. If this is true, then we should research followership and also teach it in our various courses within the university. We do not, however, just as companies will not, pay to have someone come on-site and run training programs in "followership." It's just not sexy. Not glitzy. Nobody wants to think about being a follower. Nobody wants to be told that they are a follower. The same politics keep us from considering the possibility that leaders may be deficient with respect to the basic ability to do their jobs (and leadership effectiveness therefore best enhanced not by teaching theories of leadership but by teaching essential job-related knowledge, skill, and ability).

I believe that one of the factors that explains the popularity of the comic strip "Dilbert" is its comedic relevance in showing that bosses are often without ability or technical competence, yet they are still the boss (despite their incompetence) and, consequently, they still rule people's lives. Maybe it's time for leadership theory and research to drop its comic strip assumption about leader ability and face head on the issue of including explicit consideration of leader competence in our various theories, models, and frameworks. Again, this suggestion is likely to be greeted like the plague, but it is a proposition worth considering nonetheless.

ASSUMED LEADER MOTIVATION AND COMMITMENT

As the sixth and final reason why leadership research is generally irrelevant for leadership practice, let me briefly note that leadership involves the personal investment of time, energy, and emotion in followers. Talk to people about their real-life experiences with leaders and you will typically hear that the greatest leader that your conversational partner ever had was great because he or she took a personal interest and made personal investments in the follower that simply were not required or expected (and in some cases not even condoned) by the employing organization. However, despite this being one of the hallmarks of great leadership, many managers are simply unwilling or unable to do so, or they define their jobs in a way that doesn't require such investments in their followers.

Paralleling this real-world phenomenon, leadership research invariably ignores the personal costs of following the prescriptions (implicit or explicit) of most leadership approaches (the personal investment of time, attention, etc. in followers). However, providing subordinates with individualized consideration (Bass, 1985), mentoring (Scandura & Schriesheim, 1994), or just plain old supportive leadership (House, 1971) is not cost free. It takes time and effort, both physical and emotional. But, leaders, as all employees, have to balance work against personal life. Time spent providing individualized consideration and such may require a longer workday and is often seen as not "paying off" in terms of career advancement and other organizational rewards. Consequently, manager motivation and commitment to provide coaching, counseling, guidance, and mentoring need to be explicitly treated in leadership theory and research. This might even lead us to consider studying organizational reward systems for leadership and the processes through which managers are socialized into seeing leadership as involving (or not involving) personal commitment to and investment in subordinates. Although this has generally not characterized work in the leadership domain, if we do not change in this regard we will continue to construct theories, models, and frameworks that are not relevant to most managers because they do not recognize and incorporate the realities of organizational life.

CONCLUSION AND SOME SUGGESTIONS

I've probably rambled on too long already to further burden the reader with a lengthy conclusion and set of recommendations, particularly since solutions to the deficiencies described earlier are pretty simple and obvious to all but the dead. Thus, I will offer some brief ideas, organized again around the six problems I've described. However, before doing so let me add my belief that each of these concerns must be addressed if leadership research is to begin informing managers and those interested in leadership development—rather than merely informing other leadership researchers. The choice, after all, is ours: Do we want to just talk among ourselves or do we want our work to impact and help those who are trying to enhance their leadership effectiveness?

Language

One obvious solution to the language problem discussed earlier is to start talking and writing in English! However, we all know that this is an impossible solution for academics to implement, because "science" is seen as requiring its own language (and its own sense-making mechanisms). The example of Fred Fiedler suggests that one way to talk to practitioners and still not abandon science is to write and publish in two literatures: that read by other scientists and that read by managers and students. Thus, there is no reason why we should not continue publishing abstract academic works—provided that we also publish translations that are accessible to our ultimate customers. Although writing "applied works" takes time and therefore may impair scholarly productivity a bit, my experience is that such works generally can be written very quickly (especially once the scholarly research has been completed), and therefore the cost in terms of foregone scientific publications should be minimal. This seems a small expense to incur to make what we do relevant to those who ultimately foot the bill for our research.

Goals and Objectives

If pushed against the wall and forced to vote to continue or abandon significance testing in scientific research, I would vote to continue it. It is true that if a finding is not "statistically significant" then you cannot assume that you have found anything at all (McNemar, 1969). On the other hand, practical significance is also critical! Who cares if a truly trivial relationship can also be said to be other than zero? It is still trivial. It strikes me that one way of dealing with the goals/objectives issue is to look for research topics from among those problems that are currently plaguing management. This would help ensure relevance to our key constituency outside academia. Perhaps we should also consider holding our research to a higher standard of "significance" and ask that findings not only reject the null hypothesis but also meet some standard of size or potential meaningfulness.

This is clearly uncharted ground. Sure, we have rules of thumb about the meaningfulness of various statistics when they reach certain magnitudes (e.g., factor loadings in excess of .3 or .4), but this is very ad hoc, and such rules are typically used in a haphazard and inconsistent manner at best. As an example of what we might do, scholars interested in this issue should give a closer look at the work of Dansereau, Alutto, and Yammarino (1984). They developed a coherent system of performing within- and between-groups analysis ("WABA") and of interpreting obtained results based on both statistical and practical significance. Dansereau et al. also dared to take a clear stand on practical significance by providing new standards and tests of practical significance for their analytic system. Surely, our need to talk about meaningful findings should prompt others to emulate or, perhaps, extend the ideas and approach of Dansereau et al. (1984) to other types of analyses.

Irrelevance of Validity

One of my favorite jokes is about two men who come out of a bar and see another man on his hands and knees, searching for something around the base of a lamppost. One of the two Samaritans asks, "What are you looking for?", at which point the searcher says, "My car keys." After a few minutes of fruitless searching, also on their hands and knees, the second Samaritan asks, "I don't see the keys. Where did you drop them?" At this point the keyless man responds, "Over there, in that alley, next to my car." Puzzled, the first Samaritan again speaks up, "Then, why are you looking here?" The answer comes back, "Because the light is much better!"

I wonder to what extent we are mimicking this scenario by our almost obsessive quest for scientific validity in our theories, models, and frameworks, and our total lack of concern for developing approaches that help managers stop, see the world differently, think, and formulate new strategies for dealing with their leadership problems. No, I am not saying that we should abandon the search for scientific truth. However, if the principal applied value of scholarly works is to stop habituated behavior on the part of managers and cause them to consider new approaches to leading subordinates, then perhaps we should consider whether our work has action implications and whether it is likely to lead to "startling insights" and to thinking before acting.

Excessive Intricacies

Fred Fiedler (1967) once wrote to the effect that "a pretzel-shaped world needs a pretzel-shaped hypothesis." It is clearly true that leadership processes are complex and, consequently, capturing that complexity requires complex theories. Thus, if we do not abandon the quest for scientific validity, it naturally follows that our scientific works must continue to be highly intricate.

One possible way of handling a dual concern for detail and for simplicity is to develop abbreviated or simplified versions of our more complex ideas. Fiedler's example of simplifying the situations in which leaders find themselves (from eight octants that are used in his scientific research to three aggregate levels of situational favorability—high, medium, and low) comes to mind (cf. Fiedler, 1967; Fiedler & Chemers, 1984; Fiedler et al., 1976). Another possibility is for us to develop an understanding of priorities among the various factors that we research. For example, it would be highly useful to know which of the behaviors summarized in Table 10.1 are most important and which are not. Knowing possible compensatory tradeoffs among the behaviors would also help us communicate to managers which behaviors they should emphasize. Of course, such specifications may not be possible with all of our theories, models, and frameworks, or with all aspects of each approach, but it seems clear that we need to consider how we can trim excessive detail from our scientific theories so that they can become remembered and useful for everyday management practice.

Assumed Leader Competence and Commitment

I am going to discuss these last two problems together because they seem to have a similar solution: Stop assuming! If leader task competence and commitment toward subordinates are important variables that need to be incorporated into our various theories, models and frameworks, let's begin to do so. We should stop building and using approaches that sidestep the important fact that a leader's competence does strongly impact on how well he or she leads. Similarly, it makes no sense to ignore leader motivation. Be it due to organizational reward systems, time pressures, socialization processes, organizational norms, or other factors, not all leaders are committed to making the personal investments that are often necessary to effectively lead followers. Thus, if we are going to develop approaches that mirror the realities of life in most work organization, we need to begin considering the pivotal roles that leader competence and commitment play in leadership processes. To not do so is to continue constructing castles in the sand—pretty but functionally useless, a good time diversion but hardly one of enduring value to anyone (including the builder).

ACKNOWLEDGMENTS

This paper is based upon a talk given at the Kravis-deRoulet Leadership Conference, Claremont McKenna College, Claremont, CA, in 2001, and is dedicated to Fred E. Fiedler, whose dedication to science, professional norms, work ethic, mentoring of new talent, and scholarly contributions are an inspiration to all who study, teach, and practice leadership.

REFERENCES

Bass, B. M. (1985). *Leadership and performance beyond expectations*. New York: Free Press.

Behling, O., & Schriesheim, C. A. (1976). *Organizational behavior: Theory, research, and application*. Boston: Allyn & Bacon.

Bycio, P., Hackett, R. D., & Allen, J. S. (1995). Further assessments of Bass' (1985). Conceptualization of transactional and transformational leadership. *Journal of Applied Psychology, 80*, 468–478.

Campbell, J. P., Dunnette, M. D., Lawler, E. E., III, & Weick, K. E. (1970). *Managerial behavior, performance, and effectiveness*. New York: McGraw-Hill.

Castro, S. L., & Schriesheim, C. A. (1998). What is transformational leadership? An examination and summary of the multiple dimensions of the transformational leadership construct. *Proceedings of the Southern Management Association*. New Orleans: Academy of Management, Southern Division.

Cummings, L. L. (1975). Assessing the Graen/Cashman model and comparing it with other approaches. In J. G. Hunt & L. L. Larson (Eds.), *Leadership frontiers* (pp. 181–185). Carbondale: Southern Illinois University Press.

Dansereau, F., Alutto, J. A., & Yammarino, F. J. (1984). *Theory testing in organizational behavior: The variant approach*. Englewood Cliffs, NJ: Prentice-Hall.

Dansereau, F., & Yammarino, F. J. (Eds.) (1998). *Leadership: The multiple level approaches* (Vol. B). Stamford, CT: JAI Press.

Erdogan, B., & Liden, R. C. (2002). Social exchanges in the workplace: A review of recent developments and future research directions in leader-member exchange theory. In L. L. Neider & C. A. Schriesheim (Eds.), *Research in management* (Vol. 2) (pp. 65–114). Hartford, CT: Information Age Publishing.

Fiedler, F. E. (1967). *A theory of leadership effectiveness*. New York: McGraw-Hill.

Fiedler, F. E. (1977). A reply to Schriesheim and Kerr's premature obituary of the contingency model. In J. G. Hunt & L. L. Larson (Eds.), *Leadership: The cutting edge* (pp. 46–50). Carbondale: Southern Illinois University Press.

Fiedler, F. E., & Chemers, M. M. (1984). *Improving leadership effectiveness: The leader match concept* (Rev. ed.). New York: Wiley.

Fiedler, F. E., Chemers, M. M., & Mahar, L. (1976). *Improving leadership effectiveness: The leader match concept*. New York: Wiley.

Filley, A. C., House, R. J., & Kerr, S. (1976). *Managerial practice and organizational behavior* (2nd ed.). Glenview, IL: Scott, Foresman.

French, J. R. P., & Raven, B. (1959). The bases of social power. In D. Cartwright (Ed.), *Studies in social power* (pp. 150–167). Ann Arbor: University of Michigan Press.

Gerstner, C. R., & Day, D. V. (1997). Meta-analytic review of leader-member exchange theory: Correlates and construct issues. *Journal of Applied Psychology, 82*, 827–844.

Graen, G., & Uhl-Bien, M. (1995). Relationship-based approach to leadership: Development of leader-member exchange (LMX) theory of leadership over 25 years: Applying a multi-level multi-domain perspective. *Leadership Quarterly, 6*, 219–247.

House, R. J. (1971). A path-goal theory of leader effectiveness. *Administrative Science Quarterly, 16*, 321–338.

House, R. J. (1996). Path-goal theory of leadership: Lessons, legacy, and a reformulated theory. *Leadership Quarterly, 7*, 323–352.

House, R. J., & Mitchell, T. R. (1974). Path-goal theory of leadership. *Journal of Contemporary Business, 3*, 81–97.

House, R. J., & Podsakoff, P. M. (1994). Leadership effectiveness: Past perspectives and future directions for research. In J. Greenberg (Ed.), *Organizational behavior: The state of the science* (pp. 45–82). Hillsdale, NJ: Lawrence Erlbaum Associates.

Kerlinger, F. N., & Lee, H. B. (2000). *Foundations of behavioral research* (4th ed.). Fort Worth: Harcourt College Publishers.

Kerr, S., & Schriesheim, C. A. (1974). Consideration, initiating structure, and organizational criteria— An update of Korman's 1966 review. Personnel Psychology, 27, 555–568.

Kerr, S., Schriesheim, C. A., Murphy, C. J., & Stogdill, R. M. (1974). Toward a contingency theory of leadership based upon the consideration and initiating structure literature. *Organizational Behavior and Human Performance, 12*, 62–82.

Lowe, K. B., Kroeck, K. G., & Sivasubramaniam, N. (1996). Effectiveness correlates of transformational and transactional leadership: A meta-analytic review of the MLQ literature. *Leadership Quarterly, 7*, 385–425.

McNemar, Q. (1969). *Psychological statistics* (4th ed.). New York: Wiley.

Mintzberg, H. (1982). If you're not serving Bill and Barbara, then you're not serving leadership. In J. G. Hunt, U. Sekaran, & C. A. Schriesheim (Eds.), *Leadership: Beyond establishment views* (pp. 239–259). Carbondale: Southern Illinois University Press.

Rice, R. W., & Kastenbaum, D. R. (1983). The contingency model of leadership: Some current issues. *Basic and Applied Social Psychology, 4*, 373–392.

Scandura, T. A., & Schriesheim, C. A. (1994). Leader-member exchange and supervisor career mentoring as complementary constructs in leadership research. *Academy of Management Journal, 37*, 1588–1602.

Schriesheim, C. A., Castro, S. L., & Cogliser, C. C. (1999). Leader-member exchange (LMX) research: A comprehensive review of theory, measurement, and data-analytic practices. *Leadership Quarterly, 10*, 63–113.

Schriesheim, C. A., Castro, S. L., & Yammarino, F. J. (2000). Investigating contingencies: An examination of the impact of span of supervision and upward controllingness on leader-member exchange using traditional and multivariate within- and between-entities analysis. *Journal of Applied Psychology, 85*, 659–677.

Schriesheim, C. A., Castro, S. L., Zhou, X., & Yammarino, F. J. (2001). The folly of theorizing "A" but testing "B": A selective level-of-analysis review of the field and a detailed leader-member exchange illustration. *Leadership Quarterly, 12*, 515–551.

Schriesheim, C. A., & Kerr, S. (1977a). R. I. P. LPC: A reply to Fiedler. In J. G. Hunt & L. L. Larson (Eds.), *Leadership: The cutting edge* (pp. 51–56). Carbondale, IL: Southern Illinois University Press.

Schriesheim, C. A., & Kerr, S. (1977b). Theories and measures of leadership: A critical appraisal. In J. G. Hunt & L. L. Larson (Eds.), *Leadership: The cutting edge* (pp. 9–45). Carbondale, IL: Southern Illinois University Press.

Tepper, B. J., & Percy, P. M. (1994). Structural validity of the multifactor leadership questionnaire. *Educational and Psychological Measurement, 54,* 734–744.

Vroom, V. H., & Jago, A. G. (1988). *The new leadership: Managing participation in organizations.* Englewood Cliffs, NJ: Prentice-Hall.

Vroom, V. H., & Yetton, P. W. (1973). *Leadership and decision making.* Pittsburg: University of Pittsburgh Press.

Yammarino, F. J., Dionne, S., & Chun, J. U. (2002). Transformational and charismatic leadership: A levels-of-analysis review of theory, measurement, data analysis, and inferences. In L. L. Neider & C. A. Schriesheim (Eds.), *Research in management* (Vol. 2) (pp. 23–63). Hartford, CT: Information Age Publishing.

Yukl, G. (2002). *Leadership in organizations* (5th ed.). Englewood Cliffs, NJ: Prentice-Hall.

V

Leadership Development: Applications & Practice

11

Leadership Development in Higher Education Institutions: A Present and Future Perspective

Roya Ayman, Susan Adams, Bruce Fisher,
and Erica Hartman
*Institute of Psychology and Leadership Academy
Illinois Institute of Technology*

For centuries all over the world, societies have had an interest in developing leaders (Ayman, 1993, 2000). In ancient Greece, Plato in his *Republic* discussed the lifelong process necessary to develop the philosopher-king. This process of education, according to Plato, consisted of required stages and time periods necessary for the evolution of a person into a leader of society. In his estimation a person would not achieve a sufficient level of maturity to become a leader until the age of 45 or 50. The curriculum presented by Plato was broad based and long term; it focused on developing the body as well as the mind. Thus, to foster development in a leader, a program needs to start early and be holistic (Plato, trans. 1993).

Today, leadership development programs are widespread (Day, 2000). Most large companies (e.g., Anonymous, 1999; Egan, 1999) and business schools have some type of executive development program (e.g., Smith, 2000). Some agencies, such as the Center for Creative Leadership, in collaboration with companies and universities, have extensive programs to assist aspiring executives and managers to learn about effective leadership (e.g., Anonymous, 2000). These types of adult development programs abound. For example, Honan (1998) stated that there are "nearly 700 leadership development programs at American academic institutions today" (p. 20), which he assessed was double the number of programs existing 4 years prior. However, some would argue that the supply of programs is still not keeping up with the high demand. In fact, Zimmerman-Oster and Burkhardt (1999) proposed, "One thing is certain, however. The nation's ability to respond and prosper will depend on the quality of leadership demonstrated at all levels of society" (p. i).

The overwhelming concern for effective leadership brings attention to the need for a systematic curriculum for leadership development in institutions of higher education (see Riggio, Ciulla, & Sorenson, chap. 12, this volume). The Center for Creative Leadership's compilation of existing leadership programs within universities (Schwartz, Axtman, & Freeman, 1998) showed the number and variation in these types of leadership development programs. Although there were a great number of programs, there were a limited number of systematic assessments of leadership development programs in higher education. The scarcity of clear assessments makes it difficult to demonstrate that these programs are developing effective leaders. In the current chapter we review two studies that provide assessment for programs in higher education. In addition, we examined leadership development programs at several highly ranked institutions of higher education by examining these programs based on principles of development, validated theories of leadership effectiveness, and program evaluation.

There are only two studies to date that have investigated leadership development programs in higher education (Olson, 1999; Zimmerman-Oster & Burkhardt, 1999). The W. K. Kellogg Foundation sponsored the first evaluation study. Between 1990 and 1998, the W. K. Kellogg Foundation, funded 31 leadership development programs for young adults in response to the need for developing leaders in our society. Zimmerman-Oster and Burkhardt (1999) conducted an independent evaluation of the foundation's funded programs. The W. K. Kellogg Foundation developed a review panel of nine external experts in leadership development and program evaluation. A description of each program was collected, and each program representative completed an informational survey. The programs held diverse goals and utilized various types of settings or samples (i.e., community groups, high schools, colleges, and universities). The programs included various methods for leadership development such as the use of mentors, guest speakers, and community service opportunities. Of the funded programs, 77% were directed or co-directed by students, and 72% of the programs used their graduates as mentors. For those in academic settings, 58% developed new courses, 14% developed leadership minor and major areas of study, and 35% used faculty awards and grants.

Although the Kellogg report showed that all programs they reviewed included some form of self-evaluation, in addition, the report summarizes the results of two independent evaluation studies. One was a short-term pre- and posttest study that was conducted with the Leadershape Institute for Engineers. The results demonstrated that the participant training experience was positive and their scores on transformational leadership skills improved. Another long-term study, over a 3-year period (in 1994 and from 1997 to 1998), compared 10 institutions that had received a W. K. Kellogg grant and implemented leadership training and development programs to similar institutions that did not. The students were evaluated on 14 individual measures related to leadership such as "understanding self, ability to set goals, sense of personal ethics and willingness to take risks, personal and social values, leadership skills, civic responsibilities, community orientation and multicultural awareness" (p. 12). In comparing participating and nonparticipating institutions, the students of the institutions participating "were much more likely to report significant changes on the measured leadership outcomes" (p. 12).

The Kravis Leadership Institute study focused on undergraduate leadership programs that offered leadership degrees, minors, or certificates (Olson, 1999). This study identified 49 institutions with formal academic programs, of which they conducted interviews with a select 10 institutions. In describing these programs, there are a few notable highlights: Only 3 out of 10 schools conducted systematic follow-up with alumni, all had community service requirements, the majority had an internship component, experiential learning and research were included in several of the programs, and over 90% at least had a course on leadership. Some of the changes programs sought to make for improving the program included an increase in financial support and the number of faculty, innovation in the method of instruction, more rigorous assessment and evaluation, and the use of methods, such as 360-degree feedback.

In summary, these two studies had different objectives with differing samples. The W. K. Kellogg study was broad reaching, including community, high school, and college programs, whereas the Kravis Leadership Institute was exclusively focused on higher education institutions. Program content and delivery were more comprehensive in the W. K. Kellogg programs. The Kravis Leadership Institute primarily focused on programs that offered courses or degrees in leadership. The W. K. Kellogg study only focused on programs that were funded by their foundation.

Although both studies were valuable and met important objectives, there are remaining unanswered questions regarding leadership programs in higher education, such as, how do students juggle their existing majors with the additional requirements of leadership programs. Can we expose our college students to leadership skills and experiences without expecting them to get a second degree? There are many graduates of colleges and universities who move up the career ladder and have not been prepared for the ensuing responsibilities that come with a more prestigious position. Therefore, the focus of this project examines leadership programs that are not based on academic courses or degrees in leadership in highly ranked institutions of higher education.

To embark on this task, a brief explanation of essential ingredients of leadership development programs is presented by highlighting the differences among training, education, and development programs. In addition, the various learning processes that we recommend be incorporated within the delivery of program content are briefly reviewed. After presenting the methodology of the study, the results of our investigation are described. In the results, we identify the number of programs adhering to our criteria, and moreover, we note which principles of theory and research in leadership are included in the programs. In concluding, some future directions for program development and evaluation are offered.

DIFFERENCES AMONG TRAINING, EDUCATION, AND DEVELOPMENT

Before we examine the various programs, it may be of value to consider the differences among training, education, and development. These terms are often used interchangeably (Wexley & Latham, 1991), though each can reflect a unique requirement and objective. Nadler (1984) said that without clear objectives and expectations, it would be difficult to design an appropriate program. He further expanded on these terms and provided a definition for each. His elaborations demonstrated the implications of training, education, and development on the resources, audience, and evaluation strategies of the learning program.

Nadler's definition of training is "learning related to the present job" (p. 18). The learners should be individuals that need the training to improve their performance. There should be an agreement on what the training is about, and the supervisor should have a plan to use the skill of the trained employee once the training is completed. The evaluation of training should be directly reflected in improved performance on the particular aspect of the job for which the employee was trained.

On the other hand he defined education as "learning to prepare the individual for a different but identified job" (p. 19). The distinction made is in regard to timing: Training is for the present and education is for the future. In addition, it seems that education encompasses more content areas than training. The learner under this condition should be an individual who is targeted for changes and future plans. In this setting the learning may not result in improvement of performance in the present job. In this situation, the learner should be considered as a potential resource or human capital. The knowledge, skills, and awareness gained through an education program will prepare participants for the future. The evaluation of this program should focus on whether the learner has learned the skills and knowledge. However, it may not be easy to immediately determine its transferability into results or even behavior. Perhaps the promotion and future success of the learner are more relevant.

Nadler's (1984) definition of development is different from the other processes of learning. He defined it as "learning for growth of the individual but not related to a specific present or future job" (p. 22). So, although both education and development are future oriented, an education program is more focused on an eventual career, but development is more focused on the person's growth. Unfortunately, this term has been misused at times. For example, management development programs in companies are more similar to training and education programs, than to leadership development programs, due to their focus on teaching participants how to manage and attend to different management functions. Development also inherently requires time. Although one could give a training and education program within a short period of time (e.g., half a day or a 40-hr program), development is a long-term process. For example, Avolio (1999) and McCauley, Moxley, and Van Velsor (1998) described leadership development as a process where life experiences are integrated into an individual's leadership capacity. The evaluation of developmental programs is more difficult. Some assessments of developmental programs could be interim assessments of learning, and commitment to the goal of personal development and change.

Therefore, it seems that the similarity and differences of these approaches are based on the time frame and the breadth of exposure to a given domain. Clearly training compared to education is more focused on the present and is more specifically focused on a task or a skill. Developmental programs seem to be focused on a longer time period of learning, and the goal is more general, such as an individual's growth.

When comparing training to education, it could be said that training may be part of an educational curriculum, or it could be free standing. In turn, educational programs seem to also be part of the developmental plan of an individual on a particular path in life. Presumably one could say that education is included within developmental programs. If the goal is development, then the process is an educational curriculum and training is a more specific component of the education process.

In addressing leadership development programs specifically, McCauley et al. (1998) identified three components of a development program: assessment, challenges, and support. Assessment provides an awareness of the level of an individual's performance at a given time. It provides identification of strengths and weaknesses. Development cannot take place if one does not know at what level he or she is performing compared to the standard or ideal. Among the many assessment strategies acknowledged, 360-degree feedback, or multisource rating, provides the needed qualities of insight, self-reflection, and self-awareness (see Conger & Toegel, chap. 3, this volume; Atwater et al., chap. 4, this volume). Assessment centers are another highly valued assessment method that provides participants with developmental feedback. An essential feature of the assessment center method is the use of situational tests (i.e., simulations) to observe specific behaviors. In addition, assessment centers involve trained raters who make independent observations and ratings of participant's behaviors and then reach consensus on their ratings (Thornton, 1992).

McCauley et al. (1998) found that challenge, defined as experiences that force people out of their comfort zone, is an important component of leadership development. Challenge can be due to a lack of experience in an area or to the level of difficulty in the goal. So diversity of experiences and range of difficulty will enrich the challenging experiences. A challenge can also be due to experiences of conflicts or hindrances. A person who has engaged in multiple challenging experiences will be more mature and aware of strategies to succeed. For leadership development, the more a person has been in various leadership positions, the more they have had a chance to develop their ability and knowledge.

Finally, McCauley and colleagues (1998) believe that development could not occur without support. They identified challenging experiences as creating disequilibrium; a condition needs to be offset with a message of lessons learned. A confirming message is needed to ensure that the individual, even at a time of error, has not failed but can grow and develop. The presence of sympathetic others can help the person persevere. Support systems help motivation by giving emotional strength and learning resources. These may come from other participants, such as a coach or a mentor.

Across authors (Avolio, 1999; Day, 2000, McCauley et al., 1998) several characteristics seem to be needed in a leadership development program (see also Day & O'Connor, chap. 1, this volume). It needs to happen over a period of time. It needs to provide self-awareness and confidence through insight and self-reflection. The experiences need to be diverse and realistic. Individuals need to have tools to evaluate, plan, and take action in a systematic way and should also be provided with a support system.

DIFFERENT STYLES OF LEARNING

In the previous sections, we made reference to the learner and learning. It seems apt to elaborate further on the various modes of learning and relate them to learning in leadership development programs. To address the different learning methods, we considered Kolb's (1984) model of learning modes. The model incorporates two dimensions: prehension and transformation. Prehension includes apprehension and comprehension, and transformation includes intension and extension. The former, prehension, is about building skills, knowledge, and understanding. The latter, comprehension, requires a deeper integration of information or new skill. And finally, the transformation dimension refers to incorporating what is learned into one's own self-concept and actions.

From these two dimensions, four learning processes emerge: abstract conceptualization, reflective observation, concrete experience, and active experimentation. In the first process, abstract conceptualization, the learning objective is more cognitive. The concrete experience allows the learner to reflect on experiences and match them to the knowledge gained. In reflective observation, the learner gains wisdom through observation of others either directly in person or through case analysis. The learner notices others' strengths and weaknesses, and this assists the learner in reinforcing his or her own mental map of the concept. Finally, active experimentation is when the learner actually implements what he or she has learned. In this learning process, participants test their newly gained behavior (i.e., knowledge and skill) by acting on it. However, no action should be left without assessment and reflection. This process can give the learners both the confidence and the ability to further integrate what has been learned into their own self-concept. The support system, mentioned earlier by McCauley et al. (1998), is critical to this process.

Combining these learning processes in the leadership development program will allow learners with different learning styles to achieve the learning objectives. In addition, all will have a chance to apprehend, comprehend, as well as assimilate the new concept into their own. Step by step, they will build the values, character, and skills of an effective leader. A learning program with these four processes is conducive to all types of learning experiences and all levels of learning goals (affective, cognitive, behavioral, and results; see Kirkpatrick, 1976). Therefore, it is not surprising that the W. K. Kellogg Foundation requires their grantees to have multimethod delivery as part of their proposed program in order to cover all styles of learning (Zimmerman-Oster & Burkhardt, 1999).

PRESENT STUDY

The need for this study arose partially from the paucity of published research on leadership development programs in higher education. As stated earlier, the W. K. Kellogg Foundation report (Zimmerman-Oster & Burkhardt, 1999) and the Kravis Leadership Institute study (Olson, 1999) both made valuable contributions to the study of leadership development. However, both studies left questions unanswered, which leads to the ideas explored in this chapter. The current study has two primary objectives. The first objective was to examine the presence of leadership development programs at highly ranked institutions of higher education in the United States as rated by U.S. News and World Report 2001 College Rankings (n.d.) as well as by the technical universities that are members of the Association of Independent Technological Universities (AITU). Technology is recognized as a major force for economic advancement. Among the top 50 CEOs, as determined by their companies' performance (Cringely, 1999), about half of them were CEOs of companies in the technological arena. How did these CEOs develop their leadership skills and become so successful? How many aspiring engineers were developed as leaders when in college? Many of the engineers who seek to become leaders have gained their potential unsystematically either by informal means or by pursuing an additional degree such as an Executive MBA or an Engineering Management degree. Accreditation Board for Engineering and Technology (ABET) has very demanding requirements for majors. Thus, the number of credit hours available for undergraduate engineering students to take nonscience electives is limited. Taking extra classes or choosing a minor in leadership may mean more time in school. This may discourage some of these students from pursuing the development of their leadership potential while studying their engineering major. Second, we focused on universities with leadership development programs with multiple-year duration that students of all majors can participate in without any financial or credit hour cost.

Individuals in college are in a learning mode. This state of mind can make them ready and eager to try new things and to think outside of the box. Piaget (1967) and

Vygotsky (1986) identified the adolescent years as the start of the development of abstract and higher order thinking. Therefore, college years are the time when emerging adults can put to use these newly developed cognitive abilities. At this time in their lives they have all the basic perceptual and cognitive skills to analyze and understand more complex and abstract challenges. In addition, for most, this is still a time when they have less family and social responsibilities. Students have more time and energy to devote to building their capabilities for leadership. Therefore, due in part to their age and choice, most college students devote time and energy toward learning. Thus, programs that can seize this opportunity and time to help students develop the skills, knowledge, and wisdom required for leadership are invaluable to our society.

In addition, within the present study we compared the competencies and curricula of the leadership development programs to existing leadership theories. The rationale for this was to explore the relevance between the wealth of knowledge present in a century of research on leadership, with the practical programs that have been designed to develop leaders.

METHOD

Sample

The final sample of participating institutions was 30 colleges and universities. This sample originated from the top 50 colleges and universities as rated by U.S. News and World Report 2001 College Rankings (n.d.). Due to a tie in the ratings, 51 schools were extracted from this ranking. In addition, 17 schools that make up AITU were included. The method of selection of these programs will be delineated in the following section. After eliminating several schools or programs using the following procedures and criteria, the final sample included 20 programs, giving us a response rate of 67%.

Instruments

Two instruments were used to assess the programs included in our sample: the Internet and a semistructured interview. The Internet was used to find relevant information regarding leadership development programs. This enabled us to perform an initial classification of each of the 63 original programs. Based on this classification, selected programs were then assessed using a semistructured interview. The interview included questions that were related to the following topics: admission requirements, number of participants, inclusion of relevant leadership theories, competencies, methods of training, cost, length of program, feedback, and program assessment.

TABLE 11.1
Listing of Complete Sample

Top Schools in Rank Order

---

 1. Princeton University
 2. Harvard University
 3. Yale University
 4. California Institute of Technology[a]
 5. MIT[a]
 6. Stanford University
 7. University of Pennsylvania
 8. Duke University
 9. Dartmouth College
10. Columbia University
11. Cornell University
12. University of Chicago
13. Northwestern University
14. Rice University
15. Brown University
16. Johns Hopkins University
17. Washington University-St Louis
18. Emory University
19. University of Notre Dame
20. University of California-Berkeley
21. University of Virginia
22. Vanderbilt University
23. Carnegie Mellon University[a]
24. Georgetown University
25. University of California-Los Angeles
26. University of Michigan-Ann Arbor
27. University of North Carolina-Chapel Hill
28. Wake Forest
29. Tufts University
30. College of William and Mary
31. Brandeis University
32. University of California-San Diego
33. New York University
34. University of Rochester

35. Georgia Institute of Technology
36. University of Southern California
37. University of Wisconsin-Madison
38. Boston College
39. Case Western Reserve University[a]
40. Lehigh University
41. University of California-Davis
42. University of California-Irvine
43. University of Illinois-Urbana
44. Penn State University-University Park
45. Tulane University
46. University of California-Santa Barbara
47. University of Washington
48. Yeshiva University
49. Pepperdine University
50. Rensselaer Polytechnic Institute[a]
51. University of Texas-Austin

Association of Independent
  Technological Universities
    Cooper Union for the Advancement of
      Science and Art
    Drexel University
    Embry-Riddle Aeronautical University
    Harvey Mudd College
    Kettering University
    Illinois Institute of Technology
    Milwaukee School of Engineering
    Polytechnic University
    Rose-Hulman Institute of Technology
    Worcester Polytechnic Institute
    Rochester Institute of Technology
    Stevens Institute of Technology

---

[a]Indicates school found on both lists included in sample.

Procedure

Sixty-three programs represent the final pool of colleges under examination (Table 11.1). This number corrects for the duplication of five schools found on both listings. The first step was a thorough examination of the available colleges' web sites, searching for the term "leadership" on each site's search engine. Links were followed, on average, five result pages deep. To optimize the search procedure, a different researcher conducted the same search again. In addition, the following sources were reviewed for further information to supplement the initial web searches (*National Clearinghouse for Leadership Programs'* [n.d.] web site; Olson, 1999; Schwartz et al., 1998; Zimmerman-Oster & Burkhardt, 1999). At the time of the second search, the 63 schools were classified into categories based on the level of leadership education and training. Some programs were classified into multiple categories.

If when searching the web, no information was found, that school was placed into Category 1. Category 2 refers to programs with leadership courses as their primary base of leadership development. Category 3 incorporates programs that offer a degree in leadership. These degrees or certificates usually involve credit hours and financial expenses. Category 4 includes programs that had a leadership development program that was not based on course credits. Therefore, Category 4 comprises the sample for our investigation.

Guided by the components of leadership development programs identified by McCauley et al. (1998), the following were necessary for inclusion into Category 4: multiple delivery methods and inclusion of any formal assessment of or feedback for participants. By incorporating multiple methods of delivery, the challenge component identified by McCauley et al. (1998) can be achieved. Requiring individuals to participate in a variety of activities and learning environments, programs may indeed be challenging students. This includes requiring students to participate in new activities they have little or no experience with, or learning from different sources of information. In addition, providing individuals with feedback inherently requires an assessment of skills and support, assessment and support being the other two components identified by McCauley et al. (1998).

In addition to the required criteria, the following program characteristics were assessed: program content based on the use of a leadership theory or principle, presence of admission requirements, leadership competencies included, cost of the program to students (i.e., financial and time), and presence of program evaluation.

The 30 programs were initially classified as members of Category 4 and were researched on the Web for specific information based on our selection criteria for leadership development programs. To verify information found on the Internet and to gather responses to questions unanswered by the Web-based search, these 30 programs were contacted via phone or e-mail. These interviews lasted approximately 15 min, some taking less time due to nearly complete and accurate information available on their web sites, or the programs were determined to be nondevelopmental in nature. Some interviews took longer than 15 min for such reasons as the programs were developmental, and thereby the entire questionnaire was relevant to their program efforts, or the web site described little about the program in terms of our relevant questions. Ten programs did not return our repeated phone calls or e-mails. After over 1 month of attempts, these institutions were then dropped from the sample, leaving us with a total of 20 completed interviews.

RESULTS

The results of this study cover the category dispersion of the originally studied 63 higher education institutions based on the aforementioned procedure. The qualitative results gathered from the interviews demonstrate an inspection of each leadership development program on the qualifying questions based on the three components of leadership development programs. For instance, assessment and support will be addressed under feedback, as feedback requires assessment and coaching. In addition, other pertinent descriptive questions concerning the program(s) will be discussed.

Classification into Category 1, No Program, occurred for 15 of the 63 (or 24%) programs, based on our initial search using each school's search engine. Twenty-six programs (or 41%) met the second category criteria of offering a course(s) in leadership. We classified 8 programs (13%) into Category 3, which as previously mentioned, pertains to institutions that offer a formal degree such as a major or minor in leadership and/or a certificate program involving credit hours. Last, 30 programs were classified as Category 4, developmental leadership programs. As previously mentioned, 20 interviews were completed, and of those 20 programs only 9 remained in Category 4. These 9 programs will be the focus of our qualitative results.

DELIVERY METHODS AND UNIQUE PROGRAM REQUIREMENTS

As previously mentioned, one of the main criteria for classification into Category 4 included the requirement of both academic (structured) and nonacademic (experiential) components within their program(s). A point of clarification is that academic activities represent those activities that include a cognitive component (e.g., lecture, discussion, seminar, or classes), whereas nonacademic activities include those activities with a behavioral component (e.g., community service activities, mentoring, and experiential learning). What follows is a sampling of the various delivery methods and a description of program requirements for the nine Category 4 programs.

Of the nine programs, all included some form of a class or seminar on leadership and/or other competencies that are critical to the goals of the program. In addition, five of the nine programs had an experiential learning retreat. Other experiential activities included internships, community service projects, mentoring, and individual leadership projects. One program, that stood out in quality from the rest of the programs, utilized weekly labs that were integrated into the program's activities. These labs provided the opportunity for the students to practice group facilitation techniques and receive feedback from multiple sources on their performance.

The requirements placed on the participants varied across programs. In general, the programs differed in the choices that were offered to the students. Some of the programs determined required activities based on goals that were set between a student and a mentor. Other programs, however, let students decide which activities they wanted to attend based on interest level. Two programs emphasized in the interview that they require their students to attend everything offered in order to fulfill their commitment. However, the remaining 7 programs allow participants to pick and choose the programs/activities suited for their needs. For instance, the program that requires students to create a "10-point educational plan" with their club advisor mandates participation in those 10 workshops over the course of 3 semesters. Another program offered 2 tracks for program completion. In order to earn a certificate the participant must complete 2 courses, 2 retreats, and 2 quarters of not-for-credit seminars. However, all of these activities are recorded on participants' transcripts, and if individuals do not complete all the requirements, they have a record of their participation on their academic transcript. Another example of a more long-term program was one that requires those admitted in their freshman year to participate for 4 years and complete an internship over the summer.

Feedback Component

The feedback component of the programs was what distinguished the "true" development programs from the rest of the programs. Feedback is essential to the learning environment, whether through formal graded work or through informal verbal feedback. Feedback implicitly involves an assessment of one's skills and knowledge level with the additional quality of providing both support and information for further development of one's skills and knowledge. Each of the nine programs contain various forms of feedback, which will be described in greater detail beginning with more informal feedback examples and ending with examples of more formal feedback systems.

The minimum amount of feedback involved oral feedback given to participants at the end of each program or activity. Another method of ongoing feedback was delivered through frequent meetings with the participant's club advisor in order to process and apply material learned to their own leadership situations.

Additionally, many programs considered the influence of time on leadership development in their individual implementation of programs. For example, one program offered the chance to receive feedback and be questioned in regard to students' future leadership or career goals. Two programs required the students to complete a battery of questionnaires and assessments including a leadership skills inventory. This information is supplemented by feedback from others including peers and instructors.

As previously mentioned, one program utilized weekly group labs in which the entire group is debriefed on its performance followed by a written e-mail with strategies for improvement. In addition, the nominal group leader examines the videotape of the group discussion and is provided with one-on-one feedback regarding his or her facilitation skills. Another program delivered feedback on a group level after completion of their team challenge course including "ropes courses" and other team activities.

The more formal side of feedback arose in programs where academic feedback was given to students. Five programs encouraged the completion of credit-earning classes with such titles as "Foundations of Leadership" and "Historical Studies of Leadership" in addition to the other program components. Another example of formal feedback implementation was found in two programs that mentioned a capstone feedback component of the program usually signifying the end of the individual's participation. One program initiated this process near the end of program completion, whereas the other program assessed a change in leadership skills by administering the battery upon entrance and upon completion of the program. Similarly, another program instituted both pre- and postassessment of goals over the course of 1 year.

Based on the results of this study, all nine schools had some form of feedback. However, the amount of feedback varied from oral feedback given after programs and activities, to peer and mentor feedback after facilitation, to formal academic types of feedback. Therefore, it seems that all of the schools recognize the importance and contribution that feedback can have in the development of the students. This feedback offers both assessment and support, which are both critical components of leadership development.

The following qualitative information pertains to those interview questions not necessary for inclusion into Category 4 but represents additional areas of interest to the present authors. These included the assessment of admission criteria, evaluation processes surrounding the entire leadership development program, and the foundation of the individual program(s) on core competencies and/or leadership theories.

Admission Assessment

Admission was found to be generally open to all students with an emphasis being placed on enrolling first-year or second-year students. However, we did find two programs that targeted junior-year students in order for these students to better transfer their leadership skills to their professional lives. Seven of the nine programs required that students complete some sort of application. Often this application was not a screening agent but rather an information-gathering tool. However, the programs did not typically use this material as selection criteria.

Two programs were characterized by rather extensive selection criteria. One program used a 2.5 out of a 4.0 grade-point average, a requirement of being a member or leader of a student activities-registered organization, and last, completing an application with a "10-point educational plan" with their club advisor.

Another program with selection criteria included the use of a resume and a comprehensive interview, which together are assessed for past leadership, industry and co-curricular experience, future leadership potential, patterns of leadership behavior, high academic achievement, ability to manage time, and motivation for participation.

In conclusion, six out of nine (or 77%) of the programs interviewed have open enrollment, with a first-come-first-served waitlist and an informal application process. Additionally, participation in all of the programs is free to students; however, in institutions where programs encouraged their students to enroll in leadership related courses, there were the obvious tuition costs.

Program Evaluation

Regarding program evaluation, the focus of evaluation varied. Some programs surveyed participants' reactions pertaining to the environmental context of the activity (such as evaluation of the time devoted to the program or the facilitator's performance). Others surveyed participants' reactions toward the entire program in terms of meeting their expectations or satisfaction. Seven out of the nine programs indicated that the entire program or program components (e.g., workshops, seminars or courses) were evaluated. When asked if individual competencies were evaluated, most programs referred to the feedback given to participants concerning their performance within the program. Specific examples of programs evaluations are shared later. Again, these evaluations ranged from informal to more formal, similar to the range of feedback that was given to program participants.

Examples of informal program evaluations frequently contained quick and unstructured assessments. One program utilized informal open-ended questions to gather information such as what aspects of the program were working, what aspects needed to be improved, and specific suggestions for such improvement. Two programs utilized focus groups to gauge the programs' success and to gather ideas for improvement.

On the other hand, formal program evaluations examined individuals' change over time. One program evaluated the occurrence of thought and behavior change after each activity, which is in line with the five stages of the Prochaska Model (see later; Prochaska, 1979). Another program interviewed the alumni of the program every 5 years to assess the long-term impact of the program. This same program also created an advisory group consisting of students, faculty, and staff to give feedback on the program and to guide its future development.

Program Core Competencies

In response to the question, "Is your leadership development program guided by leadership theories and research?" most schools responded by saying that they provide workshops on competencies but they did not choose these competencies based on any leadership research or theory. Only one school focused on transformational leadership theory as the core for their program's components. However, two models of development (i.e., Social Change Model of Leadership Development and Prochaska Model) dominated the direction that these schools took in developing their programs.

1. *Social Change Model of Leadership Development*—A model originating at The University of California, Los Angeles, that focuses on citizenship behaviors and community involvement. The focus is on becoming an effective leader while servicing the good of the public, basically aligns leadership to make an impact in the community (service orientation). This includes seven dimensions such as collaboration, citizenship, common purpose, communication, civility, consciousness of self, and congruence of self. This model was used by five of the nine schools as the foundation of their programs and/or aspects of their program. One of the aforementioned schools utilizing the social change model extended their program to allot attention to multicultural and global issues.

2. *Prochaska Model*—This is a model that entails five steps: precontemplation, contemplation, preparation, action, and follow-up. Basically, this model uses different approaches to get a person committed to change. Once they are ready to change, they then examine if a change has occurred in their thinking and/or behavior. The model incorporates feedback the entire way through (e.g., students are assessed after completion of each program to see if they are ready to change or if have changed behavior). The model is more of an approach to learning/training. It seems like you can use whatever competencies you wish. This model used in one particular program included nine competencies such as oral and written communication, decision making and judgment, team building, problem identification, analysis and problem solving, leadership theory, stress management, self-assessment, integrity, goal setting, and strategic planning.

Other programs' competencies closely resemble those listed here. One program stressed group facilitation and discussion skills and brainstorming techniques as the main competencies of their program. When asked about competencies, many of the programs substituted the topics of their workshops as a listing of competencies they are attempting to foster in the participating students. One program listed organizational understanding, communication skills, appreciation of diversity, ethic of service, personal integrity, self-awareness, networking, public speaking, and creative problem solving.

DISCUSSION

This study had two overall objectives. The first was to describe the present status of leadership development programs in high-ranking universities, as well as technical universities, based on the components of assessment, experience, and support

(McCauley et al., 1998). Additionally, these leadership development programs were analyzed on criteria beyond that of assessment, experience, and support, namely, the use of evaluation systems and leadership theories and models to guide program content. Therefore, the second purpose of this study was to use this additional information to suggest guidelines for the future success of leadership development programs in higher education.

Leadership Theories and Competencies

Of the 30 programs originally classified as Category 4 according to our criteria, only 9 were in fact truly developmental programs. Most surprising, out of the 9 leadership development programs, only 1 mentioned a leadership theory as central to their program (e.g., transformational leadership). For a century, leadership researchers have examined the relationship between traits, competencies and behaviors associated with leader effectiveness (Ayman, 2000; Bass, 1990; Chemers, 1997). More recently, Leadership Quarterly (Vol. 11, 2000) dedicated an issue to leadership with a focus on the skills and knowledge needed for leadership (Mumford, Zaccaro, Harding, Jacobs, & Fleishman, 2000). Yet, when practitioners are designing a curriculum of leadership development at higher education institutions, they did not acknowledge this body of knowledge. To explore the reason for this disparity is beyond the scope of this chapter. However, we compared the competencies listed in the leadership development programs to the competencies that leadership models, theories, and research support.

Relating the aforementioned competencies included in the leadership development programs to leadership theories, we first categorized them into six competency categories. These competences included: communication skill, teamwork (collaboration, common purpose, team building and team dynamic, civility), problem solving, ethics and integrity or moral leadership, self-awareness, and strategic planning and goal setting.

The importance of communication and team building is inherent in several components of transformational leadership theory (Bass & Avolio, 1993). In particular, it is through effective communication and skills of team facilitation that a leader can express the components of transformational leadership, namely, individual consideration, inspirational motivation, and idealized influence. Another leadership theory that also strongly advocates communication and team building in the role-making and relationship-building process is the Leader–Member Exchange model (Graen & Uhl-Bien, 1995; Cogliser & Scandura, chap. 8, this volume; Uhl-Bien, chap. 7, this volume). To build effective relationships, it is important to have effective communication skills and the ability to work cooperatively. Therefore, communication skills and teamwork are competencies that have empirical support in well-known leadership theories.

Articulating a vision is another element of communication and team building and occurs in transformational leadership through idealized influence and intellectual stimulation (Bass & Avolio, 1993). A vision requires a clear plan and an articulation of goals. It could also be said that the initiating structure behavior of a leader, as reflected in the Ohio State studies (Bass, 1990), alludes to similar principles of setting clear expectations. The choice of problem-solving strategy is well discussed in Vroom and Yetton's (1973) leadership decision-making model. In this model, leaders are advised to choose the extent to which they involve their team in the problem-solving process. More recently in a study of military officers (Zaccaro, Mumford, Connelly, Marks, & Gilbert, 2000) more specific skills and abilities related to problem-solving were identified. These included complex problem-solving skills, solution characteristic skills, social judgment skills, and knowledge.

Self-awareness has received a great deal of attention in recent years especially with rise of 360-degree feedback or multisource ratings (Atwater & Waldman, 1998; Dalton & Hollenbeck, 2001; also see this volume, chap. 4, Atwater et al., and chap. 3, Conger & Toegel). In leadership research, the contingency model of leadership effectiveness (Ayman, Chemers, & Fiedler, 1998; Fiedler, 1978) and its training model, Leader-Match (Fiedler & Chemers, 1986), incorporate self-awareness. In his model, Fiedler provided tools such as the LPC (Least Preferred Co-Worker) scale and situational control measures to help leaders become aware of their leadership orientation (task or relationship) as well as of the features of the situations in which they lead. The concept of self-awareness in leadership has received support for assisting leaders to be successful (London, 2002).

The area of moral leadership or ethics and leadership has not received as much direct empirical attention, but is often mentioned as an important component of existing leadership theories. Bass and Steidlmeier (1999), for example, recently described moral leadership as a leader with characteristics such as humility, being virtuous, a person with integrity, possessing loyalty, being generous, forgiving, and helping others. Moreover, they believe that transformational leadership must be based on principles of virtuosity and morality to be truly effective. Similarly, Kanungo and Mendonca (1996) acknowledged transformational and charismatic leadership as potentially related to ethical and moral leadership, describing that leaders are ethical when they are concerned for others. In fact, this concern for others, or altruism, taken to the extreme is a requirement of an ethical leader "even if it results in some cost to self" (p. 35). Furthermore, this concept of self-sacrifice in the context of leadership is said to be manifested in the leader's actions with respect to division of labor, rewards distribution, and exercise of power (Choi & Mai-Dalton, 1998). Use of skills and competencies related to transformational leadership seem to also have relevance to moral leadership. Servant leadership and moral leadership are labels for skills and behaviors related to values such as empathy toward others, inclusiveness, and tolerance of others.

In general, institutions in our study did not articulate the various theories and research that were the basis of their choice of competencies. However, the competencies chosen seemed to be supported with past empirical research and theory.

Therefore, on one hand, the relevance of the explicit connectivity of theories and research to competencies in curriculum was absent. On the other hand, as assessors of the leadership development programs, we felt assured that the competencies in the curriculum had solid scientific background.

Program Evaluation

In our review of the various programs in our sample we noticed that there was always some form of program evaluation present. However, it was not clear whether the program managers had made a conscious choice as to which level of assessment to include. If Kirkpatrick's model (1976) of training evaluation were to be considered, it seems the majority of the programs used the first level (affective reaction) and third level (behavior change). Very few programs mentioned the use of the fourth level (results), beyond the use of alumni follow-up surveys that may or may not include such information as job positions, salary, or promotions. This review seems to show that the programs overall were fairly well monitored.

Limitation

Due to time constraints and funding we were not able to survey or interview all universities. Additionally, we were dependent on Web information for our categorization. To the extent that these universities have information readily accessible, our study has validity. However, to the extent that the information was not accurately communicated via Web or interview, the study is limited.

CONCLUSIONS

In closing, the reviewed leadership development programs demonstrated a significant number of positive attributes, including the use of multiple approaches for the delivery of program content and the provision of opportunities for students to apply their leadership knowledge base. The current review also uncovered key areas for improvement within leadership development programs. Perhaps the most serious deficiency of the reviewed leadership development programs was the absence of a foundation based on leadership theory(ies). Other program limitations concern a lack of individualized feedback, the need to adhere to continual process learning, and the need for more complete program evaluation.

In general, university-based leadership development programs give greater consideration to learning theories than to leadership theories. Most of the universities studied adopt a multimethod approach to the delivery of their programs. The inclusion of traditional academic methods (e.g., seminars, lectures) as well as experiential methods (e.g., community service, internships) ensures attention to both the cognitive and the behavioral learning domains. Indeed, what most university-based leadership development programs appear to offer are learning experiences that are distinct from the traditional academic structure. As compared to most university coursework, there is a far greater reliance on experiential learning and field experiences (e.g., mentoring, community service, internships) within leadership development programs. The university model for leadership development generally conforms most closely with principles of adult learning (Kolb, 1984). Programs already incorporating multimethod approaches for program content delivery should continue on this path. Those programs that are more limited in their methodology could further develop the impact of their program on students by providing multiple means of information transfer.

As previously mentioned, it is especially noteworthy that many university-based leadership development programs focus on experiential learning to reinforce leadership principles taught or trained in a more cognitive domain. Such experiences provide students with an opportunity to act on and utilize leadership principles previously studied within seminars or discussed within workshops.

One such example, community service, was ubiquitous within the reviewed programs. Consistent with a general trend toward a greater emphasis on citizenship and values, many university programs have adopted a servant leadership focus. Indeed, since 1987, sixty-nine of W. K. Kellogg Foundation grantees have defined themselves as servant–leader organizations (Spears, 1995). Additional positive side effects of instituting community service are opportunities to see oneself as a leader in action, to practice leadership skills with real situations, and to connect and build networks with other leaders and with the community in general. Another commonly found experiential component, mentoring partnerships, also fosters positive benefits for the students. Opportunities such as observing another's leadership and management skills in action or gaining self-awareness through another's perspective are just a few of the benefits of mentoring partnerships. These activities support Kolb's (1984) learning processes and needed elements in leadership development programs in organizations (Day, 2000). Community service, mentoring partnerships, and other experiential learning activities, embraced by many leadership development programs in the institutions of higher education, are critical to the successful transfer of leadership principle knowledge to practice. These experiences can increase their potential impact by integration of individual performance feedback.

As represented in the reviewed programs, formal individualized feedback was lacking. Self and others' assessment of the various skills and competencies are generally needed to enhance student learning. This type of feedback should be combined with coaching and plans for enhancing student mastery and confidence.

Another weakness lies in the fact that the majority of programs are short-term, consisting of a single course or independent workshop. Although these activities are valuable and enhance the students' knowledge base, the students' behavior and values may not be affected with such brief exposure. Future programs should be more process driven over a period of time rather than conducted as a one-time event. Assessment procedures should be implemented prior to and after the program to evaluate individual and program-level outcomes. Program content should be sequenced to build upon previously acquired skills. A continual learning process not only benefits program impact but also provides information for individual feedback, information for overall program evaluation, and a platform for integrating leadership theories into program content.

With few exceptions, leadership theories are not incorporated into the design of university-based leadership development programs. This disconnect between leadership theory and the content of many leadership development programs provides further evidence of the gap between theory and practice in the field of leadership (see Schriesheim, chap. 10, this volume). Still, despite the fact that academic research and theory are not formally recognized in most university-based leadership development programs, these programs do nonetheless focus on competencies that are suggested by a variety of popular leadership theories (e.g., transformational leadership, contingency model of leadership). Perhaps more integrative models of leadership, such as those of Chemers (1997), will provide guidance for more theory-based and comprehensive leadership curricula.

The increased focus on leadership development within our institutions of higher learning is exciting. As our universities stretch beyond traditional academic subjects to focus on leadership, personal growth and development, and even values, higher education is positioned to play a more pivotal role in the development of a leadership culture in our society. Still, greater attention must be given to systematic program evaluation with a focus on longitudinal research and higher order outcomes. Attention to outcome criteria such as income, career advancement, and intellectual patents is appropriate, but programs should also include criteria such as community service, philanthropy, and mentoring of others. It is at this level that the university-based leadership development programs may provide the broadest impact on our society.

Many excellent and remarkable leadership development programs have been established in various institutions. Therefore, leadership development programs in higher education institutions need to learn from each other. The programs with not only strong learning principles but also solid curricula should increase. The evolution and advancement in our leadership development programs in higher education institutions will contribute toward meeting our society's goal of developing leaders in all walks of life.

ACKNOWLEDGMENTS

We would like to thank Dr. Iraj Ayman and Dr. Saba Ayman-Nolley for their comments.

REFERENCES

Anonymous (1999, October 11). Molding global leaders. *Fortune*, p. 270.

Anonymous (2000, February). Creating a university to train tomorrow's leaders. *HR Focus*, pp. 11–13.

Atwater, L. E. & Waldman, D. A. (1998). Introduction: 360 degree feedback and leadership development. *The Leadership Quarterly, 9*, 423–426.

Avolio, B. J. (1999). *Full leadership development: Building the vital forces in organizations.* Thousand Oaks, CA: Sage.

Ayman, R. (2000). Leadership. In E. F. Borgatta & R. J. V. Montgomery (Eds.), *Encyclopedia of sociology: Vol. 3* (2nd ed., pp. 1563–1575). New York: Macmillan Reference U.S.A.

Ayman, R. (1993). Leadership perception: The role of gender and culture. In M. M. Chemers & R. A. Ayman (Eds.), *Leadership theory and research: Perspectives and directions* (pp. 137–166). New York: Academic Press.

Ayman, R., Chemers, M. M., & Fiedler, F. E. (1998). The contingency model of leadership effectiveness: Back to the future. In F. Yammarino & F. Dansereau (Eds.), *Leadership: The multi-level approaches* (pp. 135–144). New York: JAI Press.

Bass, B. M. (1990). Bass & Stogdill's *Handbook of leadership: Theory, research and managerial applications* (3rd ed.). New York: The Free Press.

Bass, B. M., & Avolio, B. J. (1993). Transformational leadership: A response to critiques. In M. M. Chemers & R. Ayman (Eds.), *Leadership theory and research: Perspective and directions* (pp. 49–80). New York: Academic Press.

Bass, B. M., & Steidlemeier, P. (1999). Ethics, character, and authentic transformational leadership behavior. *The Leadership Quarterly, 10*, 181–218.

Chemers, M. M. (1997). *An integrative theory of leadership.* Mahwah, NJ: Lawrence Erlbaum Associates.

Choi, Y., & Mai-Dalton, R. R. (1998). On the leadership function of self-sacrifice. *The Leadership Quarterly, 9*, 475–502.

Cringely, R. X. (1999, May). The Best 50 CEO's. *Worth: Financial Intelligence*, 106–148.

Dalton, M., & Hollenbeck, G. P. (2001). A model for behavior change. In D. W. Bracken & C. Timmreck (Eds.), *The handbook of multisource feedback: The comprehensive resource for designing and implementing MSF processes* (pp. 352–367). San Francisco: Jossey-Bass.

Day, D. V. (2000). Leadership development: A review in context. *The Leadership Quarterly: Yearly Review of leadership*, 11, 581–613.

Egan, M. D. (1999, October 18). Leadership training increases in popularity. *National Underwriter*, pp. 30.

Fiedler, F. E. (1978). The contingency model and the dynamics of the leadership process. In L. Berkowitz (Ed.), *Advances in experimental social psychology: Vol. 11* (pp. 59–96). New York: Academic Press.

Fiedler, F. E., & Chemers, M. M. (1986). *Improving leadership effectiveness: The leader match concept* (2nd ed.). New York: Wiley.

Graen, G. B., & Uhl-Bien, M. (1995). Relationship–based approach to leadership: Development of leader-member exchange (LMX) theory of leadership over 25 years: Applying a multi-level multi-domain perspective. *The Leadership Quarterly, 6*, 219–247.

GVU's 8th WWW user survey. (n.d.). Retrieved August 8, 2000, from http://www.cc.gatech.edu/gvu/usersurveys/survey1997-10

Honan, W. H. (1998, September 30). Programs that make leadership their goal. *New York Times* pp. 20.

Kanungo, R. N., & Mendonca, M. (1996). *Ethical dimensions in leadership.* Beverly Hills, CA: Sage.

Kirkpatrick, D. L. (1976). Evaluation of training. In R. L. Craig (Ed.), *Training and development handbook: A guide to human resource development* (pp. 18–27). New York: McGraw-Hill.

Kolb, D. A. (1984). *Experiential learning: Experience as the source of learning and development.* Engelwood, NJ: Prentice-Hall.

London, M. (2002). *Leadership development: Paths to self insight and professional growth.* Mahwah, NJ: Lawrence Erlbaum Associates.

McCauley, C. D. Moxley, R. S., & Van Velsor, E. (Eds.). (1998). *Handbook of leadership development.* San Francisco: Jossey-Bass.

Mumford, M. D., Zaccaro, S. J., Harding, F. D., Jacobs, T. O., & Fleishman, E. A. (2000). Leadership skills for a changing world: Solving complex social problems. *The Leadership Quarterly, 11*, 11–36.

Nadler, L. (1984). Human resource development. In L. Nadler (Ed.),*The handbook of human resource development* (pp. 1–47). New York: Wiley.

National Clearinghouse for Leadership Programs. (n.d.). Retrieved January 16, 2001, from http://www.inform.umd.edu/CampusInfo/Departments/OCP/NCLP/CampusLinks.htm

Olson, D. A. (1999). *Overview of undergraduate leadership studies programs: Preparing tomorrow's leaders.* Unpublished manuscript, Kravis Leadership Institute, Claremont McKenna College, CA.

Piaget, J. (1967). *Six psychological studies* (A. Tenzer, Trans.). New York: Vintage Books. (Original work published 1964).

Plato (1993). *Republic* (Waterfield, R., Trans.). Oxford: University Press. (Original work published).

Prochaska, J. O. (1979). *Systems of psychotherapy: A transtheoretical analysis.* Homewood, IL: Dorsey Press.

Schwartz, M. K., Axtman, K. M., & Freeman, F. H. (Eds.). (1998). *Leadership education: A source book of courses and programs* (7th ed.). Greensboro, NC: Center for Creative Leadership.

Smith, R. (2000, May 8). College to offer leadership class. *Chicago Tribune*, p. 2NW3.

Spears, L. (1995). *Reflections on leadership: How Robert K. Greenleaf's theory of servant-leadership influenced today's top management thinkers* (pp. 352). New York: Wiley.

Thornton, G. C. (1992). *Assessment centers in human resource management.* Reading, MA: Addison–Wesley.

U.S. News and World Report 2001 College Rankings. (n.d.). Retrieved December 23, 2000, from http://www.usnews.com/usnews/edu/college/rankings/natunivs/natu_a2.htm

Vroom, V. H., & Yetton, P. W. (1973). *Leadership and decision-making.* Pittsburgh, PA: University of Pittsburgh Press.

Vygotsky, L. S. (1986). *Imagination and creativity in the adolescent* (F. Smolucha, Trans.). Unpublished manuscript, University of Chicago. (Original work published 1931).

Wexley, K. N., & Latham, G. P. (1991). *Developing and training human resources in organizations.* Palo Alto, CA: Scott, Foresman.

Zaccaro, S. J., Mumford, M. D., Connelly, M. S., Marks, M. A., & Gilbert, J. A. (2000). Assessment of leader problem solving capabilities. *The Leadership Quarterly, 11*, 37–64.

Zimmerman-Oster, K., & Burkhardt, J. C. (1999). *Leadership in the making: Impact and insights from leadership development programs in U.S. colleges and universities.* Battle Creek, MI: W. K. Kellogg Foundation.

12

Leadership Education at the Undergraduate Level: A Liberal Arts Approach to Leadership Development

Ronald E. Riggio
Kravis Leadership Institute
Claremont McKenna College

Joanne B. Ciulla
Jepson School of Leadership Studies
University of Richmond

Georgia J. Sorenson
James MacGregor Burns Academy of Leadership
University of Maryland

The number of recognized leadership development programs in institutions of higher education is rapidly nearing 1,000. This includes all three forms of leadership programs—training, education, and development, as outlined by Ayman, Adams, Hartman, and Fisher (chap. 11, this volume; also see Mangan, 2002; Sorenson, 2000). Yet, relatively few of these programs are curricular-based undergraduate programs offering academic credit in the form of a bachelor's degree, academic minor, or certificate. The purposes of this chapter are (a) to provide an overview of the historical and conceptual development of undergraduate leadership studies programs, (b) to connect college-based leadership studies programs with

the larger literature on leadership development via a model, (c) to provide guidelines for undergraduate curricular programs, and (d) to provide specific examples
of leadership studies curricula with a liberal arts focus.

A BRIEF HISTORY
OF LEADERSHIP STUDIES

Throughout history, scholars from Plutarch to Carlyle have studied leaders and
leadership. Leadership studies as we know it today emerged from social science research conducted primarily in the United States and almost exclusively
since the turn of the 20th century.[1] Explanations for the strong role played by the
United States range from the individualistic (and thus leader-focused) nature of the
American experience, the relative stability of the American economy and demo-
cratic system, neoliberalism (DeMott, 1993), and the stream of leadership funding
from American foundations and government. Leadership studies also evolved as
a result of America's powerful and innovative business culture, which was always
hungry for new and productive ways to manage the workplace. Management research was heavily subsidized by big business, and some of this work formed the
building blocks of leadership studies (Ciulla, 2000).

The first large-scale research projects on leadership in the United States were
funded by the government in the 1940s, principally as a means of improving
wartime efficiency.[2] Later, in 1966, the Smith Richardson Foundation supported
Ralph Stodgill's systematic review of literature on leadership, resulting in the
seminal *Handbook of Leadership* published in 1974 (Troyer, 1997).

Several large public universities played pioneering roles in the evolution of the
empirical study of leadership, notably, Ohio State, Southern Illinois at Carbondale, and Michigan State. In small teams in these and other public universities,
researchers, chiefly in the fields of psychology and sociology, conducted early
research on leadership, in part the result of robust postwar funding (Sorenson &
Howe, 2001).

There was independent work undertaken in small liberal arts colleges as well.
In 1978, James MacGregor Burns of Williams College published *Leadership*, a
book embraced by academics and the general public alike for its interdisciplinary
effort. It was a revolutionary book in many ways and continues to be among the
five top books used in leadership studies classes around the country (Sorenson,
2000).

---

[1] Indeed, the hegemony of the American construction of leadership is a serious problem in eliciting
and understanding culturally based views of leadership. Even U.S.-based programs by and large lack
an international perspective (see Gamaliel Perruci's excellent paper, "Leadership Studies Programs in
the Context of Globalization," available from the International Leadership Association, 1999.)

[2] See the Office of Naval Research and the Army Research Institute, especially the efforts of Owen
Jacobs.

Despite Burns' effort, the study of leadership continues today to be multidisciplinary for the most part rather than truly interdisciplinary. Scholars in academic fields as divergent as political science, psychology, business, education, history, agriculture, public administration, management, anthropology, biology, military sciences, philosophy, and sociology have contributed to an understanding of leadership. Subfields within disciplines (e.g., educational leadership, political leadership, business leadership) are taking hold and providing academic niches for leadership research. But even in departments that house scholars of various disciplines, the integration of their work is still rare. One notable exception is the so-called "general theory of leadership" group that began meeting in 2002 (Mangan, 2002).

Rise of Leadership Programs

The work by researchers and scholars, such as Bass, Fiedler, Hollander, Hunt, Burns, and others over time, contributed to the rise of leadership programs in academe. And to some degree, higher education organizations and private foundations contributed to the establishment of early programs as well. In 1976, an American College Personnel Association (ACPA) Taskforce produced one of the first surveys of the field, *Leadership Programs in Higher Education*. The number of sessions on leadership at the American Educational Research Association conferences doubled between 1985 and 1995[3] and the Center for Creative Leadership inaugurated the Leadership Education Conference. The W. K. Kellogg, Ford, and Carnegie Foundations produced seminal reports and provided early funding. Leadership courses for credit emerged shortly thereafter. Gonzaga University started offering a liberal arts-oriented Ph.D. program in leadership studies in 1980. In 1986, the McDonough Leadership Program at Marietta College was established as one of the first undergraduate liberal arts leadership programs. The Academy of Leadership, now called the James MacGregor Burns Academy, was established in 1981 and soon began offering a variety of leadership educational programs. Courses on leadership continued to proliferate on college campuses through the early 1990s. But it was not until 1992, however, that the Jepson School of Leadership Studies at the University of Richmond, with money from Richmond alumnus Robert Jepson, became the first autonomous degree-granting School of Leadership Studies.

"Leadership programs are now embedded in every imaginable discipline," according to *Leadership Education: A Source Book of Courses and Programs*, the most comprehensive compendium on educational leadership efforts (Schwartz, Axtman, & Freeman, 1998). The number of programs continues to grow exponentially, with more than double the number of only 4 years ago.[4] In fact, today

---

[3] Private communication with William Howe, 1999.

[4] Interview with Mary Schwartz, Center for Creative Leadership, Greensboro, North Carolina, August 2000.

there are more than 100 programs that offer some sort of academic recognition for students in leadership studies.[5] These efforts now range from single leadership resource centers to graduate degree programs in leadership studies (Honan, 1998). There is tremendous growth in liberal arts, history, agriculture, literature, and philosophy in particular, as well as in the original base of business and the social sciences.[6] Double degrees, leadership majors, minors and certificates, and increasingly graduate degrees and Ph.D's in leadership studies are offered in these pioneering programs. Many of the graduate degrees with leadership in the title are area specific, such as organizational leadership and educational leadership. Although there are many new players, in a recent analysis of the disciplinary base of leadership faculty by William Howe (1997), the behavioral and social sciences and business management continue to drive most leadership coursework in America.

We must conclude that growth of leadership research and leadership education has been nothing short of revolutionary. In the last 2 decades, the study of leadership has spawned thousands of publications across numerous disciplines. Professional journals, such as *Leadership Quarterly* and *The Journal of Leadership Studies*, and new ones, such as the *Leadership Review*, an online journal, have been established and are devoted exclusively to leadership research. A professional association, the *International Leadership Association*, was launched in 1999 with the goal of establishing an independent professional association in the near future. Clearly, the area of leadership studies has come of age. The challenge before us is to develop a coherent and useful model that integrates the research, pedagogy, and best practices of our accumulated experience.

A MODEL FOR COLLEGE-BASED LEADERSHIP DEVELOPMENT

Day (2000) distinguishes between *leader* development and *leadership* development. Leader development has a more individual focus, whereas leadership development focuses on the development of leadership capacity in the context of a group or organization. For the most part, in undergraduate leadership programs, the focus is on developing the individual student's leadership potential via imparting knowledge, skills, abilities, and values. Most students are not currently in professional leadership positions (although many students in leadership programs may hold student leadership posts), so typically the emphasis in undergraduate programs is on preparing students for future leadership positions, or simply increasing their understanding of leadership. Therefore, what is delivered in most undergraduate leadership programs is consistent with Day's definition of leader development. Van Velsor, McCauley, and Moxley (1998) have a similar individual

---

[5] Ibid.
[6] Ibid.

focus and view leadership development "as the expansion of a person's capacity to be effective in leadership roles and processes" (p. 4). In sum, the college-based leadership development programs that we discuss are those that are offered as part of the college's or university's regular curricular offerings, and they usually lead to some sort of major or minor in the subject, other academic credit such as a certificate of completion, or in the case of the Jepson School a bachelor's degree in leadership studies. This is a very different focus from that of the Ayman et al. chapter in this volume that focuses on noncredit programs. Putting this into the larger context, Brungardt (1996) views these curricular *leadership education* programs as only a small subset of the larger area of leadership development.

There are many "philosophies" driving leadership education programs. Some programs are guided by business models of leadership, with heavy reliance on a management approach to leadership education. These programs emphasize educating students to lead organizations with a curriculum that is heavily grounded in research from the areas of management and organizational psychology.

A second type of program is more multidisciplinary than the management-based programs and focuses on citizenship as the core of leadership education—emphasizing an understanding of and an engagement in democracy, values of social responsibility, and social action (Rost & Barker, 2000; Welch, 2000). Astin and Astin (1996) advocate this approach in what they call a "social change model of leadership development"—increasing students' potential for developing into leaders through a combination of classroom learning and social and civic engagement via service learning.

A third type of leadership education, and one that will be discussed more fully in this chapter, uses a liberal arts model—emphasizing that a broad educational experience is essential to leadership development (Gardner, 1990).

In creating guidelines for university- and college-based leadership education programs we attempt to draw on what is known about effective leadership development, as well as on sound educational practices and pedagogy for undergraduate education. We have tried to learn from our experiences in developing and coordinating leadership studies programs and the experiences of our colleagues at other institutions. We offer six basic guidelines.

Leadership Studies Should Be Multidisciplinary

As we have seen, the study of leadership is not limited to a single discipline. As mentioned earlier, faculty from a plethora of disciplines have contributed to research and education in leadership. In the same way that one cannot do competent research in leadership without surveying literature across multiple disciplines, it is very difficult to teach leadership from a single disciplinary view. This is not to say that programs cannot be "slanted" toward a particular disciplinary emphasis. Indeed, some leadership studies programs are housed in particular academic departments. This multidisciplinary emphasis is most consistent with other academic programs, most notably women's studies, American studies, ethnic studies programs, and public administration.[7]

Not only is the multidisciplinary approach to leadership education important because it provides curricular "breadth," but also there is evidence from cognitive psychology that suggests that learning is enhanced by the presentation of a particular construct from multiple perspectives and contexts (deWinstanley & Bjork, 2002; Halpern, in press). In other words, studying leadership from political, psychological, and historical perspectives should enhance students' more general understanding of the leadership construct.

Leadership Studies Students Should Be Authorized Academically

Leadership studies should be a recognized academic pursuit. Therefore, it is essential that completion of a program of leadership studies be recognized on a student's academic record via a major, minor, or academic certificate of accomplishment. There are instances where leadership programs are offered by undergraduate offices of student affairs or through the Dean of Students office. However, these constitute pure leadership development programs, as outlined by Ayman et al. (chap. 11, this volume), and would not be considered leadership *studies* programs, as valuable as these might be to student development. If leadership studies is truly an emerging discipline—and we believe it is—then academic credit must be offered, as well as academic authorization.

Leadership Studies Programs Are Guided by Theories and Research on Leadership

This point has two meanings. First, it concerns what is taught in a leadership studies program. A leadership studies curriculum should present important theories of leadership, and the content should be well grounded in leadership research. In other words, a sound leadership studies curriculum should avoid relying on "faddish" concepts and techniques and should give primary attention to teaching theories, concepts, and their applications that have been subjected to rigorous and objective evaluation and, where possible, empirical testing.

Second, the leadership studies curriculum and pedagogy should be consistent with the results of leadership research. In other words, when it comes to leadership education we should "practice what we preach." For instance, effective and ethical decision making, ability to think critically, and interpersonal skills are all believed to be important for successful leadership (Cavenagh, 1997; Ciulla, 1996;

---

[7]Note that Public Administration has emerged as a core discipline, but in its early days the field was clearly multidisciplinary.

Conger & Benjamin, 1999; Hughes, Ginnett, & Curphy, 2003; McVey, 1995). Therefore, these topics, and many others, should be included in the leadership curriculum. Moreover, leadership is an applied discipline. Leadership is both a topic of study and a set of knowledge and skills to be applied to leading groups and organizations effectively. Therefore, attention to the development of leadership skills should be a focus of leadership studies programs—producing graduates who possess knowledge of leadership studies, but who also have enhanced their personal leadership capacity.

It is important here to mention the critical role of experiential learning in leadership studies. Indeed, some undergraduate leadership development programs, such as those offered for student leaders through student affairs offices, are often substantially, or primarily, experiential in nature. We believe that effective leadership education has a balance of classroom-based instruction and relevant experience. Moreover, it is crucial that the two types of learning be interwoven. We will discuss this more fully later.

Leadership Programs Should Be Driven by Proven Models of Learning/Development

Leadership studies programs have flourished, not only because of interest in the topic of leadership but also because students have an interest in developing their personal leadership to help them in their future careers and/or in effecting social change. Furthermore, many professors in leadership studies programs are motivated to prepare students for future leadership roles—producing "tomorrow's leaders." The purpose of a liberal arts education is to prepare educated citizens, as well as educated professionals who will be leaders (Brungardt, Gould, Moore, & Potts, 1997). Often, colleges and universities focus on developing leaders as part of their mission. For example, the mission of Claremont McKenna College is "developing leaders for business, government, and the professions"—a mission that greatly facilitated the development of a multidisciplinary leadership studies program. The Jepson School's mission is "to educate for and about leadership as service to society." Marietta College's model aims at producing responsible citizen-leaders who can identify and solve the problems that face them.

Emphasis on experiential education in higher learning can be traced back to John Dewey (1938, 1958). Leadership is a discipline where it is particularly important that students receive some form of structured opportunities to apply theories and concepts learned in the classroom. Brungardt et al. (1997) argue that "liberal learning" is important for a successful leadership studies program, incorporating both classroom-based learning and experiential coursework (e.g., internships, service learning experiences, etc.). Once again, this assertion is supported by research in learning that suggests that opportunities to apply concepts learned in the classroom, via leadership experiences, promotes learning (although it is important to integrate the two by relating the experiences back to the classroom material; Halpern, in

press). In addition, leadership experiences, such as case studies, leadership simulations or "games" designed to illustrate a point, can also promote learning, by
offering an opportunity to apply learned concepts, as well as increasing students'
motivation to learn (i.e., by making learning both "fun," and relevant to life outside
of the college; Cantor, 1995; Halpern, in press).

Leadership Programs Should Cultivate the Values of the Field

All leadership programs aspire to produce good leaders, meaning leaders who are
both effective and ethical (Ciulla, 1998). However, how programs do this depends
on the location of the program in the university and the disciplines of its faculty. For
example, at Claremont McKenna College (CMC) the leadership studies program
is overseen by the Kravis Leadership Institute—one of the college's nine research
institutes, with core faculty who are also members of the Psychology Department.
Because of this, CMC emphasizes the importance of empirical research in aiding
understanding of leadership and the leadership process. Students are encouraged
to take nonrequired courses in research methodology and to work with faculty
on collaborative leadership research. At the Jepson School all of the faculty have
different academic disciplines—half of them from the humanities and half from
the social sciences. Its program is modeled on the liberal arts and requires students
to take courses in everything from research methods to history. However, since
one third of the faculty have academic backgrounds in ethics, there is a strong
emphasis one ethics and social responsibility throughout the curriculum.

Many, if not most, leadership studies programs are influenced by values regarding social responsibility. Students are expected to become engaged in the larger
community, both during their tenure as students and in their future careers and lives
after college. The James MacGregor Burns Academy, due in part to the interests
of its founder and its proximity to Washington, DC, drew upon the value of public
service. Internships in local, state, national, and international venues undergirded
coursework on political action and leadership

Service learning is one of the most prevalent features of leadership programs
today. Some programs, such as the Hart Leadership Program at Duke University,
have been built around service learning. Over the past 10 years service learning
has been a rapidly growing part of the educational landscape in high schools
and universities. But the case for service learning in leadership programs goes
back much further into Western and Eastern models of servant leadership found
in texts such as the *Holy Bible* and the *Tao-te-ching* (1989). Robert Greenleaf
(1977) popularized this traditional notion of "Servant Leadership" in contemporary
leadership literature. Most leadership studies programs emphasize instilling in their
students the value of service to the larger community.

Another value that guides many leadership programs concerns global
awareness—critically important in our increasingly internationalized world. Many

leadership studies programs offer service learning and internships in other countries, but this is an area that needs to be developed more. If we are to better understand the nature and values of good leadership, programs will have to make a strong effort to learn from students, faculty, and practitioners from other cultures. Most of the literature in the field is American or Western. The field still has a long way to go in fostering work on leadership by people in other cultures.

Leadership Studies Programs Should Be Focused on Outcomes

Perhaps more than any other discipline, there is intense skepticism about the ability to teach "leadership" (see, e.g., Cronin, 1984). Some of the reasons given are that leadership is seen as too complex and abstract to be taught effectively, that leaders are born and not made, or that leadership is thought to be something that can only be learned through direct experience. In addition, critics of leadership education feel that the only way to truly justify the efficacy of these programs is by demonstrating that leadership education programs produce practicing leaders. Therefore, it is critical, for a number of reasons, that leadership studies programs conduct outcomes assessment, to both determine the effectiveness of a particular program and to engage graduates in a lifelong learning process.

As mentioned in the Ayman et al. chapter (this volume), evaluations of the effectiveness of leadership education programs have been scarce. In addition to the W. K. Kellogg Foundation evaluation (Zimmerman-Oster & Burkhardt, 1999a, 1999b), that demonstrated some positive leadership development outcomes for program graduates, a smaller scale evaluation of graduates from Fort Hays State University's program also found some evidence of successful outcomes for leadership studies graduates (Brungardt & Crawford, 1996). Obviously, more of this sort of evaluation needs to be done. Moreover, because many of the outcomes that would be typically associated with evaluation of a leadership education program, such as attainment of a leadership position in one's profession, elected or appointed leadership positions in a community or civic-based organization, (or perhaps more importantly, being engaged in social change, whether they are formal leaders or not) are not likely to occur until many years after graduation, evaluations of leadership education programs need to have a long-term perspective—following alumni for several years postgraduation. One way to successfully engage leadership studies alumni in ongoing, longitudinal assessment is to offer continuing education in leadership for alumni. Another way to engage alumni in a "lifelong," collaborative learning relationship, is to allow alumni to serve as a resource to current students, as guest lecturers in leadership courses, as potential supervisors for internship and service learning placements, as mentors, and as contacts for career opportunities.

Of course, merely measuring the achievements of leadership studies program graduates is not enough, because many of these students would have ended up in leadership positions without leadership studies. The challenge is to conduct well-designed, longitudinal evaluations that use sound methodology, such as quasi-experimental designs with matched comparison students who did not receive leadership education, to demonstrate the added value of leadership studies to the student's academic experience and later life achievements.

Clearly, there is a need for sound evaluation of leadership studies programs. To this end, the Gallup organization has recently sponsored an ongoing, longitudinal evaluation of college- and university-based leadership studies programs. It is hoped that in the not-too-distant future there will be useful data to support the efficacy of leadership studies programs.

There is another important concern when evaluating the impact of leadership studies, and that is that collegiate leadership education, particularly the liberal arts approach that we are focusing on, contributes to solidifying the social position and opportunities of elites. Therefore, it is important to ask the question of whether leadership studies programs reach students who would not otherwise consider themselves to be leaders or potential leaders and to provide access to students who might not have either the opportunity or the inclination to study leadership.

CURRICULAR GUIDELINES

Before providing guidelines for a sound leadership studies curriculum, let us first mention that these guidelines assume a liberal arts approach to leadership studies. As mentioned earlier, many leadership education programs are discipline based (e.g., programs in leadership education, or programs, usually in business schools that focus on leadership in management; etc.) and the curricular guidelines presented here would not be applicable, although some of these guidelines might be useful in designing or revising a discipline-based leadership program.

In addition, these guidelines are meant to be prescriptive, but not dogmatic. We draw heavily on our own programs, and other similar programs, to construct these curricular guidelines. However, specific programs may need to deviate from these guidelines because of a special mission or focus, such as an institution possessing a particular religious orientation, or by necessity due to limitations in faculty resources (e.g., a limited number of faculty in only select disciplines).

Key Curricular Components

Leadership Foundations. Leadership foundations consist of some core course or courses that present core leadership theories and concepts. At the Jepson School, this involves a Foundations of Leadership course and a History and Theories of Leadership course. This foundations course exposes students to the concept of leadership, various definitions, as well as some understanding of the leadership process and how it is practiced (see Wren, 1994). At Claremont McKenna College, we have substituted two "foundations" courses in our core disciplines of Government/Political Science and Psychology.

Ethics Coursework.   Courses in ethics have been an important part of many leadership education programs (Hackman, Olive, Guzman, & Brunson, 1999). Issues of ethics are critically important to nearly all aspects of leadership, ranging from studies contrasting the "dark" and "light" sides of leadership (e.g., Conger, 1990; Hogan, Curphy, & Hogan, 1994) to research on the intersection of ethics and culture (e.g., Casmir, 1997), to concepts of social responsibility and moral leadership (e.g., Gini, 1998). Moreover, Ciulla (1996) argues that studying ethics enhances critical thinking skills—both core elements of leadership education. Ethics can also serve as a capstone course because it allows students to review what they have learned in the program through critical examination of ethical issues related to groups, individuals, cultures, service, and leadership theories.

Service Learning/Experiential Coursework.   As mentioned earlier, sound leadership education combines classroom-based learning with opportunities to apply leadership concepts to actual or simulated leadership experiences. However, it is critically important that the classroom and experiential components be integrated (Kolb, 1984; Markus, Howard, & King, 1993). In addition to providing practical leadership experiences, it has been argued that service learning can help teach students social responsibility and increase multicultural awareness—critical for leadership development in an increasingly diverse society (Simmons & Roberts-Weah, 2000). Courses on leadership in a global society taught in partnership with the University of Maryland's Burns Academy of Leadership and the University of Capetown, for example, brought students together to learn about and contribute to the elimination of AIDS in southern Africa.

Understanding of Group Dynamics.   Leadership cannot be learned, either as a skill set or as a knowledge set, without an understanding of group functioning. We do not see leadership as a set of habits or as a list of traits, but rather as a rich human experience in relationship with others. The Burns Academy, Jepson, and Claremont McKenna offer required and elective coursework either wholly or focusing in part on group dynamics, and often these are the most sought-after courses in our programs. These courses stress learning about leadership, followership, and membership of groups as the rich template of experience from which leadership arises.

Different Disciplinary Approaches/Electives.   In keeping with our liberal arts emphasis, an important component of a leadership studies program is to study leadership from different disciplinary perspectives. Our programs offer a wide range of courses offering different historical, philosophical, religious, political, international, and organizational perspectives on leadership, from nearly every academic discipline. As one might imagine, many courses are taught by faculty in disciplines typically associated with leadership, such as psychology, sociology, and political science. Other courses, however, include one from a professor of literature that looks at how leadership is portrayed in classic literature and films; another looks at leadership and religious values; and another elective course focuses on African-American leadership.

CONCLUSIONS

As leadership study continues to emerge as a recognized academic discipline, it has important implications for the larger field of leadership development. Traditionally, the bulk of attention in leadership development has been focused on the continued development of leadership skills and ability for persons who are already identified in positions of leadership, such as higher level business managers, organizational administrators, elected officials, and the like. This is also evident in the focus of many of the chapters of this book. As more and more graduating college students enter the workforce with degrees in leadership, it will help move the focus of leadership development "downward" to younger individuals who are identified as "potential leaders," due primarily to their educational degrees and accompanying leadership experience (e.g., leadership internships, service learning, etc.). This creates both opportunities, such as the early identification of persons who might fill leadership positions, and risks, such as the possible exclusion of potential leaders because they do not possess a leadership degree (i.e., the "elitism" discussed earlier) and the dangers of having a narrowly defined approach to developing leaders. Despite the scarcity of research on younger, college-aged leaders, some leadership development researchers are arguing the importance of studying leadership at an even earlier age, focusing on school-age children and adolescents (e.g., Schneider, Paul, White, & Holcombe, 1999; Schneider, Ehrhart, & Ehrhart, 2002).

We offer these guidelines for undergraduate leadership studies programs not only as a means of helping those interested in developing leadership programs but also as part of an ongoing dialogue about best practices in the field of leadership studies. It is only by sharing what works and doesn't work that we can save some from reinventing the wheel or repeating the missteps of others.

REFERENCES

Astin, H. S., & Astin, A. (1996). *A social change model of leadership development: Version III: Guidebook*. Los Angeles: Higher Education Research Institute, University of California.

Brungardt, C. (1996). The making of leaders: A review of the research in leadership development and education. *Journal of Leadership Studies, 3*, 81–95.

Brungardt, C., & Crawford, C. B. (1996). A comprehensive approach to assessing leadership students and programs: Preliminary findings. *Journal of Leadership Studies, 3*, 37–48.

Brungardt, C. L., Gould, L. V., Moore, R., & Potts, J. (1997). The emergence of leadership studies: Linking the traditional outcomes of liberal education with leadership development. *Journal of Leadership Studies, 4*, 53–67.

Cantor, J. A. (1995). *Experiential learning in higher education: Linking classroom and community.* ASHE-ERIC Higher Education Report No. 7. Washington, DC: The George Washington University, Graduate School of Education and Human Development.

Casmir, F. L. (Ed). (1997). *Ethics in intercultural and international communication.* Mahwah, NJ: Lawrence Erlbaum Associates.

Cavenagh, T. D. (1997). Establishing leadership studies in the liberal arts curriculum through conflict resolution education. *Journal of Leadership Studies, 4,* 132–139.

Ciulla, J. B. (1998). Leadership ethics, mapping the territory. In J. B. Ciulla (Ed.), *Ethics: The heart of leadership.* Westport, CT: Praeger.

Ciulla, J. B. (1996). Ethics and critical thinking in leadership education. *Journal of Leadership Studies, 3,* 110–119.

Ciulla, J. B. (2000). *The working life: The promise and betrayal of modern work.* New York: Crown Business Books.

Conger, J. A. (1990). The dark side of leadership. *Organizational Dynamics, 19,* 44–55.

Conger, J. A., & Benjamin, B. (1999). *Building leaders: How successful companies develop the next generation.* San Francisco: Jossey-Bass.

Cronin, T. E. (1984). Thinking and learning about leadership. *Presidential Leadership Studies, 14,* 22–34.

Day, D. V. (2000). Leadership development: A review in context. *Leadership Quarterly, 11,* 581–613.

DeMott, B. (1993, December). Choice academic pork. *Harper's,* p. 61.

Dewey, J. (1938). *Experience and education.* Kappa Delta Pi. (Reprinted, 1997, Scribner)

Dewey, J. (1958). *Experience and nature.* New York: Dover.

deWinstanley, P. A., & Bjork, R. A. (2002). Successful lecturing: Presenting information in ways that engage effective processing. In D. F. Halpern & M. D. Hakel (Eds.), *Applying the science of learning to university teaching and beyond* (pp. 19–31). San Francisco: Jossey-Bass.

Gardner, J. (1990). *On leadership.* New York: The Free Press.

Gini, A. (1998). Moral leadership and business ethics. In J.B. Ciulla (Ed.), *Ethics: The heart of leadership* (pp. 27–45). Westport, CT: Praeger.

Greenleaf, R. K. (1977). *Servant leadership.* New York: Paulist Press.

Hackman, M. Z., Olive, T. E., Guzman, N., & Brunson, D. (1999). Ethical considerations in the development of the interdisciplinary leadership studies program. *Journal of Leadership Studies, 6,* 36–48.

Halpern, D. F. (in press). The development of adult cognition: Understanding constancy and change in adult learning. In D. V. Day, S. J. Zaccaro & S. Halpin (Eds.), *Leadership Development for Transforming* Organizations. Mahwah, NJ: Erlbaum Associates.

Hogan, R. T., Curphy, G. J., & Hogan, J. (1994). What do we know about personality: Leadership and effectiveness? *American Psychologist, 49,* 493–504.

Honan, W. (1998, September 30). Programs that make leadership their goal. *New York Times,* p. C20.

Howe, W. (1997). Leadership education: A look across the courses. In F. Freeman et al. (Eds.), *Leadership education: A source book, 1996–1997* (Sixth edition, Vol. 2, p. 286). Greensboro, NC: Center for Creative Leadership.

Hughes, R. L., Ginnett, R. C., & Curphy, G. J. (2002). *Leadership: Enhancing the lessons of experience* (4th ed.). Boston: Irwin/McGraw-Hill.

Kolb, D. A. (1984). *Experiential learning: Experience as the source of learning and development.* Englewood Cliffs, NJ: Prentice-Hall.

Lao Tzu. (1989). *The Lao Tzu (Tao-te-ching)* (Robert G. Henricks, Trans.). New York: Ballantine.

Mangan, K. S. (2002, May 31). Leading the way in leadership education: The unending quest of the discipline's founding father. *Chronicle of Higher Education,* A10–A12.

Markus, G. B., Howard, J. P. F., & King, D. C. (1993). Integrating community service and classroom instruction enhances learning: Results from an experiment. *Educational Evaluation and Policy Analysis, 15,* 410–419.

McVey, R. S. (1995). Critical thinking skills for leadership development. *Journal of Leadership Studies, 2*, 86–97.

Perruci G. (1999). "Leadership Studies Programs in the Context of Globalization," *Selected Proceedings of the international Leadership Association* (College Park: The James MacGregor Burns Academy of Leadership, University of Maryland), pp. 55–62.

Rost, J. C., & Barker, R. A. (2000). Leadership education in colleges: Toward a 21st century paradigm. *Journal of Leadership Studies, 7*, 3–12.

Schneider, B., Ehrhart, K. H., & Ehrhart, M. G. (2002). Understanding high school student leaders II. Peer nominations of leaders and their correlates. *Leadership Quarterly, 13*, 275–299.

Schneider, B., Paul, M. C., White, S. S., & Holcombe, K.M. (1999). Understanding high school student leaders. I: Predicting teacher ratings of leader behavior. *Leadership Quarterly, 10*, 609–636.

Schwartz, M. K., Axtman, K. M., & Freeman, F. H. (Eds.). (1998). *Leadership education: A source book of courses and programs* (7th ed.). Greensboro, NC: Center for Creative Leadership.

Simmons, V. C., & Roberts-Weah, W. (2000). Service-learning and social reconstructionism: A critical opportunity for leadership. In C. R. O'Grady (Ed.), *Integrating service learning and multicultural education in colleges and universities* (pp. 189–207). Mahwah, NJ: Lawrence Erlbaum Associates.

Sorenson, G. (2000). *An intellectual history of leadership studies: The role of James MacGregor Burns.* Presented at meeting of the American Political Science Association, Washington, DC.

Sorenson, G., & Howe, W. (2001). *As strange a maze as e'er men trod: A history of leadership studies.* Presented at meeting of the International Leadership Association, Miami, FL.

Troyer, M. (1997). *The growth of leadership development programs in higher education.* Unpublished paper. University of Kentucky.

Van Velsor, E., McCauley, C. D., & Moxley, R. S. (1998). Our view of leadership development. In C. D. McCauley, R. S. Moxley, & E. Van Velsor (Eds.), *The center for creative leadership handbook of leadership development* (pp. 1–25). San Francisco: Jossey-Bass.

Welch, R. L. (2000). Training a new generation of leaders. *Journal of Leadership Studies, 7*, 70–81.

Wren, J. T. (1994). Teaching leadership: The art of the possible. *Journal of Leadership Studies, 1*, 73–93.

Zimmerman-Oster, K., & Burkhardt, J. C. (1999a). *Leadership in the making: Impact and insights from leadership development programs in U.S. colleges and universities.* Battle Creek, MI: W. K. Kellogg Foundation.

Zimmerman-Oster, K., & Burkhardt, J. C. (1999b). Leadership in the making: A comprehensive examination of the impact of leadership development programs on students. *Journal of Leadership Studies, 6*, 50–66.

13

Putting the Development in Leadership Development: Implications for Theory and Practice

Michael D. Mumford and Gregory G. Manley
The University of Oklahoma

Without the efforts of George C. Marshall, Europe as we know it today, might not exist. The success of General Electric owes much to the efforts of Jack Welch, as well as to earlier leaders such as J. P. Morgan. The decisions made by Franklin Roosevelt and Dwight Eisenhower have shaped life in the 21st century in so many ways that we often loose sight of their significance. Although other examples of such high impact leadership come to mind, our foregoing examples suffice to illustrate the point that leadership makes a difference—potentially a big difference (Day & Lord, 1988; Strange & Mumford, 2002).

When one recognizes the potential impact of leaders on society and social organizations, a new question immediately comes to fore (see Locke, chap. 2, this volume). How can we go about developing more effective leaders? Of course, any serious, scholarly attempt to answer this question requires one to address a number of substantive issues. We must know something about how leaders' careers unfold over time (Gardner, 1995; Howard & Bray, 1988). We must establish the skills needed by people occupying leadership roles and determine how these skills change as people move through different roles (Mumford, Marks, Connelly, Zaccaro, & Reiter-Palmon, 2000; Yukl, 2001). And, we must know how acquisition of these skills is influenced by broader developmental processes (Jacobs & Jaques, 1990; Simonton, 1984).

Of course, these substantive concerns indicate that the development of effective leaders is not a simple, nor a necessarily straightforward, problem. Nonetheless, the literature on leadership development has adopted a distinctly pragmatic approach to the problem of leader development focusing most research on an attempt to answer a single question. Exactly what kind of interventions will develop the skills needed for effective performance in organizational leadership positions? The current focus on this rather pragmatic question is aptly illustrated in Day's (2000) review of the leadership development literature where the extant literature is examined with respect to the techniques commonly used to influence skill acquisition, such as mentoring, networking, action learning, and multirater feedback. This distinctly practical orientation is also evident in many of the chapters presented in the present volume. For example, Atwater, Brett, and Waldman (see chap. 5, this volume) provide a detailed assessment of the effectiveness of multirater feedback, whereas Conger and Toegel (see chap. 6, this volume) examine the potential limitations of current action-learning techniques.

We do not wish to dispute the value of work along these lines. By the same token; however, we would argue that an undue focus on the technology of leader development has become a cause for concern. Because we lack an understanding of leadership development as an instantiation of broader developmental processes, we cannot say, with any certainty, exactly how the experience provided by various interventions affects the course of people's careers. Moreover, it becomes difficult to structure, and time, experiences in such a way as to maximize the long-term growth of leadership capabilities. To make matters worse, lacking a viable developmental framework, the task of formulating new intervention strategies becomes difficult and is, more often than not, a simple matter of happenstance.

If it is granted that there is a need to address these concerns, then it seems reasonable to conclude that we must begin formulating a more substantive, theory-driven approach to leader development. When one recognizes that leadership in most complex, "real-world" settings is a rare event before age 25 and commonly occurs in mid to late adulthood (O'Connor, 1993; Simonton, 1984), it seems reasonable to suggest that available models of adult development might provide a plausible point of departure for attempts to formulate a substantive basis for studies of leadership development. Accordingly, our intent in this chapter is to examine the implications of current theories of adult development for recent work on leadership development. In the course of this venture we hoped to achieve two somewhat more specific goals. First, we hoped to use available research on adult development to identify some promising new approaches to leader development. Second, we hoped that a careful examination of available models of adult development might be used to identify some necessary extensions, or revisions, of extant intervention techniques.

ADULT DEVELOPMENT

Meta-Theoretical Assumptions

Studies of adult development do not have a particularly long history. Historically, development, or regularities in patterns of behavioral change over time, was seen as primarily an attribute of childhood. Interest in *adult* development emerged in the 1950s with the seminal work of scholars such as Ericsson (1950) and Havinghurst (1953). They argued that certain social and biographical forces induced regularities in the behavioral changes observed over the course of people's adult lives. Thus, we see regularities in the time at which people seek to establish a career, establish families, or move into organizational leadership positions. Initial models of adult development tended to apply one of two basic approaches to account for these regularities—approaches Reese and Overton (1970) have referred to as the mechanistic and organismic models. Typically, mechanistic theorists see adult development proceeding along similar lines for most people with temporarily related behavioral changes emerging from a fixed set of biosocial demands—for example, social expectations for the timing of life events (e.g., George, 1993). Organismic theorists, in contrast, emphasize the plasticity of adult development holding that the meaning imputed to events, and the context in which they occur, may give rise to quantitatively different patterns of developmental change (e.g., Gutman, 1993).

The results emerging from longitudinal and cohort-sequential studies of adult behavior, however, have not been fully consistent with either of these two general models. For example, numerous studies have demonstrated age-related declines in cognitive abilities beginning in late middle age: specifically, fluid abilities as assessed by standardized test performance (Salthouse, 1998; Schaie, 1994; Verhaegan & Salthouse, 1997). However, these age-related decrements, commonly attributed to declines in processing speed, are not necessarily observed for all adults, particularly adults who remain engaged in intellectually challenging tasks (Schooler, Mulatu, & Oates, 1999). Moreover, these declines in cognitive ability may not lead to performance decrements if expertise provides a basis for compensation (Colonia-Willner, 1998; Salthouse, 1986).

Along somewhat different lines, Elder and Clipp (1989) examined the long-term effects of differential exposure to significant life events using participants in the Berkley Longitudinal study. They contrasted study participants who had, and who had not, been exposed to combat during the Second World War. In the period immediately following the war, combat veterans were found to have more behavioral and emotional problems. In their 40s and 50s, however, these combat veterans evidenced better coping skills and greater autonomy. These subsequent gains appeared to be linked to greater resilience among combat veterans who used their war experiences as a vehicle for adapting to later life demands.

Findings of this sort, along with those obtained in other studies of adult development (e.g., Block, 1971; Caspi, Bem, & Elder, 1989; Magnusson, 1988; Mumford, Stokes, & Owens, 1990; Valliant, 1977), have led most students of adult development to reject both the strict organismic and the strict mechanistic models. Instead, most current theorists have adopted a strong, or dynamic, interactional model (Lerner, Freund, Stefanis, & Habermas, 2001; Lerner & Tubman, 1989). Within this model, individuals are seen as an active entities selecting environments and adapting their behavior to opportunities and constraints imposed by biosocial demands. Learning, and the active appraisal of environmental events, coupled with the actions of the individual, in turn, shape the individual's environment. Coherent patterns of development emerge as this experience acts to shape future opportunities and people draw upon their unique experience as a vehicle for adapting to these opportunities.

One key implication of this kind of interactional model is that one would expect to see, in adulthood, coherent patterns of differential development (Magnusson, 1988). In an initial test of proposition, Mumford et al. (1990) examined the emergence of coherent patterns of differential development between ages 18 and 35. They found, in accordance with a dynamic interactional model, that coherent patterns of adult development could indeed be identified. Moreover, change in response to shifting life tasks was apparently contingent on the patterns of prior behavior and experiences evidenced by individuals at earlier points in their lives. More recently, Mumford, Zaccaro, Johnson et al. (2000) examined the emergence of developmental patterns in a sample of organizational leaders, specifically 1818 Army officers between the ages of 20 and 55. They found that developmental patterns characterizing different types of leaders over the course of their careers were related to survival, promotion, and performance. These differential outcomes, furthermore, appeared to be based on differences across types in the rate and timing of the growth of requisite leadership skills.

INTERACTIONAL VARIABLES

Given these findings, it seems reasonable to conclude that strong or dynamic interactional models might provide a viable framework for understanding both adult development as a general phenomenon and leader development as a specific instantiation of this more general phenomenon. With the widespread acceptance of strong interactional models, however, students of adult development have begun to search for those variables that represent noteworthy influences on the nature and implications of these interactions. Broadly speaking, four general approaches have been used to identify these variables that might be referred to as (a) the process approach, (b) the content approach, (c) the structural approach, and (d) the capacities approach. Although these four approaches describe interrelated, interactive influences on adult development, each provides a unique frame of reference for understanding the kind of variables that shape the course of adult development.

Process Variables

The process approach specifies key variables based on the kind of actions that shape development over the life span. Perhaps the most widely accepted process model might be found in the selection, optimization, and compensation (SOC) theory proposed by Baltes and his colleagues (e.g., Baltes, 1997; Baltes & Carstensen, 1996; Freund & Baltes, 1996; Lerner, Freund, Stefanis, & Habermas, 2001; Marsiske, Lang, Baltes, & Baltes, 1995; Schultz & Heckhausen, 1996). Within the SOC model, development is held to proceed as a function of three key processes: (a) selection, (b) optimization, and (c) compensation.

The emphasis on selection proceeds from the proposition that time is inherently limited, but adults are presented with numerous options. Thus, adults must choose which situations, or activities, they will engage in with these choices, in turn, shaping subsequent opportunities. Within this framework, the selection of activities is held to depend on the evident goals and rewards, the values of the individual, and restrictions on goal attainment implied by opportunity costs, prior commitments, and time demands. The impact of these choices on development is richly illustrated in Feldman's (1999) finding that committed high achievers often sacrifice family in the pursuit of professional goals, in the process losing a potentially critical support mechanism. Within this framework, moreover, it is assumed that the goals and values driving these choices may change over time. Thus, maintenance and gerativity goals appear to drive decisions made in later adulthood, whereas growth and mastery goals seem to drive the decisions made in young adulthood (Baltes, 1997; McAdams, 2001).

Optimization processes are concerned with the events following initial selection of a set of activities. Optimization is reflected in those activities that make it possible for people to increase the efficiency and effectiveness of chosen actions. Of course, the optimization process is held to depend, in part, on the acquisition of new knowledge and skills, as well as on the social and financial resources that support skill growth. However, other variables, particularly variables influencing effective deployment of these resources also appear to play a role in optimization including attentional focus, energy, time allocation, performance modeling, and motivation for self-development. Thus, Hershey, Walsh, Read, and Chulef (1990) found that expert financial planners more rapidly recognized applicable planning models.

The assumption that development involves both gains and losses, as well as ongoing adaptation to change, leads to the third variable included in this model—compensation. In fact, compensation has been found to represent a critical aspect of adult development. For example, Salthouse (1986) found that loss in response speed with age may be compensated for by more accurate event prediction. Along similar lines, declines in sheer information-processing speed may be compensated for by a greater awareness of error consequences and the pragmatic, social considerations influencing solution implementation (Staudinger & Baltes, 1996). These compensatory efforts, however, may involve a number of other actions aside from information utilization such as the use of external aids, shifts in attentional and time allocation, and the reliance on others who have somewhat different skill sets.

Content Variables

As might be expected, based on our foregoing observations, most current theories of adult development consider content as well as process with content after being referenced against expertise. Expertise, however, is not simply an accumulation of discrete bits of information. Instead, it represents the *organization and structuring* of information into principle-based knowledge structures that promote both the acquisition of new knowledge and the subsequent application of this knowledge to novel problems (Mumford, Zaccaro, Harding et al., 2000). From a developmental perspective, however, three noteworthy characteristics of expertise acquisition need to be borne in mind. First, in most "real-world" settings the acquisition of sufficient expertise to permit noteworthy contributions is a rather time-consuming process requiring 7 years, or more, and substantial practice (Ericsson & Charness, 1994; Weisburg, 1999). Second, acquisition of expertise appears to move through four distinct stages with novices struggling to construct basic concepts, journeymen struggling to apply a limited number of base concepts, experts extending and elaborating concepts, and, finally, automizing process application (Anderson, 1993). Third, with the acquisition of expertise, a number of complex facilitative effects emerge including more rapid situational diagnosis, greater awareness of critical errors, and more rapid identification of key causes, relevant restrictions, and the potential consequences of proposed solutions (Isenberg, 1986; Mumford, Schultz, & Osburn, 2002; Thomas & McDaniel, 1990).

The significance of these complex facilitative effects of expertise is illustrated in a study by Oura and Hatano (2001). They contrasted novice and expert musicians with respect to the processes involved in executing a piece of classical music. They used performance observations and interviews to compare these groups. Although novices and experts were found to differ in execution skills and reliance on extant, given principles, the more noteworthy finding emerging in this study was distinctly social in nature. More specifically, it was found that experts were better able to formulate and phrase their performance with respect to audience reactions. Thus, expertise apparently provides the time and awareness needed to think about others.

In addition to the influence of expertise on social awareness, it appears that people, with time, may develop expert structures bearing on the appraisal of others and their intentions. More specifically, it appears that people have beliefs about why others behave as they do. These beliefs, commonly referred to as a theory of mind, represent a form of social cognitive knowledge arrived at vis-à-vis event analysis, practice, imitation, role modeling, retrospective autobiographical analysis, and prototype acquisition (Lillard, 1998; Schwitzgebel, 1999). Nelson, Plesa, and Hensler (1998), in a study of adults' performance on theory-of-mind tasks, tasks intended to elicit beliefs about other people's actions, found that logical causal reasoning about people's actions developed with experience. Moreover, the causal reasoning applied was phrased in a narrative, contextual fashion stressing the kind of real-life, experientially based cases, commonly found to provide a foundation for planning (Berger & Jordan, 1992; Hammond, 1990; Mumford, Schultz, & Van Doorn, 2001). Thus, the abstraction of goals, causes, restrictions, and consequences from personal experience may play a key role in adult's interpretation of social events and their subsequent planning of adaptive responses.

Although some of the events applied in this case-based reasoning about people and social systems may be derived from external events such as role models and social prototypes, it also appears that internal, autobiographical material is used by adults to understand their world (Habermas, 2001; Habermas & Bluck, 2000; McAdams, 2001). In adolescence, people begin to construct narratives that serve to organize their lives to date while permitting the creation of life plans along with specification of the positive and negative events implied by these plans (Arnett, 2000; Oyserman & Markus, 1990). This autobiographical narrative, referred to as a life story, is, in turn, used as a structure for interpreting and evaluating subsequent life events. Although these narratives may be organized on a variety of bases, including temporal coherence, cultural coherence, outcome themes, and event explanations (Singer & Bluck, 2001), actions based on these narratives typically seem to depend on the specific events used as reference points for imputing meaning.

In keeping with this proposition, Pillemer (2001) argues that certain key kinds of events, defined with respect to these life stories, provide an accessible, emotionally evocative short-hand, guiding responses to emerging situations. These event types include (a) originating events (events tied to the definition of long-term goals and action plans), (b) turning points (events leading to salient modifications of goals and plans), (c) anchoring events (events that illustrate fundamental beliefs and values), (d) analogous events (preferred case models for behavior in different situations), (e) redemption events (apparently bad events with positive downstream effects), and (f) contamination events (apparently positive events with negative downstream effects). Of course, some events, for example, contamination and redemption events, may be acquired rather slowly—suggesting that the utility of autobiographical information in guiding development improves over time. Other events, for example, anchoring and turning-point events, may evoke rather powerful emotions—suggesting that the activation of some events may have a disproportionate impact on interpretation and action. Finally, definitional events may change with current life demands and expectations. Thus, one finds that career events are particularly salient to younger adults, whereas generativity events are particularly salient to older adults (McAdams, 2001).

Structural Variables

Implicit in our foregoing observations about life events is the notion that people have conceptions about the kinds of events that represent critical developmental markers at different points in the life span. In one study intended to test this hypothesis, Settersten (1997) had 319 men and women, ranging in age from 18 to more than 70, participate in interviews examining the centrality of age to some 20 life events (e.g., leaving home, settling on a career, and raising children), falling in five spheres: family, education, work, health, and death. He found that age was generally considered a significant aspect of all these life events with age proving particularly important for events involving family and careers. Thus, the age-grading of social expectations for the completion of various life tasks appears to represent an overarching goal structure that may serve as a general directive mechanism, providing some structure to the course of adult development (Freund, 1997).

In addition to culturally based expectations for the completion of various life tasks, at least three other structural regularities have commonly been identified in studies of people's movement through the life course. First, resources, including financial resources, personal resources (e.g., expertise), and social resources (e.g., acquaintances) appear to increase into late middle age. As a result, middle-aged adults, in contrast to young adults, display greater confidence, a more positive outlook on life, and better coping skills (Gallagher, 1993). Second, accompanying these increases in resources, one finds an increase in perceived control and autonomy (Bray, Campbell, & Grant, 1974; Grob, Krings, & Bangerter, 2001). Third, as critical life tasks involving establishment of a family and career are completed, life events involving prosocial relationships and contributions to others acquire greater significance (Ericsson, 1950; McAdams, 2001).

The simple passage of time appears to induce some noteworthy regularities in the structure of adult development. More specifically, as the time available to people decreases, it appears that shifts occur in the strategies people use to complete various tasks and the goals pursued during task completion. One illustration of this principle may be found in Carstensen, Isaacowitz, and Charles (1999), who noted that, as people perceive limitations in available time, their goals shift from the acquisition of knowledge and performance capabilities to socioemotional enhancement. Along similar lines, Gollwitzer (1999) has found that time constraints limit abstract planning activities as individuals shift their focus to practical task accomplishment. Indeed, prior studies of the task strategies used by older adults, including organizational leaders, indicate that age is associated with a more pragmatic implementation orientation as well as a greater reliance on past experience (Baltes, 1997; Mumford, Marks et al., 2000). In keeping with these observations, Bluck and Habermas (2001) found that older adults were more likely to view the past favorably, as compared to younger adults, and were more likely to try to understand events in terms of past experience.

Capacity Variables

In contrast to studies examining the timing and structure of life experience, other scholars have posed a distinctly different, differential, question. In these capacity studies, they examine the differential characteristics that make it possible for people to profit from experience. As is the case in virtually all studies of development, general intellectual capacities, specifically intelligence, seem to represent noteworthy influences on the individual's ability to profit from experience accruing over the life course (Terman, 1959). These intellectual capacities, moreover, include specific instantiations of intelligence with emotional and practical intelligence representing potentially noteworthy influences on the later phases of adult development (Sternberg, 2002; Zaccaro, 2002).

In addition to general intellectual capacities, two discrete cognitive skills appear to represent potentially noteworthy influences on adult development. One of these skills is planning, which not only serves to direct developmental activities, such as activity selection (Pea, 1982), but also exerts a far more complex set of effects. One illustration of this point may be found in Taylor, Phan, Rivkin, and Armor (1998). They found that the mental simulation of processes for reaching goals increases adaptive capacity and coping. Other work by Gollwitzer (1999) and Mumford, Schultz, and Van Doorn (2001) indicates that planning activities, such as forecasting, identification of restrictions, and specification of marker events, increases motivation, facilitates identification of the requirements for solution implementation, and promotes the growth of expertise. The other discrete cognitive skill held to represent a noteworthy influence on adult development is judgment. The impact of judgment on development is illustrated in studies by Bass (1985) and Jacobs and Jaques (1990). Their findings indicate that awareness of tradeoffs and risks allows people to pursue more effective courses of action while ensuring the judicial application of available expertise.

Related to judgment, of course, is the more global construct of wisdom. Although different definitions of wisdom have been proposed over the years (Arlin, 1993; Baltes & Staudinger, 2000; Cook, 1993; Sternberg, 1998), most theorists hold that wisdom involves more than judgment. In addition to judgment, wisdom is commonly held to require an awareness of self and others, objectivity, and the capacity to evaluate contextual influences on events. All of these characteristics promote the application of experience in problem solving. In accordance with this observation, Mumford, Marks et al. (2000) found not only that these wisdom-related capacities increased with age and experience in organizational leadership positions but also that the acquisition of these capacities was a crucial influence on performance.

Wisdom is closely related to the capacity for self-reflection, in that self-reflection is held to promote the growth of wisdom and judgment. Unlike wisdom and judgment, however, the capacity for self-reflection does not show change as people move through adulthood (Baltes, Staudinger, Maercker, & Smith, 1995).

Instead, self-reflection appears to promote the abstraction of knowledge, particularly self-knowledge, throughout the life span. What does change with age, however, is the application of self-reflection. Thus, Staudinger (2001) found that, early in adulthood, self-reflection was focused on activity selection and problem solving, whereas in later adulthood, self-reflection provided a basis for finding meaning in experience and integrating different life experiences.

Development, as reflected in the individual's ability to profit from life experiences, is not solely a matter of cognition. It may also be influenced by certain dispositional characteristics. Certainly, it is difficult to profit from experience if one has not acquired a diverse base of different kinds of experiences. Moreover, effective reaction to the demands imposed by new or diverse experiences requires a controlled appraisal of the situation at hand. Thus, it is not surprising that both openness (McCrae, 1996) and self-regulation (Baugh & Chartrand, 1999) have been found to contribute effective, successful development across the life span. In fact, Mumford, Baughman, Uhlman, Costanza, and Threlfall (1993) have provided some support for this conclusion with their finding that openness and self-regulation contribute to both adaptation and the acquisition of expertise during practice.

LEADERSHIP DEVELOPMENT

To this point, our primary concern has been examining what we know about the nature of adult development. At this juncture, however, it would seem germane to return to the basic question posed at the outset of this paper. More specifically, what do the findings emerging from studies of adult development tell us about how we should go about developing leaders? In the ensuing discussion, we will attempt to provide a preliminary answer to this question examining the implications of the various chapters presented in this volume with respect to the three key processes, selection, optimization, and compensation, that appear to represent the best available overarching structure for understanding adult development.

Selection

Because experience in certain types of situations represents a pivotal force driving adult development, one would expect that the kind of situations individuals are exposed to over the course of their careers would represent potentially powerful influences on leader development. Indeed, prior studies by McCauley, Ruderman, Ohlott, and Morrow (1994) and Mumford, Marks et al. (2000) indicate that exposure to assignments where people are required to solve complex, novel organizational problems contribute to the development of leadership skills. These findings in turn, however, suggest that the selection of situations will also influence leader development. In organizations, situation exposure is conditioned by two basic processes: (a) the actions of the organization in selecting leaders and (b) the actions of the individual in selecting situations. In the ensuing discussion, we will consider the implications of both these forms of selection for leader development.

Organizational Selection. Organizational selection of leaders has a long and proud history as a leader development intervention (e.g., Owens, 1976). Indeed, much of the work on assessment centers is explicitly concerned with the development of procedures to select leaders or qualify leaders for advancement (Bray et al., 1974). However, in recent years the design of leader selection systems has received somewhat less attention as a potentially significant developmental intervention. In light of this trend, Locke's (see chap. 2, this volume) chapter represents a particularly significant contribution by reminding us that the assessment of leaders with respect to traits such as intelligence, creativity, autonomy, and ethical values must represent a core component of any viable leadership development program.

In this regard, however, it seems important to bear in mind two points emerging from our review of the available literature on adult development. First, as useful as it is to structure leader selection based on traits underlying performance, it may be desirable to extend this approach to incorporate those capacities that seem to represent potentially significant influences on further development, particularly when leaders are being selected for early- or midcareer positions. Thus, extension of current selection systems to include characteristics such as openness, self-regulation, self-awareness, planning, wisdom, and decision making might prove of value. Efforts along these lines are, of course, especially likely to prove valuable if they examine how these skills are applied by appraising experience in leadership positions.

Second, although systems for leader selection have traditionally focused on differential capacities, examination of the leader development literature suggests that experience, or content, represents a particularly powerful influence on development and subsequent performance. One implication of this observation is that, because older individuals tend to rely on experience (Baltes, 1997; Bluck & Habermas, 2001), selection systems may find it useful to place a greater emphasis on experience in selecting people for senior, as opposed to more junior, leadership roles. Another implication of this observation pertains to the kind of content considered in making these selection decisions. The kinds of content shaping adult development are not restricted to simple work experience but, instead, include the autobiographical experience that people use to impute meaning to events (Pillemer, 2001). Accordingly, one might expect that "depth" interviews intended to reveal key life experiences, such as anchoring events, turning points, and redemption events, might provide a potentially viable technique for selecting leaders, especially when people are being considered for more senior leadership positions.

In considering the role of experiential content in selecting leaders, however, a point made by Avolio and Kahai (see chap. 3, this volume) and Spreitzer (see chap. 4, this volume) needs to be borne in mind. Both these authors point out that technology, technology as manifested in the emergence of virtual work groups, has resulted in some significant changes in leaders' roles and the problems leaders confront in interacting with followers. This observation, in turn, suggests that we may, with changes in leader role demands, require new kinds of capacities and new kinds of experiences. Given the time lags, potentially substantial lags, involved in developing leaders, it would seem prudent to take these changes into account even in the initial selection of leaders.

Individual Selection. Within the model of adult development presented earlier, selection is not simply a matter of a decision made by the organization. Selection, from a developmental perspective, involves choices by the individual as to the type of activities he or she will engage in. In the leadership literature, where it is *assumed* that all individuals seek the power and prerogative attached to organizational leadership, the role of individual preferences as a force driving leadership development has received scant attention.

Bearing this point in mind, Cox, Pearce, and Sims (see chap. 9, this volume) make a potentially noteworthy contribution. They remind us that there may not be one type of desirable leader and that, indeed, to survive and thrive, organizations may require multiple types of leaders working together as a team. In keeping with this proposition, Mumford, Zaccaro, Johnson et al. (2000) have shown that at least one organization, the United States Army, seems to value at least three distinct types of leaders. Other research by Bartel (1994) and Murray (1989), moreover, suggests that the availability of these diverse styles, and the implied experiential differences, in fact contributes to the decision-making performance of executive teams, at least in complex and turbulent environments.

The need for, and existence of, different types of leaders occupying different roles, and bringing different experiences to bear, is not of interest simply as change in our common meta-theories. It is also of interest because recognition of the need for different styles opens up some new horizons for work on leader development. Given the fact that a substantial portion of adult development is driven by the individual's selection of activities, it seems plausible to argue that one way we might facilitate leader development is by accurately describing both the positive and the negative aspects of different leadership roles. This material might then be used to provide realistic role previews to leaders to be used as a basis for role selection. The utility of these realistic previews might subsequently be enhanced by arranging for exposure to preferred roles either by assignment to positions stressing requisite role activities or, alternatively, by arranging shadowing or mentoring relationships with individuals currently occupying these roles. Although interventions of this sort seem likely to have some value in maximizing the self-selection process in leader development, it seems important to bear in mind two points made earlier. More specifically, interventions of this sort are more likely to prove effective (a) if they are accompanied by the kind of systematic feedback needed to promote self-reflection and (b) if they are timed to occur relatively early in a leader's career, typically before age 40, when self-reflection is geared to a search for optimal roles.

Later in leaders' careers, the impact of selective functions on development is likely to be based less on structured experiences and more on the leaders' day-to-day interactions with followers, peers, and superiors. As Uhl-Bien (see chap. 7, this volume) and Cogliser and Scandura (see chap. 8, this volume) point out, however, from an exchange perspective where dyadic relationships are independently defined, the success of a leader is knowing who to form relationships with, at what time, and for what purpose. Accordingly, by allowing leaders' reasonable discretion in relational formation, and subsequently encouraging analysis of key characteristics of these relationships, such as trust, development of the follower, ease of working relations, conflict sources, etc., acquisition of a key leadership skill may be accomplished by capitalizing on the selective aspect of adult development. Although necessarily somewhat speculative at this juncture, it is possible that the impact of this kind of intervention will increase when leaders are asked to articulate the redemptive and contaminating events occurring in these relationships. Of course, the potential value of this extended relational analysis arises from the contribution of such events to defining the autobiographical narratives that guide subsequent decisions about relational formation.

Optimization

Although selection issues have been of some concern in the design of leadership development programs, selection has clearly received substantially less attention than optimization. Optimization in this context, of course, refers to interventions intended to enhance the effectiveness and efficiency with which leaders execute various activities required for successful performance in leadership roles. Thus, under this rubric, one may subsume a host of interventions including formal educational programs, training courses, simulation exercises, assignments, networking, and mentoring (Day, 2000). From a developmental perspective, however, it appears that these experiences may be broken into two broad categories: (a) performance interventions and (b) relational interventions.

Performance Interventions. As Ayman, Adams, Hartman, and Fisher (see chap. 11, this volume), Conger and Toegel (see chap. 6, this volume), and Schriesheim (see chap. 10, this volume) point out, experientially based intervention for the enhancement of leader performance has become one of the preferred techniques for leader development. One prototypic illustration of this approach may be found in action learning. Conger and Toegel (see chap. 6, this volume) provide a relatively detailed description of this technique noting that it involves presenting individuals with special projects where project assignments are used to increase the range of available knowledge while developing the expertise and problem-solving skills needed in upper-level leadership roles.

From a developmental perspective, action learning, along with special assignments, represents attractive intervention strategy for three reasons. First, development is based on the kind of autobiographical experience that seems to represent a key aspect of adult development. Second, if these experiences are managed carefully in terms of individual needs and readiness, they may provide not only useful case analogies but also the kind of turning point and anchoring experiences that represent powerful forces shaping adult development. Third, because action learning and assignments embed learning in practical real-world events, they provide experience in a fashion consistent with the older adult learning style.

As attractive as these features of action learning, and assignments, may be, from a developmental perspective, these learning techniques are also hobbled by a fundamental characteristic of all human learning. Expertise acquisition is not simply a matter of acquiring experience. Instead, it requires the organization of experience in terms of underlying principles. Although it does appear that people can construct principles from experience, the abstraction of principles from past experience is apparently quite difficult (Reeves & Weisburg, 1994). To abstract these principles and effectively apply them in any skilled performance, (a) people must have multiple experiences, (b) these experiences and feedback must be structured to articulate key principals involved, (c) diagnostic and work heuristics must be provided or articulated, and (d) key features of each experience must be distinguished from other related principles (Mumford & Gustafson, in press).

When one considers these requirements for the acquisition of expertise, it seems unlikely that either action learning or assignments will provide an adequate basis for learning and expertise acquisition in novice, or journeyman, populations. Instead, these techniques are most likely to prove valuable in experienced populations, at the expert or subexpert level, where requisite base principles have been provided through formal classroom instruction. Moreover, even in this population, the effectiveness of these experiences may depend on the availability of adequate time for feedback and reflection as well as requisite coaching (see Conger & Toegel, chap. 6, this volume).

Of course, the obvious implication of these observations is that action learning and assignments are more likely to prove effective when they are used as one type of learning exercise within a broader developmental program (see Ayman, Adams, Hartman, & Fisher, chap. 11, this volume). Moreover, such long-term, multifaceted developmental programs, if they are to prove effective, are likely to require a substantial investment in classroom training. This classroom training should be based on lectures and exercises intended to illustrate core principles. In this regard, however, the tendency of adults to rely on events, or real-life cases, as a basis for action suggests that effective interventions along these lines will require multiple, carefully selected cases and simulation exercises that illustrate principle application in a "real-world" context where active analysis and planning of potential actions are required. Moreover, given the importance of self-reflection, judgment, and wisdom to adult development and leader performance, it seems likely that these training programs will prove more effective if they are explicitly designed to encourage self-analysis of individual or team performance.

Social Interventions.   In contrast to assignments, action learning, and formal training, all techniques intended to facilitate expertise acquisition, other optimization interventions seek to develop social skills or social awareness. Given the fact that people, with experience, develop theories of the causes underlying their own, and others', behavior (Nelson, Plesa, & Hensler, 1998), and given the impact of these beliefs about the causes of people's behavior on leader performance (Zaccaro, Gilbert, Thor, & Mumford, 1991), it seems reasonable to conclude that social interventions have a place in virtually all leadership development programs.

Of the available social interventions, multisource feedback has received the most attention in recent years. The logic underlying this approach is quite straightforward. It assumes that people's beliefs about others' reactions to their behavior may be erroneous. Thus, by providing behavioral feedback from multiple alternative perspectives, one can change behavior and increase the individual's understanding of their impact on others. As Atwater, Brett, and Waldman (see chap. 5, this volume) point out, some evidence is available for the ability of multisource feedback to induce behavioral change. However, the technique suffers from various problems such as the rejection of feedback, failure to induce change in the cases of the greatest discrepancies, etc.

From a developmental perspective, however, it is open to question whether multisource feedback techniques are necessarily a desirable, or effective, intervention. Because these techniques point out discrepancies between self and others' beliefs and perceptions, it can be expected that they will induce self-regulation (Baugh & Chartrand, 1999). Self-regulation, however desirable from an organizational perspective, may not induce developmental change if the individual simply uses a means ends analysis intended to provide a psychological reduction of the observed discrepancy. Instead, what is required is an active analysis where the individual seeks to *understand* the origins and implications of the observed discrepancies and uses the causes identified in this analysis as a basis for change.

This apparently straightforward statement, however, has two implications. First, multisource feedback is unlikely to prove effective developmentally if threat is induced. Second, the success of interventions along these lines will be contingent on the inclusion of activities intended to induce active analysis of discrepancies. Thus, participants in such programs should be required to produce change plans, and coaching and feedback should be provided bearing on the beliefs and assumptions embedded in these plans.

Of course, multisource feedback is not the only technique available for acquiring an understanding of others in the workplace. More often than not, such knowledge structures emerge through collaborative work with others. In fact, early studies on mentoring expressly noted the role of the mentor in providing an understanding of people, their relationships, and the causal variables operating in social settings (Zuckerman, 1977). As Day (2000) points out, mentoring, along with other techniques for promoting an understanding of the social causes operating in complex systems, such as networking, do appear to represent potentially effective leadership development interventions.

The question that arises at this juncture, however, is exactly what steps might be taken to ensure the effectiveness of mentoring and networking, in developing an understanding of the causes shaping people's actions. Based on the available developmental research, three key conclusions come to fore (Lillard, 1998; Nelson et al., 1998; Schwitzgebel, 1999). First, such interventions are most likely to prove effective when the leader or peers not only role model behavior but also explain the reasons underlying their actions. Second, leaders and peers should encourage people to analyze the causes of personal and social events. Third, an attempt should be made by leaders, peers, and, perhaps, coaches and trainers to provide protypic cases illustrating the origins and consequences of interactional patterns frequently encountered in the workplace.

Timing of Interventions. These observations about mentoring and networking, however, bring to the fore a crucial developmental issue—one we often lose sight of based on the mistaken belief that development is a universal good. In an examination of the influence of network exposure on adolescent development, Lerner et al. (2001) found that an individual's involvement in peer networks outside their zone of readiness typically leads to negative developmental outcomes. Along similar lines, Mumford, Marks et al. (2000) have argued that mentoring, to be effective, requires a mentor only moderately but not extremely advanced beyond the mentee. These observations are not surprising when it is recognized that the success of social interventions depends on the individual's ability to grasp, and act on, the concepts about relationships being provided by others. Thus, leadership development programs must structure and time optimize interventions with respect to developmental needs.

These observations about timing, however, also point to a broader set of concerns related to the structural regularities commonly observed in adult development. As noted earlier, a number of structural regularities are observed in the course of adult development. It seems likely that the success of optimization interventions will, to some extent, depend on the ability of these interventions to respond to the developmental needs of people at different points in the careers. For example, earlier we noted that older adults focus on integration and generativity concerns stressing practical outcomes and practical experience in decision making. This observation, in turn, suggests that somewhat different developmental experiences will be required for more experienced, senior, leaders than their less experienced counterparts. For example, given the concerns of older adults, exercises that stress strategies for developing the organization as a whole based on industry benchmarks might prove particularly beneficial.

Along similar lines, it seems reasonable to expect that the success of some interventions may be contingent on the individual's career phase. For example, the greater autonomy of senior leaders suggests that networking interventions might prove more successful in the early career period. In contrast, by virtue of their greater resources, and interactional concerns, multisource feedback might prove more beneficial for senior, as opposed to less experienced, leaders. Although other examples of this sort might be cited, the foregoing examples seem sufficient to make our basic point—effective optimization requires considering the timing of interventions.

Compensation

No matter how well designed, it is unlikely that leadership development programs can provide all of the skills needed in leadership roles. Thus, leaders, like adults in all other walks of life, must find ways of compensating for their deficiencies if they are to prove successful. Although the application of compensation strategies has received some attention in discussions of leadership development, a point illustrated by research on derailment factors (McCall & Lombardo, 1983), it is also clear that compensation has received less attention than optimization and selection strategies. What work does exist, however, seems to reflect one of two general approaches: (a) identification of leader strengths and weaknesses and (b) the use of situational variables as a mechanism for counteracting evident weaknesses.

Identification of Strengths and Weaknesses. One of the traditional applications of assessment centers is to provide managers with reports describing their strengths and weaknesses as leaders (Campbell & Bray, 1993). The potential utility of such feedback with respect to leader performance has been provided by the Gallup Organization (Buckingham & Clifton, 2001). They examine the business impact of introducing assessment techniques in several large organizations and report findings indicating that the application of these techniques may result in motivation and productivity gains.

As valuable as these techniques appear to be, from a strictly developmental perspective, a number of questions arise with respect to their optimal application. Perhaps the first and most basic question in this regard pertains to how feedback should be provided—should one report strengths, report weaknesses, or report a mix of both. Although, from a developmental perspective, identification of weakness is attractive, it is open to question whether people can adequately cope with negative feedback. Thus, a mixed or a strengths-oriented approach, where weaknesses are identified, seems most appropriate.

Simply providing people with information about weaknesses may stimulate some compensatory efforts. The value of this information, however, seems likely to be enhanced if three additional steps are taken. First, because people do not normally seek, or readily accept, information about weaknesses, feedback of this sort of information is only likely to be effective if the self-reflection, self-objectivity, and wisdom are already in place. Because these capacities emerge relatively late in life (Connelly, 1995), it seems reasonable to expect that interventions of this sort are likely to prove more useful later, rather than earlier, in leaders' careers.

Second, an awareness of weaknesses, however laudable, will not prove of value if this knowledge cannot be incorporated in the leaders' day-to-day actions. The implication of this statement is that leaders should be encouraged to reflect on failure and incorporate failure experiences into career narratives. One way this might be accomplished is by asking people to identify common attributes of situations where they performed less effectively than expected. Another way these events might be incorporated in narratives is by asking leaders to identify the experiences that lead them to reject certain career options. Regardless of the specific strategy applied, given the findings of Russell (e.g., Russell & Kuhnert, 1992) concerning the impact of negative life events on leaders' self-image, it seems likely that interventions of this sort will prove of some value in development programs.

Third, although the availability of accessible, meaningful failure concepts is required for compensation, taken by itself, simple concept availability may not prove fully sufficient. For this kind of self-knowledge to be valuable, leaders must respond to situations based on this information changing either their actions or certain conditions of the situation at hand. This requirement, in turn, suggests that, in addition to self-reflection, successful leadership development programs will require interventions intended to develop self-management skills as they are related to the kind of problems likely to be encountered (Yukl, 2001).

Situational Variables.   Our foregoing observations about the need for self-management skills in leadership development also point to the role of effective situational management in compensatory efforts. The notion that leaders must select, appraise, and change situations based on their unique patterns of strengths and weaknesses is by no means new to the leadership literature. In fact, this concept plays a noteworthy role in Fiedler's contingency theory (Fiedler, 1967; Fiedler & Chemers, 1982). However, studies of adult development do suggest some new approaches that might be applied in efforts along these lines.

Baltes (1997) notes that one of the most commonly applied compensatory strategies is for the individual to rely on others to accomplish certain tasks. Given the fact that leadership occurs in a group setting where dyadic relationships represent a basis for many activities (see Uhl-Bien, chap. 7, this volume, and Cogliser & Scandura, chap. 8, this volume), one viable compensatory strategy would be for leaders to establish close exchange relationships with subordinates who do not share their weaknesses. An alternative approach is suggested by work on leader substitutes (Kerr & Jermier, 1978). Here leaders might seek to change subordinate, task, or organizational characteristics that would neutralize, or substitute for, a personal deficiency. Thus, leaders who lack technical expertise might explicitly seek subordinates who have a strong technical background or, alternatively, seek to impose greater structure on work activities.

What should be recognized in this regard, however, is that the feasibility of leaders engaging in effective compensatory actions will, to some extent, be contingent on broader characteristics of the organization. For example, one highly effective compensation strategy is for the leaders to withdraw from situations that play to their weaknesses. However, use of this strategy depends, in part, on the autonomy and discretion granted the occupants of leadership roles. Alternatively, compensation can occur through the use of technology. For example, a leader may use email to avoid initial overreaction (see Spreitzer, chap. 4, this volume). Again, however, the feasibility of applying this strategy depends on the organization's business strategy and culture. The implications of these observations, of course, is that effective compensation will, in part, depend on an understanding of the organization's operating environment as it relates to personnel capacities.

Aside from changing the situation, people may compensate for deficiencies by acting to change their own capabilities. These targeted, remedial interventions are not commonly considered a part of leadership development programs. However, in cases where specific deficiencies are amenable to developmental remediation, the implementation of person-specific training interventions may prove of some value. Of course, implementation of this approach implies the need for a trusting environment that stresses the value of development. Accordingly, creation of a developmental climate may, as suggested by Cogliser and Scandura (see chap. 8, this volume), represent a necessary foundation for compensatory development and, perhaps more generally, any kind of systematic leadership development program.

CONCLUSIONS

Before turning to the broader conclusions flowing from the present effort, certain limitations should be noted. To begin with, the present effort should not be viewed as a complete extended review of the adult development literature. Instead, in the present study, the adult development literature is reviewed with a specific purpose in mind—its potential implications for current studies of leadership development. Moreover, in the course of this review, clarity of presentation required distinguishing among the selection, optimization, and compensation processes underlying adult development. In the course of a person's life, however, these processes operate in a dynamic, interactive fashion. It seems likely that similar interactive effects will also be observed in leadership development.

Even bearing these limitations in mind, we believe the conclusions flowing from this review have some noteworthy implications for the current literature on leadership development. To begin with, the leadership development literature has, from time to time, been criticized as little more than a simple accumulation of clever technologies. In fact, the present review suggests a somewhat different view of this issue. Multiple leadership development techniques may have emerged as a way of addressing the multiple considerations involved in creating a system of interventions that take into account multiple developmental processes: processes we have labeled selection, optimization, and compensation.

This observation, however, brings us back to a question presented at the outset of the present effort. More specifically, can current models of adult development provide the theoretical framework needed to promote future work in the field of leadership development? Although one cannot answer this kind of framing question in an absolute sense (Fleishman & Quaintance, 1984), it does appear that theories of adult development provide a plausible and potentially useful framework for understanding leadership development. To begin with, current models of adult development, specifically process-oriented models, appear to provide a viable framework for organizing common leadership development techniques. Moreover, the organizing framework appears sufficiently comprehensive that it can readily be extended to account for some of the more novel developmental techniques examined in this volume such as those proposed by Cogliser and Scandura (see chap. 8, this volume), Day and O'Connor (see chap. 1, this volume), and Locke (see chap. 2, this volume).

Of course, a viable theoretical framework should not only provide a basis for organizing the relevant phenomenon but also allow us to formulate hypotheses capable of explaining observed anomalies (Kuhn, 1970). One illustration of this point may be found in the apparent preference of organizations for older leaders. This preference, however, is not especially surprising given their prosocial, integrative orientation along with the experience, practicality, and forecasting skills of older adults. Still another illustration of the ability of developmental theory to meet this criteria may be found in the notion of narratives and cases. It has long been recognized that leaders prefer case-based, or exercise-based, instruction. However, if one accepts the tendency of adults to rely on practical experience in problem-solving (Baltes, 1997), the origins of this preference become evident. Along similar lines, it has proven difficult to explain the mixed findings obtained in many studies of multisource feedback (see Atwater, Brett, & Waldman, chap. 5, this volume). The literature on adult development, however, suggests these mixed effects may raise because the specific implementation strategies applied do not necessarily serve to develop explanations, or understanding, of the reasons for people's perceptions.

It appears not only that models of adult development provide a basis for explaining at least some of the anomalies found in the literature on leadership development but also that these models serve to illustrate the contingencies shaping effective application of these techniques. In this regard, our observations about the kind of structural regularities observed in adult development appear noteworthy. Given their concerns with generativity and integration, as opposed to mastery, the kind of developmental interventions likely to prove useful for their more senior executives are not those that will prove most useful for more junior, less experienced counterparts. Along similar lines, the success of techniques such as action learning appear to depend on the prior acquisition of requisite principle-based structures for organizing and interpreting experience (see Conger & Toegel, chap. 6, this volume).

Given the fact that models of adult development can organize the literature, account for anomalies, and establish the boundary conditions required for successful interventions, it does, indeed, seem reasonable to conclude that models of adult development might provide a useful framework for understanding leadership development. The value of applying models of adult development in studies of leadership development becomes even more attractive when it is recognized that they provide a useful framework for identifying gaps in the extant literature and requisite extensions of current techniques.

At a macro level, this point is aptly illustrated by our division of developmental techniques in terms of selection, optimization, and compensation processes. Clearly the literature on leadership development has devoted substantial effort to the development of optimization techniques such as action learning, multisource feedback, and mentoring. By the same token, however, it seems clear that selection and compensation techniques warrant somewhat more attention than has traditionally been the case. Indeed, there would seem to be some value in studies contrasting the relative merits of these three approaches.

At a more micro level, however, application of the principles derived from models of adult development suggests some promising extensions to current approaches. For example, the role of selection in adult development suggests that realistic previews of the demands of different leadership roles represent a promising new line of research. Along similar lines, the importance of life events in shaping the selection and interpretation of situations suggests that attempts to assess, or have leaders articulate, events such as turning points, anchoring events, and redemptive events might provide a new, potentially powerful, assessment and development tool.

Although other examples of this sort might be cited, the foregoing examples seem sufficient to illustrate our key point. Although models of adult development do not represent the only potential framework for understanding leadership development, they do provide a promising framework for efforts to build a more comprehensive and sophisticated approach to the development of leaders across the life span. The present effort, by illustrating the promise of this approach, will hopefully provide an impetus for further work along these lines.

REFERENCES

Anderson, J. R. (1993). Problem-solving and learning. *American Psychologist, 48*, 35–44.

Arlin, P. K. (1993). Wisdom and expertise in teaching: An integration of perspectives. *Learning and Individual Differences, 5*, 341–349.

Arnett, J. J. (2000). Emerging adulthood: A theory of development from the late teens through the twenties. *American Psychologist, 55*, 469–480.

Baltes, P. B. (1997). On the incomplete architecture of human ontogeny. *American Psychologist, 52*, 366–380.

Baltes, M. M., & Carstensen, L. L. (1996). The process of successful aging. *Aging and Society, 16*, 397–422.

Baltes, P. B., & Staudinger, U. M. (2000). Wisdom: A metaheuristic to orchestrate mind and virtue toward excellence. *American Psychology, 55*, 122–136.

Baltes, P. B., Staudinger, U. M., Maercker, A., & Smith, J. (1995). People nominate as wise: A comparative study of wisdom-related knowledge. *Psychology and Aging, 10*, 155–166.

Bartel, K. A. (1994). Strategic planning openness: The role of top team demography. *Group and Organization Management, 19*, 406–424.

Bass, B. M. (1985). *Leadership beyond expectations*. New York: The Free Press.

Baugh, J. A., & Chartrand, T. L. (1999). The unbearable automativity of being. *American Psychologist, 54*, 462–479.

Berger, R. M., & Jordan, J. M. (1992). Planning sources, planning difficulty, and verbal fluency. *Communication Monographs, 71*, 1–31.

Block, J. (1971). *Lives through time*. Berkeley, CA: Bancroft.

Bluck, S., & Habermas, T. (2001). Extending the study of autobiographical memory: Thinking back about life across the life span. *Review of General Psychology, 5*, 135–147.

Bray, D. W., Campbell, R. J., & Grant, D. W. (1974). *Formative years in business: A long-term AT&T study of managerial lives*. New York: Wiley.

Buckingham, M., & Clifton, D. O. (2001). *Now, discover your strengths*. New York: The Free Press.

Campbell, R. J., & Bray, D. W. (1993). Use of an assessment center as an aid in management selection. *Personnel Psychology, 46*, 691–649.

Carstensen, L. L., Isaacowitz, D. M., & Charles, S. T. (1999). Taking time seriously: A theory of socio-emotional selectivity. *American Psychologist, 54*, 165–181.

Caspi, A., Bem, N. J., & Elder, G. H. (1989). Continuities and consequences of interactional styles across the life course. *Journal of Personality, 57*, 375–406.

Colonia-Willner, R. (1998). Practical intelligence at work: Relationship between aging and cognitive efficiency among managers in a bank environment. *Psychology and Aging, 13*, 45–57.

Connelly, M. S. (1995). *Wisdom as a predictor of leadership performance*. Unpublished doctoral dissertation, George Mason University, Fairfax, VA.

Cook, A. (1993). *Canons and wisdom*. Philadelphia: University of Pennsylvania Press.

Day, D. V. (2000). Leadership development: A review in context. *Leadership Quarterly, 11*, 581–613.

Day, D. V., & Lord, R. G. (1988). Executive leadership and organizational performance: Suggestions for a new theory and methodology. *Journal of Management, 14*, 453–464.

Elder, G. H., & Clipp, E. C. (1989). Combat experience and emotional health: Impairment and resilience in later life. *Journal of Personality, 57*, 311–342.

Ericsson, E. (1950). *Childhood and society*. New York: Norton.

Ericsson, K. A., & Charness, N. (1994). Expert performance: Its structure and acquisition. *American Psychologist, 49*, 725–747.

Feldman, D. H. (1999). The development of creativity. In R. J. Sternberg (Ed.), *Handbook of creativity* (pp. 169–188). Cambridge, England: Cambridge University Press.

Fiedler, F. E. (1967). *A theory of leadership effectiveness*. New York: McGraw-Hill.

Fiedler, F. E., & Chemers, M. M. (1982). *Improving leadership effectiveness: The leader-match concept*. New York: Wiley.

Fleishman, E. A., & Quaintance, M. K. (1984). *Taxonomies of human performance: The description of human tasks*. Potomac, MD: Management Research Institute.

Freund, A. M. (1997). Individuating age salience: A psychological perspective of the salience of age in the life course. *Human Development, 40*, 287–292.

Freund, A. M., & Baltes, P. B. (1996). *Selective optimization and compensation as a strategy for life management: Prediction of subjective indicators of successful aging*. Unpublished manuscript, Max Plank Institute for Human Development and Education, Berlin.

Gallagher, U. (1993). Midlife myths. *Atlantic Monthly, 102*, 51–69.

Gardner, H. (1995). *Leading minds*. New York: Basic Books.

George, L. K. (1993). Life events. In R. Kastenbaum (Ed.), *The encyclopedia of adult development* (pp. 274–278). Phoenix, AZ: Oryx.

Gollwitzer, P. M. (1999). Implementation intentions: Strong effects of simple plans. *American Psychologist, 54*, 493–503.

Grob, A., Krings, F., & Bangerter, A. (2001). Life markers in biographical narratives of people from three cohorts: A life span perspective in its historical context. *Human Development, 44*, 171–190.

Gutman, D. (1993). Mastery types, development, and aging. In R. Kastenbaum (Ed.), *The encyclopedia of adult development* (pp. 311–320). Phoenix, AZ: Oryx.

Habermas, T. (2001). History and life stories. *Human Development, 44*, 191–194.

Habermas, T., & Bluck, S. (2000). Getting a life: The emergence of the life story in adolescence. *Psychological Bulletin, 126*, 748–770.

Hammond, K. J. (1990). Case-based planning: A framework for planning from experience. *Cognitive Science, 14*, 385–443.

Havinghurst, R. (1953). *Human development and education*. New York: Longmans.

Hershey, D. A., Walsh, O. A., Read, S. J., & Chulef, A. S. (1990). The effects of expertise on financial problem-solving: Evidence for goal-directed problem-solving scripts. *Organizational Behavior and Human Decision Processes, 46*, 77–101.

Howard, A., & Bray, D. W. (1988). *Managerial lives in transition: Advancing age and changing times*. New York: Guilford.

Isenberg, D. J. (1986). Thinking and managing: A verbal protocol analysis of managerial problem-solving. *Academy of Management Journal, 29*, 775–788.

Jacobs, T. O., & Jaques, E. (1990). Military executive leadership. In K. E. Clark & M. B. Clark (Eds.), *Measures of leadership* (pp. 281–295). West Orange, NJ: Leadership Library of America.

Kerr, S., & Jermier, J. M. (1978). Substitutes for leadership: Their meaning and measurement. *Organizational Behavior and Human Performance, 22*, 375–403.

Kuhn, T. (1970). *The structure of scientific revolutions*. Chicago, IL: University of Chicago Press.

Lerner, R. M., Freund, R. M., Stefanis, I. D., & Habermas, T. (2001). Understanding developmental regulation in adolescence: The use of the selection, optimization, and compensation model. *Human Development, 44*, 29–50.

Lerner, R. M., & Tubman, J. G. (1989). Conceptual issues in studying continuity and discontinuity in personality development across life. *Journal of Personality, 57*, 343–373.

Lillard, A. (1998). Theories behind theories of the mind. *Human Development, 41*, 40–46.

Magnusson, D. (1988). Individual development from an interactional perspective. In D. Magnusson (Ed.), *Paths through life* (pp. 1–21). Hillsdale, NJ: Lawrence Erlbaum Associates.

Marsiske, M., Lang., F. R., Baltes, M. M., & Baltes, P. B. (1995). Selective optimization with compensation: Life span perspectives on successful human development. In R. A. Dixon & L. Backman (Eds.), *Compensation for psychological defects and declines: Managing losses and promoting gains* (pp. 35–79). Hillsdale, NJ: Lawrence Erlbaum Associates.

McAdams, D. P. (2001). The psychology of life stories. *Review of General Psychology, 5*, 100–123.

McCall, M. W., & Lombardo, M. M. (1983). *Off the track: Why and how successful executives get derailed*. Greensboro, NC: Center for Creative Leadership.

McCauley, C. D., Ruderman, M. N., Ohlott, P. J., & Morrow, J. E. (1994). Assessing the developmental components of managerial jobs. *Journal of Applied Psychology, 79*, 544–560.

McCrae, R. R. (1996). Social consequences of experiential openness. *Psychological Bulletin, 120*, 323–337.

Mumford, M. D., Baughman, W. A., Uhlman, C. G., Costanza, D. P., & Threlfall, K. V. (1993). Personality variables and skill acquisition: Performance on well-diffused and ill-defined problem-solving tasks. *Human Performance, 6*, 345–381.

Mumford, M. D., & Gustafson, S. B. (in press). Creative thought: Cognition and problem solving in a dynamic system. In M. A. Runco (Ed.), *Creativity research handbook*. Cresskill, NY: Hampton Press.

Mumford, M. D., Marks, M. A., Connelly, M. S., Zaccaro, S. J., & Reiter-Palmon, R. (2000). Development of leadership skills: Experience and timing. *Leadership Quarterly, 11*, 87–114.

Mumford, M. D., Schultz, R. A., & Osburn, H. K. (2002). Planning in organizations: Performance as a multi-level phenomenon. *Annual Review of Research in Multi-Level Issues, 1*, 3–63.

Mumford, M. D., Schultz, R. A., & Van Doorn, J. R. (2001). Performance in planning: Processes, requirements, and errors. *Review of General Psychology, 5*, 316–341.

Mumford, M. D., Stokes, G. S., & Owens, W. A. (1990). *Patterns of life adaptation: The ecology of human individuality*. Hillsdale, NJ: Lawrence Erlbaum Associates.

Mumford, M. D., Zaccaro, S. J., Harding, F. D., Jacobs, T. O., & Fleishman, E. A. (2000). Leadership skills for a changing world: Solving complex social problems. *Leadership Quarterly, 11*, 11–36.

Mumford, M. D., Zaccaro, S. J., Johnson, J. F., Diana, M., Gilbert, J. A., & Threlfall, K. V. (2000). Patterns of leader characteristics: Implications for performance and development, *Leadership Quarterly, 11*, 115–134.

Murray, A. I. (1989). Top management team heterogeneity and firm performance. *Strategic Management Journal, 10*, 125–141.

Nelson, K., Plesa, D., & Hensler, S. (1998). Children's theory of mind: An experimental interpretation. *Human Development, 41*, 7–29.

O'Connor, J. A. (1993). *A sample for a historiometric study of charismatic leaders*. Fairfax, VA: Center for Behavioral and Cognitive Studies.

Oura, Y., & Hatano, G. (2001). The construction of general and specific mental models of other people. *Human Development, 44*, 144–159.

Owens, W. A. (1976). Biographical data. In M. A. Dunnette (Ed.), *Handbook of industrial and organizational psychology* (pp. 612–642). Chicago: Rand-McNally.

Oyserman, O., & Markus, H. R. (1990). Possible selves and delinquency. *Journal of Personality and Social Psychology, 59*, 112–125.

Pea, R. D. (1982). What is planning development the development of? *New Directions in Child Development, 18*, 5–27.

Pillemer, D. B. (2001). Momentous events and the life story. *Review of General Psychology, 5*, 123–134.

Reese, H. W., & Overton, W. F. (1970). Models of development and theories of development. In L. R. Goulet & P. B. Baltes (Eds.), *Life-span developmental psychology: Research and theory* (pp. 115–145). New York: Academic Press.

Reeves, L. M., & Weisburg, R. W. (1994). The role of content and information in analogical transfer. *Psychological Bulletin, 115*, 381–400.

Russell, L. J., & Kuhnert, K. W. (1992). Integrating skill acquisition and perspective taking capacity in the development of leaders. *Leadership Quarterly, 3*, 109–135.

Salthouse, T. A. (1986). Shifting levels of analysis in the investigation of cognitive aging. *Human Development, 35*, 321–342.

Salthouse, T. A. (1998). Independence of age-related influences on cognitive abilities across the lifespan. *Developmental Psychology, 34*, 851–864.

Schaie, K. W. (1994). The course of adult intellectual development. *American Psychologist, 49*, 304–313.

Schooler, C., Mulatu, M. S., & Oates, G. (1999). Continuing effects of substantively complex work on the intellectual functioning of older workers. *Psychology and Aging, 14*, 483–506.

Schultz, R., & Heckhausen, J. (1996). A life span model of successful aging. *American Psychologist, 51*, 702–714.

Schwitzgebel, E. (1999). Gradual belief change in children. *Human Development, 42*, 283–296.

Settersten, R. A. (1997). The salience of age in the life course. *Human Development, 40*, 257–281.

Simonton, D. K. (1984). *Genius, creativity, and leadership: Historiometric inquiries*. Cambridge, MA: Harvard University Press.

Singer, J. A., & Bluck, S. (2001). New perspectives on autobiographical memory: The integration of narrative processing and autobiographical reasoning. *Review of General Psychology, 5*, 91–100.

Staudinger, U. M. (2001). Life reflection: A social-cognitive analysis of life review. *Review of General Psychology, 5*, 148–160.

Staudinger, U. M., & Baltes, P. B. (1996). Interactive minds: A facilitative setting for wisdom-related performance. *Journal of Personality and Social Psychology, 71*, 746–762.

Sternberg, R. J. (1998). A balance theory of wisdom. *Review of General Psychology, 2*, 347–365.

Sternberg, R. J. (2002). Successful intelligence: A new approach to leadership. In R. Riggio, S. Murphy, & F. Pirozollo (Eds.), *Multiple intelligences and leadership* (pp. 9–28). Mahwah, NJ: Lawrence Erlbaum Associates.

Strange, J. M., & Mumford, M. D. (2002). The origins of vision: Charismatic versus ideological leadership. *Leadership Quarterly, 13*, 1–35.

Taylor, S. E., Phan, L. B., Rivkin, I. D., & Armor, D. A. (1998). Harassing the imagination: Mental simulation, self-regulation, and coping. *American Psychologist, 53*, 429–439.

Terman, L. M. (1959). *The gifted group at mid-life*. Stanford, CA: Stanford University Press.

Thomas, J. B., & McDaniel, R. R. (1990). Interpreting strategic issues: Effects of strategy and the information processing structure of top management teams. *Academy of Management Journal, 33*, 286–306.

Valliant, G. E. (1977). *Adaptation to life*. Boston: Little Brown.

Verhaegan, P., & Salthouse, T. A. (1997). Meta-analysis of age-cognition relations in adulthood: A test of alternative models. *Psychological Bulletin, 122*, 231–249.

Weisburg, R. W. (1999). Creativity and knowledge: A challenge to theories. In R. J. Sternberg (Ed.), *Handbook of creativity* (pp. 226–250). Cambridge, England: Cambridge University Press.

Yukl, G. (2001). *Leadership in organizations*. Englewood Cliffs, NJ: Prentice-Hall.

Zaccaro, S. J. (2002). Organizational leadership and social intelligence. In R. Riggio, S. Murphy, & F. Pirozollo (Eds.), *Multiple intelligences and leadership* (pp. 29–54). Mahwah, NJ: Lawrence Erlbaum Associates.

Zaccaro, S. J., Gilbert, J. A., Thor, K. K., & Mumford, M. D. (1991). Leadership and social intelligence: Linking social perspectives and behavioral flexibility to leader effectiveness. *Leadership Quarterly, 2*, 317–342.

Zuckerman, H. (1977). *Scientific elites: Nobel laureates in the United States*. New York: The Free Press.

Author Index

Hoel, W., 157, *159*
Hoenig, C., 49, *68*
Hogan, J., 233, *235*
Hogan, R. T., 233, *235*
Hogarth, R. M., 111, *123*
Holcombe, K. M., 234, *236*
Hollander, E. P., 20, *27*, 131, 133, 134, 136, *146*
Hollenbeck, G. P., 217, *221*
Holtz, B. C., 24, *28*
Homans, G. C., 137, *146*, 165, 169, *177*
Honan, W. H., 201, *221*, 226, *235*
Hooijberg, R., 13, *27*
House, R. J., 52, 58, *68*, 131, 137, *146*, 164, 165, 169, *177*, *179*, 183, 186, 190,191, *196*
Howard, A., 237, *259*
Howard, J. P. F., 233, *235*
Howe, W., 224, 226, *235*, *236*
Howell, J. M., 169, *177*, *179*
Hox, J. J., 23, *27*
Hughes, R. L., 229, *235*
Hunt, J. G., 13, *27*, 129, *146*, 163, 165, *177*
Huselid, M. A., 23, *26*
Hy, L. X., 16, 24, *27*

I

Iacono, C. S., 52, 54, *69*
Ilgen, D. R., 98, *105*, *106*
Isaacowitz, D. M., 244, *258*
Isenberg, D. J., 242, *259*
Ivancevitch, J. M., 165, *176*

J

Jackson, S. E., 113, *124*
Jacobs, R. R., 15, *28*
Jacobs, T. O., 216, *222*, 237, *242*, 245, *259*, *260*
Jago, A. G., 188, 189, *197*
Jaques, E., 237, 245, *259*
Jarvenpaa, S. L., 77, 81, *85*
Jefferson, T., 21, *27*
Jensen, M., 43, 44, *46*
Jermier, J. M., 61, *69*, 173, *177*, 254, *259*
Johnson, J. F., 240, 248, *260*
Johnson, J. W., 92, 94, 100, *105*
Jones, E., 117, 120, *124*
Jordan, J. M., 243, *258*
Judge, T., 115, 118, *119, 123, 124*
Julin, J. A., *113, 124*
Jung, D. I., 58, *66, 69*

K

Kahai, S., 49, 53, 57, 58, 59, 61, 62, *68, 69, 70*, 247
Kahn, R. L., 64, *69*, 132, *146*
Kahneman, D., 121, *124*
Kahwajy, J. L., 174, *177*
Kane, J., *92*, 96, *105*
Kanungo, R. N., 35, *46*, 171, *176*, 217, *221*
Karoly, P., 135, *147*
Kastenbaum, D. R., 187, *196*
Katz, D., 64, *69*, 132, *146*, 165, *177*
Kay, E., 100, *105*
Kazdin, A. E., 165, *177*
Kegan, R., 16, *17*, 19, 24, *27*
Kelly, G., 24, *27*
Kennedy, J., 139, *147*
Kerlinger, F. N., 182, *196*
Kerr, S., 61, *69*, 164, 173, *177, 179*, 183, 184, *196, 197*, 254, *259*
Kets de Vries, M., 155, *159*
Kiesler, S., 78, 79, *86*
King, D. C., 233, *235*
King, P. M., 15, *27*
Kirker, W., 120, *124*
Kirkman, B. L., 171, 172, *177*
Kirkpatrick, D. L., 72, *85*, 217, 218, *221*
Kirkpatrick, S. A., 30, *46*
Kitchener, K. S., 15, *27*
Klein, E. B., 15, 21, *27*
Klimoski, R. J., 1, *7*
Kluger, A., 90, 92, 93, 95, *105*, 119, *123*
Knetsch, J., 121, *124*
Kolb, A., 111, *124*
Kolb, D. A., 111, *124*, 206, 219, *221*, 233, *235*
Konovsky, M., 136, *146*
Korukonda, A. R., 165, *177*
Kotter, J., 41, *46*, 132, 133, *146*
Kozlowski, S. W. J., 21, *27*
Krackhardt, D., 129, 131, 136, *145*
Kraimer, M. L., 22, *28*
Kram, K. E., 157, *159*
Kreitner, R., 165, 169, *178*
Krings, F., 244, *259*
Kroeck, K. G., 186, *196*
Kuhn, T., 256, *259*
Kuhnert, K. W., 254, *260*
Kuiper, N., 120, *124*
Kurland, N. B., 78, 79, 80, 82, *85*

Subject Index

A

Abstract conceptualization, 206
Action learning, 107–109, 153
  advantages, 109–110
  failures, 110–114
  performance interventions, 249–250
Active experimentation, 206
Active mind, 36
Actor-observer bias, 120
Adaptability, 16
Adaptive Structuration Theory (AST), 52, 55–59
Adult development, *see also* Higher education
    programs
  capacity approach, 240, 244–245
  content approach, 240, 242–243
  ego development, 16
  history of, 14, 239
  leadership programs, 201–202
  life stories and events, 243, 244
  models of, 239–240
  orders of consciousness, 16–18
  paradox of, 15
  postformal approaches to, 14
  process approach, 240, 241–242
  reflective judgment, 15–16
  structural approach, 240, 244
Advanced information technology (AIT),
    see also E-leadership; Technology
  anonymity, 61
  appropriation of structures, 56–59
  challenges to leaders, 50
  defined, 53
  effects of, 49, 52
  group leadership and, 61–63
  interpretation of, 54
  social systems and, 54–57, 63
  spirit of structural features, 56, 58
  structural features, 56
  user response to, 55
Age, 244
Agee, William, 38
Agenda setting, 41
Ambition, 37
Analogous events, 243
Anchoring events, 243
Anonymity
  feedback, 89, 90, 93
  group dynamics and, 61–62
Appraisal motive, 117
Appropriation of structures, 56–59
Assessment
  of leadership studies programs, 231–232
  performance, 205
Assessment centers, 205, 253
Associations, professional, 226
AST, *see* Adaptive Structuration Theory
Authority, formal, 42

B

BB&T, code of values, 34
Bounded rationality, 187
Brick walls, 154–155

C

Capacity approach, 240, 244–245
Cascading leadership, 152
CEOs, *see* Chief Executive Officers
Challenge, 205

273

L

LarLanguage, academic *vs.* manager, 182–184, 192
Leader development, *vs.* leadership development, 19–22, 130
Leader-Match, 217
Leader-Membership Exchange (LMX), 130, 150–151
  communication, 216
  differentiation, 135–136
  feedback ratings' influence on, 100
  implications for, 143–144
  linking-pin positions, 151
  validity, 186–187
Leader participation model, 188
Leader performance, 24–25
Leader substitutes, 254–255
Leaderplex model, 13
Leaders, *see also* Virtual leaders
  compared to managers, 133
  competency of, 190–191, 194–195
  effective, 137, 144
  job performance, 25
  motivation and commitment of, 191–192
  relationships, 135–136, 137
  as role models, 42
  roles of, 29–30
  selection of, 246–249
  technological challenges, 50
  traits of successful, 35–38
Leadership, *see also* E-leadership
  adaptation to new technology, 58–61
  change and, 132–133
  defined, 29, 132–133
  domains of, 30
  e-leadership *vs.*, 49
  influence and, 132–135
  politics of, 190–191
  types of organizational, 30
Leadership (Burns), 224
Leadership development, *vs.* leader development, 19–22, 130
Leadership effectiveness, 136, 144
Leadership systems, 58
Learning processes, 206–207
Learning styles, 206–207
Life events, 243, 244
Life stories, 243
Linking-pin positions, 151

Listening, 40
LMX, *see* Leader-Membership Exchange
Lost potential, 136

M

Managers
  compared to leaders, 133
  use of academic research, 182–186
Marietta College, 229
Mechanistic model, 239
Mental models, shared, 82
Mentoring, 251–252
  in higher education programs, 219
  virtual workplace, 82
Military, information dissemination, 50–51
Mission statements, university, 229
Monitoring, employee, 76–77, 80
Moral leadership, *see* Ethics
Morale, 44
Motivation
  employee, 42–44
  to lead, 13
  leader, 191–192
Multidimensionality, 18–23
Multiple-action learning, 110–111
Multirater feedback, *see* 360-degree feedback
Multisource feedback, *see* 360-degree feedback

N

Normative decision-making, 188

O

Optimization, 241, 249
  performance interventions, 249–251
  social interventions, 251–252
  timing of interventions, 252–253
Orders of consciousness, 16–18
Organismic model, 239
Organizational processes and technology, 55–57
Organizational selection, 247–248
Organizations, *see also* Virtual organizations
  actions, 41–45
  core values, 34–35
  development needs, 20–21
  goals, 30